Originally advertised as *Ireland and Romanticism*, Patrick Rafroidi's work is a revised and updated translation of his much acclaimed *L'Irlande et le romantisme* (1972). It is now published for the first time in English in two volumes, the first a study of the period and its authors, and the second an important work of reference on all the Irish literary figures of the time.

The study is divided into three sections, 'Prelude to Romanticism', 'Nationalist Romanticism', and 'The Impact of Irish Romanticism', with extensive notes and an index. Professor Rafroidi studies the causes of the movement, how it was influenced by political and literary landmarks of the time, and how the authors themselves influenced others, not only in England but also in the United States, in France and in Germany, and their re-discovery and use of Ireland's early history and myths. The reference section contains a general bibliography, bio-bibliographies of the Irish authors whose work was published between 1789 and 1850, and information as to the performances of their plays in the most important theatres in the British Isles, and a list of the princible Irish periodicals of the time.

This is therefore a most useful book for all those interested in the period, and the bibliographies make it an essential work of reference which all libraries and students of Anglo-Irish Literature will need on their shelves, for continuous referal.

Patrick Rafroidi is Professor of English and Anglo-Irish Literature and Vice-Chancellor of the University of Lille (France), where he has founded Centre d'Études et de Recherches Irlandaises de l'Université de Lille III and edits *Études Irlandaises*. He was Chairman of the International Association for the Study of Anglo-Irish Literature 1976–1979. He has already published, and contributed to a number of books of Irish interest, and is currently working on Part II of *Irish Literature in English*, entitled *The Second Coming, 1850–1912*.

IRISH LITERATURE IN ENGLISH
THE ROMANTIC PERIOD
(1789–1850)

VOLUME II

IRISH LITERATURE IN ENGLISH

THE ROMANTIC PERIOD

(1789–1850)

VOLUME II
PART IV

Patrick Rafroidi

HUMANITIES PRESS

Atlantic Highlands, N.J.

Copyright © 1972 Patrick Rafroidi
English translation copyright © 1980 Colin Smythe Ltd.

First published in France in 1972 under the
title *L'Irlande et le Romantisme*

First published in the U.S.A. and Canada by
Humanities Press Inc., 171 First Avenue,
Atlantic Highlands, N.J. 07716

Library of Congress Cataloging in Publication Data

Rafroidi, Patrick.
  Irish literature in English.

  Translation of L'Irlande et le romantisme.
  The bibliography has been rev. and updated.
  Bibliography: v. 2.
  Includes index.
  1. English literature—Irish authors—History and criticism.   2. English
literature—19th century—History and criticism.   3. Romanticism—Ire-
land.
  I. Title.
  PR8750.R313   820 .9 007   79–12605
  ISBN 0–391–01032–8 (v. 1)
  ISBN 0–391–01033–6 (v. 2)

Printed in Great Britain

Contents

Volume II

PART IV: REFERENCE SECTION

1. General bibliography   3

2. Irish authors (1789–1850), works, criticism,   35
    bio-bibliographical notes

3. Irish authors (1789–1850),   359
    principal French translations

4. Principal Irish periodicals   379
    from 1789 to 1850

(revised and updated by the author for the period 1970–1978)

PART IV

REFERENCE
SECTION

N.B. The general bibliography does not include mention of

- works by authors appearing in the second section of the bibliography

- monographs devoted to these authors and listed under their names

- very specialised studies the references for which have been provided in the body of the work

1

GENERAL BIBLIOGRAPHY
(Historical and critical studies,
works of reference, anthologies)

ALDUS, JUDITH B.:
    'Anglo-Irish Dialects, a bibliography'.
    Regional Language Studies, Newfoundland, II, 15 Sept. 1969.
    (Special number.)

ALLIBONE, S. A.:
    A Critical Dictionary of English Literature.
    (1859) new edition, Detroit: Gale Research Co;
    Guildford: Ch. W. Trayler, 1965, 3 v. + 2.
    (Supplement by J.-F. Kirk.)

ALSPACH, RUSSEL K.:
    Irish Poetry from the English Invasion to 1798.
    Philadelphia: University of Pennsylvania Press (1943), 2nd
    ed.: 1959.

Annual Bibliography of English Language and Literature.

ARCHER, WILLIAM:
    The Old Drama and the New, an Essay in Re-valuation.
    London: Heinemann, 1923.

ARNOLD, BRUCE:
    A Concise History of Irish Art.
    London: Thames & Hudson, 1969, ill.

ARNOLD, MATTHEW:

On the Study of Celtic Literature, (London, 1867),
The Complete Works of Matthew Arnold, III, Lectures and
Essays in Criticism edited by R. H. Super.
Ann Arbor: University of Michigan Press, 1962.

AUDEN, W. H., ed.:

XIXth Century Minor Poets, notes by G. R. Greeger.
London: Faber & Faber, 1967 (anthology).

BAKER, ERNEST, A.:

History in Fiction. A Guide to the Best Historical Romances,
Sagas, Novels and Tales.
London: G. Routledge; New York: E. P. Dutton, n.d.
[=1907].

The History of the English Novel.
New York: Barnes and Noble, 10 v., (1924–39), 1960.
Vol. VI: Edgeworth, Austen, Scott.
Vol. VII: The Age of Dickens and Thackeray (Ch. I: 'The
Irish Novelists', pp. 11–61).

BALZAC, HONORÉ DE:

Œuvres.
Paris: Club français du Livre, 1962.

BARAT, EMMANUEL:

Le Style poétique et la révolution romantique.
Paris: Hachette, 1904.

BARBIER, AUGUSTE:

Iambes et Poèmes.
7e éd., Paris: P. Masgana, 1852.

BARTLEY, J. O.:

Teague, Shenkin and Sawney. Being an Historical Study of
the Earliest Irish, Welsh and Scottish Characters in English
Plays.
Cork University Press, 1954.

BARZUN, JACQUES:

Race, A Study in Superstition.
Revised, with a new Preface, New York, etc.: Harper & Row,
1965.

BEACH, JOSEPH WARREN:
   The Concept of Nature in XIXth Century English Poetry.
   New York: The Macmillan Company, 1936.
   New York: Pageant Book Company, 1956.

BEAUMONT, GUSTAVE DE:
   L'Irlande sociale, politique et religieuse.
   4ᵉ éd., Paris: C. Gosselin, 1841, 2 v.

BECKETT, J. C.:
   The Making of Modern Ireland, 1603–1923.
   London: Faber, 1966, paperback ed.: 1969.

BEHAN, BRENDAN:
   Brendan Behan's Island, an Irish Sketch-Book with drawings
   by Paul Hogarth.
   London: Hutchinson & Co, 1962.

BERNBAUM, ERNEST:
   Guide Through the Romantic Movement (1930).
   2nd ed., New York: The Ronald Press Company, 1949.

BESSAI, DIANE E.:
   ' "Dark Rosaleen" as Image of Ireland.' *Eire-Ireland*, X, 4,
   Winter 1975, 62–84.

The Bibliographical Society of Ireland Publications.
   Dublin: Three Candles, 1918, etc.

Bibliographie de la France, initially published under the title:
   Bibliographie de l'Empire français ou *Journal de l'imprimerie
   et de la librairie* (1811–14, Volumes I, II, III) receives its
   present title in 1815, from Vol. IV; photographic reprint by
   permission of Cercle de la Librairie, Paris: Nendeln;
   Liechtenstein: Kraus Reprint Ltd, 1966.

BIRKHEAD, E.:
   The Tale of Terror. A Study of the Gothic Romance.
   London: Constable & Co, 1921.

BLACAM, AODH DE:
   *A First Book of Irish Literature. (Hiberno-Latin, Gaelic,
   Anglo-Irish) from the Earliest Times to the Present Day.*
   Dublin: Talbot Press, n.d. (reprinted by the same publisher,
   1973).

BLAKE, WILLIAM:
  Works.
  G. KEYNES ed., London: Nonesuch Press, 1957.

BLOOM, HAROLD:
  The Visionary Company. A Reading of English Romantic Poetry.
  London: Faber & Faber, 1962.

BÖLL, HEINRICH:
  Journal irlandais.
  Translated from the German by Charles Bladier.
  Paris: Editions du Seuil, 1969 (in German: *Irisches Tagebuch,* 1957).

BOLSTER, RICHARD:
  'French Romanticism and the Ireland Myth', *Hermathena,* XCIX, 1964, pp. 42–8.

BOURNIQUEL, CAMILLE:
  Irlande.
  Paris: Seuil, «Petite planète», 1955.
  Ireland.
  London: Vista Books; New York: Viking Press, 1960.

BOWRA, C. M.:
  The Romantic Imagination.
  London: Oxford University Press, 1950.

BOYD, ERNEST A.:
  Ireland's Literary Renaissance.
  Dublin and London: Maunsel and Co, 1916.
  Reprinted in 1969 by Allen Figgis.

BOYLAN, HENRY:
  A Dictionary of Irish Biography.
  Dublin: Gill & Macmillan, 1978.

BOYLE, ANDREW:
  An Index to the Annuals. Vol. I, 1820–50.
  Andrew Boyle, 1967.

BRANDES, G.:
  Main Currents in XIXth Century Literature.

Vol. IV: *Naturalism in England* (1875).
London: Heinemann, 1905.

BRIGGS, K. M.:
The Fairies in Tradition and Literature.
London: Routledge & Kegan Paul, 1967.

BROMWICH, RACHEL:
Matthew Arnold and Celtic Literature. A Retrospect, 1865–1965.
(The O'Donnell Lecture, Oxford, 7 May 1964).
Oxford: Clarendon Press, 1965.

BROOKE, STOPFORD A. & ROLLESTON, T. W.:
A Treasury of Irish Poetry in the English Tongue.
London: Smith, Elder & Co, 1900: (anthology).

BROWN, MALCOLM
The Politics of Irish Literature from Thomas Davis to W. B. Yeats.
London: Allen & Unwin, 1972.

BROWN, STEPHEN J. (S. J.):
Ireland in Fiction.
1st ed. 1915; 2nd ed. 1919, Dublin & London: Maunsel, reprinted with an introduction by Desmond J. Clarke: Shannon: Irish University Press, 1969.

BROWN, TERENCE:
Northern Voices: Poets from Ulster.
Dublin: Gill & Macmillan, 1975, 248p.

BROWNE, R. B.; ROSCELLI, W. J.; LOFTUS, R., eds.:
The Celtic Cross.
Purdue, Indiana: Purdue University Studies, 1964.

BUCKLEY, MARY:
'Attitudes to Nationality in Four XIXth c. Novelists'. *Journal of the Cork Historical Archaeological Society*, 78, 227, 1973, pp. 27–34, etc.

BYRON, Lord:
Poetical Works, ed. E. H. Coleridge.
Letters & Journals, ed. R. E. Prothero.
1898–1904.

CAILLOIS, ROGER:
Anthologie du fantastique.
60 tales of terror, collected and introduced by R.C.
Paris: Le Club Français du Livre, 1958 (anthology).

Catalogues and card indexes of the following libraries:
Bibliothèque Nationale, Paris.
British Museum.
Library of Congress.
National Library of Ireland, Dublin.
Queens University, Belfast.
Trinity College, Dublin.

Cambridge Bibliography of English Literature and *New Cambridge Bibliography of English Literature,* ed. G. Watson, 1969.

CARASSO, JEAN-PIERRE:
La Rumeur irlandaise.
Paris: Champ Libre, distribution by Denoël, 1970.

CARPENTER, ANDREW, ed.:
Place, Personality and the Irish Writer.
Gerrards Cross: Colin Smythe, 1977, 'Irish Literary Studies I'.

CARR, JOHN:
The Stranger in Ireland, 1803.
(Recently reprinted by Irish University Press.)

CARRÉ, JEAN-MARIE:
Goethe en Angleterre.
Paris: Plon, 1920.

Bibliographie de Goethe en Angleterre.
Paris: Plon, 1920.

CARTY, JAMES:
Ireland from Grattan's Parliament to the Great Famine (1783–1850). A Documentary Record.
Dublin: C. J. Fallon Ltd, 1949, 3rd ed. 1957, ill.

Catalogue Général de la Librairie Française pendant 25 ans (1840–65), compiled by Otto Lorenz. Paris: O. Lorenz, 1867, etc.

CHASTENET, JACQUES:
«L'Irlande au milieu du XIXᵉ siècle».
Revue des Deux Mondes, 1 Feb. 1961, pp. 396–408.

CHATELAIN, CHEVALIER DE:
Beautés de la Poésie anglaise.
London: Rolandi, 1860–72, 5 v.

CHAUVIRÉ, ROGER:
L'Irlande.
Paris: Didier, 1936.

CHORLEY, HENRY F. & COLLAS, ACHILLE:
The Authors of England. A Series of Medallion Portraits of
Modern Literary Characters, engraved from the works of
British Artists, by Achille Collas, with illustrative notices by
Henry F. Chorley.
London: Charles Tilt, 1838.

CLARK, WILLIAM SMYTH:
The Irish Stage in the County Towns 1720–1800.
Oxford University Press, 1965.

CLEEVE, BRIAN:
Dictionary of Irish Writers.
1st series (Fiction), 1967. 2nd series (Non Fiction), 1969. 3rd
series (Writers in the Irish Language), 1971.
Cork: The Mercier Press.

COLBY, VINETA:
Yesterday's Woman: Domestic Realism in the English Novel.
Princeton: Princeton University Press, 1973.

CONNELL, K. H.:
Irish Peasant Society. Four Historical Essays.
Oxford: Clarendon Press, 1968.

CORKERY, DANIEL:
*The Hidden Ireland. A Study of Gaelic Munster in the
XVIIIth Century.*
4th ed. Dublin: Gill, 1956.

Synge and Anglo-Irish Literature.
London: Longmans, 1931. Cork University Press, 1955, etc.

COSTIGAN, GIOVANNI:
'Romantic Nationalism: Ireland and Europe'.
Irish University Review, III, 2, Autumn 1973, 141–152.

COURTHOPE, W. J.:
A History of English Poetry.
Vol. VI: *The Romantic Movement in English Poetry. Effects of the French Revolution.*
London: Macmillan, 1913.

CRAIG, MAURICE:
Social and Architectural History of Dublin, 1660–1860.
New edition, Dublin: Allen Figgis, 1969.

CRONE, J. S.:
A Concise Dictionary of Irish Biography.
New York: Longmans, Green and Co, 1928.
Revised and enlarged ed., Dublin: The Talbot Press, 1937.

CURTIS, EDMUND:
A History of Ireland.
London: Methuen, 1936, 1960.

DEVONSHIRE, M. G.:
The English Novel in France, 1830–70.
London: University of London Press, 1929.

Dictionary of American Biography.

Dictionary of National Biography.

DROZ, JACQUES:
Le Romantisme politique en Allemagne.
Paris: A. Colin, 1963, «U 2».

DUGGAN, G. C.:
The Stage Irishman, A History of the Irish Play and Stage Characters from the Earliest Times.
Dublin: The Talbot Press, 1937.

DURRETT, FLORENCE:
The Irish Question as Portrayed in the Fiction of 1800–50.
M.A. thesis, Columbia University, 1924.

EAGER, ALAN R.:
A Guide to Irish Bibliographical Material.
Library Association, 1964.

EDWARD, R. D. & WILLIAMS, T. D., eds.:
The Great Famine. Studies in Irish History, 1845–52.
Dublin: Browne & Nolan, 1956.

EDWARDS, OWEN D., etc.:
Celtic Nationalism.
London: Routledge & Kegan Paul, 1968.

ELKINGTON, MARGERY E.:
Les Relations de société entre la France et l'Angleterre sous la
Restauration (1814–1830).
Paris: H. Champion, 1929 (Bibliothèque de la Revue de
Littérature Comparée, 56).

ELKINS, Jr, A. C., et al.:
The Romantic Movement Bibliography, 1936–1970.
Epping, Bowker Publishing Co.

Encyclopaedia of Ireland:
(V. MEALLY, etc., eds.), Dublin: Allen Figgis, 1968.

ESTILL, ADELAIDE D.:
The Sources of Synge.
Philadelphia, 1939.

FACKLER, HERBERT V.:
'Wordsworth in Ireland, 1829: A Survey of his Tour'.
Eire-Ireland, Vl, 1, Spring 1971, 53–64.

FAIRCHILD, HOXIE N.:
The Romantic Quest. A Study of English Romantic
Literature.
New York: Columbia University Press, 1931.

FARREN, ROBERT:
The Course of Irish Verse in English.
New York: Sheed and Ward, 1947.

FEUILLIDE, JEAN G. CAPO DE:
L'Irlande.
Paris, 1839, 2 v.

FINNERAN, RICHARD J., ed.:
Anglo-Irish Literature. A Review of Research.
New York: M.L.A., 1976.
(particularly pp. 24–47: 'Nineteenth-Century Writers' by James F. Kilroy).

FLANAGAN, THOMAS:
The Irish Novelists 1800–1850.
New York: Columbia University Press, 1959.

FLOOD, W.-M. H. GRATTAN:
A History of Irish Music.
2nd ed., Dublin: Browne and Nolan, 1906; 3rd ed., Irish University Press, 1970.

FOAKES, R. A.:
The Romantic Assertion. A Study in the Language of XIXth Century Poetry.
London: Methuen, 1958.

FOSTER, JOHN WILSON:
Forces and Themes in Ulster Fiction.
Dublin: Gill & Macmillan, 1974.

FOX, C. M.:
Annals of the Irish Harpers.
London: Smith, 1911.

FRÉCHET, RENÉ:
Histoire de l'Irlande.
Paris: Presses Universitaires de France, «Que Sais-Je» n° 394, 1970.

FREEMAN, T. W.:
Ireland. A General and Regional Geography.
London: Methuen, 1950, 1960.

GALLACHER, KENT G.:
The Foreigner in Early American Drama. A Study in Attitudes.
The Hague: Mouton, 1966. (Studies in American Literature, 3.)

GÉRARD, ALBERT:

L'idée romantique de la poésie en Angleterre. Etudes sur la théorie de la poésie chez Coleridge, Wordsworth, Keats et Shelley.
Paris: Les Belles Lettres, 1955.
(Bibliothèque de la Faculté de Philosophie et Lettres de l'Université de Liège, Fasc. CXXXVI.)

GRAVES, A. P.:

Irish Literary and Musical Studies.
London: Elkin Mathews, 1913.

GRAVES, CHARLES L.:

Humours of Irish Life.
London, etc.: The Gresham Publishing Company, n.d.
(The Irish Library) (anthology.)

GREENE, DAVID & O'CONNOR, FRANK:

A Golden Treasury of Irish Poetry, A.D. 600 to 1200.
London: Macmillan, 1967. (Gaelic anthology.)

GREENE, DAVID H.:

An Anthology of Irish Literature.
New York: The Modern Library, 1954.

GUICHARD, LÉON:

La Musique et les Lettres au Temps du Romantisme.
Paris: Presses Universitaires de France, 1955. (Université de Grenoble, Publications de la Faculté des Lettres, 12.)

GUIFFAN, J.; VERRIÈRE, J.; RAFROIDI, P.:

L'Irlande, Vol. I: Milieu et Histoire.
Paris: A. Colin, 1970, «U 2».

GWYNN, DENIS:

Young Ireland and 1848.
Cork University Press, 1949.

GWYNN, STEPHEN:

Irish Books and Irish People.
Dublin: Talbot Press; London: Fisher Unwin, n. d. [1919 or 20].

Irish Literature and Drama in the English Language, a Short History.
London, etc.: Nelson, 1936.

HAMILTON, C. J.:
Notable Irishwomen.
Dublin: Sealy, Bryers & Walker, n.d. [1904].

Women Writers, Their Works and Ways.
London: Ward, Lock & Co, 1892–3, 2nd series.

HARMON, MAURICE:
'Aspects of the Peasantry in Anglo-Irish Literature from 1800 to 1916'. *Studia Hibernica*, XV, 1975.

Select Bibliography for the Study of Anglo-Irish Literature.
Portmarnock: Wolfhound Press, 1977.

HARRISON, S. J. C.:
Irish Women Writers, 1800–1835.
Typewritten Ph.D. thesis, Dublin, Trinity College, 1935.

HAYES, RICHARD:
Bibliographical Dictionary of Irishmen in France.
Dublin: M. H. Gill, 1949.

Old Irish Links with France. Some Echoes of Exiled Ireland.
Dublin: M. H. Gill, 1940.

Ireland & Irishmen in the French Revolution, with a preface by H. Belloc.
London: E. Benn, 1932.

HAYLEY, BARBARA:
'Irish Periodicals from the Union to the *Nation*'. *Anglo-Irish Studies,* II, 1976, 83 seq.

HAZLITT, WILLIAM:
The Complete Works.
Ed. P. P. Howe, 1931, 21 v.

HEALY, JAMES N.:
The Mercier Book of Old Irish Street Ballads.
Cork: The Mercier Press, 1967, etc. 3 v.

HEASLIP, K. W.:
> *Irish Gaelic Literature (verse) in Translation. A bibliography of Translations of a Literary Nature and a Critical Assessment of the More Important Works.*
> Typewritten B.Litt. thesis, Dublin: Trinity College, 1952.

HEATH-STUBBS, JOHN:
> *The Darkling Plain, a Study of the Later Fortunes of Romanticism in English Poetry from G. Darley to W. B. Yeats.*
> London: Eyre & Spottiswoode, 1950.

HENRY, P. L.:
> 'A Linguistic Survey of Ireland'.
> *Lochlann*, I, Oslo, 1958, pp. 49–208.

HERRING, I. J.:
> *History of Ireland.*
> Belfast: W. Mullan & Sons, 1937, 1954.

HEWITT, JOHN:
> *Ulster Poets, 1800–1870.*
> Typewritten M.A. thesis, Belfast: Queen's, 1951.

HOARE, DOROTHY, M.:
> *The Works of Morris and of Yeats in Relation to Early Saga Literature.*
> Cambridge University Press, 1937.

HOGAN, ITA MARGARET:
> *Anglo-Irish Music, 1780–1830.*
> Cork University Press, 1966.

HOGAN, JEREMIAH, J.:
> *The English Language in Ireland.*
> Dublin: Education Co of Ireland, 1927.

HORN-MONVAL, MADELEINE:
> *Répertoire bibliographique des traductions et adaptations françaises du théâtre étranger du XVe siècle à nos jours.*
> Paris: C.N.R.S., 1958 etc. Vol. 5: *Théâtre anglais, théâtre américain,* 1963.

HOUGHTON, WALTER E., ed., etc.:
The Wellesley Index to Victorian Periodicals, 1824–1900.
University of Toronto Press; London: Routledge & Kegan
Paul, 1966.

HOUTCHENS, C. W. & L. H., eds.:
*The English Romantic Poets and Essayists. A Review of
Research and Criticism.*
New York: The Modern Language Association of America,
1957.

HOVELAQUE, H.:
*Anthologie de la Littérature irlandaise des origines au XXᵉ
siècle.*
Paris: Delagrave, 1924.

HUGO, VICTOR:
Œuvres complètes.
Paris: J. Hetzel, n.d.

HUNT, LEIGH:
Dramatic Criticism.
L. H. & C. W. Houtchens eds., New York, 1949.

Literary Criticism.
Id., ibid., 1956.

HYDE, DOUGLAS:
*A Literary History of Ireland from Earliest Times to the
Present Day.* 1st ed., London: Fisher Unwin, 1899.
New edition with introduction by Brian O'Cuív, London: E.
Benn; New York: Barnes & Noble, 1967.

*The Irish Book-Lover. A Monthly Review of Irish Literature and
Bibliography,* edited by John S. Crone.
London: Salmond; Dublin: Hanna & Neale, 1909–1928, 16 v.

JACK, IAN:
English Literature 1815–1832.
London: Oxford University Press, 1963 ('Oxford History of
English Literature').

JOHNSTON, ARTHUR:

Enchanted Ground. The Study of Medieval Romance in the XVIIIth Century.
London: Athlone Press, 1964.

JOHNSTON, EDITH M.:
Irish History, A Selected Bibliography.
London: The Historical Association, 1969.

JOYCE, JAMES:
The Critical Writings, ed. E. Mason & R. Ellmann.
New York: The Viking Press; London: Faber & Faber, 1959.

The Essential James Joyce, ed. H. Levin.
Harmondsworth: Penguin Books, 1963, etc.

The Letters, ed. S. Gilbert, ibid., 1957.

JOYCE, P. W.:
English As We Speak It in Ireland.
3rd ed., Dublin: Talbot Press; London: Longmans, Green & Co, n.d. [1910].

KAVANAGH, PATRICK:
Collected Pruse (sic).
London: Macgibbon & Kee, 1967.

KAVANAGH, PETER:
The Irish Theatre. Being a History of the Drama in Ireland from the Earliest Period up to the Present Day.
Tralee: The Kerryman Ltd, 1946.

KELLEY, Sister MARY EDITH:
The Irishman in the English Novel of the XIXth Century.
Washington D.C.: The Catholic University of America, 1939.

KENNELLY, BRENDAN, ed.:
The Penguin Book of Irish Verse.
Harmondsworth: Penguin Books, 1970 (anthology).

KETTLE, T. M.:
Irish Orators and Oratory.
London, etc.: The Irish Library, the Gresham Publishing Co., n.d. (anthology).

KILLEN, A. M.:

Le Roman «terrifiant» ou roman «noir» de Walpole à Anne Radcliffe et son influence sur la littérature française jusqu'en 1840.
Paris: G. Crès & Co., 1915.

KINSELLA, THOMAS:

(See YEATS, W. B. & KINSELLA.)

KRANS, HORATIO SHEAFE:

Irish Life in Irish Fiction.
New York: Columbia University Press; London: Macmillan, 1903.

KRAUSE, DAVID:

Introduction to The Dolmen Boucicault.
Dublin: Dolmen Press, 1964.

KUNITZ, STANLEY J.; HAYCRAFT, HOWARD:

British Authors of the XIXth Century.
New York: The H. W. Wilson Co., 1936.

Les Langues Modernes:

LXI, n° 2, March–April, 1967, «Irlande» (special number).

LECLAIRE, LUCIEN:

A General Analytical Bibliography of the Regional Novelist of the British Isles, 1800–1950.
Le Roman régionaliste dans les Iles Britanniques, 1800–1950.
Paris: Les Belles Lettres, 1954.

Les Lettres:

Paris, Librairie Les Lettres.
N°ˢ 5 and 6, 1946, «Le Romantisme anglais».

LEVY, MAURICE:

Le Roman 'gothique' anglais, 1764–1824.
Toulouse: Publications de la Faculté des Lettres, Série A, Vol. 9, 1968.

LOFTUS, RICHARD J.:

Nationalism in Modern Anglo-Irish Poetry.
Madison & Milwaukee: The University of Wisconsin Press, 1964.

LUCY, SEÁN, ed.:
> *Irish Poets in English.*
> Cork & Dublin: Mercier Press, 1973.

LUKACS, GEORG:
> *The Historical Novel.*
> Translated from the German by H. S. Mitchell,
> London: Merlin Press, 1962, 1965.

Mc CAFFREY, LAWRENCE J.:
> *Daniel O'Connell and the Repeal Year.*
> University of Kentucky Press, 1966.

Mc CARTHY, JUSTIN, etc.:
> *Irish Literature.*
> Chicago: Debower-Elliott Co., 1904, 10 v. (annotated anthology).

Mac DONAGH, DONAGH & ROBINSON, LENNOX:
> *The Oxford Book of Irish Verse, XVIIth Century-XXth Century.*
> Oxford: Clarendon Press, 1958 (anthology).

Mac DONAGH, Thomas:
> *Literature in Ireland – Studies Irish and Anglo-Irish.*
> Dublin: Talbot Press, 1916.

Mc DOWELL, R. B., ed.:
> *Social Life in Ireland.*
> Dublin: Three Candles, 1957.

MACLEAN, MAGNUS:
> *The Literature of the Celts.*
> New ed., London, Glasgow, Bombay: Blackie & Son, 1926.

MacLIAMMÓIR, MICHEÁL:
> *Theatre in Ireland.*
> Dublin: Three Candles, 1950 ('Irish Life and Culture').

Mac MANUS, DIARMUID, A.:
> *The Middle Kingdom. The Faerie World of Ireland.*
> London: Max Parrish, 1959; reprinted Gerrards Cross: Colin Smythe, 1973.

MAIGRON, LOUIS:
Le Roman historique à l'époque romantique. Essai sur l'influence de W. Scott.
Paris: Hachette, 1898.

MANSERGHI, NICHOLAS:
The Irish Question, 1840–1921.
London: Allen & Unwin, 1965.

MARKALE, JEAN:
L'Epopée celtique d'Irlande.
Paris: Payot, 1971.

MASEFIELD, MURIEL:
Women Novelists from Fanny Burney to G. Eliot.
London: Ivor Nicholson & Watson, 1934 (The University Extension Library).

MAXWELL, CONSTANTIA ELISABETH:
The Stranger in Ireland from the Reign of Elizabeth to the Great Famine, 1580–1842.
London: Cape, 1954.

MERCIER, VIVIAN:
The Irish Comic Tradition.
Oxford: Clarendon Press, 1962.

MEYER, KUNO:
A Primer of Irish Metrics.
Dublin: Hodges, Figgis and Co.; London: David Nutt, 1909.

MICHELET, JULES:
Sur les Chemins de l'Europe.
Paris: Marpon & Flammarion, 1893.

MONAHAN, MICHAEL:
Nova Hibernia. Irish Poets and Dramatists of Today and Yesterday.
New York: Kennerley, 1914.

MONGLOND, ANDRÉ:
La France révolutionnaire et impériale. Annales de Bibliographie méthodique et description des livres illustrés.
Grenoble: B. Arthaud, 1930–63, 9 v.

MONTAGUE, JOHN:
  The Faber Book of Irish Verse.
  London: Faber & Faber, 1974 (anthology).

MOODY, T. W. & MARTIN, F. X., eds.:
  The Course of Irish History.
  Cork: The Mercier Press, 1967, ill.

MORAUD, MARCEL:
  La France de la Restauration d'après les visiteurs anglais ...
  1814–21.
  Paris: H. Champion, 1933.

  Le Romantisme français en Angleterre de 1814 à 1848.
  Paris: H. Champion, 1933 (Bibliothèque de la Revue de
  Littérature Comparée, 90).

MORGAN, BAYARD QUINCY:
  A Bibliography of German Literature in English Translation.
  Madison: University of Wisconsin Studies in Language &
  Literature, n° 16, 1922.

MORTON, DAVID:
  The Renaissance of Irish Poetry, 1880–1930.
  New York: Ives Washburn, 1929.
  (Contains a few pages on precursors, Ferguson in particular.)

NICOLL, ALLARDYCE:
  A History of English Drama, 1660–1900.
  Cambridge University Press, 1952, Vol. 3 and 4.

NOWLAN, KEVIN, B.:
  The Politics of Repeal. A Study in the Relations between
  Great Britain and Ireland.
  London: Routledge & Kegan Paul, 1965.

NOYES, RUSSEL, ed.:
  English Romantic Poetry and Prose.
  New York: Oxford University Press, 1956 (anthology).

O'CASEY, SEÁN:
  Autobiographies.
  London: Macmillan, 1963, 2 v.

O'CONNOR, FRANK:

The Backward Look. A Survey of Irish Literature.
London: Macmillan, 1967.

A Book of Ireland.
London & Glasgow: Collins, 1959, etc., ill. (anthology).

Kings, Lords, and Commons. An Anthology from the Irish.
Dublin: Gill & Macmillan, 1970.

An Only Child. An Autobiography.
London: Macmillan, 1958, 1965.

O'DONOGHUE, D. J.:

The Humour of Ireland selected, with introduction, biographical index and notes.
London: Walter Scott, 1894 (Library of Humour) (anthology).

*The Poets of Ireland: A Biographical and Bibliographical
Dictionary of Irish Writers of English Verse.*
Dublin: Hodges Figgis; London: H. Frowde, Oxford Univer-
sity Press, 1922.

Sir Walter Scott's Tour in Ireland in 1825.
Glasgow: Gowans and Gray; Dublin: O'Donoghue, Gill &
Son, n.d., ill.

O'GRADY, STANDISH:

The Story of Ireland.
London: Methuen, 1894.

Óh-AODHA, MICHEÁL:

Plays and Places.
Dublin: Progress House, 1961.

O'HEGARTY, P. S.:

'Synge and Irish Literature'.
Dublin Magazine, VII, n° 1, January–March 1932, pp. 51–6.

OLIPHANT, Mrs.:

*Annals of a Publishing House: William Blackwood and his
Sons, Their Magazine and Friends.*
Edinburgh & London: W. Blackwood, 1897.

Ó LOCHLAINN, COLM:

Anglo-Irish Song-Writers since Moore.
Dublin: Three Candles, 1950 (The Bibliographical Society of Ireland Publications, Vol. VI, n° 1).

O'NEILL, J. J.:

Irish Theatrical Literature.
Dublin: Three Candles, 1920 (The Bibliographical Society of Ireland Publications, Vol. I, n° 6, pp. 57–88).

O'NEILL, PATRICK:

'German Literature & the *Dublin University Magazine*, 1833–1850: a Checklist and Commentary'. *Long Room*, 1976, 20–31.

'The Reception of German Literature in Ireland 1750–1850'. *Studia Hibernica*, 16, 1976, pp. 122–139 (to be concluded).

O'SULLIVAN, DONAL:

Irish Folk Music & Song.
Dublin: Three Candles, 1952, etc. ill.

Songs of the Irish. An Anthology of Irish Folk Music.
Dublin: Browne & Nolan, 1959.

O'SULLIVAN, SEÁN:

Folktales of Ireland.
The University of Chicago Press, 1966.

The Folklore of Ireland.
London: Batsford, 1974.

PAKENHAM, THOMAS:

The Year of Liberty. The Story of the Great Irish Rebellion of 1798.
London: Hodder & Stoughton, 1969.

PARTRIDGE, ERIC:

The French Romantics' Knowledge of English Literature, 1820–1848, According to Contemporary French Memoirs, Letters and Periodicals.
Paris: Champion, 1924 (Bibliothèque de la Revue de Littérature Comparée, 14).

PASTON, GEORGE [= Miss E. M. SYMONDS]:
Little Memoirs of the XIXth Century.
London: Grant Richards; New York; E. P. Dutton, 1902.

PAULY, MARIE-HÉLÈNE:
Les Voyageurs français en Irlande au temps du Romantisme.
Paris: G. Ernault, 1939.

PENZOLDT, PETER:
The Supernatural in Fiction.
New York: Humanities Press, 1952, 1965.

POE, EDGAR A.:
Poems & Essays.
London: Dent, 1927, etc., 'Everyman's'.

POWER, PATRICK C.:
A Literary History of Ireland.
Cork: The Mercier Press, 1969.

The Story of Anglo-Irish Poetry, 1800–1922.
Cork: The Mercier Press, 1967.

PRAZ, MARIO:
The Romantic Agony.
Oxford University Press, 1933, 2nd ed.: 1951, 1954.
Translated by Angus Davidson.

RAFROIDI, PATRICK:
«Chronique irlandaise».
Langues Modernes LXI, 2, March–April 1967, pp. 196–206.

English Romantic Poets.
Paris: O.C.D.L., 1969 (anthology).

L'Irlande, Tome II: Littérature.
Paris: A. Colin, 1970, «U 2»

Les Poètes anglais du XIXe siècle. I. Les Romantiques.
Paris: Europe Universitaire, 1968.

'The Uses of Irish Myth in the Nineteenth Century', *Studies*,
Autumn/Winter 1973, pp. 251–261.

RAFROIDI, PATRICK; FEHLMANN, GUY; MacCONMARA,
MAITIU, eds.:

France–Ireland, Literary Relations.
Lille: P.U.L., Paris: Editions Universitaires, 1974.

RAFROIDI, PATRICK & HARMON, MAURICE, eds.:
The Irish Novel in Our Time.
Lille, P.U.L., 1976.

RAFROIDI, PATRICK; POPOT, RAYMONDE; PARKER,
WILLIAM, eds.:
Aspects of the Irish Theatre.
Lille: P.U.L.; Paris: Editions Universitaires, 1972.

RAILO, EINO:
*The Haunted Castle. A Study of the Elements of English
Romanticism.*
London: Routledge; New York: E. P. Dutton, 1927.

Rann, an Ulster Quarterly, Poetry & Comment.
Edited by Barbara Hunter and Roy McFadden, n° 20, June
1953 (*Ulster Writing*).

READ, CHARLES A.:
The Cabinet of Irish Literature.
London: Blackie ... 1879, 4 v. (annotated anthology).

READ, HERBERT:
*The True Voice of Feeling. Studies in English Romantic
Poetry.*
London: Faber, 1953.

REBOUL, PIERRE:
*Le Mythe anglais dans la Littérature française sous la
Restauration.*
Lille: Bibliothèque Universitaire, 1962. (Travaux et Mémoires
de l'Université de Lille, Series in-4°, n° 1.)

REMAK, HENRY:
'A Key to West European Romanticism'.
Colloquia Germanica, 1968.

RENAN, ERNEST:
Souvenirs d'Enfance et de Jeunesse.
Paris: Calmann Lévy, 1883.

RENWICK, W. L.:
> *English Literature, 1789–1815.*
> London: Oxford University Press, 1963 ('Oxford History of English Literature').

Revue des Sciences Humaines
> Faculté des Lettres de Lille. Nouvelle série, Fasc. 62–3, August–September 1951, «Problèmes du Romantisme».

RIVOALLAN, ANATOLE:
> *L'Irlande.*
> Paris: A. Colin, 1934, 2nd ed. 1950.

> *Présence des Celtes.*
> Paris: Nouvelle Librairie Celtique, n.d. [1957].

ROCHEDIEU, CHARLES-ALFRED E.:
> *Bibliography of French Translations of English Works, 1700–1800,* with an introduction by Donald F. Bond.
> Chicago: University of Chicago Press, 1948.

ROSA, MATTHEW WHITING:
> *The Silver-Fork School. Novels of Fashion Preceding 'Vanity Fair'.*
> New York: Morningside Heights, Columbia University Press, 1936.

RUER, JEAN:
> «Plaidoyer pour la littérature à sensation».
> *Bulletin de la Faculté des Lettres de Strasbourg,* XLVII, n° 4, January 1969, pp. 233–47.

> *Sensation in English Fiction in the Eighteen Sixties.*
> Typewritten M.A. thesis, University of Manchester, June 1957.

RUFF, MARCEL A.:
> Introduction to *Bertram*: «Maturin et les Romantiques français».
> Paris: José Corti, 1955.

RYAN, DESMOND:
> *The Phoenix Flame. A Study of Fenianism and John Devoy.*
> London: Arthur Barker, 1937.

The Sword of Light. From the Four Masters to Douglas Hyde, 1636–1638.
London: Arthur Barker, 1939.

SADLEIR, MICHAEL:
XIXth Century Fiction, a bibliographical record.
London: Constable, 1957.

SAINTE-BEUVE:
Volupté.
Ed. Olivier Centlivres, Lausanne: Rencontre, 1964.

SAINTSBURY, GEORGE:
A History of English Prosody from the 12th Century to the Present Day.
Vol. III: *From Blake to Mr Swinburne.*
London: Macmillan, 1923.

SHAW, BERNARD:
Man and Superman.
John Bull's Other Island.
Standard Edition: London: Constable; also: Penguin.

The Matter with Ireland.
Hitherto Uncollected Writings edited by D. H. Greene & Dan H. Laurence.
London: Rupert Hart Davis, 1962.

SHELLEY, P. B.:
The Complete Works.
R. Ingpen & W. E. Peck, eds.
London: E. Benn; New York: Ch. Scribner's Sons, 1928.

Poetical Works.
Ed. by Thomas Hutchinson, Oxford University Press, 1967.

SIGERSON, GEORGE:
Bards of the Gael and Gall. Examples of the Poetic Literature of Erin Done into English after the Metres and Modes of the Gael.
2nd ed. London: Fisher Unwin, 1907. Reprinted, New York: Lemma, 1973.

SJOESTEDT, MARIE-LOUISE:

In Memoriam, suivi de *Essai sur une Littérature nationale, la Littérature irlandaise contemporaine.*
Paris: Droz, 1941.

SNYDER, EDWARD D.:

The Celtic Revival in English Literature, 1760–1800.
Cambridge, Mass: Harvard University Press, 1923, ill.

'The Wild Irish: A Study of Some English Satires against the Irish, Scots and Welsh'.
Modern Philology.
The University of Chicago Press, Vol. XVII, n° 12, April 1920, pp. 147–185.

SPENSER, EDMUND:

Works.
London: Collier, 1862.

STALLKNECHT, NEWTON PHELPS & FRENZ, HORST:

Comparative Literature: Method and Perspective.
Carbondale: Southern Illinois University Press, 1961.

STENDHAL:

De l'Amour.
Ed. Michel Crouzet, Paris: Garnier-Flammarion, 1965.

STEPHENS, JAMES:

'A Conversation with George Moore'.
The Listener, 16 Jan. 1947.

STEWART, J. D. etc.:

British Union Catalogue of Periodicals. A Record of the Periodicals of the World, from the XVIIth Century to the Present Day, in British Libraries.
London: Butterworths Scientific Publications, 1955, 5 v.

STOCKLEY, W. F. P.:

Essays in Irish Biography.
Cork University Press, 1933.

STOKOE, F. W.:

German Influence in the English Romantic Period, 1788–1818, with special reference to Scott, Coleridge, Shelley and Byron.
Cambridge University Press, 1926.

STRICKLAND, W. G.:
A Dictionary of Irish Artists.
Dublin and London: Maunsel & Co, Ltd. 2 v., ill.
Reprinted by Irish University Press in 1969 (with a critical introduction by Theo Snoddy).

Studies in Romanticism.
The Graduate School, Boston University.

SULLIVAN, DANIEL *et al.:*
The Anglo-Irish Novel.
Dublin: The Education Times, 1974 (11 p.)

SUMMERS, M.:
A Gothic Bibliography.
London: The Fortune Press, n.d.

The Gothic Quest. A History of the Gothic Novel.
London: The Fortune Press, n.d. [1938].
New York: Russell & Russell, 1964.

SYMONS, ARTHUR:
The Romantic Movement in English Poetry.
London: Constable, 1909 (annotated anthology).

SYNGE, JOHN MILLINGTON:
Collected Works.
London: Oxford University Press, 1962–68, 4 v.

TALMON, J. L.:
Romanticism and Revolt.
London: Thames & Hudson, 1967, ill.

TAYLOR, GEOFFREY, ed.:
Irish Poets of the XIXth Century.
London: Routledge & Kegan Paul, 1951 (anthology).

THACKERAY, WILLIAM MAKEPEACE:
Works.
London: Smith, Elder & Co, 1873, 12 v.

THOMPSON, L.F.:
Kotzebue. A Survey of his Progress in France and England Preceded by a Consideration of the Critical Attitude to him in Germany.

Paris: Champion, 1928. (Bibliothèque de la Revue de Littérature Comparée. Volume 51.)

THOMPSON, WILLIAM IRWIN:
The Imagination of an Insurrection: Dublin, Easter 1916. A Study of an Ideological Movement.
New York: Oxford University Press, 1967.

THOMSON, DERRICK, S.:
The Gaelic Sources of Macpherson's 'Ossian'.
Edinburgh, London: Oliver & Boyd, 1952.
(Aberdeen University Studies, n° 30).

THORLBY, A.K.:
The Romantic Movement.
London: Longmans, 1966. ('Problems and Perspectives in History'.)

THORPE, C. D.; BAKER, C.; WEAVER, B., eds.:
The Major English Romantic Poets. A Symposium in Reappraisal.
Carbondale: Southern Illinois University Press, 1957.

THORSLEV, PETER L. Jr:
The Byronic Hero. Types and Prototypes.
Minneapolis: University of Minnesota Press, 1962, 1965.

THRALL, MIRIAM, M. H.:
Rebellious Fraser's. Nol Yorke's Magazine in the Days of Maginn, Thackeray & Carlyle.
New York: Columbia University Press, 1934. (Columbia University Studies in English and Comparative Literature, n° 117.)

TIMBS, JOHN:
Anecdote Lives of the Later Wits and Humourists.
London: R. Bentley, 1874, 2 v.

TROLLOPE, ANTHONY:
(Trollope's 'Irish' novels mentioned in Chapter 6 of the present study have recently been reprinted by Garland Publishing, Inc. of New York.)

TRUNNINGER, ANNELISE:
Paddy and the Paycock. A study of the Stage-Irishman from Shakespeare to O'Casey.
Bern: Francke, 1976.

UNWIN, RAYNER:
The Rural Muse. Studies in the Peasant Poetry of England.
London: Allen & Unwin, 1954.

UTTER, R. P. & NEEDHAM, G. B.:
Pamela's Daughters.
London: Lovat Dickson, 1937.

VAN TIEGHEM, P.:
Ossian en France.
Paris (publisher unknown), 1917.

Le Préromantisme. Etudes d'Histoire littéraire européenne.
Paris: Ed. Sfelt, 1947.

Le Romantisme dans la Littérature européenne.
Paris: Albin Michel, 1948, 1969, («L'évolution de l'humanité»).

VARMA, DEVENDRA, P.:
The Gothic Flame. Being a History of the Gothic Novel in England: Its Origins, Efflorescence, Disintegration, and Residuary Influences.
London: A. Barker Ltd, 1957.

VAX, LOUIS:
La Séduction de l'étrange. Etude sur la Littérature fantastique.
Paris: Presses Universitaires de France, 1964.

VENEDEY, J.:
Ireland & the Irish During the Repeal Year, 1843.
Translated (from the German) and with notes by W. B. MacCabe.
Dublin: J. Duffy; London: Ch. Dolman, 1844.

VIGNY, ALFRED DE:
Œuvres complètes.
Ed. Conard, Paris, 1914.

VOISINE, Jacques:
J. J. Rousseau en Angleterre à l'époque romantique. Les écrits autobiographiques et la légende.
Paris: Didier, 1956.

VOLTA, Ornella & RIVA, Valerio:
Histoires de Vampires.
Présentées par R. Vadim, Paris: R. Laffont, 1961 (anthology).

WALSH, T. J.:
Opera in Dublin, 1705–1797, the social scene.
Dublin: Allen Figgis, 1973.

WEBB, Alfred:
A Compendium of Irish Biography. Comprising Sketches of Distinguished Irishmen and of Eminent Persons Connected with Ireland by Office or by their Writings.
Dublin: Gill, 1878.
Photographic reprint available: Hildesheim (West Germany); G. Olms, also Lemma Publishing Corp., New York, 1970.

WHITMORE, Clara H.:
Woman's Work in English Fiction from the Restoration to the Mid-Victorian Period.
New York & London: G. P. Putnam's Sons, The Knickerbocker Press, 1910.

WILDE, Oscar:
Complete Works.
London: Collins, 1966.

WITTKE, Carl:
The Irish in America.
Baton Rouge: Louisiana State University Press, 1958.

WOODHAM-SMITH, Cecil:
The Great Hunger.
London: Hamish Hamilton, 1962.
London: The New English Library (paperback), 1968.

The Year's Work in English Studies.

YEATS, W. B.:
Collected Plays.
London: Macmillan, 1953.

Collected Poems.
London: Macmillan, 1958.

Essays and Introductions.
London: Macmillan, 1961.

Explorations selected by Mrs W. B. Yeats.
London: Macmillan, 1962.

Irish Fairy and Folk Tales.
New York: The Modern Library, n.d. (anthology), published in
England with *Irish Fairy Tales* as *Fairy and Folk Tales of
Ireland*; Gerrards Cross: Colin Smythe, 1973.

The Letters, edited by Allan Wade.
London: Rupert Hart Davis, 1954.

Uncollected Prose, Vol. I, edited by J. P. Frayne.
London: Macmillan, 1970. Vol. II, edited by J. P. Frayne &
Colton Johnson, ibid., 1975.

YEATS, W. B. & EGLINTON, JOHN:
Literary Ideals in Ireland.
London: Fisher Unwin; Dublin: Daily Express Office, 1899.

YEATS, W. B. & JOHNSON, LIONEL:
Poetry and Ireland.
Dundrum: Cuala Press, 1908.

YEATS, W. B. & KINSELLA, THOMAS:
Davis, Mangan, Ferguson?
Dublin: Dolmen Press, 1971.

YOUNG, ARTHUR:
A Tour in Ireland, 2 v.
Recently reprinted by Irish University Press (A. W. Hutton,
ed.).

ZELLWEGER, RUDOLF:
*Les Débuts du roman rustique, Suisse-Allemagne-France,
1836–1856.*
Paris: E. Droz, 1941.

ZIMMERMANN, GEORGE-DENIS:
Irish Political Street Ballads & Rebel Songs.
Genève: Imprimerie La Sirène, 1966.
Hatboro, Pennsylvania: Folklore Associates, Inc., 1967.

2

IRISH AUTHORS (1789–1850)
works, criticism
BIO-BIBLIOGRAPHICAL NOTES

N.B. Dramatic works are listed with the date of their first performance where this is known. The name of the theatre appears before the name of the play. The town is mentioned only when it is other than London or Dublin.

Non-dramatic works are listed with the date of their first publication.

In both cases, the place of performance or publication, the publisher, the number of pages and, occasionally, in brackets, a description of the contents, are given. The format is indicated only when it is unusual. The main titles of the volumes described are given in SMALL CAPITALS, their subtitles and the titles of secondary works in *italics*.

In the case of a work, or the first edition of a work, that the present author has been unable to see himself, all particulars taken from previous works of reference appear in square brackets.

The abbreviations are those in current use and do not call for individual explanation, (e.g., *infra:* below; *n.d.:* not dated, date unknown; *q.v.:* see; *seq.:* and following; *supra:* above, etc.) except for the names of theatres shown as follows:

ADEL.:   Adelphi
CAP.S.:   Capel Street, Dublin
C.G.:   Covent Garden
COB.:   Coburg
C.S.:   Crow Street, Dublin
D.L.:   Drury Lane

E.O.H.:   English Opera House
F.S.:   Fishamble Street, Dublin
HAY: Haymarket
GRIM.:   Grimston
LYC.:   Lyceum
N.N.T.:   New National Theatre, New York
OLYM.:   Olympic
PRIN.:   Princess
P.W.:   Prince of Wales
QU.:   Queen's
R.A.:   Royal Amphitheatre
ROY.:   Royalty
R.V.:   Royal Victoria
S.A.:   Smock Alley, Dublin
S.W.:   Sadler's Wells
STR.:   Strand
St.J.:   St James'
SUR.:   Surrey

As a rule, and for the first time, complete accounts of each author *of the period 1789–1850* mentioned in the body of the present work and of a few others are to be found in the following pages. However, writers who were not essentially men of letters are given only limited space and it has not been deemed necessary to re-introduce a name when no documentation exists to support a previous reference. Also, works anterior to 1789 and posterior to 1850 are only given as a reminder and only where they are of relevance to Ireland.

Garland Publishing Inc. of New York have recently reprinted a number of nineteenth-century Anglo-Irish novels. Those that fall within the scope of this bibliography have been noted in the text by an asterisk after the title of the work.

ADDISON (Henry-Robert – 1805(?)–1876)

BIOGRAPHY

According to D. J. O'Donoghue, Addison was born about 1805 in Calcutta, of Irish parents and this is the reason for his being mentioned here as his work shows no specifically Irish qualities.

This dramatist who, if Nicoll is to be believed, was also a military man (captain, then lieutenant-colonel), wrote for the *Dublin University Magazine* and compiled a *Who's Who* in 1849–50. He had previously lived for some time in Belgium where he is said to have inspired Lever's creation of the character of Captain Bubbleton in *Tom Burke.*

He died in London on June 24, 1876.

BIBLIOGRAPHY

(a) Dramatic works previous to 1850:

1830. (22.7) LO ZINGARO, a petite opera, in 2 acts ...
music composed by A. Lee.
London: J. Duncombe & Co, n.d., 26 p.

1833. (26.8, ADEL.) JESSIE, THE FLOWER OF DUMBLAINE; *or, Well May the Keel Row,*
a petite opera, in 1 act ...
London: J. Duncombe & Co, n.d., 20 p.

(28.9, R.V.) WHO WOULD BE MARRIED?
(unpublished)

1834. (25.11, D.L.) TAM O'SHANTER,
a musical farce, in 2 acts ...
music composed and selected by P. Cook.
London: W. Kenneth, 1834, 30 p.

1835. (20.1, D.L.) THE KING'S WORD,
from the French ...
London: J. Miller, 1835, 24 p.

1836. (13.2, C.G.) SIGISMOND AUGUSTUS
(unpublished)

(27.2, C.G.) MARIE, *a Tale of the Pont Neuf,*
an original comedietta, in 1 act ...
London: J. Duncombe & Co, 1836, 20 p.

1846. (20.7, ADEL.) ABRAHAM PARKER
(unpublished)

1848. BRITISH BEAUTY; *or, The Seraglio in an Uproar*
(unpublished version of *Les Trois Sultanes*, music by Lee).

A PRETTY COUPLE (unpublished)

(27.9, SUR.) DID YOU EVER? (id.)

1849. (30.4, SUR.) SOPHIA'S SUPPER, a farce in 1 act.
London: T. H. Lacy, n.d. (vol. XVI).

(b) Miscellanea:

1838. HANDBOOK FOR RESIDENTS AND TOURISTS IN BELGIUM.
Brussels: Pratt & Barry, 1838, 421 p.
(dedicated to King Leopold)

1839. THE RHINE, *its Banks and Environs.*
Brussels: Belgian Company of Booksellers,
Hauman & Co, 1839, 168 p.

1843. BELGIUM AS SHE IS.
Brussels & Leipzig: C. Muquardt, 1843, 316 p.

ALEXANDER (Cecil Frances – 1818(?)–1895)

BIOGRAPHY

Cecil Frances Humphreys who was to marry William Alexander (1824–1911), future Professor of Poetry at Oxford, Protestant Bishop of Armagh and Primate of all Ireland, was born in County Wicklow in 1818 according to some accounts, and in Tyrone in 1823 according to others. She had started writing before her marriage in 1850, but it is particularly after this date that she published hymns and religious poems of which some ('There is a green hill far away' for example or 'The burial of Moses' that Tennyson would have liked to have written) are very well known.

She died in Derry on October 12, 1895.

BIBLIOGRAPHY

1838. THE BARON'S LITTLE DAUGHTER, *and Other Tales, in Prose and Verse.*
London: J. Masters, 1838, IV + 176 p.

1846. VERSES FOR HOLY SEASONS, *with questions for examination,* by Cecil Frances Humphreys, edited by Walter Farquhar Hook, D.D., Vicar of Leeds.
London: F. & J. Rivington, 1846, XI + 232 p.

1848. HYMNS FOR LITTLE CHILDREN.
London: J. Masters, 1848, 72 p.

THE LORD OF THE FOREST AND HIS VASSALS, an Allegory.
London: J. Masters, 1848, 118 p. (prose).

Noteworthy after 1850 are:

1853. NARRATIVE HYMNS FOR VILLAGE SCHOOLS.
London: J. Masters.

1858. HYMNS DESCRIPTIVE AND DEVOTIONAL ...
ibid.

1859. THE LEGEND OF THE GOLDEN PRAYERS AND OTHER POEMS.
London: Bell & Daly.

There exists a complete edition:

1896. POEMS.
London: Macmillan & Co, 1896, XLIII + 463 p.
    Part I: 'Hymns (1–62)'.
    Part II: 'Poems on Sacred Subjects' (65–127).
    Part III: 'Poems Narrative and Imaginative' (130–334).
    Part IV: 'Memorial Verses' (346–373).
    Part V: 'Occasional & Miscellaneous' (375–429).
    Part VI: 'Translations' (432–48).
    Part VII: 'Songs for Children' (451–63).

and an anthology of poetry by William Alexander and his wife:

SELECTED POEMS OF W. ALEXANDER, ARCHBISHOP OF ARMAGH ... AND C. F. ALEXANDER, edited by A. P. Graves.
London: Society for Promoting Christian Knowledge, 1930, X + 118 p.

note also the following article:

MC MAHON (Sean): 'All Things Bright and Beautiful', *Eire-Ireland*, X, 4, Winter 1975, 101–108.

ALLINGHAM (John Till)

BIOGRAPHY

According to D. J. O'Donoghue who bases himself on *The Thespian Dictionary*, and from information given in *The Life of John Kemble* by L. Boaden (1825), J. T. Allingham was the son of an Irish wine merchant settled in London.

He was destined for the Bar but died young, his intemperance having hastened his death. He is the author of ten mediocre plays.

BIBLIOGRAPHY

(a) Published Works:

1799.   (25.5, C.G. and HAY.) FORTUNE'S FROLIC, a farce, in 2 acts.
London: James Ridgway, 1799.

1800.   (17.6, HAY.) 'TIS ALL A FARCE,
a farce, in 2 acts ...
London: Ridgway, 1800, 36 p.

1803.   (16.4, D.L.) THE MARRIAGE PROMISE,
a comedy in 5 acts ...
London: Ridgway, 1806, 80 p.

(27.5, HAY.) MRS WIGGINS, a comic piece, in 2 acts.
London: Ridgway, 1808, 49 p.

(19.11, D.L.) HEARTS OF OAK, a comedy, in 5 acts.
London: Ridgway, 1804, 71 p.

1805.   (18.11, D.L.) THE WEATHERCOCK, a farce, in 2 acts ...
the music by M. P. King,
London: Lackington, Allen & Co, n.d. (1805), 27 p.

1808.   (25.2, C.G.) THE WIDOW; *or, Who Wins?*, a farce, in 2 acts,
London: Cumberland's British Theatre, Vol. 32, 36 p.

(b) Unpublished Works:

1806.   (11.1, C.G.) THE ROMANTIC LOVER; *or, Lost and Found.*

1809.   (9.3, HAY.) INDEPENDENCE; *or, The Trustee.*

1810.   (30.11, LYC.) TRANSFORMATION; *or, Love and Law.*

ALLINGHAM (William – 1824–1889)[1]

Born in Ballyshannon on March 19, 1824, the future author of the famous *Laurence Bloomfield* (1864) and of a no less famous *Diary* that has just been re-published, and friend of the greatest Victorian poets, the chief editor of *Fraser's*, is deserving of a mention in the period with which we are concerned only by virtue of his first collection of poems of 1850:

POEMS. London: Chapman & Hall, 1850, XII + 299 p.

A complete list of his works is to be found in:

O'HEGARTY (P. S.): *A Bibliography of William Allingham*, privately printed by Alex. Thom & Co, Ltd, Dublin, 1945, 12 p.

To be supplemented by:

WARNER (Alan): 'William Allingham: A Bibliographical Survey'. *Irish Booklore*, II, 2, 1975

Recent reissues include:

W. ALLINGHAM'S *Diary*, introd. by Geoffrey Grigson. London: Centaur Press, 1967, 404 p.

There is an anthology:

The Poems of William Allingham. Edited with an introduction by John Hewitt. Dublin: The Dolmen Press, 1967, 102 p.

And a critical volume:

WARNER (Alan): *William Allingham*. Lewisburg: Bucknell University Press, 1975, 90 p.

[1] Updated by Alan Warner.

ANKETELL (Rev. John – 1750–?)

BIOGRAPHY

Born in County Tyrone. Studied at Trinity College, Dublin (B.A. 1773). He reappears as curate of Donaghendry, again in Tyrone. Published three mediocre works in neo-classical vein.

BIBLIOGRAPHY

1793. POEMS ON SEVERAL SUBJECTS ... *to which are added 'The Epistle of Yarico to Inkle', and 'The English and Latin Songs of Chevy Chase'.*
Dublin, printed for the author by William Porter, Skinner Row, 1793, LVII + 333 p.

1799. VERSIFICATION OF THE BOOK OF JOB AND CHRIST'S SERMON ON THE MOUNT.
Dublin, printed by W. Porter, 1799, 107 p.

1806. [ESSAYS IN PROSE AND VERSE.
Belfast, 1806.]

ANSTER (John – 1793–1867)

BIOGRAPHY

Born in 1793 at Charleville, County Cork. Studied at Trinity College, Dublin (B.A. 1816) where, in 1850, he was to become Regius Professor of Civil Law. Died in Dublin on June 9, 1867, aged 73.

BIBLIOGRAPHY

John Anster contributed to several magazines: *Blackwood's* (1820) in which his first translations of Goethe appeared, *Amulet* (poems: 1826–8), *Dublin University Magazine* (1837–56, articles and poems), *North British Review* (1847, etc., articles on the Irish situation then literary chronicles on Shelley, Swift, Southey, Campbell, Leigh Hunt, etc.).

His works collected in book form comprise poems, translations and essays.

(a) Poems:

1818. LINES ON THE DEATH OF HER ROYAL HIGHNESS THE PRINCESS CHARLOTTE OF WALES: to which was adjudged the prize, proposed by the Provost and senior fellows of Trinity College, Dublin, for the best English poem on the subject.
Dublin: R. Milliken; London: Longman, 1818, 24 p.

1819. POEMS WITH SOME TRANSLATIONS FROM THE GERMAN ...
Edinburgh: W. Blackwood; London: Cadell and Davies; Dublin: R. Milliken, 1819, VIII + 244 p.
(According to the preface to this anthology, some of the poems included had already been collected and published in Dublin in 1815, but the author withdrew the edition from circulation.)

1837. XENIOLA. *Poems, including translations from Schiller and de la Motte-Fouqué ...*
Dublin: Milliken, 1837, X + 174 p.
(This collection duplicates the thin volume of 1818, most of the poems of 1819 and adds a very few new pieces.)

(b) Translations:

The volumes of 1819 and 1837 contain translations among the original poems. Note also:

1835. FAUSTUS, *a dramatic mystery, 'The Bride of Corinth', 'The First Walpurgis Night'* translated from the German of Goethe, and illustrated with notes ...
London: Longman, 1835, XLIV + 491 p.

1864. FAUSTUS, *the second part*, from the German of Goethe.
London: Longman, 1864, LXXXVII + 485 p.
This double translation is the author's greatest claim to fame as much for its novelty as its quality. Cf. what A. Symons (*The Romantic Movement*, p. 338) said of it:

'John Anster besides writing some valueless verse of his own, did a translation of Goethe's "Faust" which remains one of the best for lightness of touch on rhymes and rhythm.'

(c) Essays:

1850. INTRODUCTORY LECTURE ON THE STUDY OF THE ROMAN CIVIL LAW.
Dublin: Hodges and Smith, 1850, 51 p.

1864. 'German Literature at the close of the last century and the commencement of the present' in THE AFTERNOON LECTURES ON LITERATURE AND ART ...
S. Stephen's Green ...
London: Bell and Daly; Dublin: Hodges and Smith, X + 277 p.
Anster's lecture: pp. 151–195.

ARCHDEACON (Matthew – 1800(?)–1853(?))

BIOGRAPHY

Born in Castlebar, County Mayo, round about 1800. A teacher by profession. Died in 1853 according to some accounts or, 1862–1863 according to others.

BIBLIOGRAPHY

1830. CONNAUGHT, a tale of 1798.
Dublin: printed for M. Archdeacon and sold by all booksellers, 1830, 394 p.
(current title: 'Connaught in 1798').

1839. LEGENDS OF CONNAUGHT, Irish Stories, by the author of 'Connaught in 1798'.
Dublin: J. Cumming, 1839, XV + 406 p.
(contains:
'Fitzgerald' (1–165)
'The Banshee' (166–180)
'The Election' (181–277)
'Alice Thompson' (278–296)
'McMahon' (297–353)
'The Rebel's Grave' (354–371)
'The Ribbonman' (372–382)
Appendix (on G. R. Fitzgerald)
O'Donoghue and Brown give the date of 1829(?) for this work, as does B. Cleeve).

1835. [EVERARD: an Irish Tale of the XIXth century.
Dublin, 1835, 2 v.
The reference is to be found in O'Donoghue and Brown;
the present author has not seen this work.]

1844. THE PRIEST-HUNTER, an Irish Tale of the Penal Times.
Dublin: J. Duffy, 1844, 8 + 416 p. In 1862, a new edition
(ibid.) alternates this title with *Shawn na Soggarth; or,
The Priest Hunter.*

ARCHER (Henry Playsted)

Author of:

EMMET, THE IRISH PATRIOT; *and Other Poems* by the late Henry
Playsted Archer.
Canterbury: R. Colegate, 1832, VIII + 64 p.
(The title-poem is divided into 3 cantos and runs from pages 9 to
50. Its literary interest is slender, the author wrote it at the age of
17, but it illustrates the hold that the young hero Emmet had over
the Irish imagination. The rest of the volume (14 p.) is taken up by
either lyrical or occasional verse.)

ARCHER (William – ?, 1874)

Born in Dublin, author of *The Orange Melodist* (1852).

ARMSTRONG (A. W.)

Author of:

THE POETICAL WORKS OF A. W. ARMSTRONG OF NORTH
SHIELDS. North Shields: Printed by W. Orange, 1816, XXII +
216 + 12 p.
(The last 12 pages comprise the poem 'O'Neil's Farewell', the
parting song of a young Irishman about to be executed for

theft. The rest of the collection consists of witty epigrams, lamentations, etc.)

THE PARTICULARS OF THE ARREST AND EXAMINATION OF A. W. ARMSTRONG *on a charge of high treason on June 13, 1818, for threatening the life of the Prince Regent ...*
London: R. Carlile, n.d. [1818?], 16 p. (including an introductory poem).

ASHE (Rev. Nicholas)

Author of:

PANTHEA; *or, The Susan Captive*, a tragedy in 5 acts ...
Dublin: Printed by John Halpen, 1800, 70 p.
(This verse-play, in the purest neo-classical tradition, is set partly in the Persian camp and partly in the African one.)

A FUNERAL SERMON *preached in the Parish Church of Maynooth, the 28th October, 1804, to his Grace the Late W. Robert, Duke of Leinster.*
Dublin: printed by J. & J. Carrick, n.d. (1804?), 20 p.

ATKINS (John)

Born in Cork, studied at Trinity College, Dublin; a lawyer by profession, author of:

THE PILGRIMS OF ERIN *and Other Poems ...*
London: W. H. Dalton, 1832, VII + 120 p.
(Pages 9 to 53 of this anonymous collection consist of the 153 Spenserian stanzas of the poem that gives the volume its title. They describe, sometimes movingly, the woes of Ireland. Twenty pages of explanatory notes follow, the remainder of the work being taken up by short lyrical pieces.)

ATKINSON (Joseph – 1743–1818)

BIOGRAPHY

Born in Dublin. An army officer by profession and a friend of Moore who wrote his epitaph (Cheadle cemetery, Staffs.) and who speaks of him in his diary. Also frequented Lady Morgan's circle (Fitzpatrick mentions him in his biography of the former).

BIBLIOGRAPHY

(a) Poetry:

1778. CONGRATULATORY ODE TO GENERAL SIR WILLIAM HOWE, *on his return from America.*
Dublin: printed by James Hoey, 1778, IV + 15 p.

1790(?) KILLARNY, a poem by an officer in the army.
Dublin, n.d., printed for Thomas Ewing, 18 p.
(1790 is the date suggested by the catalogue in the British Museum. The only dated edition (and there are considerable differences in the text) is of 1798:
KILLARNEY, a poem by J. Atkinson Esq.
Dublin: printed by W. Porter, 1798, v + 28 p.)

1818. A POETIC EXCURSION.
Dublin: R. Milliken, 1818, 8 + 5 + 58 p. (a description of Wicklow, in verse).

(b) Dramatic Works:

1785. (2.3, S.A.) THE MUTUAL DECEPTION.
London: Dilly, 1785, VII + 96 p.
(A comedy inspired by *Le Jeu de l'Amour et du Hasard* by Marivaux.)

1786. (17.4, S.A.) A MATCH FOR A WIDOW; *or, The Frolics of Fancy.*
London: Dilly, 1788, 61 p. + epilogue.
(A musical comedy adapted from *L'Heureuse Erreur* by Patrat; music by Didbin.)

1799. (29.5, C.S.) LOVE IN A BLAZE.
Dublin: printed by W. Porter, 1800, 4 + 79 p.
(A musical comedy inspired by *Le Naufrage* by Lafont; music by Sir John Stevenson.)

AUSTIN (Thomas – 1794–1881)

BIOGRAPHY

Born on December 18, 1794. A military career: Middlesex militia (1810), battle of Merxem (1814) as a result of which one of his legs was amputated. After his marriage in 1816, he commanded Fort Duncannon until about 1869. Settled in Bristol on retirement. A distinguished geologist and author of several books on the subject.

BIBLIOGRAPHY

1848. THE WOUNDED SOLDIER'S DREAM; *The Irish Emigrant; Prince Charlie and Other Poems.*
London: Hamilton, Adams & Co, 1848, IX + 154 p.

1926. OLD STICK-LEG. *Extracts from the Diaries of Major Thomas Austin*, arranged by Brigadier-General H. H. Austin.
London: Geoffrey Bles, 1926, 206 p.

BALFOUR (Mary – 1780–1819)

BIOGRAPHY

Daughter of a clergyman, was born in Derry; she was head-mistress of a school in Newton Limavady, then in Belfast. She is especially known for her verse translations from the Irish (among the first) and for the lyrics which, like Th. Moore, she wrote for certain of Bunting's airs.

1810. HOPE, *a Poetical Essay; with Various Other Poems.*
Belfast: printed by Smith & Lyons, 1810, 192 p.
('Hope' (1–40) is a neo-classical poem inspired from Campbell; 'Kathleen O'Neil' (no connection with the play of the same name) introduces Irish fairy-lore (41–87); there are several adaptations from the Gaelic including a pleasant 'Ellen a Roon' (172–3).)

1814. (9.2, Belfast) KATHLEEN O'NEIL, a grand national melodrama, in 3 acts ...
Belfast: printed by Archbold & Duncan, 1814, 54 p.

(Some obvious flaws: badly introduced incidents, rudimentary characterisation, songs in verse clumsily inserted in the prose, over-numerous reminiscences, etc., but the play justifies the epithet 'national' of the sub-title: it is an authentically Celtic work.)

BANIM (John – 1798–1842)[1]
(Michael – 1796–1874)

BIOGRAPHY

Both born in Kilkenny. Father a prosperous farmer.

JOHN began by studying the fine arts which he abandoned in 1820. Stayed a long time in London where he was a friend of Gerald Griffin and frequented literary circles. Died in Kilkenny (he seems to have returned to Ireland in 1835) on August 13, 1842. Considered in his time and since as one of the three or four great names in the nineteenth-century Irish novel.

MICHAEL studied law before entering business and, much later, in 1852, being nominated Postmaster in Kilkenny. Less talented, less well versed in literature than his brother, more learned however in the subject of history and in Irish problems, he was, for John, a valued collaborator during the latter's lifetime, and a conscientious custodian of his memory. Michael's career was confined to Ireland where he died, in County Dublin, on August 30, 1874.

BIBLIOGRAPHY

Most of the works of the Banim brothers having appeared under the common pseudonym of 'The O'Hara Family', it is difficult to dissociate them. However, this has been done here, in the interests of clarity, but not without some uncertainty of erroneous attribution: there are, in fact, notable divergences of opinion among bibliographers and critics consulted by the present author, divergences sometimes about the dates of the works' publication: Brown, *D. N. B.* (Read's) *Cabinet of Irish Literature*, Krans, Leclaire,

---

[1] Revised by Bernard Escarbelt who has edited *The Boyne Water* and *The Fire Club* (q.v. infra), is engaged on a general study of the authors and has already published: 'La Superstition et Le Paysan irlandais dans l'oeuvre des frères Banim'. *La Raison et l'Imaginaire*, S.A.E.S., *Actes du Congrès de Rennes (1970)*, Paris, Didier, n.d., pp. 167–176.

Flanagan ... Murray's biography of J. Banim (Patrick Joseph Murray: *The Life of John Banim, the Irish Novelist* ... with extracts from his correspondence general and literary, London: William Lay ... 1857, 334 p., portr.) does not give a systematic list. Anna Steger's more recent German thesis: *John Banim ein Nachahmer Walter Scotts. Auf Grund der wichtigsten ... 'O'Hara Tales'* ... Erlangen. Karl Dores, 1935, 87 p., offers a bibliography which is incomplete and devoid of scientific value.

Where there is a doubt, the present author has, then, followed the most widely held or most amply endorsed opinion, making use of internal evidence where possible.

JOHN BANIM

(a) **Poetry:**

1821. THE CELT'S PARADISE, in 4 duans.
London: John Warren, 1821, 96 + XXVI p. (notes).

1831. CHAUNT OF THE CHOLERA (etc.) by the authors of 'The O'Hara Tales' ...
London: James Cochrane and Co, 1831, 92 p.

(b) **Prose** (novels, novellas, miscellany):

1824. REVELATIONS OF THE DEAD ALIVE.
London: J. Simpkin and R. Marshall, 1824, 376 p.
(These essays in a novelistic framework, which anticipate W. Morris's *News from Nowhere*, were subsequently going to appear under the title:
London and its Eccentricities in the Year 2023; or, Revelations of the Dead Alive.)

1825. THE FETCHES.*
Vol. II, pp. 109–392 of *Tales by the O'Hara Family* containing: 'Crohoore' ... 'The Fetches' and 'John Doe', in 3 v., London: Simpkin and Marshall, 1825.
(As with J.B.'s other novels, there is much to be gained from a consultation of the editions published in 1865, etc., by Duffy, Dublin, with prefaces and notes by Michael Banim.)

THE BOYNE WATER.*
London: Simpkin & Marshall, 1826, 3 v.
I: XXIX + 375 p.; II: 421 p.; III: 436 p.

Reprinted with an introduction and notes by Bernard Escarbelt, Lille, P.U.L. ('Anglo-Irish Texts'), 1976, 600 p.

1826. THE NOWLANS.*
Vol. I complete (1–318) and Vol. II complete (1–360) of *Tales by the O'Hara Family, 2nd series* comprising 'The Nowlans' and 'Peter of the Castle', in 3 v.; London: Colburn, 1826.

1828. THE ANGLO IRISH OF THE XIXTH CENTURY.*
London: Colburn, 1828, 3 v. (anon).
Vol. I: 308 p.; II: 305 p.: III: 303 p.

1830. THE DENOUNCED, by the authors of *Tales by the O'Hara Family* in 3 v.*
London: Colburn and Bentley, 1830.

THE LAST BARON OF CRANA.
Vol. I (complete), VIII + 309 p.; Vol. II to p. 187.

THE CONFORMISTS.
Vol. II: p. 189 to 315; Vol. III (complete): 292 p.

1831. THE SMUGGLER, a tale in 3 v.
London: Colburn and Bentley, 1831.
Vol. I: IV + 302 p.; II: 299 p.; III: 326 p.

(c) Dramatic works:

1821. (25.8, C.G.) DAMON AND PYTHIAS, a tragedy, in 5 acts.
London: John Warren, 1821, 67 p.
(An anonymous publication by our author in collaboration with R. L. Sheil who revised it. Macready and Kemble acted in this play in blank verse.)

1824. (24.7, E.O.H.) THE SERGEANT'S WIFE, a drama, in 2 acts ... taken from the author's Tales of the *'O'Hara Family'*.
London: T. H. Lacy, n.d., Lacy's Acting Edition, Vol. 23, N° 335, 36 p. (prose) (music by Goss).

A consultation of Nicoll and Kavanagh reveals the titles of other plays listed here for information: *Turgesius, The Prodigal, The Death Fetch* (1825), *The Last Guerilla* (1826), *Sylla* (1826), *The Sister of Charity* (1830), *The Conscript's Sister* (1832), *The Ghost Hunter* (1833), *The Irish Widow* (1835), *The Duchess of Ormond* (1836).

It appears that none of these works has been printed.

MICHAEL BANIM

1825. CROHOORE OF THE BILL-HOOK in:
Tales by the O'Hara Family containing 'Crohoore of the Bill-Hook', 'The Fetches' and 'John Doe', in 3 v.
London: Simpkin and Marshall, 1825.
Vol. I complete (1–367) and p. 1 to 107 of Vol. II.

1828. THE CROPPY, a tale of 1798 by the authors of *The O'Hara Tales* ...*
London: Colburn, 1828, 3 v.
Vol. I: 314 p.; Vol. II: 299 p.; Vol. III: 318 p.

1833. THE GHOST-HUNTER AND HIS FAMILY by the O'Hara Family*.
London: Smith, Elder and Co (The Library of Romance edited by Leitch Ritchie, Vol. I), 330 p.

1835. THE MAYOR OF WINDGAP (and *Canvassing*)*
by the O'Hara Family, in 3 v.
London: Saunders and Otley, 1835.
Vol. I ('The Mayor'): 336 p.; Vol. II: 401 p. ('The Mayor'; cont.: 1–222), ('Canvassing': 223–401); Vol. III ('Canvassing'): 316 p.
('Canvassing' is not, however, by Michael Banim but by Harriet L. Martin, q.v. Michael Banim himself attests to this fact.)

1852. 'CLOUGH FION: *or, The Stone of Destiny*'.
Dublin University Magazine, August to December.

1864. THE TOWN OF THE CASCADE by Michael Banim, survivor of the 'O'Hara Family' ... in 2 v.
London: Chapman and Hall, 1864.
Vol. I: XI + 284 p.; Vol. II: VIII + 284 p.

1976. THE HELL FIRE CLUB (fragment of a novel) edited by B. Escarbelt in *Etudes Irlandaises*, new series, 1, 1976, pp. 51–61.

JOHN AND MICHAEL BANIM, WORKS WRITTEN IN COLLABORATION

1825. JOHN DOE; *or, The Peep o' Day* in *Tales by the O'Hara Family* containing 'Crohoore' ... 'The Fetches' and 'John Doe', in 3 v.*
London: Simpkin and Marshall, 1825, (Vol. III).

1826. PETER OF THE CASTLE in *Tales by the O'Hara Family*, 2nd series, comprising 'The Nowlans' and 'Peter of the Castle', in 3 v.*
London: Colburn, 1826, (Vol. III: 381 p.)

1838. THE BIT O' WRITIN' *and Other Tales**
by the O'Hara Family, in 3 v.
London: Saunders and Otley, 1838.

(Comprises:

Vol. I (304 p.): 'The Bit of Writin''. 'The Irish Lord Lieutenant and his Double'. 'The Family of the Cold Feet'.

Vol. II (305 p.): 'The Harehound and the Witch'. 'The Soldier's Billet'. 'The Hall of the Castle'. 'The Half-Brothers'. 'Twice Lost but Saved'. 'The Faithful Servant'. 'The Roman Merchant' (Orig. published in *Dublin Penny Journal* I, 8 (Aug. 18, 1832), pp. 61–3. The same magazine printing in the next issue (Aug. 25, 1832, n° 9, pp. 66–7): 'A Peasant Girl's Love'.) 'Ill Got, Ill Gone'.

Vol. III (296 p.): 'The Last of the Storm'. 'The Rival Dreamers'. 'The Substitute'. 'The White Bristol'. 'The Stolen Sheep'. 'The Publican's Dream'. 'The Ace of Clubs'.)

The 1865 edition (Dublin: Duffy) with foreword and notes by Michael, contains an additional tale: 'A Peasant Girl's Love'.

1842. FATHER CONNELL,
by the O'Hara Family, in 3 v.
London: Newby and Boone, 1842.
Vol. I: 303 p.; II: 273 p.; III: 333 p.

BARRETT (Eaton Stannard – 1786–1820)

BIOGRAPHY

Born in Cork. Studied at Trinity College, Dublin, then at the Middle Temple in London, but abandoned law in favour of literature at the time of his first satirical poem which gave the government the name of 'Ministry of All the Talents'. It was in this satirical vein that he pursued a brilliant career in London. Died of tuberculosis, in Wales.

BIBLIOGRAPHY

1807.   ALL THE TALENTS; a satirical poem, in three dialogues.
London: J. J. Stockdale, 1807, XIII + 99 p.
(The pseudonym used is 'Polypus'. The eighteenth edition,
of the same year, by the same publisher, contains an
engraving by Rowlandson, XVII + 152 pages, the title being
identical but the subtitle being changed as follows: 'A
satirical poem in four dialogues, to which is added a
pastoral epilogue'. There were at least 19 editions in 1807
since *The Poetical Register* wrote that year:

'The 19th edition!!! Mercy on us! If this be true, there is more
folly in the world than we supposed ... Perhaps, however ... *only
the title page* has gone through 19 editions.'

This is followed by fierce criticism ... The number of
imitations, attacks, counter-attacks, etc., in any case
testifies to the pamphlet's success.)

ALL THE TALENTS IN IRELAND; a satirical poem, with
notes.
London: J. J. Stockdale, 1807, VIII + 44 p.
(Pseudonym: 'Scrutator').

THE RISING SUN, a serio-comic satiric romance.
London: Appleyards, 1807, 2 v., I: 197 p., II: 171 p.
(Pseudonym: 'Cervantès Hogg').

THE SECOND TITAN WAR; *or, The Talents Buried Under
Portland-Isle,* by the Author of 'The Rising Sun'.
London: H. Colburn, 1807, II + 63 p.
(Satirical poem).

1808.   THE COMET: by the Author of 'All the Talents'.
London: J. J. Stockdale, 1808, 86 p.
(A sort of pseudo-newspaper, a series of satirical tracts,
some in prose, others in verse.)

THE MIS-LED GENERAL; a serio-comic, satiric, mock-
heroic romance by the author of 'The Rising Sun'.
London: H. Oddy, 1808, 197 p.

1809.   THE SETTING SUN; *or, Devil Amongst the Placemen,* to
which is added, a New Musical Drama; being a parody on
The Beggar's Opera, as lately acted, with universal éclat,
at the Theatre Royal; with Hints for a Masquerade
Jubilee, on a grand scale. London: Hughes, etc., 1809, 3 v.,
I: XXIX + 122 p., II: 141 p., III: 148 p.

(Pseudonym: 'Cervantès Hogg'. A mixture of prose and verse.)

THE TARANTULA; *or, The Dance of Fools* ... a satirical work in 2 v.
London: Hughes, 1809, I: II + 157 p., II: 137 p. (Prose).

1810. WOMAN, a poem.
London: Murray, etc., 1810, XV + 85 p.
(A later edition:
Woman, a Poem. Occasional Poems.
London: H. Colburn, 1818, 121 p., includes, besides: 'Song' (107–8), 'Fanny' (109–11), 'Sonnet, to the Moon' (112–3), 'Sonnet, the Butterfly' (114–5), 'The Farewell' (116–21).)

1813. THE HEROINE; *or, Adventures of a Fair Romance Reader.*
London: Colburn, 1813, 3 v., I: XX + 224 p., II: 239 p., III: 302 p.
(A parody presented within the framework of an epistolary novel. The second edition is:
The Heroine; or, Adventures of Cherubina.
With considerable additions and alterations.
London: Colburn, 1814, 3 v., I: XXIII + 235 p., II: 258 p., III: 266 p.)

1815. (25.7, HAY.) MY WIFE! WHAT WIFE? a comedy in 3 acts.
London: printed for C. Chapple, 1815, 60 p.

1816. THE TALENTS RUN MAD; *or, Eighteen Hundred and Sixteen.*
A satirical poem by the author of 'All the Talents' in three dialogues, with notes.
London: Colburn, 1816, X + 70 p.

1817. SIX WEEKS AT LONG'S by a Late Resident.
London: printed for the author, 1817, 3rd edition, 3 v., I: XII + 230 p., II: 228 p., III: 222 p.
(1817 is the date also given by the bibliographers, for the first edition that the present author has been unable to trace.)

Some also attribute to Barrett an anonymous poetical collection of 1821, that the present author has been unable to consult:

Henry Schultze, a tale. *The Savoyard*, a French Republican's story, with other poems.

As for:

The Hero; or, The Adventures of a Night, this parodical novel is not by him as has been believed.

To the present author's knowledge, Barrett has not yet been the object of the study that he deserves. However, there is much to be gained from a reading of the pages devoted to him by E. Railo in *The Haunted Castle* and E. Birkhead in *The Tale of Terror*.

BARRINGTON (Sir Jonah – 1760–1834)

BIOGRAPHY

The most famous memorialist of Ireland, after some studies at Trinity College, was, in turn, a lawyer, a member of Parliament, and a judge at the Court of Admiralty. His excessive spending led him, in 1830, to some imprudent actions that cost him his post. He died at Versailles on April 8, 1834.

BIBLIOGRAPHY

1827. PERSONAL SKETCHES AND RECOLLECTIONS OF HIS OWN TIME.
London: H. Colburn, 1827, 2 v., I: XXVII + 476 p., II: XII + 474 p.
(A third volume was added in 1832.)
There exists an improved edition, dating from 1809, and published by Routledge: with a Memoir of the Author; an Essay on Irish Wit and Humour; Notes and Corrections by the editor: Townsend Young. 2 v., I: XXXVIII + 376 p., II: XVII + 464 p.

1833. HISTORICAL ANECDOTES AND SECRET MEMOIRS OF THE LEGISLATIVE UNION BETWEEN GREAT BRITAIN AND IRELAND ... with engravings ... by J. Heath, illustrated with curious letters and papers in facsimile.
London: pub. by R. Bentley for H. Colburn, 1833, 2 v. (in 4°), I: XI + XLII + 358 + XXVIII, II: IX + 464 + Index.
RISE AND FALL OF THE IRISH NATION.
Paris: G. C. Bennis, 1833, 494 p.

Note also the following anthology:

STAPLES (Hugh B.) ed.: *The Ireland of Sir Jonah Barrington.*
London: Peter Owen, 1968, 328 p.

BARRON (Philip F. – 1797–1860(?))

Editor of the magazine *Ancient Ireland* (q.v. periodicals) in
which almost all the articles are by him.
Author of AN IRISH PRIMER (Dublin: J. S. Folds, 1836).
D. Ryan speaks of him at some length in *The Sword of Light.*

BARRY (Michael-Joseph – 1817–1889)

BIOGRAPHY

Born in Cork in 1817. Contributed to *The Dublin University
Magazine* (1842–43), then to *The Nation* and *The (Cork) Southern
Reporter* (1848, etc.) of which he was the editor. An enthusiastic
member of the Young Ireland party, he subsequently returned to
more conservative opinions and obtained an appointment as
magistrate in Dublin. He died on January 23, 1889.

BIBLIOGRAPHY

1842–7. THE KISHOGE PAPERS.
(First published in *The Dublin University Magazine* – (1):
XIX. 109, Jan., 1842, pp. 18–26. (2): id. 114, June,
pp. 724–8. (3): XX. 117, Sept., pp. 321–26. (4): id. 119,
Nov., pp. 574–82. (5): XXI. 123, Mar., 1843, pp. 299–306.
(6): id. 124, Apr., pp. 501–5. (7): XXII. 132, Dec., pp.
677–84. (8): XXVII. 161, May, 1846, pp. 535–42. (9): XXX.
180, Dec., 1847, pp. 706–9. – These poems probably
appeared in book form, in Dublin, at this time, under the
pseudonym 'Bouillon de Garçon' before being re-issued, in
London, in 1872.)

1845. IRELAND, AS SHE WAS, AS SHE IS, AND AS SHE SHALL
BE.
Dublin: J. Duffy, 1845, 112 p.

(an essay on the Repeal that won its author 1st prize in the competition organised by the Repeal Association.)

THE SONGS OF IRELAND edited by Michael Joseph Barry. Dublin: ... J. Duffy, 1845, XVI + 238 p.

(It was Thomas Davis who had begun to prepare this volume as a complement to Duffy's *The Ballad Poetry of Ireland.* Dedicated to Th. Moore, the anthology comprises 38 anonymous songs and a certain number of signed pieces (Banim, Callanan, Curran, Davis, Drennan, Furlong, Griffin, Lover, Lysaght, M'Carthy, Milliken, Lady Morgan, Moore, Ogle, Orr, Wolfe, etc.). The Gaelic refrains are printed in Irish characters, Eugene O'Curry coming to the assistance of Barry for the 2nd revised edition of 1846, which was reprinted in 1869.)

1849. Several poems by the author in the anthology that he edited:
ECHOES FROM PARNASSUS, Cork: Southern Reporter, 1849, VIII + 92 p.

Beside a few legal works, Barry was also to publish:

1854. A WATERLOO COMMEMORATION FOR 1854.
London: W. S. Orr & Co (verse).

1856. LAYS OF THE WAR AND MISCELLANEOUS LYRICS.
London: Longman & Co.

1871. SIX SONGS OF BÉRANGER.
Dublin: printed for private circulation.

1886. HEINRICH AND LEONORE, *an Alpine story. Corregio: and some miscellaneous verses, original and translated.*
Dublin: Hodges Figgis & Co.

BELL (Robert – 1800–1867)

BIOGRAPHY

Born in Cork on January 16, 1800. Father a magistrate. Studied at Trinity College Dublin (B.A.: 1818).

A journalist, he left the capital of Ireland, where he had contributed to the reorganisation of the Dublin Historical Society and founded *The Dublin Inquisitor*, for London where he stayed from 1828. There, he was in charge of *The Atlas* and presided, with

Bulwer-Lytton and Lardner, at the founding of *The Monthly Chronicle* (1838–41) before directing the *Home News*. A tireless writer, playwright, biographer (his biography of Canning in 1846 is the best known), compiler of anthologies (cf. *The Annotated Edition of the English Poets*, 1854–7, 29 vols.), he was also interested in spiritualism on which subject he published an interesting article in *The Cornhill Magazine* (II (Aug. 1860), pp. 211–24).

Died April 12, 1867. Buried at Kensal Green beside his friend Thackeray.

BIBLIOGRAPHY

(The biographies and anthologies that have just been mentioned are omitted, and so are works like *History of Russia* (1836).)

(a) **Dramatic works:**

1816. (19.10, D.L.) THE WATCHWORD; *or, Quito-Gate*, a melo-drama in 2 acts ...
London: Effingham Wilson, 1816, 28 p.
(of doubtful authorship.)

1838. [MACBETH MODERNIZED: a most illegitimate drama.
(privately printed).]

1842. (27.1, HAY.) MARRIAGE,
a comedy in 5 acts ...
London: Longman & Co, 1842, XII + 164 p.

1843. (24.1, C.G.) MOTHERS AND DAUGHTERS, a comedy in 5 acts ...
London: Cunningham & Mortimer, 1843, 128 p.
(A 2nd edition, in 1844, adds a preface (XXV p.) to explain the reasons for the withdrawal of the play.)

1847. (17.5, HAY.) TEMPER, a comedy in 5 acts ...
London: T. H. Brown, 1847, 73 p.

(b) **Miscellanea:**

1849. WAYSIDE PICTURES THROUGH FRANCE, BELGIUM AND HOLLAND.
London: R. Bentley, 1849, XII + 456 p.
(France: pp. 3–346. There are illustrations by G. Meason.)

1850. THE LADDER OF GOLD, an English story.
London: R. Bentley, 1850, 3 v.
I (Books I & II): 336 p.; II (Books III & IV): 315 p.; III
(Books V & VI): 324 p.

1852. HEARTS AND ALTARS, a narrative in 3 v.
London: Colburn & Co, 1852.

I: A. 'Phantoms and Realities' (Autobiography) – 1.
'Morning' (5–93), 2. 'Noon' (97–270), 3. 'Night'
(273–302).

II: A. id. (continued) (5–129); B. 'The Armourer of
Münster', a page from the history of fanaticism (the action
takes place in 1534) (133–336: int.+ch. 1 to 18).

III: B. (continued) (3–100: ch. 19–32); C. 'Love to the
Rescue' (103–207); D. 'Love Laughs at Monarchs'
(211–233); E. 'The Bride that the Rain Rained on'
(237–286); F. 'The Careless Word' (289–348).

(reprinted from *Fraser's*.)

BICKERSTAFF(E) (Isaac – 1735(?)–1812(?))

BIOGRAPHY

Denis Johnston (*In Search of Swift*, Dublin: Hodges Figgis,
1959, p. 7) notes the following about this author:

> 'The fanciful has a way of coming to life, as in the case of Isaac
> Bickerstaff, who began as an imaginary astrologer, invented by
> the Dean to annoy an Almanack maker, and who now appears to
> have a place in the "D.N.B." as the author of several plays.'

Bickerstaffe II, much later than his Swiftian ancestor, was well
established in the literary and fashionable society of his time after
the success of his comic operas. He was expelled from the Navy for
'ignominious conduct', but we do not know in what exact cir-
cumstances. Then, suspected of having committed 'a capital crime',
he took refuge on the continent in 1772. From St-Malo he wrote a
letter, in French, to David Garrick who did not reply:

> 'Ayant perdu mes amis, mes espérances, tombé, exilé et livré au
> désespoir comme je suis, la vie est un fardeau presque insup-
> portable.'

We do not know where he spent the rest of his wretched days.

BIBLIOGRAPHY

(a) Comic operas (prior to the period under discussion):

1762. (8.12, C.G) LOVE IN A VILLAGE.
(Published 1763; inspired by *The Village Opera* by Charles Johnson, *The Dancing Master* by Wycherley and *Le Jeu de l'Amour et du Hasard* by Marivaux.)

1765. (31.1, C.G.) THE MAID OF THE MILL.
(Published in 1765; inspired by Richardson's *Pamela*.)

1768. (25.2, C.G.) LIONEL AND CLARISSA.

(b) Plays (of the period under discussion):

1790. (22.3, D.L. and S.A.) THE FARCE OF THE SPOIL'D CHILD, in two acts,
as performed at the Theatre-Royal, Smock-Alley,
printed for the bookseller, 1792, 31 p.
(The name of the author does not appear. It is part of the book *A Volume of Farces*, as they are performed at the Theatre Smock Alley, Dublin. Of doubtful authorship.)

BLACKER (Colonel William – 1777–1855, 'FITZSTEWART')

BIOGRAPHY

Colonel Blacker has been called 'The Orange Minstrel' (cf. *Irish Book Lover.* IV, 10, May 1913, pp. 163–5) and it is, in fact, as the author of some vigorous Orangist ballads that he is best known (cf. 'Oliver's Advice', *Dublin University Magazine*, IV, 24, December 1834, pp. 700–1, recalling Cromwell's recommendation:

> 'So put your trust in God, my boys
> And keep your powder dry.'

cf. also 'The Battle of the Boyne', *Dublin University Magazine*, XIII, 75, March 1839, pp. 302–3, poems signed 'Fitzstewart').

He was born on September 1, 1777, at Carrickblacker, in County Armagh, studied at the 'Royal School' in the county town and at Trinity College, Dublin (B.A.: 1799, M.A.: 1803). He had a military career and was also interested in economics (several essays on this subject). Died November 25, 1855.

BIBLIOGRAPHY
1848.   ARDMAGH, a chronicle; *The Fire Towers; Carmel; The Goldsmith*, an Indian tale and *The Fourth Sword*.
Armagh, printed at 'The Guardian' office by J. Thompson, 1848.

1853.   EARLY PIETY. Portadown, printed by G. Wilson, 1853, 12 p.

1854.   A TALE OF WOE, for children, ibid., 1854, 12 p.

1855.   EMMAUS, a tale for Easter, ibid., 1855, 12 p.

BLESSINGTON (Marguerite Power, Countess of – also: 'Gardiner, M.' – 1789–1849)

BIOGRAPHY

Born in Knockbrit, near Clonmel, in County Tipperary, on September 1, 1789.

Her father, a Catholic but won over to the English cause, acquired a frightful reputation, before and after 1798, through the inclemency, indeed the sadism, with which he carried out his functions as magistrate. The old dandy, nicknamed 'Shiver the Frills' and 'Beau Power' by turns, did not spare his household in his abuse of power since he forced Marguerite to marry an officer when she was 15. The marriage lasted only three months, the young woman refusing to remain any longer at the conjugal residence. A widow, she was married for the second time in 1818, to Count Blessington whose large house at 11 St James's Square, in London, would become, thanks to her, a literary and fashionable circle.

In 1822 began a long European tour that was to take her to Genoa, where in 1823 she was one of Byron's intimate friends, and to Paris where her husband died in 1829.

From 1831 she settled in London again, the focus of famous gatherings, first in Mayfair, then at Gore House, Kensington and pursued her literary activities. Financial ruin followed hard upon the ruin of her reputation, and a few months before her death, to flee her creditors, she was compelled to return to France in the company of her companion, the Comte d'Orsay. She died in Paris and her remains rest in Chambourcy, near Saint-Germain-en Laye.

BIBLIOGRAPHY

(a) Poetry:

1836. FLOWERS OF LOVELINESS; twelve groups of female figures, emblematic of flowers: designed by E. T. Parris, Esq. With poetical illustrations by the Countess of Blessington.
London: Ackerman & Co, 1836 seq., unpaginated, folio.

GEMS OF BEAUTY; displayed in a series of twelve highly finished engravings from designs by the first artists (successively: Parris, Edward Corbould) ... with fanciful illustrations in verse, by the Countess of Blessington.
London: Longman, Rees, Orme, Brown, Green & Longmans, 1836 seq., unpaginated, folio.

HEATH'S BOOK OF BEAUTY ...
London: Longman, etc., 1836 seq.
(Here, Lady Blessington's work is in prose as well as in verse.)

1840. THE BELLE OF A SEASON; a poem, by the Countess of Blessington. ill. by A. E. Chalon.
London: Longman, etc., 1840, 93 p.

THE KEEPSAKE ... edited by Lady E. Stuart Wortley (1840), edited by the Countess of Blessington (1841–9), edited by the Late Countess of Blessington (1850).
London: Longman, etc., 1840 seq. (verse and prose).

As well as some individual pieces in *Amulet, Forget Me Not,* and a posthumous collection (1867) AMABEL and *Other Poetical Pieces.*

(b) Prose (novels and miscellanea):

1822. JOURNAL OF A TOUR THROUGH THE NETHERLANDS TO PARIS, IN 1821 ... (anon.)
London: Longman, Hurst, Rees, Orme & Brown, 1822, 171 p.

THE MAGIC LANTERN; *or, Sketches of Scenes in the Metropolis* ... (anon.)
London: Longman, etc., 1822, 105 p.

SKETCHES AND FRAGMENTS ... (anon.)
London: Longman, etc., 1822, VIII + 139 p.

1833. THE REPEALERS. A novel by the Countess of Blessington.

London: Bentley ..., 1833, 3 v.; I: 316 p.; II: 348 p.; III: 320 p.
(The 1834 edition has the title: *Grace Cassidy; or, The Repealers.*)

1834.   CONVERSATIONS OF LORD BYRON WITH THE COUNTESS OF BLESSINGTON.
(Current title: 'Journal of Conversations with Lord Byron'.)
London: published for Henry Colburn by R. Bentley, 1834, 409 p.
(Note the later edition: *A Journal of the Conversations ...* a new edition, revised, and annotated to which is prefixed a Contemporary Sketch of Lady Blessington, by her sister, and a Memoir of her by the editor ... With several portraits engraved on steel.)
London: R. Bentley & Son, 1893, LXIV + 376 p.
Princeton University Press re-issued this text in 1969 (Ernest J. Lovell, ed.).

1835.   THE TWO FRIENDS, a novel ...
London: Saunders & Otley, 1835, 3 v., I: 282 p.; II: 258 p.; III: 275 p.

1837.   THE VICTIMS OF SOCIETY ...
London: Saunders & Otley, 1837, 3 v., I: VII + 288 p.; II: 288 p.; III: 290 p.

1838.   THE CONFESSIONS OF AN ELDERLY GENTLEMAN. Illustrated by 6 female portraits, from highly finished drawings by E. T. Parris.
London: Longman, etc., 1838, 287 p.

THE CONFESSIONS OF AN ELDERLY LADY. Illustrated by 8 portraits, from highly finished drawings by E. T. Parris.
London: Longman, etc., 1838, 342 p.

1839.   DESULTORY THOUGHTS AND REFLECTIONS.
(The current title is: 'Maxims, Thoughts and Reflexions'.)
London: Longman, etc., 1839, 122 p.

THE GOVERNESS.
London: Longman, etc., 1839, 2 v., I: 308 p.; II: 331 p.

THE IDLER IN ITALY.
London: H. Colburn, 1839, 2nd edition (But the *Cambridge Bibliography* gives the same date for the 1st).

2 v., I: XI + 363 p.; II: X + 358 p.
The 1840 edition has a 3rd volume (IV + 371 p.).

1841. THE IDLER IN FRANCE.
London: H. Colburn, 1841, 2 v., I: 356 p.; II: 270 p.

1842. THE LOTTERY OF LIFE.
London: H. Colburn, 1842, 3 v.

I: 312 p.
  'The Lottery of Life' (3–279)
  'Veronica of Castille' (281–312)

II: 308 p.
  'Scenes in the Life of a Portrait Painter' (1–34)
  'Galeria; or, The Deserted Village' (35–55)
  'The Dream' (57–64)
  'The Honeymoon' (65–82)
  'Mary Lester' (83–101)
  'Isota Grimani' (103–136)
  'Matrimony' (137–190)
  'The Gamesters' (191–239)
  'The Coquette' (241–268)
  'The Beauty and her Sister' (Part I) (269–308)

III: 337 p.
  'The Beauty and her Sister' (Part II) (1–35)
  'The Antidote to Love' (37–115)
  'The Old Irish Gentleman (117–149)
  'Madelina' (151–182)
  'Annette; or The Galerian' (183–194)
  'The Young Mother' (195–217)
  'The Chalet in the Alps' (219–239)
  'Remorse, a Fragment' (241–250)
  'Thoughts on Lord Byron' (251–258)
  'A propos of Bores' (259–266)
  'The Bay of Naples in the Summer of 1824'
    (267–270)
  'The Parvenue' (271–337)

1843. MEREDITH.
London: Longman, etc., 1843, 3 v., I: 311 p.; II: 306 p.; III:
325 p.

1845. STRATHERN; *or, Life at Home and Abroad.* A story of the
Present Day.
London: H. Colburn, 1845, 4 v.; I: 315 p.; II: 305 p.; III:
314 p.; IV: 295 p.

1846. LIONEL DEERHURST; *or, Fashionable Life under the Regency.*
Edited by the Countess of Blessington.
London: R. Bentley, 1846, 3 v.; I: 300 p.; II: 289 p.: III: 269 p.

MEMOIRS OF A FEMME DE CHAMBRE, a novel.
London: R. Bentley, 1846, 3 v., I: 315 p.; II: 315 p.; III: 318 p.

1847. MARMADUKE HERBERT; *or, The Fatal Error.* A novel, founded on fact.
London: R. Bentley, 1847, 3 v., I: 304 p.; II: 297 p.; III: 304 p.

1850. COUNTRY QUARTERS, a novel ... With a Memoir by her niece, Miss Power.
London: W. Shoberl, 1850, 3 v., I: XXIII (Memoir)+ 312 p.; II: 304 p.; III: 375 p.
(*Country Quarters* is Lady Blessington's second 'Irish' novel, the first being *The Repealers.*)

Note also:

1838. THE WORKS OF LADY BLESSINGTON, in two volumes.
Philadelphia: E. Carey & A. Hart, 1838.

Vol. I:
'The Two Friends' (5–150)
'The Repealers' (153–325)
'The Confessions of an Elderly Gentleman'
    (329–387)

Vol. II:
'The Confessions of an Elderly Lady' (5–75)
'The Victims of Society' (79–233)
'Conversations with Lord Byron' (237–329)
'The Honey-Moon' (333–337)
'Galeria' (338–342)

1895. In: THE COLLECTION OF AUTOGRAPH LETTERS AND HISTORICAL DOCUMENTS, formed by Alfred Morrison ...
London, 1895, Vol. 2, second series (current title: 'The Blessington Papers'), 234 p.

(c) Secondary material:

Beside general works on English Romanticism, CHORLEY (H. F.):
The Authors of England, MAGINN (W.) etc.: *A Gallery*, ROSA (M.
W.): *The Silver-Fork School*, q.v. in the general bibliography.

MADDEN (R. R.): *The Literary Life and Correspondence of the
　　Countess of Blessington.*
　　London: T. C. Newby, 1855, 3 v., I: VIII+491 p.; II: VI+
　　484 p.; III: VI+555 p.

MOLLOY (J. F.): *The Most Gorgeous Lady Blessington.*
　　London: Downey & Co, 1896, 2 v., I: XIV+290 p.; II: VII+
　　319 p.

SADLEIR (M.): *The Strange Life of Lady Blessington*, 1933.

BOUCICAULT (or Bourcicault)
(Dyonysius Lardner – 1820–1890)

BIOGRAPHY

　　Dion Boucicault's mother was Anne Darley, sister of the poet
George Darley and wife of Samuel Smith Boursiquot, of Huguenot
descent. But his father was Dionysius Lardner, author of the
Cyclopœdia, as W. J. Lawrence establishes in his article in *Ireland
Saturday Night* (October 28, 1922) and as subsequent biographers
have reiterated.

　　Born in Dublin on December 26, 1820, studied at the Academy
of Dr Geoghegan, then in London and Brentford. Returned to
London, to the University this time, to become an engineer.
However, in 1837 he joined a touring company where he began to
play comic parts which were to win him fame as an actor, and to
write plays.

　　His first success in London came in 1841 with *London
Assurance*. 1844–8: then, there was a stay in France and a first
marriage to a woman much older (and richer) than himself and
who had the courtesy to die forthwith in the course of a trip to the
mountains; his first adaptations of French plays now began to
appear.

　　1853: eloped with Charles Kean's ward, the actress Agnes
Robertson and reached America where henceforth he was to have

his principal residence. The plays from his 'realist' period, like his 'Irish' dramas later, were to be highly successful there.

Judging from the evidence, Dion Boucicault's emotional passion did not diminish with age. 1885: a second escapade – and third marriage – to Miss Thorndyke, more than thirty years his junior. Boucicault's popularity declined towards the end of his life and he was compelled to set up as a teacher of elocution and dramatic art. Died in 1890.

BIBLIOGRAPHY

(a) Varia:

D. J. O'Donoghue points out one or other poems by the author in *Bentley's Miscellany*, Vol. IX, *The Musical Examiner* and *The Musical World* of 1843, etc.

There are also articles and tracts on the theatre (after 1850) that may be found in Walsh or Krause (q.v. below).

(b) Dramatic works prior to 1850:

1838. (Brentford) NAPOLEON'S OLD GUARD.

(Cheltenham) HARD UP.

(Brighton) A LEGEND OF THE DEVIL'S DYKE.
London: Dick's Standard Plays, N° 1043, n.d., 15 p.

1839. (Hull) JACK SHEPPARD.

(London) LODGINGS TO LET.

1841. (4.3, C.G.) LONDON ASSURANCE,
a comedy in 5 acts.
London: J. Andrews, 1841, VIII + 86 p.
Note also the following re-issue used for the 1970 production at the Aldwych Theatre, London (opening night: June 23, 1970):
London Assurance, the full original text adapted for the modern stage and edited by Ronald Eyre with an introduction by Peter Thomson, London: Methuen & Co, 1971, XXIII + 87 p.

1842. (4.3, C.G.) [THE IRISH HEIRESS.
London, 1842.]

(21.4, HAY.) A LOVER BY PROXY.
London: National Acting Drama, Vol. 9, n.d., 28 p.

(19.9, HAY.) ALMA MATER; *or, a Cure for Coquettes,* an original comedy in 3 acts.
London: Webster, n.d. (1842), 48 p.

(24.9, HAY.) CURIOSITIES OF LITERATURE, an original farce, in 1 act.
London: Webster, n.d. (1842), 20 p.

(19.12, HAY.) THE BASTILE.

1843. (2.10, C.G.) WOMAN.

(9.10, PRIN.) THE OLD GUARD, a drama in 1 act.
London: Dick's Standard Plays, N. 1056, n.d.

(London) SHARP'S THE WORD.

(2.11, HAY.) VICTOR AND HORTENSE.

(15.11, HAY.) LAYING A GHOST.

1844. (6.2, HAY.) USED UP, a petit comedy in 2 acts ...
London: National Acting Drama, Vol. 15, n.d., 33 p.

(25.3, HAY.) LOLAH.

(22.4, HAY.) LOVE IN A SACK.

(30.9, ADEL.) MOTHER AND SON.

(2.10, ADEL.) THE FOX AND THE GOOSE; *or, the Widow's Husband,* a comic operetta in 1 act by Benjamin Webster and Dion Boucicault. The music composed by Ambroise Thomas ...
London: National Acting Drama, Vol. 10, n.d. (1814) 20 p.

(14.10, ADEL.) COESAR DE BAZAN; *or, Love and Honour,* a drama, in 3 acts by B. Webster and D. Boucicault ...
London: National Acting Drama, Vol. 10, n.d., 40 p.
(Adapted from Dumanoir.)

(18.11, HAY.) OLD HEADS AND YOUNG HEARTS, a comedy in 5 acts ...
London: National Acting Drama, Vol. 13, n.d., 63 p.

1845. (London) FOUND OUT AT HOME.

(London) THE WATER CURE.

(6.2, ADEL.) A SOLDIER OF FORTUNE.

(25.8, LYC.) ENQUIRE WITHIN.

1846. (5.2, HAY.) THE OLD SCHOOL.

(London) SHAKESPEARE IN LOVE.

(London) LOVE AND MONEY.

(11.5, ADEL.) UP THE FLUE; *or, What's in the Wind?*
(1st title: *Felo de Se*, written in collaboration with J. Kenney.)

1847.   (4.2, HAY.) THE SCHOOL FOR SCHEMING, in 5 acts.
London: National Acting Drama, Vol. 13, n.d., 59 p.

1848.   ((2.5, HAY.) CONFIDENCE.

(22.11, ADEL.) THE KNIGHT OF ARVA, a comic drama in 2 acts.
New York: Samuel French, n.d., 28 p.

1849.   (26.11, ADEL.) THE WILLOW COPSE.
(Adapted from *La Closerie des Genêts* by Frédéric Soulié).

(London) SALAMANDRINE.

1850.   (London) THE INVISIBLE HUSBAND.

(London) A RADICAL CURE.

(London) LA GARDE NATIONALE.

(12.9, HAY.) GIRALDA; *or, The Miller's Wife.*
(In collaboration with B. Webster; revived in 1870 under the title *A Dark Night's Work.*)

(c) Later 'Irish' plays and modern editions:

1851.   (21.4, ADEL.) O'FLANNIGAN AND THE FAIRIES.

1860.   (27.3, N. York, Laura Keen's) THE COLLEEN BAWN; *or, The Brides of Garryowen*, a domestic drama in 3 acts ...
London: Lacy's Acting Edition of Plays, 63, n.d. (1865).
(This is, at least, the oldest edition in the possession of the British Museum, but there was another (or others) anterior to it since the French translation *Le Lac de Glenaston* dates from 1861. (Paris: Michel Lévy, 86 p.). The play had been performed at the Ambigu Comique on October 17, 1861. It is a stage adaptation of *The Collegians* by G. Griffin. Benedict would make a famous opera out of it, *The Lily of Killarney*, in 1862.)

1864.   (7.11, Dublin) ARRAH-NA-POGUE; *or, The Wicklow Wedding.*
London (publisher impossible to determine, the title page of the edition in the British Museum is missing), 1865, 44 p.

(The play was also to be performed in Paris, in translation, at the Gaité theatre (June 20, 1866). Eugene Nus was the translator. Title: *Jean la Poste*. Published the same year in Paris in the 'Librairie Dramatique'.)

1870.   (9.9, PRIN.) THE RAPPAREE; *or, The Treaty of Limerick.*

1871.   (Manchester) NIGHT AND MORNING,
(revised as *Kerry, or, Night and Morning*, 1893),
published with an introduction by Hilary Berrow in *Irish University Review*, III, 1, Spring 1973, 31–50.

1873.   (N. York, Booth's) THE O'DOWD; *or, Life in Galway.*

1874.   (14.11, N. York, Wallack's) THE SHAUGHRAUN,
an original drama in 3 acts.
London: Lacy's Acting Edition, Vol. 123, n.d., 64 p.

1884.   (4.11, Prince of Wales, Greenwich) ROBERT EMMET.

1887.   (Boston) FIN MACCOOL,
(revision of *Belle Lamar*, a play produced by Boucicault in 1874).

There are two modern collections of plays by Dion Boucicault:

1940.   FORBIDDEN FRUIT AND OTHER PLAYS by Dion Boucicault, edited by Allardyce Nicoll and F. Theodore Cloak. Princeton, New Jersey: Princeton University Press, 1940, ('America's Lost Plays' series') VIII + 313 p.
The volume contains a short general introduction by A. Nicoll, a short introduction to each play by F. T. Cloak and the text of the following works: *Forbidden Fruit* (3 seq.), *Louis XI* (51), *Dot* (109), *Flying Scud* (153), *Mercy Dodd* (231), *Robert Emmet* (263).

1964.   *The Dolmen Boucicault* edited by David Krause, with an essay by the editor on the theatre of Dion Boucicault and the complete authentic text of Boucicault's three Irish plays: *The Colleen Bawn, Arrah na Pogue, The Shaughraun.*
Dublin: The Dolmen Press, 1964, 253 p., ill.

(d) Secondary material:

There is to be found in Kavanagh (Part V, Ch. III, pp. 402–6) a study and, as in the *D.N.B.*, a list of old articles on the author.

The two most interesting monographs are:

WALSH (T.): *The Career of Dion Boucicault.* New York: The Dunlap Society, 1915, XVIII + 224 p., ill.

HOGAN (Robert): *Dion Boucicault.* New York: Twayne, 1969.
See also:

ÓH-AODHA (Micheál): *Plays and Places.* Dublin: Progress House, 1961 (pp. 1–17).

The last three critics mentioned as well as A. Nicoll and David Krause seem to place D. Boucicault higher than did their predecessors or than P. Kavanagh who is very stringent. All are in any case of one mind in recognising his innovating role as a producer and playwright, and in acknowledging in him a master of melodrama.

BOYD (Rev. Henry – 1749–1832)

BIOGRAPHY

Born in Ireland in 1749 (according to Hewitt; O'Donoghue says 1756). Studied at Trinity College, graduated in 1776. A minister of the Reformed Church. Had to flee at the time of the rebellion of 1798. Drumgath was one of the parishes to which he was appointed, and he was chaplain to the Right Honourable Viscount Charleville. Died in Ballitemple near Newry on September 18, 1832.

BIBLIOGRAPHY

(a) Translations:

E. Boyd worked especially as a translator, and of Dante in particular (*The Inferno*, 1785, *The Divina Commedia*, 1802). He also edited the works of Milton.

(b) Original works:

1793. POEMS CHIEFLY DRAMATIC AND LYRIC.
Dublin, printed by Graisberry and Campbell, 1793, VIII + 646 p.
The collection comprises:
'The Helots', a tragedy in blank verse (1–152).
3 biblical plays in blank verse:

'The Temple of Vesta', a dramatic poem (153–238).
'The Rivals', a religious drama (239–295).
'The Royal Message', a dramatic poem (297–446, including a postscript).
'Prize Poems, Odes, Elegies', etc. (447 seq.).

1805. THE WOODMAN'S TALE after the Manner of Spenser to which are added, *Other Poems*, chiefly Narrative and Lyric and *The Royal Message*, a drama.
London: Longman, Hurst, Rees and Orme, 1805, XXVI + 449 p.
(The collection includes:
'Woodman's Tale',
'Milesian Tales' (The Knight of Feltrim, The Dead Man's Belt, The Moon-Flower, The Recognition, The Fairy Favour).
'The Royal Message'.)

BOYD (Percy – ?–1876)

Studied at Trinity College (B.A.: 1840).
Author of:

A BOOK OF BALLADS FROM THE GERMAN.
Dublin: J. M'Glashan, 1848.
A lengthy review of this will be found in the *Dublin University Magazine* (XXXI, 183, March 1848, pp. 305–14).
The same periodical would also publish (XXXII, 187, July 1848, pp. 61–7) his 'A Wreath of Student Songs' also translated from the German.
A friend of Dickens and Thackeray. Died in London on June 1, 1876.

BRENAN (Joseph – 1828–1857)

Born in Cork, was one of the talented writers of *The Nation* in which several of his poems appeared under the signature J. B., Cork or J. B. —n. A friend of Mangan. Editor of *The Irishman* (1849) which he launched after *The Nation* was banned. Was forced to flee to the United States where he pursued his journalistic career until 1853. Died in New Orleans. Had been blind for several years.

BRITTAINE (Rev. George – 1790(?)–1847)

BIOGRAPHY

Not much is known about the life of this novelist. A minister in Kilcormack, he devoted his literary energies to painting the blackest picture of the Irish peasants and to hysterically denouncing Catholicism. He died in Dublin in 1847.

BIBLIOGRAPHY

1829(?) RECOLLECTIONS OF HYACINTH O'GARA.
Dublin: R.M. Tims, 1829, 84 p., 3rd edition, enlarged.
(The first edition has not been found by the present author.)

1829. THE CONFESSIONS OF HONOUR DELANY.
Dublin: R. M. Tims, 1829, 129 p.

1830. IRISH PRIESTS AND ENGLISH LANDLORDS.
Dublin: R. M. Tims, 1830, 249 p.
(There exists another edition of these three works, in one volume, of 1839, by the same publisher, 'corrected by the author', 4 + 3 + 350 p.)

1831(?) IRISHMEN AND IRISHWOMEN.
Dublin: R. M. Tims, 1831, 219 p. 2nd edition.
(The first edition has not been found by the present author.)

1833. JOHNNY DERRIVAN'S TRAVELS.
Dublin: R. M. Tims, 1833, 36 p.

MOTHERS AND SONS.
Dublin: R. M. Tims, 1833, 297 p.

NURSE MCVOURNEEN'S STORY.
Dublin: R. M. Tims, 1833, 33 p., 2nd edition.
(The first edition has not been found by the present author.)

1837.   'Some Doings Long Ago at Currahbeg'
by the author of 'Hyacinth O'Gara'.
Dublin   University   Magazine,   IX,   53,   May   1837,
pp. 559–70.

'The Orphans of Dunasker'
by the author of 'Hyacinth O'Gara' ... (etc.)
Dublin University Magazine
Ch. 1–4, X, 59, Nov. 1837, pp. 537–56.
Ch. 5–7, X, 60, Dec. 1837, pp. 635–51.

1838.   Ch. 8–10, XI, 61, Jan. 1838, pp. 54–69.
Ch. 11–13, XI, 63, Mar. 1838, pp. 271–90.
Ch. 14, 15, XI, 65, May 1838, pp. 543–54.
Ch. 16, 17, XI, 66, June 1838, pp. 736–46.

1840.   THE ELECTION.
Dublin: R. M. Tims, 1840, VI + 331 p.

BRONTË (Rev. Patrick – 1777–1861)

BIOGRAPHY

The Rev. Patrick Brontë has received more critical attention
than his colourless works deserve, at least three biographies and
several bibliographies ... It is, of course, primarily because the
fame of his daughters was reflected on the father; it is also the case
that his ill-established origins are at the root of the dispute as to the
Celtic and familial sources of *Wuthering Heights.*

This is not to hark back to the 'Irish' theory concerning these
sources, supported by Dr William Wright: *The Brontës in Ireland,*
or Facts Stranger than Fiction (London: Hodder and Stoughton,
1893, XX + 308 p.), attacked in *Bronteana* (see below), taken up
again, with no new evidence, by Cathal O'Byrne in *The Gaelic*
Source of the Brontë Genius (Edinburgh and London: Sands and
Co, 1933, 45 p.), and abandoned too hastily, perhaps, by modern
critics.

What is certain is that the Rev. Patrick Brontë really was Irish,
that he was born in Ireland on March 17, 1777, that he spent his
childhood and adolescence there, that he even started teaching
there before going to Cambridge, and that he retained his Irish
accent, his attachment to his motherland (his works testify to this)
and his links with his Irish relations.

Everything is known of his subsequent existence, his pastoral functions in Yorkshire, his life at the vicarage in Haworth. He died in 1861.

One notes that the surname 'Brontë' only appears with the Rev. Patrick's arrival at Cambridge. From its origins to the entry to Cambridge, the name seems to have undergone countless transformations: O'Prointy, O'Prunty, Prunty, Pronty, Brontë.

There is a recent biography by Annette B. Hopkins: *The Father of the Brontës*, published for Goucher College by the Johns Hopkins Press, Baltimore, 1958, XI + 179 p.

BIBLIOGRAPHY

This has been established by

Thomas James Wise: *A Brontë Library*. A catalogue of Printed Books, Manuscripts and Autograph Letters by the Members of the Brontë Family ...
London: printed for private circulation only, 1929, XXIII + 82 p., numerous facsimiles.
(The Rev. Patrick Brontë figures in Part IV, pp. 48–57.)

1810.   WINTER-EVENING THOUGHTS, a miscellaneous poem ...
London: printed for Longman, Hurst, Rees and Orme, and John Hurst, Wakefield, 1810, 23 p.
(The author's name does not appear. The poem recurs, much altered, in the following volume.)

1811.   COTTAGE POEMS ...
Halifax: printed and sold by P. K. Holden, for the author, 1811, 136 p.

1813.   THE RURAL MINSTREL, a miscellany of descriptive poems ...
Halifax: printed and sold by P. K. Holden, for the author.
Sold also by B. and R. Crosby and Co ...
London, 1813, XII + 108 p.
(The intention that his works might 'profit, whilst he pleased', expressed by the author on p. xi of his 'advertisement', accurately defines the two collections in each of which appear some Irish pieces: cf. in 1811 'The Irish Cabin' (pp. 69–86), in 1813 'The Harper of Erin'.)

1815.   THE COTTAGE IN THE WOOD *or, The Art of Becoming Rich and Happy* ...
Bradford: printed and sold by T. Inkersley ... 1815, 68 p.

(A rather poor tale, certain episodes of which are repeated in verse from p. 49 onwards.)

1818. THE MAID OF KILLARNEY; *or, Albion and Flora.*
A modern tale; in which are interwoven some censory remarks on Religion and Politics ...
London: published by Baldwin, Cradock and Joy. Sold also by T. Inkersley, Bradford; Robinson and Co, Leeds ...
1818, 166 p.

1824. THE PHENOMENON; *or, an account in verse, of the extraordinary disruption of a bog, which took place in the moors of Haworth, on the 12th day of September, 1824 ...*
Bradford ... T. Inkersley ... and ... F. Westley, 1824, 12 p.

There are also various SERMONS, TRACTS, etc., collected, together with the above-mentioned works, in the following volume which is valuable, although it is not always edited with care:

BRONTEANA. *The Rev. Patrick Brontë A.B., his Collected Works and Life* ... edited etc. by J. Horsfall Turner, Idel, Bradford.
Bingley: printed for the editor by T. Harrison & Sons, 1898, 304 p.

For the CORRESPONDENCE, see:

LOCK (John) and DIXON (Canon W. T.): *A Man of Sorrow, The Life, Letters and Times of the Rev. Patrick Brontë* ...
Foreword by the Archbishop of York.
London and Edinburgh: Nelson, 1965, XIX + 566 p.

BROOKE (Charlotte – 1740–1793)

BIOGRAPHY

One of the 22 children of the prolific poet, playwright and novelist Henry Brooke (1703–83), daughterly, religious, retiring, she was the first Anglo-Irishwoman with the ability to show her compatriots the richness of Gaelic literature.

If, as far as her biography is concerned, later critics have hardly added to the 'Memoir' of Aaron Crossly Seymour (cf. below: *Reliques*, 1816) her work as translator has been considered in detail in almost all studies of Irish literature (cf. for example.: J. F.

CAMPBELL: *Leabhar na Feinne*, D.RYAN: *The Sword of Life*, etc.
See also HEASLIP).

BIBLIOGRAPHY

1786. in *Historical Memoirs of the Irish Bards* by J. C. Walker,
London: Payne, 1786.
'Carolan's Receipt' (translation) pp. 87–8.
'Carolan's Monody on the death of Mary Mac Guire'
(translation) pp. 94–5.
'Tiagharna Mhaighe-eo' (translation) pp. 103–6.

1789. RELIQUES OF IRISH POETRY consisting of heroic poems,
odes, elegies and songs, translated into English verse with
notes explanatory and historical; and the originals in the
Irish character. To which is subjoined an Irish tale. By
Miss Brooke.
Dublin: George Bonham, printer ... 1789, XXVI + 369 p.,
large format.
Preface: III-X, Subscribers' names: XI-XXIII, Contents:
XXIV-VI, 'Heroic Poems': 1–134, 'Odes': 135–186,
'Elegies': 187–226, 'Songs': 227–261, 'Irish Originals':
262–320, 'Mäon, an Irish Tale': 321–369.
Extracts from this book appear later in *Bolg an Tsohair or
Gaelic Magazine*, n° 1, Belfast: Northern Star Office,
1795.
Note subsequently:
Reliques (etc.) to which is prefixed, a Memoir of her (i.e.
Ch. Brooke's) life and writings, by Aaron Crossly Sey-
mour, Esq., author of 'Letters to Young Persons', etc.
Dublin: Printed by J. Christie ... 1816.

1791. THE SCHOOL FOR CHRISTIANS.
Dublin: printed by Bernard Dornin, 1791, 4 + 71 p.

1792. (ed) THE POETICAL WORKS OF H. BROOKE.
Dublin, 1792, 4 v.

[1796. *Dialogue between a Lady and her Pupil.*
A work mentioned by Allibone who gives no other information.]

[1803. *Emma; or, the Foundling of the Wood.* A novel.
The present author has found mention of such a work in
Allibone only.]

[**n.d.**   *Belisarius*, a play.

On this subject, see Seymour's 'Memoir', LXV.

This play has never been printed and no trace remains of the manuscript sent to Charles Kemble and which the latter must have mislaid.]

BROUGHAM (John – 1814–1880)

BIOGRAPHY

Actor and playwright born in Dublin on May 9, 1814. After studying at Trinity College he starts a medical course that, on reaching London in 1830, he abandons in favour of an acting career. In 1840, he is director of the Lyceum. 1842–60: in the United States, opens on Broadway on October 15, 1850, 'Brougham's Lyceum'. 1860–5: staying in London once again after which he settles permanently in America. Dies in New York on June 7, 1880.

BIBLIOGRAPHY

(a) Theatrical works before 1850:

1840.   (29.6, E.O.H.) THE DEMON GIFT; *or, Visions of the Future.*

(23.7, ibid.) LIFE IN THE CLOUDS: *or Olympus in an Uproar.*

(according to Nicoll, the play was published the same year.)

(30.7, ibid.) LOVE'S LIVERY.

1841.   (4.6, ibid.) THE HUNTER'S BRIDE; *or, The Rose of Altenheim.*

1842.   (9.5, ibid.) THE ENTHUSIAST.

1847.   (1.6, PRIN.) ROMANCE AND REALITY; *or, Silence Gives Consent.*

(Dicks: 730).

1848.   (27.1, R.V.) JANE EYRE; *or, The Secrets of Thornfield Manor House.*

(arranged and revived in New York (Laura Keene's Varieties) 26.5.56.)

Published: New York: S. French, n.d., 32 p.

After 1850, there were to be a few 'Irish' plays, cf:
The Irish Emigrant (pub: Lacy).
The Irish Yankee (pub: French).
A Recollection of O'Flannigan and the Fairies (pub: Lacy).

(b) Miscellanea:

1855.   A BASKET OF CHIPS.
New York: Bunce & Brothers, 1855, 408 p.
(A mixture of verse and prose, fairy stories, and also 'The Bunsby Papers' (229–408) which were to be re-issued separately, two years later.)

1857.   THE BUNSBY PAPERS, IRISH ECHOES ...
New York: Derby & Jackson, 1857, VIII + 9 + 298 p.

1881.   LIFE, STORIES AND POEMS OF JOHN BROUGHAM,
edited by William Winter.
Boston: J. R. Osgood & Co, 1881, VIII + 15 + 461 p.
    (I: 'Autobiography' (15–92)
    II: 'A Supplementary Memoir' (97–144)
    III: 'Sketch of his Club Life' (144–154)
    IV: 'Selections from his Miscellaneous Writings'
    (to 461).)

BROWN (Frances – 1816–1879)

BIOGRAPHY

'The blind poetess of Donegal' was born in Stranorlar in 1816. She seems to have lived in the north of Ireland until 1847 when she settled in Edinburgh. She died in London on April 25, 1879.

BIBLIOGRAPHY

Frances Brown contributed to numerous magazines (*Northern Whig, Irish Penny Journal, Athenaeum, Hood's, Keepsake, Chamber's Journal*).
Of her writings in book form, which are difficult to find, the present author has only been able to consult two titles and the others (collections of poems and, especially, novels for children) are

given on the strength of an anonymous article in *The Irish Book Lover* (VIII, 5, 6, December, January 1916–17, pp. 49–51.)

1844. THE STAR OF ATTEGHEI: *The Vision of Schwartz; and Other Poems.*
London: Moxon, 1844, XXII + 261 p.

1848. LYRICS AND MISCELLANEOUS POEMS.
Edinburgh: Sutherland & Knox, 1848, 144 p.

[1852. THE ERICKSENS.

1856. PICTURES AND SONGS OF HOME.

1857. GRANNY'S WONDERFUL CHAIR.

1859. OUR UNCLE THE TRAVELLER.

1860. THE YOUNG FORESTERS.

1861. MY SHARE OF THE WORLD, 3 v.

1862. THE CASTLEFORD CASE, 3 v.

1866. THE HIDDEN SIN.

1869. THE EXILE'S TRUST.

1875. MY NEAREST NEIGHBOUR.

1886. THE FOUNDLING OF THE FEN.
THE DANGEROUS GUEST.

1887. THE FIRST OF THE AFRICAN DIAMONDS.]

BROWN (John – ?–1808)

A school-fellow of Thomas Moore's, born in Belfast, and one of the translators gathered by Bunting.

BROWNE (Mary Anne, Mrs James Gray – 1812–1845)

Not Irish (born in Maidenhead, married to a Scot) but mentioned here because she was a constant contributor (poetry) to the *Dublin University Magazine* which devoted an obituary notice to her (XXV, 147, March 1845, pp. 327–41). Moreover, Mrs Gray seems to have lived in Ireland for some time and it was in Cork that she died on January 28, 1845.

Her collections are: *Mont Blanc*, London, 1827; *Ada*, ibid., 1828; *Repentance*, ibid., 1829; *The Coronal*, ibid., 1833; *The Birthday Gift*, ibid., 1834; *Ignatia*, ibid., 1838; *Sacred Poetry*, ibid., 1840; *Sketches from the Antique*, Dublin, 1844.

BUGGY (Kevin, T. – 1817–1843)

A poet born in Kilkenny, died in Belfast at 27 years of age. Published in several magazines including *The Vindicator* of Belfast and *The Nation*. Figures in *The Spirit of the Nation*.

BUNBURY (Selina – 1802–1882)

BIOGRAPHY

A Protestant novelist born in County Louth in 1802, into a family of 15 children and to a father who was a minister. A great traveller, she alternated accounts of journeys with moralising tales and novels some of which are set in Ireland, others exploiting an historical or contemporary vein, etc.

Also contributed to various periodicals.

BIBLIOGRAPHY

(a) Works before 1850:

Selina Bunbury began her career with pious works: *Early Recollections, Stories from Church History* ...

1827.   CABIN CONVERSATIONS AND CASTLE SCENES. An Irish story ...

London: J. Nisbet, 1827, 173 p.

(An anti-Catholic novel set in the West of Ireland round about 1815.)

[»   MY FOSTER BROTHER.]

(This is the date given by Brown. The present author has only seen the third edition: Dublin: R. M. Tims, 1833, 134 p.)

[**1828.** THE ABBEY OF INNISMOYLE, a story of another century ...]
Dublin: W. Curry, Jun. & Co, 2nd edition: 1829, 336 p.
(The date 1828 (Brown) is confirmed by the National Library. In this novel, it is the Jesuits who come under attack from Miss Bunbury. The abbey is situated on the north-west coast of Ireland. The story begins in the twelfth century.)

1829. RETROSPECTIONS; a Soldier's Story ...
Dublin: W. Curry ..., 1829, 294 p.

[**1830.** ANNOT AND HER PUPIL.]
Edinburgh: W. Oliphant, 1830, 2nd edition, 179 p.

ELEANOR.
Dublin: W. Curry ..., 1830, 113 p.

1833. TALES OF MY COUNTRY.
Dublin: W. Curry ..., 1833, VII + 301 p.
(1. 'A Visit at Clairville Park, and the story of Rose Mulroon' (11–74). 2. 'Eveleen O'Connor' (77–106). 3. 'Monan-a-Glena' (109–188). 4. 'Six Weeks at the Rectory' (191–301).)

1843. COOMBE ABBEY, an historical tale of the reign of James the First (ill.)
Dublin: W. Curry, 1843, XV + 591 p.

1844. THE CASTLE AND HOVEL; or, The Two Sceptics.
London: B. Wertheim, 1844, 42 p. (in-18°)

RIDES IN THE PYRENEES.
London: T. C. Newby, 1844, 2 v., I: v + 296 p.
II: 301 p.

THE STAR OF THE COURT; or, The Maid of Honour and Queen of England, Ann Boleyn.
London: Grant & Griffith, 1844, VI + 161 p.

1845. EVENINGS IN THE PYRENEES; comprising the Stories of Wanderers from Many Lands. Edited and arranged by S. B.
London: J. Masters, 1845, IX + 305 p.
(The last of these stories is Irish: 'The Heiress of the Morelands'.)

[THE INDIAN BABES IN THE WOOD.]

1847. THE TRIUMPH OF TRUTH; *or, Henry and his Sister.*
London: R.T.S., 1847, VII + 188 p.

1849. EVELYN; *or a Journey from Stockholm to Rome in 1847–48.*
London: R. Bentley, 1849, 2 v., I: IV + 341 p.;
II: 396 p.

A VISIT TO THE CATACOMBS ... AND A MIDNIGHT VISIT TO MOUNT VESUVIUS.
London: W. W. Robinson, 1849, IV + 35p.

1850. THE BLIND MAN AND HIS LITTLE GUIDE.
London: Wertheim & Macintosh, 1850, 34 p.

(b) Principal works after 1850 (novels):

1856. OUR OWN STORY; *or, The History of Magdalene and Basil St Pierre.*
London: Hurst, etc., 1856, 3 v.

1858. SIR GUY D'ESTERRE.
London: Routledge, 1858, 2 v.
(Ireland in the Elizabethan period.)

1861. MADAME CONSTANCE, *The Autobiography of a French-woman in England ...*
London: T. C. Newby, 1861, 2 v.

1865. FLORENCE MANVERS.
London: T. C. Newby, 1865, 3 v.

BUNTING (Edward – 1773–1843)

The most important name among the Irish musicologists of the period under discussion.

Born in Armagh in February 1773, he was chosen to note down the melodies at the last congress of harpists (Belfast: 1792).

Author of:

A GENERAL COLLECTION OF THE ANCIENT IRISH MUSIC.
Dublin: W. Power, 1796, IV + 32 p. in-4°.

[A GENERAL COLLECTION OF THE ANCIENT MUSIC OF IRELAND, arranged for the piano-forte (1809).]

THE ANCIENT MUSIC OF IRELAND. Arranged for the piano forte, to which is prefixed a dissertation on the Irish harp and harpers, including an account of the old melodies of Ireland.
Dublin: Hodges and Smith, 1840, VIII + 100 + XII + 110 p. in-4°. Recently reissued by Walton's, Dublin.
(The first one hundred pages are devoted to the 'dissertation', some chapters being written by other contributors: Ferguson, Petrie. The melodies then follow.)

His work, unfinished, was continued by Petrie after 1850 and completed in the twentieth century (cf. O'Sullivan (D. J.) and Freeman (A. M.): *The Bunting Collection of Irish Folk Music and Songs*. Edited from the original manuscripts. *Journal of the Irish Folk Song Society*, Vol. 22, London, 1927).

See:

FOX (Charlotte Milligan): *Annals of the Irish Harpers*. London: Smith ..., 1911, XIV + 320 p.

Bunting had settled in Dublin in 1819, after his marriage and it was there that he died in December 1843.

BURDY (Samuel – 1754–1820)

BIOGRAPHY

Born in Dromore, County Down, of a family of tradespeople descended from the Huguenots. Studied at Trinity College. Ordained in 1783. Belonged to Percy's literary group, but was long excluded from it because he had had the unfortunate idea of falling in love with the bishop's daughter (the Belinda of his poems: cf.

'Banished from thee, whose smiles alone impart
A soothing med'cine to an aching heart.'
(*Ardglass*, pp. 99–100).)

When Percy put an end to his exile, he did not however give him his daughter, and S. Burdy remained a bachelor.

BIBLIOGRAPHY

(a) Poetry:

1802. ARDGLASS; *or, the Ruined Castles,* also *The Transformation, with some other poems.*
Dublin: printed by Graisberry and Campbell, 1802, XXVII + 128 p.

(b) Prose:

1792. [A SHORT ACCOUNT OF THE AFFAIRS OF IRELAND DURING THE YEARS 1783–1784, AND PART OF 1785.]
THE LIFE OF THE LATE REV. PHILIP SKELTON, with some curious anecdotes.
Dublin: printed for the author and sold by William Jones, 1792, (4) + 4 + 240 p.

1807. [A TOUR OF A FEW DAYS TO LONDONDERRY AND THE GIANT'S CAUSEWAY.
Dublin: printed by J. Jones, 1807.]

1817. THE HISTORY OF IRELAND FROM THE EARLIEST AGES TO THE UNION.
Edinburgh: Doig and Stirling; London: George Cowie; Dublin: J. Cumming, 1817, 574 p.

BURK (John Daly – 1775(?)–1808)

BIOGRAPHY

An important name in the history of the early theatre in the United States, where Burk had to flee in 1796 to escape political arrest.

Began by launching a newspaper in Boston (*The Polar Star and Boston Daily Advertiser*) where he also tried his hand at the theatre, then in New York (*Time Piece*). He then settled in Petersburgh, Virginia. Was killed in a duel with the Frenchman, Coquebert.

BIBLIOGRAPHY

(a) Dramatic works:

1797. (17.12, Boston: Hay-market) BUNKER HILL; *or, The Death of General Warren.*
New York: Greenleaf, 1797, 55 p. (verse).

THE DEATH OF GENERAL MONTGOMERY IN STORMING THE CITY OF QUEBEC.

1798. (N. York: Park Theatre) FEMALE PATRIOTISM; *or, The Death of Joan d'Arc.*
New York: Hurtin, 1798, 40 p.

1808. (Petersburgh) BETHLEN GABOR, LORD OF TRANSYL-VANIA; *or, The Man-Hating Palatine.*
Petersburgh: Somervell & Conrad, 1807, 49 p.

also (dates unknown):
The Fortunes of Nigel.
The Innkeeper of Abbeyville.
Which Do You Like Best, the Poor Man or the Lord?

(b) Miscellanea:

1799. HISTORY OF THE LATE WAR IN IRELAND.
Philadelphia: Bailey, 1799, 140 (+ 1) + 40 p.

1803. AN ORATION, *delivered on the 4 March, 1803.*
Petersburgh: Field, 1803, 18 p.

1804. THE HISTORY OF VIRGINIA.
-16. Petersburgh: Dickson & Pescud, 4 v.
(I: 1804, II, III: 1805, IV: 1816).

1808. 'An Historical Essay on the Character and Antiquity of Irish Songs'.
Richmond Enquirer, 27 May 1808.

(c) Secondary material:

CAMPBELL (Charles): *Some Materials to Serve for a Brief Memoir of John Daly Burk, author of a 'History of Virginia',* with a Sketch of the Life and Character of his only child, Judge John Julius Burk. Albany, N.Y.: Joel Munsel, 1868, VI + 123 p.

Dictionary of American Biography.
(III, pp. 279–80 which refers to the following:)

CLAPP (W. W. Jun.): *A Record of the Boston Stage*, 1853.

WEGELIN (Oscar): *Early American Plays*, 1900.

QUINN (Pr.): *A History of the American Drama from the Beginnings to the Civil War*, 1923.

BURKE (Edmund – 1729–1797)

The substance of the life and activities of the famous political writer is beyond the bounds of the period under discussion. However, certain works by this great Irishman are of immediate concern here. They are:

1757.   A PHILOSOPHICAL ENQUIRY INTO THE ORIGIN OF OUR IDEAS OF THE SUBLIME AND BEAUTIFUL.
London, 1757, VIII + 184 p., an excellent modern edition of which is that by J. T. Boulton: London, Routledge, 1958, University of Notre Dame Press, 1968, CXXX + 197 p.

1790.   REFLECTIONS ON THE REVOLUTION IN FRANCE.
London: J. Dodsley, 1790, IV + 356 p., to be read to advantage in the edition by Thomas H. D. Mahoney and O. Priest, Indianapolis & New York, 'The Library of liberal arts', Bobbs-Merrill Co., 1955, XLIV + 307 p.

A listing of Burke's other works will be found in all bibliographies of the English XVIIIth. century, cf.:

1791.   A LETTER TO A MEMBER OF THE NATIONAL ASSEMBLY.

1792.   A LETTER TO SIR HERCULES LANGRISHE ON THE ROMAN CATHOLICS OF IRELAND.
etc.

The 1887 London edition of the complete works in 12 v. has recently been reproduced by G. Olms, Hildesheim, West Germany, while Burke's letters are in the course of publication by Cambridge University Press.

Among RECENT STUDIES, are the following:

BROWNE (Ray, B.): 'The Paine-Burke Controversy in XVIIIth Century Irish Popular Songs', in *The Celtic Cross*, q.v. in the general bibliography (R. B. Browne, etc., ed.), pp. 80–97.

CHAPMAN (G. W.): *E. Burke: The Practical Imagination*. Cambridge, Mass.: Harvard University Press, 1968, 350 p.

BURKE (Thomas Travers –)

Probably a doctor by profession (cf., London, 1840: *The Accoucheur's Vademecum; or, Modern Guide to the Practise of Midwifery*). Author of the following Ossianids:

1818. TEMORA, an Epic Poem in eight cantos; versified from Macpherson's prose translation of 'The Poems of Ossian'.
Perth: printed by R. Morrison, for the author, 1818, II + 77 p.
(2 cantos only in the edition consulted by the present author in the British Museum.)

1820. DAR-THULA, a Poem of Ossian translated into English Verse.
London: Longman, etc.; Dublin: R. Milliken, 1820, LXXXVI + 76 p.

1844. FINGAL, an Epic Poem versified from the 'Genuine Remains of Ossian'. With notes.
London: Cowie, Jolland & Co, 1844, XIX + 194 p.

1858. OSSIAN, HIS PRINCIPAL POEMS TRANSLATED INTO ENGLISH VERSE, with introduction and notes, illustrative of the manners and customs of the Caledonians, and an account of the harp in the Highlands.
Edinburgh: Adam & C. Black, 1858, LXXXVIII + 381 p.
(This is an anthology: anonymous, Rev. Mr Holl, Mr Woodrow. Burke's contribution (8 passages) begins on p. 229.)

According to O'Donoghue, he is also the author of:

THE ROYAL VISIT, a poem on the arrival of his most gracious Majesty, George IV. Dublin: C. P. Archer, 1821, 48 p.

BURRELL (Lady Sophia Raymond – 1750(?)–1802)

BIOGRAPHY

The *D.N.B.* and P. Kavanagh after it, give 1750 as Lady Burrell's date of birth, whereas D. J. O'Donoghue has her born around 1760.
We may classify her among Irish authors on the strength of the

latter who himself relied on the list of Irish poets given by Sir John Carr in his *Stranger in Ireland* of 1803. The *D.N.B.* on the other hand, associated her with the English county of Essex.

The internal evidence is inconclusive, but rather in favour of the Irish thesis. In fact, in her *Poems*, several pieces are dedicated to some important figures in Ireland, and the Celtic vein predominates.

BIBLIOGRAPHY

(a) Poetry:

1793.   POEMS dedicated to the R. H. The Earl of Mansfield.
London: printed by J. Cooper ... sold by Leigh & Sotheby, etc. 1793.
(Vol. I (VIII + 286 p.), beside other more particularly Celtic poems, comprises:
'Abelard to Eloisa', heroic couplets, p. 12.
'Comala', a dramatic poem in 3 acts taken from a poem of Ossian, Dec. 1784, pp. 47–87, followed by Macpherson's original; blank verse.
'Connal and Crimora', about which the author says in a note, 'This poem is taken from the book of Carriethura in Ossian's *Fingal* ...', p. 139.
'The Druid', p. 159.
Also note: 'The Triumph of Nature', p. 198 seq.
Vol. II (VII + 303 p.) is entitled: *Poems by Lady Burrell.*)

(b) Dramatic works:

1800.   MAXIMIAN, a tragedy, taken from Corneille.
London: printed by Luke Hansard, sold by Leigh & Sotheby, 1800, 98 p.
5 acts in blank verse. (The name of the author does not appear on the title page, but the dedicatory letter to William Lock is signed Sophia Burrell.)

THEODORA; *or, The Spanish Daughter*, a tragedy.
London: printed by Luke Hansard, sold by Leigh & Sotheby, 1800, VIII (epilogue + dramatis personae) + 100 p.
5 acts + epilogue. (The author's name does not appear), blank verse, the action takes place mostly in Spain.

1814.   VILLARIO, a play in 5 acts.

In *The New British Theatre*, a selection of original dramas, not yet acted ... Vol. II.
London: Henry Colburn, 1814, pp. 137–88 + notes pp. 189 and 190.
The action takes place in Dalmatia.

A SEARCH AFTER PERFECTION, a comedy in 5 acts.
In *The New British Theatre*, a selection of original dramas, not yet acted ... Vol. III.
London: Henry Colburn, 1814, pp. 33–90 + observations pp. 91–94.

BUTT (Isaac – 1813–1879)

BIOGRAPHY

Born in Glenfin, Donegal, on September 6, 1813. On leaving Trinity College, engaged in some important literary activities; it was thus that, in 1834, after having published various essays and several novels, he succeeded the Rev. Charles Stuart ('Anthony Poplar') as editor of *The Dublin University Magazine*, a post that he was to occupy for four years.

Later, Isaac Butt was to abandon the conservatism of his youth for nationalism. A well-known barrister, he defended the Fenian prisoners in 1865–9; an eminent political figure, he became the leader of the Agrarian League and the party for Home Rule.

Died in Roebuck Cottage, near Dundrum, in county Dublin, on May 5, 1879.

BIBLIOGRAPHY

The work of Butt consists primarily of POLITICAL ESSAYS among which, anterior to 1850, are the following:

A VOICE FOR IRELAND. *The Famine in the Land. What has been done and what is to be done.* Dublin: McGlashan, 1847, VIII + 59 p.

(A detailed review of the above will be found in the *Dublin University Magazine*, XIX, 172, April 1847, pp. 501–540.)

Beside *Children of Sorrow* mentioned by Brown but untraced by the present author, the THREE NOVELS are:

1834. CHAPTERS OF COLLEGE ROMANCE.
(The first instalment of this narrative appeared in the *Dublin University Magazine* (IV, 23, pp. 486–501) in November 1834 under the name of Edward Stevens O'Brien, and continued at irregular intervals until November 1837 (X, 59, pp. 499–520). An edition in book form appeared under the author's real name, in London (C. J. Skeet) in 1863.)

1840. IRISH LIFE: IN THE CASTLE, THE COURTS, AND THE COUNTRY.
London: How & Parsons, 1840, 3 v., I: VII + 332 p., II: 355 p., III: 368 p.

1848. THE GAP OF BARNESMORE: A Tale of the Irish Highlands, and the Revolution of 1688.
London: Smith, etc., 1848, 3 v., I: 336 p., II: 314 p., III: 334 p.

The standard work on the author is:

De VERE WHITE (Terence): *The Road of Excess.*
Dublin: Browne and Nolan, 1946, VIII + 393 p., portr., ill.

BYRNE (P. E.)

The following works appear under this signature: in 1825, *The Western Harp; or, Songs of Erin in Bondage;* in 1830, published in Dublin: *Osmin and Leila,* a Turkish tale, with other poems.

CALLANAN (Jeremiah Joseph – 1795–1829)

BIOGRAPHY
There seems to be hardly any agreement on the author's Christian names; he is generally christened Jeremiah Joseph (MacCarthy: *Irish Literature,* Vol. II, p. 438) but also Jeremiah John *(D.N.B.).* However, we are acquainted with the broad outlines of his life thanks especially to the 'Memoir' preceding the *Poems* in the 1861 edition, and to that in *Bolster's Quarterly Magazine* (1831, pp. 280–97).
Born in Cork in 1795, spent his childhood among Gaelic peasants

whose language he learnt. His parents had decided that he had a vocation, as sometimes happens in Ireland. He thus entered Maynooth which he left at twenty years of age, without quite knowing how to re-orientate his life.

He studied for some time at Trinity College with a view to becoming a doctor, then returned to Cork, and wrote for magazines, *Bolster's Quarterly, The Literary Magnet, The Mercantile Chronicle*, resided with various people, worked here and there, between journeys into the heart of the country to gather legends and texts that he was never to publish.

Died of tuberculosis in Lisbon where he had gone as a tutor, on September 19, 1829.

With Callanan there is an almost pathological indecision, a sort of permanent mystical despair. He is the author of a slim volume of poetry, but he is not a mediocre poet. He has summarised his life in a pretty piece:

> 'A poet's eye whilst yet a child.
> A boyhood, wayward, warm and wild,
> A youth that mocked correction's rod ...
> A manhood with a soul that flies
> More high than heaven's own highest skies,
> But with a wing that oft will stoop ...'

BIBLIOGRAPHY

(a) Publications in periodicals:

During his lifetime, Callanan's writings appeared in various periodicals: very particularly in *Bolster's:*

> (I, 2, May 1826, pp. 223–9 – 'Lamentation of Felix McCarthy', 'Cusheen Loo', 'On the Last Day'.
>
> II, Jan. 1827, pp. 15–16 – 'The Lament of O'Gnive'.
>
> III, May 1828, p. 33 – 'The Outlaw of Loch Lene'; Dec. 1829, p. 283 – 'Adieu my own dear Erin', pp. 295–6 – 'De la vida del Cielo'; Mar. 1830, pp. 400–11 – 'Irish Druidism' (an article in prose).)

Beside these works and the 'Memoir' mentioned above, a long, unsigned article on his poetry is to be found in this magazine (III, August 1828, pp. 191–200).

(b) Works collected into book form (all posthumous:):

1830.   THE RECLUSE OF INCHIDONY *and Other Poems.*
London: Hurst, Chance and Co, 1830, 160 p.
(It will be noticed that the copy in the British Museum contains several of Callanan's handwritten letters, a manuscript version of his 'Gougane Barra' and the 'Memoir' from *Bolster's* of 1831, all of them documents added subsequently.)

1847.   [2nd edition of the *Poems.*
according to Mc Carthy (*Irish Literature*).
with introductions and notes by M. F. M'Carthy.
The *D.N.B.* mentions Cork as the place of publication.]

1861.   THE POEMS OF J. J. CALLANAN, a new edition with biographical introduction and notes.
Cork: published by Daniel Mulcahy ... sold by J. Duffy, Dublin and London, 1861, XVI + 167 p.
(This edition only differs from that of 1830 in its title, its introduction, the displacement of three poems (one of which, 'The Last Song of Henry Kirk White', has been lengthened), and the addition of 11 new poems at the end. Callanan's most famous poems, translations included, already appear in the 1830 edition. The 1861 edition is featured again in 1883 in *Gems from the Cork Poets.*)

(c) Secondary material:

Callanan is studied in all general works on Anglo–Irish literature, figures in all the anthologies, and receives the attention of all those concerned with translations (cf. FARREN, HEASLIP, RYAN, q.v. in general bibliography).

MONAHAN (M.) (*Nova Hibernia*, 1914) devotes a chapter to him (pp. 186–197).

Among articles should be mentioned beside B. G. MacCarthy's already referred to (*Studies*, Sept. 1946):

LEE (B.S.): 'Callanan's "The Outlaw of Loch Lene" ', *Ariel*, I, 3, July 1970, 89–100.

CAMPBELL (James – 1758–1818)

A weaver-poet from Northern Ireland whose posthumous works were published in Belfast in 1820. See HEWITT.

CARLETON (William 1794–1869)[1]

BIOGRAPHY

Born in Tyrone into a poor and numerous peasant family in which Gaelic was not yet dead. A somewhat chaotic education in the 'hedge-schools' and as a 'poor scholar'. A Catholic who had even entertained thoughts of entering the priesthood, he turned to Protestantism under the influence of, among others, the Rev. Coesar Otway (q.v.) who, from 1828, introduced him to the columns of his periodical, *The Christian Examiner.* Famous at an early age, praised by all – although sometimes with some reticence, cf. Lever – he is perhaps the only nineteenth-century Irish–English writer to have preserved intact the esteem of the discerning. That, however, did not help him make a fortune in his lifetime. Died on January 30, 1869, near Dublin.

BIBLIOGRAPHY

(a) Prose works before 1850:
The first of Carleton's writings to be published is 'A Pilgrimage to Patrick's Purgatory' (signed W.) in *The Christian Examiner* of April–May 1828. Countless other contributions by this author are to be found in this magazine; cf. also *The Dublin Family Magazine, The National Magazine, The Dublin University Review and Quarterly, The Dublin University Magazine* (from 1833), *The Citizen, The Irish Penny Journal* (from 1840), *The Nation, The Independent.*
The works collected in book form are the following:

1829.   FATHER BUTLER; THE LOUGH DEARG PILGRIM.*
           Being Sketches of Irish Manners.
           Dublin: Wm. Curry, etc., 1829, IV + 302 p.

---

[1] Revised and updated by André Boué.

(The second of these stories would figure in *Traits* from 1833. It is to be noted that its first title was 'A Pilgrimage to Patrick's Purgatory'.

'Father Butler' had first appeared in *The Christian Examiner* of August–December 1828.)

1830. TRAITS AND STORIES OF THE IRISH PEASANTRY,*
with etchings by W. H. Brooke.
Dublin: Wm. Curry, etc., 1830, 2 v.
Vol. I: XII + 275 p. Vol. II: 304 p.

(This first series comprised:

I. Preface; 'Ned Mc Keown'; 'The Three Tasks'; 'Shane Fadh's Wedding'; 'Larry Mc Farland's Wake'; 'The Battle of the Factions'.

II. 'The Party Fight and Funeral'; 'The Hedge School'; 'The Station' which had already been published in the *Christian Examiner* for Jan.–Apr.–June 1829.)

1833. TRAITS AND STORIES OF THE IRISH PEASANTRY, 2ND SERIES.*
Dublin: W. F. Wakeman, 1833, 3 v.
Vol. I: VIII + 471 p. Vol. II: 475 p. Vol. III: 448 p.

(I. 'The Midnight Mass'; 'The Donagh; or, the Horse-Stealers' (formerly published in The *National Magazine* for Dec. 1830); 'Phil Purcel, the Pig Driver'; 'An Essay on Irish Swearing' (generally incorporated to the following in later editions); 'The Geography of an Irish Oath'.

II. 'The Lianhan Shee' (*Christian Examiner*, Nov. 1830); 'The Poor Scholar'; 'Wildgoose Lodge'; 'Tubber Derg, or the Red Well'.

III. 'Dennis O'Shaughnessy going to Maynooth' (*Christian Examiner*, Sept.–Dec. 1831); 'Phelim O'Toole's Courtship'; Notes.

The 1843 edition (Dublin: Curry; London: Orr, 2 v.) would also include Carleton's very interesting autobiographical introduction, as well as 'Neal Malone' first published in the *Dublin University Review and Quarterly*, Jan. 1833, then in the book *Tales of Ireland* of '34.

Certain later editions, like the one used by the present author (with ill. by Daniel Maclise, London: Maxwell, n.d. 1 v., 780 p.) also contain:

'The Silver Acre' (*Illustrated London Magazine*, 1853)
'The Fair of Emyvale' (ibid., 1853)
'Master and Scholar' (ibid., 1853)

all three published separately in book form in 1862 under the original title.)
Traits have been reprinted in 1973 by the Mercier Press, with an introduction by Maurice Harmon.

1834.   TALES OF IRELAND.*
Dublin: Wm. Curry, etc., 1834, XIII + 366 p. ill.
('The Death of a Devotee' (*Christian Examiner*, Oct. 1829); 'The Priest's Funeral' (ibid., Jan.–Feb. 1830); 'Neal Malone' (*Dublin University Review and Quarterly*, Jan. 1833); 'The Brothers' (*Christian Examiner*, March–June 1830); 'The Illicit Distiller' (*Christian Examiner*, Dec. 1830); 'The Dream of a Broken Heart' (*Dublin University Review and Quarterly*, April 1833); 'Lachlin Murray and the Blessed Candle' (*Christian Examiner*, Aug. 1830).)

POPULAR TALES AND LEGENDS OF THE IRISH PEASANTRY, by S. Lover.
Dublin: W. F. Wakeman, 1834, 404 p.
(Contains by Carleton 'Alley Sheridan' already published in the *National Magazine*, Nov. 1830; 'Laying a Ghost' published, ibid., January 1831.)

1839.   FARDOROUGHA THE MISER; *or, the Convicts of Lisnamona**
Dublin: Wm. Curry, etc., 1839, X + 468 p.
(Had already appeared in the *Dublin University Magazine* from Feb. 1837, IX, 50, p. 212, to Feb. 1838, XI, 61, p. 250).

1841.   THE FAWN OF SPRINGVALE, *The Clarionet and Other Tales.**
Dublin: Wm. Curry, etc., 1841, 3 v.
I: VIII + 367 p. II: 351 p. III: 328 p.
(Contains I: Preface; 'Jane Sinclair'; 'Lha Dhu'. II: 'The Clarionet'; 'The Dead Boxer'. III: 'The Misfortunes of Barney Branagan'; 'The Resurrections of Barney Bradley'.
'Jane Sinclair' had appeared previously in the *Dublin*

University Magazine from Sept. 1836, VIII, 45, p. 334, to Dec. of the same year, VIII, 48, pp. 702–21.
'The Dead Boxer' in the same magazine in Dec. 1833, II, 12, p. 617.
'The Misfortunes of Barney Branagan' from January 1841, XVII, 97, p. 80, to May 1841, XVII, 101, pp. 585–98, ibid.
'The Resurrections of Barney Bradley' in February 1834, III, 14, p. 177.)

1845.   ART MAGUIRE; *or, the Broken Pledge.*
Dublin: J. Duffy, 1845, XI + 252 p.

PARRA SASTHA; *or, the History of Paddy-Go-Easy and his Wife Nancy.*
Dublin: J. Duffy, 1845, XVI + 198 p.

RODY THE ROVER; *or, the Ribbonman.*
Dublin: J. Duffy, 1845, IV + 244 p.

CHARACTERISTIC SKETCHES OF IRELAND AND THE IRISH.
(Samuel Lover, W. Carleton, Mrs Hall.)
Dublin: Hardy & Sons, 1845, 288 p.
(Contains:
   (1) 'The Horse Stealers' (*Traits*, 1833).
   (2) 'Owen Mc Carthy' (*National Magazine*, April 1831, under the title: 'The Landlord and Tenant').
   (3) 'Squire Warnock' (*Popular Tales*, 1834, under the title: 'Laying a Ghost').
   (4) 'The Abduction' (ibid., under the title: 'Alley Sheridan'.)
   (5) 'Sir Turlough' (a poem, *National Magazine*, Nov. 1830).)

TALES AND SKETCHES *Illustrating the Character, Usages, Traditions, Sports and Pastimes of the Irish Peasantry.*
(Also known as: TALES AND STORIES OF THE IRISH PEASANTRY.)*
Dublin: J. Duffy, 1845, IX + 393 p.
(Comprises:
'Mickey McRorey, the Irish Fiddler'; 'Buckramback, the Country Dancing-Master'; 'Mary Murray, the Irish Match-Maker'; 'Ben Pentland, or the Gauger outwitted';

'The Fate of Frank McKenna'; 'The Rival Kempers'; 'Frank Martin and the Fairies'; 'A Legend of Knockmany'; 'Rose Moan, the Irish Midwife'; 'Talbot and Gaynor, Irish Pipers'; 'Frank Finnegan, the Foster-Brother'; 'Tom Gressiey, the Irish Senachie'; 'The Castle of Aughentain, or a Legend of the Brown Goat'; 'Barney McHaigney, the Irish Prophecy Man.' (All these texts, with the exception of 'Talbot' appeared in *The Irish Penny Journal* in 1840–1). 'Moll Roe's Marriage, or the Pudding Bewitched' (*The Citizen*, 17 March 1841); 'Barney Brady's Goose, or Dark Doings at Slathberg' (*Dublin University Magazine*, XI, 15, May 1838, p. 604); 'Condy Cullen, or the Exciseman Defeated'. 'A Record of the Heart, or the Parent's Trial' (*The Citizen*, 8 June 1840); 'The Three Wishes' (*Dublin University Magazine*, XIV, 83, Nov. 1839, p. 600); 'The Irish Rake; Stories of Second Sight and Apparition'.)

VALENTINE MC CLUTCHY, *The Irish Agent; or, The Chronicles of the Castle Cumber Property.**
With plates by Phiz.,
Dublin: J. Duffy, 1845, 3 v.
I: XII + 300 p. II: 318 p. III: 336 p.

1847. THE BLACK PROPHET, a Tale of Irish Famine.*
With six illustrations by W. Harvey ...
London: Simms & McIntyre, 1847, XI + 455 p.
(Previously published in the *Dublin University Magazine*, May 1846: XXVII, 161, p. 600, to Dec. 1846: XXVIII, 168, pp. 717–47.) Republished with an introduction by Timothy Webb: Shannon, Irish University Press, 1972.

1848. THE EMIGRANTS OF AHADARRA, a Tale of Irish Life.*
London and Belfast: Simms & Mc Intyre, 1848, VII + 309 p.

1849. THE TITHE PROCTOR, a Novel. Being a Tale of the Tithe Rebellion in Ireland.*
(with *The Hand and Word* by Griffin).
London: Simms & Mc Intyre, 1849, XVI + 288 p.

(b) Prose – later books:

1852. RED HALL; *or, the Baronet's Daughter.*
London: Saunders and Otley, 3 v.

THE SQUANDERS OF CASTLE SQUANDER.
London: Illustrated London Library, 2 v.

1855. WILLY REILLY AND HIS DEAR COLLEEN BAWN.
London: Hope, 3 v.
(A first version appeared in *The Independent*, London,
Dec. 50, Jan. 51.)

1857. THE BLACK BARONET (a revision of *Red Hall*).
Dublin: J. Duffy.

1860. THE EVIL EYE; *or, the Black Spectre*, ibid.

1862. THE DOUBLE PROPHECY, ibid.

REDMOND, COUNT O'HANLON, THE IRISH RAPPAREE,
ibid.

THE SILVER ACRE *and Other Tales.*
London: Ward & Lock.

1889. THE RED-HAIRED MAN'S WIFE.
Dublin: Sealy ...; London: Simpkin ...

(c) Poetry:

1828. 'Retrospections' (signed: Wilton).
Christian Examiner, Sept.

'The Midnight Hour' (id.)
ibid., Nov.

1829. 'The Retrospect' (id.)
Dublin Family Magazine, Aug.

1830. 'Sir Turlough, or the Churchyard Bride'.
National Magazine, Nov.

1831. 'A Sigh for Knockmany' in 'Landlord and Tenant'.
National Magazine, April.

1834. 'A Song of Sorrow' in 'Irish Storyists'.
Dublin University Magazine, Sept.

1845. 'Willy Reilly' in
The Ballad Poetry of Ireland by C. G. Duffy.

1854. 'Taedet me Vitæ'.
Nation, 30 Dec.

1858. 'Farewell'.
Nation, 18 Dec.

1896. 'Jane Anderson' in
The Life of Carleton by D. J. O'Donoghue, q.v. below.

(d) Dramatic works:

1841. IRISH MANUFACTURE; *or, Bob McGawley's Project.*
(A comedy performed at the Theatre Royal, Dublin, on
March 25, 1841, only the prologue is printed (*The Warder*,
Dublin, April 3, 1841).)

(e) Secondary material:

D.N.B., CRONE. All works on Irish literature, particularly:
BROWN, FLANAGAN, FOSTER, KRANS, LECLAIRE (q.v. in the
general bibliography).

Also:

YEATS (W. B.): *Stories from Carleton*, with an introduction.
London: W. Scott, n.d. [= 1889], XVII + 302 p. Reprinted:
New York, Lemma, 1973.

O'DONOGHUE (David J.): *The Life of William Carleton:**
Being his autobiography and letters; and an account of his life
and writings, from the point at which the autobiography
breaks off. With an introduction by Mrs Cashel Hoey.
London: Downey & Co, 1896, 2 v. (2 portr.).
I: LXIV + 289 p. II: VIII + 362 p.

SHAW (Rose): *Carleton's Country*,
with foreword by Mr Shane Leslie.
Dublin: Talbot Press, 1930, 145 p., photos.

KIELY (Benedict): *Poor Scholar. A Study of the works and days of
William Carleton.*
London: Sheed and Ward, 1947, IX + 198 p., reprinted:
Dublin, Talbot Press, 1972.

KAVANAGH (Patrick): Preface to *The Autobiography of William
Carleton.*
London: Macgibbon and Kee, 1968, 238 p.

IBARRA-SULLIVAN (Eileen): *Realistic Accounts of the Irish
Peasantry in Four Novels of William Carleton.*
Unpublished dissertation, University of Florida, 1969, 217 p.

BOUÉ (André): *William Carleton 1794–1869, romancier irlandais.*
Lille: Service de Reproduction des Thèses, 1973, VIII + 579 p.

CHESNUTT (Margaret): *Studies in the Short Stories of William Carleton.*
Göteborg, Gothenburg Studies in English 34, 1976, 213 p.

Note also the *Carleton Newsletter* (Florida University).

CHENEVIX (Richard – 1774–1830)

BIOGRAPHY

It is primarily as a chemist and mineralogist that Richard Chenevix is known, and particularly on that score that the *D.N.B.* devotes to him two columns of its volume 10. Descended from Huguenots, born in Dublin where he completed his studies. Was 'Fellow of the Royal Society of Edinburgh', 'Fellow of the Irish Academy' and correspondent for several learned societies on the Continent.

BIBLIOGRAPHY

(R. Chenevix's scientific works are not included here.)

(a) Prose:

1832. AN ESSAY UPON NATIONAL CHARACTER, *being an inquiry into some of the principal causes which contribute to form and modify the characters of nations in the state of civilisation.*
London: James Duncan, 1832, 2 v.
I: VII + 532 p. II: IV + 590p.

(b) Dramatic works:

1802. DRAMATIC POEMS, LEONORA, a tragedy, and ETHA AND AIDALLE, a dramatic poem.
London: J. Bell, 1802, 2nd edition, 164 p.
('Leonora', a tragedy in 5 acts, in blank verse, is followed by 'Remarks by the author of the play'.

'Etha and Aidalle' (p. 103 seq.) is also in 'blank verse' and followed by remarks (p. 145 seq.).)

1812. Two Plays: Mantuan Revels, a comedy in 5 acts; Henry the Seventh, an historical tragedy in 5 acts.
London: J. Johnson & Co, 1812, 319 p.
(The comedy (pp. 1–146) is inspired partly by a novel by Cinthio and partly by an episode in *Don Quixote*; a mixture of verse and prose. id. in the tragedy (p. 147 seq.).)

Not one of the dramatic works of R. Chenevix seems to have been performed.

(c) Secondary material:
See *Edinburgh Review*, 1812 (hardly a laudatory article).

CHERRY (Andrew – 1762–1812)

BIOGRAPHY

Born in Limerick on January 11, 1762. His father was a printer and bookseller. Was linked throughout his life to the theatre: an amateur actor from the age of 14, then head of a touring company, married the daughter of a theatre director, Richard Knight. He was to be found successively in Dublin (Smock Alley) where his first part was Darby in *The Poor Soldier* by John O'Keeffe, in Manchester, Bath (1798), Drury Lane (1802). He died in Wales, where he directed a theatre, in 1812.

He is still well known primarily for the songs in certain of his plays, 'The Dear Little Shamrock' for example or more particularly 'The Bay of Biscay' (*Spanish Dollars*), and it is as a song writer that Hercules Ellis includes him six times in his *Songs of Ireland, 2nd series*, 1849. A. Cherry's most curious play from the point of view of the use of these songs is incontestably *The Travellers* (1806) in which the musical style of each country through which the hero travels is imitated by the composer Corri, and it is a wide spectrum that transports us from China to the Ireland of O'Gallagher.

BIBLIOGRAPHY

(a) Theatrical works – published plays:

1793.   [HARLEQUIN ON THE STOCKS, a pantomime.]

1804.   [THE LYRIC NOVELIST; *or, Life Epitomised.*
1804.] a play never performed.
*The Songs etc ... in the new entertainment called The
Lyric Novelist; or, Life Epitomised:* in character, song, and
sentiment, as sung by Mrs Mountain ...
London: T. Preston, n.d. (1804).
(8 composers for the melodies, including Shield and
Carolan. By the latter cf. p. 12, 'Nature and Melody'. Also,
passim, Romantic themes including p. 7 'Poor Emma, the
Maniac', in a very Ossianic style.)

(7.2, D.L.) THE SOLDIER'S DAUGHTER, a comedy in 5
acts, now performing with unbounded applause, at the
Theatre Royal, Drury Lane.
9th edition, London: printed for Richard Phillips, 1804,
86 p.
(Cherry's most popular play: it ran for thirty-five nights.)

1805.   (9.5, C.G.) SPANISH DOLLARS; or, *The Priest of the
Parish,* an operatic sketch ... The Music by J. Davy,
London: Barker & Son, 1806, 32 p.
(1 act; the action takes place on the Irish coast; all the
characters are Irish; songs in the Irish style also, cf. 'Loud
roar'd the dreadful thunder ... In the Bay of Biscay, O!')

1806.   (22.1, D.L.) THE TRAVELLERS; *or, Music's Fascination,*
an operatic drama in 5 acts ...
The music composed by Mr. Corri.
London: printed for Richard Phillips ..., 1806, 82 p.
(The preface announces that in this play will be found: 'the
national melody of various kingdoms ... introduced, and
the progress of music traced, commencing in China, and
terminating in England'.)

1807.   (8.5) PETER THE GREAT; *or, The Wooden Walls,*
an operatic drama in 3 acts.
London: R. Phillips, 1807, 74 p.

1808.   (1.3, D.L.) IN AND OUT OF TUNE.
Inspired by Dennis Lawler. (An unpublished play, figures in
the Larpent manuscripts collection.)

*Songs, duets, trios, etc ... in the new musical farce called
In and Out of Tune,* in two acts ..., music: Corri,
London: C. Lowndes, n.d. (1808), 19 p.
(Arrangements of popular tunes, including at least one
Irish one:

> 'An Irishman's all over
> A fiddle, bass, hautboy and flute ...')

(b) Unpublished plays:

1796. (1.3, C.S.) THE OUTCAST; *or, Poor Bess and Little Dick,*
an opera.

1805. (15.5, D.L.) ALL FOR FAME! *or, A Peep at the Times.*

(18.7, HAY.) THE VILLAGE; *or, The World's Epitome.*
(Withdrawn from the stage at the second performance.
Figures in the Larpent manuscripts collection.)

1806. (7.2, D.L.) THALIA'S TEARS.
(Figures in the Larpent manuscripts collection.)

1807. (9.4, D.L.) A DAY IN LONDON.
(Larpent manuscripts.)

1813. (14.6, SUR.) LLEWELLYN, *Prince of Wales; or, Gellert the
Faithful Dog.*
(A play begun by Cherry and completed by Dibdin.)

1814. (10.3, D.L.) TWO STRINGS TO YOUR BOW.

CLARKE (John Bertridge – 1780(?)—1824)

BIOGRAPHY

Born in Roscommon. Studied at Trinity College (B.A.: 1805).
Contributed to various newspapers and periodicals (*Dublin
Magazine*, 1820, *The Drama*, etc.), was also an actor and play-
wright. Died in destitution in 1824.

BIBLIOGRAPHY

(a) Poetry:

1816. [NAPOLEON AT WATERLOO, a poem in 4 cantos, with
other juvenile poems.]

1817. THE TEARS AND SMILES OF IRELAND, a poem on the death of J. P. Curran, Dublin: R. Milliken, 1817, 46 p.

1818. THE LAMENTATIONS OF THE EMPIRE, a poem on the death of H.R.H. the Princess Charlotte.
Dublin: Hodges & M'Arthur, 1821, 44 p.

(Also, according to O'Donoghue, an unpublished manuscript: *The Moorish Maid*, a metrical tale, 1820.)

(b) Dramatic works:

1822. (C.S.) RAMIRO.

1824. (3.12, C.G.) RAVENNA; *or, Italian Love.*
London: Whittaker, 1824, 80 p.
(adapted from *Kabale und Liebe* by Schiller.)

CLARKE (Lady Olivia, née Owenson – 1785(?)–1845)

Daughter of the comedian Robert Owenson, and sister of Lady Morgan, she married Sir Arthur Clarke, a Dublin doctor, in 1808, and wrote a few poems for various periodicals (*Metropolitan Magazine*, 1831–4; *Comic Offering*, 1832; *Athenaeum*, 1835) as well as a curious work: *Parodies on Popular Songs*, with a paradoxical preface dedicated to the Countess of Charleville, London and Dublin, 1836. Sir J. A. Stevenson helped with the musical parts of the book.

Before this date, she had the honour of having one of her particularly bad plays performed at the Theatre Royal, Dublin:

The Irishwoman, a comedy in 5 acts.
London: H. Colburn, 1819, 80 p.

CODE (Henry Brereton – ?–1830(?))

BIOGRAPHY

Author of poems, essays, plays; editor of the Dublin Tory newspaper, *The Warder*; particularly famous for his songs (cf. 'The Sprig of Shillelagh':

'O Love is the soul of a neat Irishman'),

so much so that some were attributed to him which he never wrote (cf. 'Donnybrook Fair'); was a widely detested character, a spy and informer in the pay of the English government, whom Th. Furlong includes in his poem: *The Plagues of Ireland.*

BIBLIOGRAPHY

1803. THE INSURRECTION OF THE 23RD JULY 1803.
Dublin: printed by Graisberry & Campbell, 1803, XIV + 110 p.

1810(?) (Peter Street, Dublin) THE PATRIOT; *or, The Hermit of Saxellen,*
a musical drama, in 3 acts.
Dublin: printed for the author, 2nd edition, 1811, XVI + 70 p.
(The action takes place in Switzerland.)

1812. (22.9, LYC.) SPANISH PATRIOTS A THOUSAND YEARS AGO,
an historical drama, in 3 acts.
London: Walker, 1812, VIII + 67 p.

1813. (C.S.) THE RUSSIAN SACRIFICE; *or, Burning of Moscow,*
an historical and musical drama.
Dublin: printed for the author, 1813, IX + 79 p.

1821. [AN ODE, to be performed at the Castle of Dublin on Monday 23rd of April, 1821 ... the birthday of ... George IV.
Dublin: 1821, in-4°. Music by Sir J. A. Stevenson.]

1824. [THE ANGLING EXCURSIONS OF GREGORY GREENDRAKE AND GEOFFREY GREYDRAKE IN THE COUNTIES OF WICKLOW, etc ... Dublin, 1824. In collaboration with Th. Ettingsall.]

COLLIER (William)

Apart from a few poems (*Bentley's Miscellany*, Sheridan's *Comic Offering*, Vol. II, 1832), the work of William Collier – whose dates are unknown – consists of plays.

1834. (23.1, R.V.) THE BLACKSMITH; *or, A Day at Gretna Green,*
a musical farce, in one act.
London: Duncombe (n.d.), 20p. (XIV).

1835. (6.4, QU.) THE QUEEN'S JEWEL; *or, The Interrupted Ball,*
a petite comedy, in one act.
London: Duncombe (n.d.), 30 p. (XXI).

(6.12, QU.) IS SHE A WOMAN? A comedy, in one act.
London: Duncombe (n.d.), 30 p. (XXI).

1836. (3.10, QU.) KATE KEARNEY; *or, The Lakes of Killarney,*
a petite opera, in two acts.
London: Duncombe (n.d.), 30 p. (XXIII).

1847. (5.4, S.W.) THE RIVAL SERGEANTS; *or, Love and Lottery,*
a musical burletta, in one act.
London: Duncombe (n.d.), 21 p. (LIX).

CONNELLAN (Owen – 1800–1869)

A linguist and historian born in Sligo. Translated the Gospel according to St John into Gaelic. Also the author of the following works:

1834. A DISSERTATION ON IRISH GRAMMAR ...
Dublin: R. Milliken & Son, 1834, 62 p.

1846. (Michael O'Clery's) THE ANNALS OF IRELAND,
translated from the original Irish of THE FOUR MASTERS ... with annotations by P. Mac Dermott, and the translator.
Dublin: B. Geraghty, 1846, 736 p., in-4°.

as well as several translations posterior to 1850.

CONYNGHAM (Mrs George Lenox – née Elizabeth Emmet Holmes – 1800–?)

BIOGRAPHY

Her father belonged to the Irish Bar (cf. 'Anthony Poplar's note book' in *Dublin University Magazine*, IV, 19, July 1834, p. 116 seq.), her mother was Robert Emmet's sister, and she seems to have known Southey well. Her poems are not without merit, she has an ear for music and refrain and delicately treats the theme of melancholy.

BIBLIOGRAPHY

1833. THE DREAM *and Other Poems.*
London: Edward Moxon, Dover Street, 1833, 166 p. (Comprises original poems (20); poems by her mother, arranged (4); Italian sonnets (5), 2 of which are translated; poems (5), translated from the German, by F. Von Matthison ('The Death Bed', 'A Summer Evening', 'To Love', 'The Tombstone', 'Faith').)

1836. HELLA *and Other Poems.*
London: Edward Churton, 1836, 241 p. (Original poems, with two exceptions: a translation from *The Trojan Women* by Euripides and *Ajax* by Sophocles.)

1859. [HORAE POETICAE, *Lyrical and Other Poems.*
London, 1859.]

1863. [EILER AND HELVIG, a Danish Legend.
London, 1863.]

COX (Walter – 1770(?)–1837)

BIOGRAPHY

Born in 1760 according to O'Donoghue and 1770 according to Brian Cleeve. He was the son of a Meath blacksmith. Joined the Society of United Irishmen for whom, in 1797, he launched *The Union Star*, the first of a fairly long series of newspapers that he was to publish and that would include *The Irish Magazine* (q.v. 1807). A book on this subject is *Watty Cox and his Publications* by Seamus O'Casaide, Dublin: Three Candles, 1935, 38 p., ill. (The Bibliographical Society of Ireland, Vol. V, n° 2.) His other works comprise some poems and pamphlets and two plays. His political position, fairly clear at first sight judging by his loyalties and the tone of a publication such as *The Irish Magazine*, has nevertheless engendered divergent interpretations and he was accused of being an agent of the government: it is true that his pen, dipped in vitriol, could only make him enemies. He died in Dublin on January 17, 1837. Had spent some time in the U.S.A. where he was chief editor of *The Exile*.

BIBLIOGRAPHY

(a) Published **some poems** in *The Irish Magazine* of which he was editor, and may have been the 'Publicola' who issued *The Tears of Erin* in 1810.

(b) Among his **prose works** are the following:

1802. ADVICE TO EMIGRANTS. Dublin: printed for the author, 1802, 33 p.

1804. REMARKS BY ONE OF THE PEOPLE. Dublin: printed by J. Shea, 1804, 36 p.

1819. A SHORT SKETCH OF THE PRESENT STATE OF THE CATHOLIC CHURCH IN THE CITY OF NEW YORK. N.Y.: 61 William St., 1819, 23 p.

1820. THE SNUFF-BOX, ibid., 16 p.
A HUMOROUS, THEOLOGICAL AND CLASSICAL REVIEW *of the Rapparee Expedients Made Use of by Certain Irish Nobility to Persecute their Bishop* ... ibid., 1820, 23 p.

1823(?) BELLA, HORRIDA BELLA. Dublin, 32 p., n.d.

1833. THE CUCKOO CALENDAR, *Anecdotes of the Liberator*, Containing some Humorous Sketches of the Religious and Political Cleverness of the Great Mendicant. Dublin: printed by J. Bryan, 1833, (2) + 46 p.

(c) Cox's dramatic works consist of:

1822. THE WIDOW DEMPSEY'S FUNERAL,
a dramatic performance in 3 acts. Dublin: printed for the author, 1822, 46 p.

(?) [THE COMING OF AIDEEN.
(a title mentioned by Kavanagh).]

COYNE (Joseph Stirling – 1803–1868)

BIOGRAPHY

A journalist and playwright born in Birr in 1803. Studied in Dungannon and Dublin. Was intended for the Bar, but preferred literature. Was active in this field primarily in London where he went in 1837 with a letter of introduction from W. Carleton. Wrote for *Bentley's Miscellany* and *Punch* and was the author of more than 50 plays. Became secretary of the Society of Dramatic Authors in 1856. Died, paralytic, in London, on July 18, 1868.

BIBLIOGRAPHY (works prior to 1850)

(a) Dramatic works:

1835. (3.6, C.S.) THE PHRENOLOGIST (farce).

1836. (7.4, ibid.) THE HONEST CHEATS (id.).

(14.4, ibid.) THE FOUR LOVERS (id.).

(28.11, ADEL.) THE QUEER SUBJECT, a farce, in 1 act.
London: Dicks (782), n.d., 9 p.

1837. (30.10, ADEL.) VALSHA; *or, The Slave Queen*, a drama in 3 acts.
London: Chapman & Hall (Acting National Drama II), n.d., 36 p. (Adapted from the French play: *La Guerre des Servantes*).

1838. (1.1, ADEL.) ALL FOR LOVE; *or, The Lost Pleiad,* a romantic drama, in 3 acts.
ibid., n.d., 76 p. (Adapted from: *Une Fille de l'Air.)*

(22.10, ADEL.) ARAJOON; *or, The Conquest of Mysore,* a grand oriental drama, in 3 acts.
London: Dicks (700), n.d., 16 p.

1840. (9.6, E.O.H.) HELEN OAKLEIGH; *or, The Wife's Stratagem,* an historical drama, in 3 acts.
London: Duncombe (XLIII), n.d., 32 p.

1841. (11.2, ADEL.) SATANAS AND THE SPIRIT OF BEAUTY, a romantic legendary spectacle, in 2 acts.
London: Lacy (XXXIX), n.d., 46 p.
(Adapted from *Le Diable Amoureux* by J. H. Vernoy de St-Georges.)

(20.7, HAY.) MY FRIEND THE CAPTAIN, *a farce* ...
London: Dicks (740), n.d.

1842. (7.6, E.O.H.) THE WATER WITCHES, an original farce, in one act.
London: Lacy (XLI), n.d., 23 p.

(13.10, ADEL.) DOBSON AND COMPANY; *or, My Turn Next*, a farce ...
London: Dicks (624), n.d.

(12.12, ADEL.) THE MERCHANT AND HIS CLERKS, a drama ...
London: Dicks (642), n.d.

1843. (13.2, ADEL.) BINKS THE BAGMAN,
a farce, in one act.
London: Lacy (VII), n.d., 19 p.

(7.12, HAY.) THE TRUMPETER'S DAUGHTER.
(farce)

1844. (8.2, ADEL.) RICHARD III.
(burlesque)
(According to Nicoll, published that same year in London.)

(8.4, OLYM.) THE SIGNAL, a drama, in 3 acts.
London: Duncombe (XLIX), n.d., 40 p.

1846. (16.3, ADEL.) DID YOU EVER SEND YOUR WIFE TO CUMBERWELL?
An original farce, in one act.
London: Acting National Drama (XII), 16 p.

(8.6, ADEL) THE QUEEN OF THE ABRUZZI, a drama, in one act.
London: Duncombe (LVIII), n.d., 30 p.

1847. (26.7, ADEL.) HOW TO SETTLE ACCOUNTS WITH YOUR LAUNDRESS,
an original farce, in one act.
London: A.N.D. (XIV), n.d., 19 p.

(9.9, ADEL.) THIS HOUSE TO BE SOLD; (THE PROPERTY OF THE LATE W. SHAKESPEARE.) INQUIRE WITHIN. A musical extravaganza in one act.
ibid., n.d., 16 p. (music by A. Mackenzie).

(6.12, ADEL.) THE TIPPERARY LEGACY, a farce, in one act.
ibid., n.d., 20 p.

1848. (27.1, ADEL.) OUR NATIONAL DEFENCES; *or, The Cock-shott Yeomanry,*
a farce, in one act.
Acting National Drama, n.d., 23 p.

(24.4, ADEL.) THE FOUNTAIN OF ZEA; *or, The Child of Air*
(an entertainment)

(26.4, HAY.) LOLA MONTES; *or, A Countess for an Hour.*
(*Pas de Fascination; or, Catching a Governor,* a farce, in one act. ibid., n.d., 20 p., is the title given to *Lola Montes* on its revival on 22.5 and in print.)

1849. (26.2, ADEL.) COCKNIES IN CALIFORNIA, a new and original 'Piece of Golden Opportunity', in one act.
ibid., n.d., 20 p.

(12.3, HAY.) SEPARATE MAINTENANCE, a farce, in one act.
London: Duncombe (LXIV), n.d., 23 p.

(15.10, ADEL.) MRS BUNBURY'S SPOONS, a slippery, tippery sketch, in one act.
London: A.N.D., n.d., 20 p.

1850. (4.2, STR.) A SCENE IN THE LIFE OF AN UNPROTECTED FEMALE,
a farce, in one act.
London: Duncombe (LXIV), n.d., 36 p.

(11.4, HAY.) THE VICAR OF WAKEFIELD; *or, The Pastor's Fireside,*
a drama in 2 acts.
London: A.N.D. (XVI), n.d., 36 p.

(14.10, OLYM.) MY WIFE'S DAUGHTER, a comedy, in 2 acts.
London: Lacy (II), n.d., 34 p.

Among the later plays, there is none of Irish interest and thus deserving of mention after this list of mediocrities unless one wishes to mention the 'stage Irishman' (Major O'Reilly) of *The Hope of the Family,* a 3-act comedy (1853).

(b) Miscellanea (Prose) prior to 1850:

1846. THE SCENERY AND ANTIQUITIES OF IRELAND,

illustrated from drawings by W. H. Bartlett, the literary portion of the work by N. P. Willis & J. S. Coyne.
London: G. Virtue, n.d., 2 v., I: 170 p. II: 186 p.

1849.   In: GAVARNI IN LONDON, Sketches of Life and Character, with illustrative essays by popular writers, edited by Albert R. Smith.
London: D. Bogue, 1849, 115 p.
(by Coyne: 'The Barmaid' (87–90) a delicious mock-heroic piece extolling the charms of the priestess of Bacchus; 'The Potato Can' (101–6), an interesting observation of the customers of an Irish potato seller in the Strand.)

CROKER (John Wilson – 1780–1857)

BIOGRAPHY

The *D.N.B.* gives him eighteen columns and he figures in the *Encyclopaedia Britannica*, etc. A monograph has ben devoted to him (Brightfield, see below). Here it will be enough to mention the main events of his life.

Born in Galway on December 20, 1780. His father was 'Surveyor General of Customs and Excise for the port of Dublin'. Studied at Trinity College and Lincoln's Inn. A member of the Irish Bar.

1807: member for Downpatrick, took up the fight, with some reservations, for Catholic Emancipation.

1809: one of the founders of the *Quarterly Review* in which his first article was a review of *Tales of Fashionable Life* by Maria Edgeworth. Between this date and 1854, was to write some 270 articles on all manner of subjects, but particularly on history (he was an expert on the French Revolution) and politics (he was an ardent Tory). His less frequent literary reports have sometimes become regretfully famous, like his critique of Keats's *Endymion* (Sept. 1818).

Became 'Secretary of the Admiralty', a post in which he showed himself to be upright and remarkable as an organiser. Had some great friends (cf. the Duke of Wellington, Cunning, etc.), rendered great services to those whom he protected (cf. Moore) but also had some bitter enemies whom – in return – he could cut to pieces. Lady Morgan was one of them as well as Macaulay and Disraeli. He died at Hampton, Middlesex, on April 10, 1857.

BIBLIOGRAPHY

A complete bibliography of Croker is to be found on pp. 451–9 of Myron F. Brightfield's *John Wilson Croker*, Berkeley: University of California Press, 1940, XIII + 464 p., portrait. The reader is referred to this monograph for a listing of the articles, the purely political works, etc., while the few separately published works having literary or Irish interest are listed below.

(a) Poetry:

1804. FAMILIAR EPISTLES TO FREDERICK J. — S, ESQ. ON THE PRESENT STATE OF THE IRISH STAGE.
Dublin: John Barlow, 1804, XIX + 78 p. (author's name not indicated.)
(The British Museum houses 5 successive editions of this personal, dramatic and acrid critique that is full of interest for the historian of Irish literature. Note the 2nd edition, of the same year, (enlarged), and the 5th, Dublin: Graisberry & Campbell, 1806, XXII + 110 p., with the title giving the name of Frederick E. Jones in full.
The first edition in the British Museum includes in a single volume:
Theatrical Tears, a poem occasioned by Familiar Epistles, Dublin: J. Parry, 1804, 47 p.
A Few Reflections occasioned by the perusal of a work, entitled Familiar Epistles, etc., Dublin: J. Parry, 1804, 77 p.
and other satires more or less connected with this work.)

1806. THE AMAZONIAD; *or, Figure and Fashion*, a scuffle in high life with notes critical and historical interspersed with choice anecdotes of bon ton ...
Dublin: John King, 1806.
(2nd edition only at the British Museum. Contains: 5 cantos in 2 v., I: cantos 1 to 3, 73 p. II: cantos 4 and 5, 72 p. It is uncertain whether this 2nd part belongs to the same edition. No indication and title page quite different. It is curious that this work does not figure in Brightfield's list.)

1809. THE BATTLE OF TALAVERA, Dublin: Mahon, 1809.
(The British Museum possesses *The 'Battle' of Talavera*, 10th edition, London: Murray, 1816, 114 p. including notes (without author's name).

The collection includes: 'Battle' (pp. 1–55), (25 stanzas of 23 verses each) and other more or less warlike poems: 'War Song', 'Songs of Trafalgar').

(b) Prose:

1803. [THE OPINION OF AN IMPARTIAL OBSERVER CONCERNING THE LATE TRANSACTIONS IN IRELAND.
Dublin: J. Parry, 1803.]

1804. AN INTERCEPTED LETTER, from J—T—, ESQ., WRITER AT CANTON, TO HIS FRIEND IN DUBLIN, IRELAND.
Dublin: M. N. Mahon, 1804, 42 p.
(Satire in prose in the tradition of *Lettres Persanes*. It contains discussions on public affairs, on the theatre, etc., in Ireland.)

1808. A SKETCH OF THE STATE OF IRELAND PAST AND PRESENT.
Dublin: M. N. Mahon, 1808, 63 p.
(A very clear insight into the history of Ireland and an examination, sometimes partisan but always lucid, of present evils.)

1854. CORRESPONDENCE *between the Right Honourable J. W. Croker and the Right Hon. Lord J. Russell on Some Passages of 'Moore's Diary' with a postscript by Mr Croker explanatory of Mr Moore's acquaintance and correspondence with him.*
London: Murray, 1854, 35 p.

1884. THE CROKER PAPERS.
The correspondence and diaries of the late R.H., J. W. Croker, LL.D., F.R.S., Secretary to the Admiralty from 1809 to 1850, edited by Louis J. Jennings, in 3 v.
London: Murray, 1884.
I: with portrait, XII + 434 p. II: VII + 423 p.
III: VII + 397 p. (With an index.)

1967. THE CROKER PAPERS 1808–1857.
Edited by Bernard Pool.
London: Batsford, 1967, 277 p.

(c) See:

RILEY, Paul, E.: 'John Wilson Croker as a Literary Critic'.
Dissertation Abstracts, 27, 1966, 1345 A.

CROKER (Thomas Crofton – 1798–1854)

BIOGRAPHY

Born in Cork on January 15, 1798. Was set to work as
apprentice accountant, at age 15, in a business house. Henceforth
devoted his spare time to visiting the countryside in search of
folklore etc., and corresponded with Thomas Moore.

In 1818 he settled in London where, thanks to his namesake J.
W. Croker, he obtained a post at the Admiralty, contributed to
various magazines and prepared his first novel. In 1825: another
journey to Ireland. Met W. Scott and, from 1827, received a whole
series of distinctions (Fellow of the Society of Antiquaries of
London, Member of the Royal Irish Society, Camden Society,
Percy Society, British Archaeological Association ...).

In 1830 married Marianne Nicholson, daughter of the water-
colour artist Francis Nicholson, and herself an artist and writer.
Died in Brompton on August 8, 1854.

Maginn devoted an article to him (pp. 29–30) and Maclise
sketched him in *A Gallery of Illustrious Characters* (1875): Croker
had, in fact, been one of the contributors to *Fraser's*.

BIBLIOGRAPHY

Croker wrote in numerous PERIODICALS: *Amulet, Christmas Box*
(1827), *Keepsake* (1828), *Gentleman's Magazine, Fraser's* (cf. in
the latter: 'Specimens of Irish Minstrelsy' I, 191, 314, 580, II: 41,
VIII: 127. 'The Nameless Fountain' (verse) II: 221. 'Ensign
O'Donoghue's Stories and Letters' IV: 79, VI: 341, VIII: 156 IX:
32, 147, 575, 711, X: 409, XI: 137, 630, XIII: 645, 657, XIV: 168,
474, XV: 339, 662, 663, XVII: 432, XVIII: 86, 140.)

The WORKS PUBLISHED IN BOOK FORM are the following:

1824.   RESEARCHES IN THE SOUTH OF IRELAND *illustrative of
the scenery, architectural remains, and the manners and*

superstitions of the peasantry. With an appendix, containing a private narrative of the rebellion of 1798.
London: J. Murray, 1824, 393 p., in-4°, ill.
(re-printed: Dublin: Irish University Press, 1968, facsimile of the 1824 edition with a critical introduction by Kevin Danaher.)

1825–8. FAIRY LEGENDS AND TRADITIONS OF THE SOUTH OF IRELAND.
London: J. Murray, Part I: 1825, VI + 363 p., Part II: 1828, XII + 326 p., Part III: 1828, XXXII + 300 p.
(This last part has no bearing on Ireland but comprises a translation of the brothers Grimm and then concerns itself with Wales.)

1826. (Christmas, ADEL.) DANIEL O'ROURKE; *or, Rhymes of a Pantomime,* founded on that story by T. C. Croker, Esq.
London: Ainsworth, 1828, 30 p. (verse).

1829. LEGENDS OF THE LAKES; *or, Sayings and Doings at Killarney* collected chiefly from the manuscripts of R. Adolphus Lynch, Esq.
London: J. Ebers, 1829, 2 v., I: VIII + 245 p. II: VI + 247 p.
(Comprises a topographical index, and pictorial and musical illustrations.)

1835. LANDSCAPE ILLUSTRATIONS OF MOORE'S 'IRISH MELODIES' with comments for the curious. Part I.
London: J. Power, 1835, ill.
(Only the 1st part seems to have been published.)

1837. THE TOUR OF THE FRENCH TRAVELLER M. DE LA BOULLAYE LE GOUZ IN IRELAND. A.D. 1644, edited by T. C. Croker with notes and illustrative extracts contributed by James Roche, the Rev. F. Mahony, Th. Wright, and the editor.
London: T. & W. Boone, 1837, VIII + 139 p.

1838. MEMOIRS OF JOSEPH HOLT, *General of the Irish Rebels, in 1798,* edited from his original manuscript in the possession of Sir William Betham ...
London: H. Colburn, 1838, 2 v.
I: LIV + 360 p. II: XII + 432 p.

1839. THE POPULAR SONGS OF IRELAND collected and edited with introductions and notes ...
London: H. Colburn, 1839, XIX + 340 p.

1841. THE HISTORICAL SONGS OF IRELAND: *illustrative of the Revolutionary Struggle between James II and William III,* edited with introductions and notes ...
London: printed for the Percy Society by C. Richards, 1841, VIII + 139 p. (Percy Society ... Vol. I).

NARRATIVES ILLUSTRATIVE OF THE CONTESTS IN IRELAND IN 1641 AND 1690 ...
London: printed for the Camden Society by J. Bowyer Nichols & Sons, 1841, 149 p.

1842–3. A DESCRIPTION OF ROSAMOND'S BOWER, FULHAM, *distant three miles from Hyde Park Corner, the Residence of T. Crofton Croker, Esq.* With an inventory of the pictures, furniture, curiosities, etc.
London: for private circulation only.
Part I: Dec. 1842, 10 p. Part II: Jan. 1843, 8 p.
Part III: Mar. 1843, pp. 9–32. (Fifteen copies.)

1843. A KERRY PASTORAL *in imitation of The First Eclogue of Virgil* ...
London: reprinted for the Percy Society by T. Richards, 1843, XV + 38 p.
(Presentation and annotated edition of a poem by Murroghoh O'Connor of Aughanagraun published in Dublin in 1719. Vol. VII in 'The Percy Society of Early English Poetry', etc.)

1844. THE KEEN OF THE SOUTH OF IRELAND *as illustrative of Irish political and domestic history, manners, music and superstitions,* collected, edited and chiefly translated by T. Crofton Croker.
London: printed for the Percy Society by T. Richards, 1844, LIX + 108 p.
('Percy Society', Vol. XIII, n° XLVI.)

1845–7. POPULAR SONGS, ILLUSTRATIVE OF THE FRENCH INVASIONS OF IRELAND ...
London: reprinted for the Percy Society by T. Richards.
(Part I: ('Memoirs of Cpt. Thurot') VIII + 44 p. Feb. 1845.
Part II: (Id., continued + songs) XXXII + 27 p. Nov. 1846.
Part III: ('The Bantry Bay and Killala Invasion') IV + 118 p. May 1847.
Percy Society, Vol. XXL, n°s LIV, LXVII, LXX.)

1850.   (24.12, GRIM) RECOLLECTIONS OF OLD CHRISTMAS,
a masque ...
(publisher unknown: 22 + X p.)

1860.   A WALK FROM LONDON TO FULHAM by the late Th. C.
Croker ... revised and edited by his son T. F. Dillon
Croker ... with additional illustrations by F. W. Fairholt.
London: W. Tegg, 1860, XX ('memoir' on the author) +
256 p.

Concerning the 'Memoir', note also the one in *The Gentleman's
Magazine* (Oct. 1854) reprinted in the form of a pamphlet (VIII p.)
with a portrait by Maclise. These 8 pages in the British Museum
(011904 a 15 (1)) have been bound with: 'Catalogue of the Greater
Part of the Library of the Late Thomas Crofton Croker ... which
will be sold by auction by Messrs Puttick and Simpson ... on
Monday, Dec 8th, 1854', (38 p.). The collection was extremely rich.

CROKER (Mrs T. C. —, née Marianne Nicholson – ?–1854)

Wife of the former. Author of two works, the first of which was
published under her husband's name:

1832.   THE ADVENTURES OF BARNEY MAHONEY ...
London: H. Fisher, n.d. (1832), 299 p.

1833.   MY VILLAGE, VERSUS 'OUR VILLAGE' by the author of
'Barney Mahoney'.
London: H. Fisher ..., 1833, 345 p.
(The first of these books presents the stage-Irishman in the
manner of S. Lover, and the second is a satirical description of Brompton. Note these two lines in the prologue,
repeated as an epigraph.

For village life is not at all à la Mitford
Or else, 'tis very plain that I'm unfit for't.)

CROLY (Rev. George – 1780–1860)

BIOGRAPHY

He whom Byron (*Don Juan*, XI, 57) would irreverently call the Reverend 'Rowley Powley' was born in Dublin in 1780. Studied at Trinity College. In 1810 moved to London. In 1835 received charge of the parish of St Stephen's, Walbrook, in the capital. Died on November 24, 1860.

BIBLIOGRAPHY

Besides a considerable number of articles in *Blackwood's Magazine*, note:

(a) Poetry:

1817– PARIS IN 1815, a poem.
  21. (*1st part:* London: Murray, 1817, XIII + 75 p.
       2nd part ... With Other Poems: London: J. Warren, 1821, XII + 110 p.
       In the preface to this second part, the author denies having plagiarised *Childe Harold*, as certain pages of his work antedate the publication of Byron's poem.)

1820. THE ANGEL OF THE WORLD; An Arabian Tale – *Sebastian*; A Spanish Tale: *With Other Poems.* London: J. Warren, 1820, 182 p.

1822. GEMS PRINCIPALLY FROM THE ANTIQUE drawn and etched by Richard Dagley with illustrations in verse by the Rev. George Croly, A.M.
       London: Hurst, Robinson & Co, 1822, VIII + 52 p.

1822– CATLINE: a tragedy in 5 acts, *With Other Poems.*
  27. London: Hurst, Robinson & Co., 1822, 232 p.
       (The play was performed at the Royal Coburg Theatre on June 4, 1827, and published the same year (London: J. Lowndes, VI + 50 p.) in an adaptation by H. M. Milner ('with alterations and additions from Ben Jonson, Voltaire and Franklin' (!)) under the title: *Lucius Catiline, The Roman Traitor*, a drama in 3 acts.)

1827. MAY FAIR, in four cantos.
London: W. H. Ainsworth, 1827, 194 p.
(satire in verse – doubtful authorship, Luttrell?)

1830. THE POETICAL WORKS of the Rev. G. Croly.
London: H. Colburn & R. Bentley, 1830, 2 v.
I: XVI + 352 p., II: XVI + 341 p.

1846. THE MODERN ORLANDO.
London: H. Colburn, 1846, 212 p.
(A pale imitation of *Don Juan.*)

1851. [SCENES FROM SCRIPTURE, *with Other Poems*, London.]

1854. [PSALMS AND HYMNS FOR PUBLIC WORSHIP.]

1863. [THE BOOK OF JOB. With a Memoir by F. W. Croly.]

(b) Prose fiction:

1828. [TALES OF THE GREAT ST BERNARD, 3 v.]

**1828–
29.** SALATHIEL. A Story of the Past, the Present and the
Future.
London: H. Colburn, 1829, new edition, 3 v.
I: VII + 316 p. II: 300 p. III: 306 p.
(A variation on the theme of the Wandering Jew.)

1846. MARSTON; *or, The Soldier and Statesman* ...
London: H. Colburn, 1846, 3 v.
I: VII + 339 p. II: 308 p. III: 296 p.
(Had originally appeared in *Blackwood's.*)

(c) Essays and sermons:

1842. HISTORICAL SKETCHES, SPEECHES AND CHARACTERS.
London: Seely & Burnside, 1842, XIII + 356 p.
(One of the rare works by Croly touching on Ireland. Cf.
Ch. VI (89–107): 'The Church of Ireland', Ch. X(204–24):
'Character of Curran and the Eloquence of Ireland.')

1848. POPERY THE ANTECHRIST.
London: J. Kendrick, 1848, 24 p.
(a sermon).

1849. THE YEAR OF REVOLUTIONS. A Sermon preached on the
last day of the year 1848, in the Church of St Stephen,
Walbrook.
London: J. Kendrick, 1849, 24 p.

(d) See:

KERRING (R.): *A Few Personal Recollections of the Late Rev. G. Croly* with extracts from his speeches and writings.
London: Longman, etc., 1861, VI + 216 p.

CROWE (Eyre Evans – 1799–1868)

BIOGRAPHY

An historian, novelist and journalist, born near Southampton of Irish parents. Studied at Trinity College, Dublin, but immediately returned to London. His first writings had appeared in *The London Examiner* and *The Dublin Magazine*. In 1823, he sent some letters from Italy to *Blackwood's* and continued to contribute to this periodical until 1834. From 1830 onwards he was the Paris correspondent for *The Morning Chronicle* and, from 1849 to 1851, editor of *The Daily News*. Died in London on February 25, 1868.

BIBLIOGRAPHY

1819. THE PLEASURES OF MELANCHOLY; *and A Saxon Tale.*
London: printed by W. Clowes, 1819, IV + 75 p. (verse).

1825. TODAY IN IRELAND.*
London: C. Knight, 1825, 3 v.
(I: pp. 1–291: 'The Carders'. II: pp. 1–158: (contin.), pp. 161–319: 'Connemara'. III: pp. 1–258: 'Old and New Light', 261–305: 'The O'Toole's Warning' (stories).)

  „   [THE ENGLISH IN ITALY.]

1828. [THE ENGLISH IN FRANCE.]
(both volumes: stories also, according to the *D.N.B.*)

1829. YESTERDAY IN IRELAND.*
London: H. Colburn, 1829, 3 v.
(I: 1–313: 'Corramahon'. II: 1–287: (contin.), 291–327: 'The Northerns of '98'. III: 1–332:(contin.).)
(two stories).

1830. [THE ENGLISH AT HOME]
(stories, according to the *D.N.B.*)

1831– THE HISTORY OF FRANCE.
58.   London: Longman, 1831–6, 3 v. in-16°.
     ibid., 1858, 5 v. in-8°.

1833–8. (contribution to:)
    LIVES OF THE MOST EMINENT FOREIGN STATESMEN.
    (by E. E. C. and G. P. R. James).
    London: Longman, 1833–8, 5 v.

1853.   CHARLES DELMER, a Story of the Day.
    London: R. Bentley, 1853, 2 v.
    I: 328 p. II: 343 p.
    (a story).

   „   [THE GREEK AND TURK.]
    (a study).

1854.   HISTORY OF THE REIGNS OF LOUIS XVIII AND
    CHARLES X.
    (a study).
    London: R. Bentley, 1854, 2 v. I: VII + 503 p.
    II: V + 474 p.

CRUMPE (Miss)

An historical novelist, daughter of a Limerick surgeon. Author
of:

GERALDINE OF DESMOND; or, Ireland in the Reign of Elisabeth,
    an historical romance.
    London: H. Colburn, 1829, 3 v., I: 13 + 352 p., II: 323 p. III:
    287 p. (anonymous)

Brown also attributes to her:

THE DEATH FLAG; or The Irish Buccaneers, for which he cites the
    1852 edition (London: W. Shoberl) which is doubtless not the
    first.

CUNNINGHAM (William – 1781–1804)

Born in Magherabeg, near Dromore, one of the members of the poetical school of Percy, author of:

POEMS, Dromore: printed by James Parks, 1803, 53 p.

CURRAN (Henry Grattan – 1800–1876)

Natural son of John Philpot Curran, lawyer then magistrate, was one of the contributors to Hardiman's *Irish Minstrelsy* and to various other anthologies. Also wrote a few original poems and some novels, of which one (the information is taken from Cleeve) is *Confessions of a Whitefoot*, 1844.

CURRAN (John Philpot – 1750–1817)

BIOGRAPHY

Born on July 24 in Newmarket, County Cork. Studied at Trinity College, Dublin, then at the Middle-Temple. A member of the Irish Parliament from 1783 to 1797, he was a liberal in the tradition of Grattan. No doubt the most famous Irish orator of his time, and an eminent figure, a patriot of integrity, a man of intellect and a friend of Byron, Mme de Staël and Moore. Died in London, Brompton, on October 14, 1817.

BIBLIOGRAPHY

None of his literary works have been published in book form.

1808.   SPEECHES.
Published for the first time in Dublin (J. Stockdale), 1808, XII + 475 p.; reprinted in this form until 1817.

Speeches, etc ... with a memoir of his life, a new edition with additions, London: Longman, 1817, XII + 486 p.

Then: *A New and Enlarged Collection of Speeches*, etc., containing several of importance in no former collection; with memoir ... London: W. Hone, 1819, XXIV + 344 p.

Finally: *The Speeches of the R.H. John Philpot Curran.*
Complete and correct edition, edited with memoir and
historical notices by Th. Davis ..., Dublin: J. Duffy, 1845,
XLIV + 603 p.

1819.   LETTERS OF CURRAN TO THE REV. H. WESTON, written
in the Years 1773 and 1774.
London: T. Hookham, 1819, IV + 45p.

But the text of his poems, sometimes first published in magazines
(cf. 'The Plate Warmer' in *Carrick's Morning Post*, Dublin, August
13th, 1816), may be found in certain STUDIES, ETC., mentioned
below:

O'REGAN (W.): *Memoirs of the Legal, Literary and Political Life
of the Late R.H. John Philpot Curran*, once master of the
Rolls in Ireland: comprising copious anecdotes of his wit and
humour; and a selection of his poetry ... by William O'Regan,
Esq., Barrister.
London: J. Harper; Dublin: R. Milliken, 1817, XVI + 315 p.
(Contains among other poems: 'The Plate Warmer':
pp. 137–150; 'To Sleep': p. 151; 'The Green Spot That Blooms
in the Desert of Life': pp. 151–52; 'The Deserter's Meditation'
is not included.)

STEPHENS (A.): *A Memoir of the Life of the R. H. John Philpot
Curran.*
London: Longman, 1817, 31 p.
(without the author's name, but with a signed dedication.)

PHILLIPS (Ch.): *Recollections of Curran and Some his Contemporaries* (sic), by Charles Phillips, Esq.
London: T. Hookham, 1818, portraits, XIII + 407 p.
(Note: 'The Deserter's Lamentations', pp. 23–4, presented in 4
stanzas, thus:

> 'If sadly thinking,
> And spirits sinking.'

The British Museum possesses the re-issues of 1850, 1851,
1857.)

CURRAN (W.H.): *The Life of the R. H. John Philpot Curran* ... by
his son, William, Henry Curran, barrister at law, in 2 v.
London: Longman; Edinburgh: Constable, 1819,
I: VIII + 448 p., II: VIII + 532 p.
(A later edition exists: 'with additions and notes by R. Shelton
Mackenzie', New York: Redfield, 1855, 1 v., 525 p. + index.)

DAVIS (Th.): *The Life of the R.H. John Philpot Curran ...* by Thomas Davis, M.R.I.A., Dublin: J. Duffy; London: Simpkin, 1846, 78 p.
(Complete title: ... and a Memoir of the Life of ... Grattan, by D. O. Madden (pp. 79 to 232).

TIMBS (J.): *Anecdote Lives of the Later Wits and Humourists* (then follows the list in which figure Maginn, Father Prout, Curran, etc.), by John Timbs, F.S.A.
London: R. Bentley, 1874, 2 v.
I: X + 340 p. (Curran, pp. 127–45). II: IV + 329 p.

W. (R. W.): *John Philpot Curran, 1750–1817*, by R.W.W. Dublin: Sealy, etc., 1907, ill., 62 p.

HALL (L.): *John Philpot Curran (1750–1817), His Life and Times.* London: J. Cape, 1958, 287 p., references, index.

D'ALTON (John – 1792–1867)

BIOGRAPHY

Lawyer, historian, translator, and occasionally poet, D'Alton was born in Bessville, in County Westmeath, on June 20, 1792. Studied at Trinity College and in London. Returned to practise in Dublin. Besides the works published in book form, he wrote for several periodicals including *The Irish Penny Magazine.* Died in Dublin on January 20, 1867.

BIBLIOGRAPHY

(a) Poetry:

1814. DERMID; *or, Erin in the Days of Boru: a poem.*
London: Longman, etc.; Dublin: J. Cumming, 1814, VIII + 504 p. in-4°.
(This poem was extolled by Walter Scott.)

1831. (contributions to)
IRISH MINSTRELSY ... by James Hardiman (q.v.)

1849. VISIT OF HER MOST GRACIOUS MAJESTY QUEEN VICTORIA, AND HIS R.H. PRINCE ALBERT TO IRELAND, AUGUST 1849.
Dublin (printed but not published), 1849, 26 p.

(b) Historical works:

Besides some monographs: *Memoirs of the Archbishop of Dublin; History of the County of Dublin; History of Drogheda; History of Dundalk*, the following will be noted:

1830. ESSAY ON THE HISTORY, RELIGION, LEARNING, ARTS AND GOVERNMENT OF IRELAND ... published for the 16th vol. of the 'Transactions of the Royal Irish Academy'. Dublin: R. Graisberry ... 1830, 379 p., in-4°.

1845. THE HISTORY OF IRELAND, *from the Earliest Period to the Year 1245, when 'The Annals of Boyle'* ... *Terminate*. Dublin: published by the author, 1845, 2 v. I: XLIV + 283 p., II: IV + 418 p.

DARLEY (George – 1795–1846)

BIOGRAPHY

Born in Dublin of Anglo-Irish parents. Studied at Trinity College (B.A. 1820). Went to London where he lived the life of a recluse, in spite of his friendship with some famous people (Carlyle, Lamb, Southey, Tennyson, etc.), dividing his time between mathematics on which subject he wrote some works of note, his contributions to various periodicals (*London Magazine, Athaeneum*, etc.) and works, poetical especially, in which are manifest an unbridled imagination and a surprising feeling for words. Poor, melancholy, suffering from a severe stammer, Darley is a fitting representative of the generation of Romantic decadence, the generation of Beddoes and Hood. He died on November 23, 1846.

BIBLIOGRAPHY

(a) Poetry and poetical drama:

1822. THE ERRORS OF ECSTASIE: *a dramatic poem. With Other Pieces*. London: G. & W. B. Whittaker, 1822, VII + 72 p.

1827. SYLVIA; *or, The May Queen*, a lyrical drama in 5 acts. London: J. Taylor, 1827, VII + 217 p.

1835. NEPENTHE.

(incomplete edition at the British Museum, without title page. London: 1835), 69 p.
Was reprinted at the end of the century: *Nepenthe*, a poem in two cantos, London: E. Matthews, 1897, XVI + 61 p.; with an introduction by R. A. Streatfeild.)

1840.   THOMAS A BECKET, a dramatic chronicle in 5 acts.
London: E. Moxon, 1840, VI + 144 p.

1841.   ETHELSTAN; *or, The Battle of Brunanburh*, a dramatic chronicle in 5 acts.
London: E. Moxon, 1841, 95 p.

After Darley's death, note:

1890.   POEMS, a memorial volume.
Liverpool: printed for private circulation, 1890, 211 p.
(with a 'Memoir' pp. 1–31).

1904.   SELECTIONS FROM THE POEMS OF G. DARLEY, with an introduction and notes by R. A. Streatfeild.
London: Methuen & Co, 1904, VIII + 180 p.

1908.   THE COMPLETE POETICAL WORKS OF GEORGE DARLEY now first collected, reprinted from the rare original editions in the possession of the Darley family and edited with an introduction by Ramsay Colles.
London: G. Routledge; New York: E. P. Dutton, 1908, XXXVII + 538 p.

(b) Prose:

1826.   THE LABOURS OF IDLENESS; *or, Seven Nights' Entertainments*.
London: J. Taylor, 1826, 330 p.
(Also contains some poetry. Contents:
    'Epistle dedicatory to the Reader' (1)
    I. 'The Enchanted Lyre' (17)
    II. 'Love's Devotion' (105)
    III. 'Pedro Ladron' (123)
    IV. 'Aileen Astore' (195)
    V. 'The Dead Man's Dream' (223)
    VI. 'Ellinore' (275)
    VII. 'Lilian of the Vale' (which would serve as a starting point for *Sylvia*) (293)
The collection appeared under the pseudonym 'Guy Penseval'.)

1829.   THE NEW SKETCH BOOK.
London: printed for the author, 1829, 2 v.
I.: 278 p. II (a reprinting of the preceding volume): 330 p.
(Appeared under the pseudonym 'Geoffrey Crayon Jr.'.)

(c) Secondary material:

STREATFEILD (R. A.): *A Forgotten Poet: George Darley.*
Reprinted from the *Quarterly Review*, 1902, 13 p.

Irish Book Lover. III, 2 (Sept. 1911), pp. 17–19.

ABBOT (Claude, C.): *The Life and Letters of G. Darley, Poet and Critic.* Oxford: University Press; London: Humphrey Milford, 1928.
Further Letters of George Darley (1795–1846) ... reprinted by permission from the *Durham University Journal,* Dec. 1940, 45 p.

GREENE (Graham): 'George Darley', *London Mercury,* XXIX, 1929.

WOLFF (L.): 'G. Darley, poète et critique d'art', *Revue Anglo-Américaine,* February 1931.

Also:

SYMONS, HEATH-STUBBS (*The Darkling Plain*), BLOOM (*The Visionary Company*) q.v. in the general bibliography as well as: Robert Bridges: *Collected Essays,* 1927 and B. Kennelly: 'G.D.: Poet & Mathematician'. *Hibernia,* Mar. 20, 1970, p. 13.

DAUNT (William Joseph O'Neill – 1807–1894)

BIOGRAPHY

Born in Tullamore, was converted to Catholicism and fought on the side of O'Connell; orator, historian and novelist. Was member for Mallow. Died in Kilcaskin.

BIBLIOGRAPHY

Works of non-fiction:

1844. A CATECHISM OF THE HISTORY OF IRELAND, ANCIENT AND MODERN.
Dublin: J. Duffy, 1844, 144 p.

1848. PERSONAL RECOLLECTIONS OF THE LATE DANIEL O'CONNELL, M.P.
London: Chapman & Hall, 1848, 2 v. in the binding: 6 + 331 p.

1896. A LIFE SPENT FOR IRELAND.
London: Unwin, 1896, 20 + 420 p.
(an autobiography made up of fragments from his diary put together by his daughter). Recently reprinted with an introduction by David Thornley, Shannon, Irish University Press.

Novels:

1838. THE WIFE HUNTER & FLORA DOUGLAS, tales by the Moriarty Family ed. by Denis Ignatius Moriarty, esq.
London: Bentley, 3 v., I: 342 p., II: 332 p., III: 316 p.
('The Wife Hunter' in Vols I, II, 'Flora': Vol. III).

1839. [THE HUSBAND HUNTER, 3 v.]

1840. INNISFOYLE ABBEY, a tale of modern times.
London: C. Dolman, 1840, 3 v., I: 300 p., II: 327 p., III: 314 p. + VII (appendix) (same pseudonym).
Note that the later volume of 1844: *Saints and Sinners* is but a digest of *Innisfoyle Abbey*.

1846. HUGH TALBOT, a tale of the Irish confiscations of the XVIIth Century.
Dublin: J. Duffy, 1846, (2) + 474 p.

1851. [THE GENTLEMAN IN DEBT].

DAVIS (Francis – 1810–1885)

Born in Belfast, contributor to *The Nation*, and later, in 1850, editor of the ephemeral *Belfast Man*, published two collections of poetry before this date:

1847.   MISCELLANEOUS POEMS AND SONGS.
Belfast: J. Henderson, 1847, XI + 168 p.
re-issued in 1852.

1849.   LISPINGS OF THE LAGAN.
Belfast: J. Henderson, 1849, VIII + 94 p.

Details for the later works have been taken from David Stewart (*Irish Book Lover*, V, March 8, 1914), but with some hesitation, the bibliographer's information concerning the two preceding titles and the re-issue of the 1st being erroneous.

[1861.   THE TABLET OF SHADOWS, a fantasy *and Other Poems*.

1863.   LEAVES FROM OUR CYPRESS AND OUR OAK.

1878.   EARLIER AND LATER LEAVES; *or, An Autumn Gathering*,
being his complete collected works with an introduction by
Rev. Columban O'Grady.]

DAVIS (Thomas Osborne – 1814–1845)

BIOGRAPHY

Born in Mallow in County Cork, on October 14, 1814, into a Protestant family. Studied at Trinity College, Dublin. Completed his law studies but never practised, devoting all his time to the nationalist cause whose figurehead he would become. A talented writer, his essays successively appeared in *The Citizen. The Dublin Morning Register* and *The Nation* of which he was one of the founders. It is in this latter paper that from October 1842 his numerous poems are to be found. Davis was not content to fight for the repeal of the Act of Union, but also fought for domestic tolerance and to restore to the Irish a sense of their cultural heritage. He seems to have been universally appreciated in his time, even ultra-conservative magazines like the *Dublin University Magazine* saving their sarcasm for other patriots. Unfortunately for the Young Ireland movement, he was carried off at 31 years of age, on September 18, 1845, by an infectious disease. His death was mourned all over the country. A statue by John Hogan commemorates Davis.

BIBLIOGRAPHY

(a) Works:

1843. In THE SPIRIT OF THE NATION (q.v. in periodicals: *The Nation*) (poems).

1845. 'Essay on Irish Songs' in THE SONGS OF IRELAND (q.v. under Barry (M. J.)).

1846. THE POEMS OF TH. DAVIS now first collected.
Dublin: Duffy, 1846, VIII + 232 p.
    (I. 'National Ballads and Songs' (3–30)
    II. 'Miscellaneous Songs and Ballads' (35–70)
    III. 'Historical Ballads and Songs'
      1st series (73–125)
    IV. id., 2nd series (131–162)
    V. 'Miscellaneous Poems' (167–203)
    Appendix.)

LITERARY AND HISTORICAL ESSAYS.
Dublin: Duffy, 1846, X + 252 p.
(Dedicated to John B. Dillon).

1847. LETTERS OF A PROTESTANT, ON REPEAL.
edited by Th. Meagher.
Dublin: printed for the Irish Confederation, 1847, VII + 36 p.
(A plea for national unity as a means of creating an independent Ireland.)

1890. PROSE WRITINGS OF THOMAS DAVIS.
edited with an introduction by T. W. Rolleston.
London: W. Scott, n.d. (1890), 285 p.

1914. ESSAYS LITERARY AND HISTORICAL. Centenary edition, with prefaces, notes by D. J. O'Donoghue and an essay by John Mitchel.
Dundalk: W. Tempest, 1914, XXIII + 456 p.
(Comprises material that had never previously been published in book form.)

THOMAS DAVIS, THE THINKER AND TEACHER.

The essence of his writings in prose and poetry selected, arranged and edited by Arthur Griffith.
Dublin: Gill, 288 p., ill.

1945.   ESSAYS AND POEMS: with a Centenary Memoir 1845–1945.
Foreword by an Taoiseach, Eamon de Valera.
Dublin: M. H. Gill & Son, 1945, XI + 236 p.

(b) Secondary material, etc.:

Nearly all works on the Irish literature, and still more the history, of the period, devote space to Thomas Davis.

Also:

MONAHAN (M.): *Nova Hibernia*, and the introductions to and memoirs in the collections of Davis's works mentioned above.

In addition:

DUFFY (Ch. G.): *Th. Davis: The Memoirs of an Irish Patriot, 1840–6.* London: Kegan Paul, Trench & Co, 1892, 6 + 398 p.

YEATS (W. B.): *Tribute to Thomas Davis* ... with an account of the Thomas Davis Centenary Meeting held in Dublin on Nov. 20, 1914 ...
Cork University Press, 1947, 22 p.

HONE (J. M.): *Thomas Davis*, London: G. Duckworth; Dublin: Talbot Press, 1934, 119 p.

AHERN (J. L.): *Thomas Davis and his Circle.*
Waterford: Carthage Press, 1945, 70 p.

MAC MANUS (M. J.), ed.: *Thomas Davis and Young Ireland.*
Dublin: Stationery Office, 1945, VIII + 127 p., ill., in-4°.

MOODY (T. W.): *Thomas Davis, 1814–45.* A centenary address delivered in Trinity College, Dublin, on June 12, 1945, at a public meeting of the College Historical Society.
Dublin: University of Dublin Historical Society, 1945, 64 p.

QUIGLEY (Michael), ed.: *Pictorial Record: Centenary of Th. Davis and Young Ireland.*
Dublin: Public Sales Office, 1945, ill.

YEATS (W. B.), KINSELLA, (Th.): *Davis, Mangan, Ferguson ?*
Dublin: Dolmen Press, 1971.

SULLIVAN (Eileen): *Thomas Davis.*
Lewisburg, Bucknell University Press, 1979, 90 p.

DERMODY (Thomas – 1775–1802)

BIOGRAPHY

This author whom no one reads any more is nevertheless mentioned in all studies of Anglo–Irish (cf. Alspach, Snyder (*The Wild Irish*), etc.). A short account of his life was written four years after his death and another in the twentieth century (see below), he has been the object of articles in *Notes and Queries* (see below) and his character has inspired A. Symons (*The Romantic Movement in English Poetry*, p. 170).

He was born in Ennis, County Clare, in January 1775. His father was a teacher. He fled to Dublin early on where he found many a disinterested patron to help him survive and start his career, but whom he wearied one after the other: it appears that with the exception of a short spell in the army, he had unruly and drunken habits.

This poet, whose precocity is amazing, died at 27, describing himself in his epitaph as:

> 'Unnoticed for talents he had, and forgot,
> But most famously noticed for faults he had not.'

BIBLIOGRAPHY

(a) Poetry:

1789. POEMS.
Dublin: printed by Chambers, 1789, 31 p.

1792. POEMS CONSISTING OF ESSAYS, LYRIC, ELEGIAC, etc.
by T. D., written between the 13th and 16th year of his age.
Dublin: printed by J. Jones, 1792, 112 p., small format.
(A great variety of subjects, as the title implies: sonnets, songs, fragments, etc. Certain dedications show that the young author was already established, cf. The Countess of Moira, Sidney Owenson, Miss Brooke.)

1800.— POEMS, MORAL, AND DESCRIPTIVE by Thomas Dermody.
London: Vernor & Hood ..., Lackington, Allen & Co, 1800, XI + 112 p., ill.
(The collection is dedicated to the Countess of Moira. The 1st poem 'A Retrospect' takes up 34 pages of the book. The 2nd 'The Pursuit of Patronage', a poetic Epistle, 30 further pages. The rest is made up of short poems.)

1802. THE HISTRIONADE; *or, Theatric Tribunal,* a Poem
Descriptive of the Principal Performers at both houses, in 2
parts, by Marmaduke Myrtle, Esq.
London: E. S. Kirby ..., C. Chapple ..., J. Ginger, 1802,
56 p.

1806. Unpublished poems, etc. in
RAYMOND (J. G.): *The Life of Thomas Dermody* interspersed with pieces of original poetry, many exhibiting
unexampled prematurity of genuine poetical talent and
containing a series of correspondence with several eminent
characters, in 2 v., London: W. Miller; Dublin: J. Archer
and M. Mahon, 1806. I: XXIV + 258 p. II: 346 p. Portrait.

1807. THE HARP OF ERIN containing the poetical works of the
late Thomas Dermody, in two volumes, London: R.
Phillips, 1807. I: XVI + 287 p. II: VII + 312 p.
(James Grant Raymond is the editor of these two volumes
in which – in spite of the title – Ireland hardly appears but
in the poems on Killeigh (I), in 'The Vision of St Patrick'
(II, 88) and in some political pieces. The theme of 'self', on
the other hand, is still very much alive.)

1818. Poems in *Harmonica* (Cork) q.v. under Millikin.
Some unpublished letters and additional information are to be
found in a series of articles by Mabbott (Thomas Ollive):

Notes and Queries: CXLIX: 154, 208, CLI: 70, CLXVI: 371,
CLXXVII: 261, 263 (7 Oct. 1939).

(b) Secondary material:
Beside Raymond (1806) and Mabbott (1939), already mentioned,
note:

BURKE (Th.): *Vagabond Minstrel, The Adventures of Thomas
Dermody.*
London: Longmans, Green & Co, 1936, 345 p.

ÓH-AODHA (M.): 'The Child-Poet from Clare' in *Plays and Places.*
Dublin: Progress House, 1961, pp. 97–101.

COLUM (Padraic): 'The Child of Sorrow' in *The Dublin Magazine,*
Autumn–Winter 1965, pp. 38–42.

DE VERE (Hunt) (Sir Aubrey – 1788–1846)

BIOGRAPHY

Born in Curragh Chase, in County Limerick, on August 28, 1788. Vere Hunt was his real name. Studied at Harrow. A friend of Wordsworth. Spent the greater part of his life efficiently looking after his estate and seems only to have started writing from the age of thirty. Died on July 28, 1846.

BIBLIOGRAPHY

(a) Aubrey de Vere contributed to a certain number of periodicals:

1830. *National Magazine.*
> (I, 1 (July) 'Sonnet to Liberty', p. 30. 2 (Aug.) 'Epitaph', p. 144; miscellanea, p. 192. 3 (Sept.) 'Sonnet: The Hill of St Patrick', p. 276; 'Sonnet: To France Arming for Liberty', p. 347; 'Lines on the Death of J. T. Waller', p. 353.)

1830–2. *Gem.*

1832–3. *Dublin Penny Journal.*
> (I, n° 17 (20 Oct. 1832) 'Sunset on the Lower Shannon', p. 129. 18 (27 Oct. 1832) 'There is no remedy for time mispent', p. 139. 19 (3 Nov. 1832) 'The Shannon', p. 150. 29 (12 Jan. 1833) 'A Sonnet on the Liberty of Press', p. 232.
>
> II, n° 54 (13 July. 1833) 'The Rock of Cashel', p. 11.) etc.

1835. *Keepsake.*

1844. *Dublin Literary Journal.*
> (cf. I, 11 (1st Feb. 1844) 'On a Visit to Wordsworth after a Mountain Excursion', p. 171), etc.

(b) Works published in book form:

1822. JULIAN THE APOSTATE, a dramatic poem.
London: John Warren, 1822, VI + 202 p.

1823. THE DUKE OF MERCIA, an historical drama.
The Lamentation of Ireland, and Other Poems.
London: Hurst, etc., 1823, VIII + 292 p.

('The Lamentations of Ireland' follows the dramatic poem (219–30). The poems end with a series of 18 sonnets (275 to the end).)

1842.   A SONG OF FAITH, DEVOUT EXERCISES AND SONNETS.
London: W. Pickering, 1842, XIII + 286 p.
('A Song of Faith', p. 1; 'Devout Exercises', p. 101;
'Sonnets':
   (1) 'Religious and Moral', p. 135.
   (2) 'On Character & Events', p. 170.
   (3) 'Descriptive', p. 190 (contains: 'The Rock of Cashel': 193; 'Gougaune Barra': 1, 210; 2, 211; 'Glengariff': 1, 215; 2, 216; 'Killarney': 217).
   (4) 'Personal and Miscellaneous', p. 218.
   (5) 'Historical', p. 237.
   (6) 'On the Lord's Prayer', p. 264.
The volume is dedicated to Wordsworth.)

1844-7. MARY TUDOR, an historical drama.
The Lamentation of Ireland and Other Poems.
London: W. Pickering, 1847, 456 p.
(written in 1844).

(c) See:

'The Poems of the De Veres'. *Dublin University Magazine*, XXI, 122 (February 1843), pp. 190–204 (unsigned).

DE VERE (Aubrey, Thomas): *Recollections of A. de Vere.*
London & New York: E. Arnold, 1897, VI + 373 p.

DE VERE (Aubrey Thomas – 1814–1902)

BIOGRAPHY

Son of the former. It is sometimes difficult to distinguish the work of one from that of the other. At first, Aubrey Thomas sometimes published at the same time as his father (cf. for instance: 'The Prayer of Moses' in *The National Magazine*, n° 3, Sept. 1830, follows 'Lines on the Death of J. T. Waller' mentioned above in the previous note); besides the middle name (Thomas) is very infrequently used. If Aubrey Thomas de Vere is of interest to our period by virtue of his early works, he is nevertheless a Victorian in all respects: a disciple of Wordsworth, closely acquainted with Coleridge's daughter, he was a champion of Tennyson and Sir Henry Taylor. From the Irish point of view, he is, with Ferguson and O'Grady, one of the major links between Romanticism and the Celtic Renaissance of the end of the century.

Studied at Trinity College, Dublin; was converted to Catholicism in 1851. Died in Curragh Chase on January 21, 1902.

BIBLIOGRAPHY

(a) Works prior to 1850:

1842. THE WALDENSES, *or, the Fall of Rora*, A Lyrical Sketch, *With Other Poems.*
Oxford: J. H. Parker; London: Rivingstons, 1842, XII + 311 p.
('The Waldenses': 1–92; 'Miscellaneous Poems': 95–225; 'Sonnets': 235–311.)

1843. THE SEARCH AFTER PROSERPINE, *Recollections of Greece, and Other Poems.*
Oxford: J. H. Parker, 1843, VII + 308 p.
('Search': 1; 'Recollections': 39; 'Miscellaneous Poems': 141; 'Songs': 202; 'Sonnets': 253.)

1848. ENGLISH MISRULE AND IRISH MISDEEDS.
Four Letters from Ireland, addressed to an English Member of Parliament.
London: J. Murray, 1848, 2nd edition, IV + 265 p.
(Essays in prose; deal in part with the famine.)

(b) Poetical works from 1850:

1855. POEMS.
London: Burns & Lambert, 1855, XII + 319 p.
(dedicated to J. H. Newman).

1857. MAY CAROLS.
London: Longman, etc., 1857.

1861. THE SISTERS, INISFAIL *and Other Poems.*
London: Longman ...; Dublin: Mc Glashan & Gill, 1861.

1864. THE INFANT BRIDAL ... *and Other Poems.*
London: Macmillan, 1864.

1872. THE LEGENDS OF ST PATRICK.

London: H. S. King; Dublin: Mc Glashan & Gill, 1872, XXX + 248 p.

1874. ALEXANDER THE GREAT, a dramatic poem.
ibid., 1874.

1876. ST THOMAS OF CANTERBURY, a dramatic poem.
London: H. S. King, 1876.

1877. ANTAR & ZARA (and a re-printing of earlier poems), ibid.

1879. LEGENDS OF THE SAXON SAINTS.
London: Kegan Paul, 1879.

1882. THE FORAY OF QUEEN MAEVE and Other Legends of Ireland's Heroic Age. ibid., 1882, XXIV + 233 p.

1884– THE POETICAL WORKS OF A. DE VERE.
98. Vol. 1–3: Kegan Paul ... 4–6: Macmillan, London, 1898.

1887. LEGENDS AND RECORDS OF THE CHURCH AND THE EMPIRE.
London: Kegan Paul ... 1887.

1888. ST PETER'S CHAINS.
London: Burns & Oates; New York: Catholic Pub. Soc., 1888.

1893. MEDIAEVAL RECORDS AND SONNETS.
London: Macmillan, 1893.

(c) Secondary material:

REILLY (Sister M. Paraclita – C.S.J.): *Aubrey de Vere, Victorian Observer.*
Dublin: Clomore & Reynolds; London: Burns, Oates and Washbourne, 1956, 180 p.

FACKLER (Herbert V.): 'Aubrey De Vere's *The Sons of Usnach* (1884), a heroic narrative poem in six cantos'.
Eire–Ireland, IX. 1, Spring 1974, 80–9.

DILLON (John Blake – 1816–1866)

One of the members of Young Ireland who founded and contributed to *The Nation*. Was active in the 1848 rising.

LYONS (F. S.): *John Dillon.* London: Routledge & Kegan Paul, 1968, 516 p.

DOBBS (Francis – 1750–1811)

An author whose works bear on an earlier period. Note, however, *The Patriot King; or, The Irish Chief,* a tragedy in verse (1773–4).

DOHENY (Michael – 1805–1863)

A member of Young Ireland, one of the poets of *The Nation* and the author of the famous *Felon's Track* or *History of the Attempted Outbreak in Ireland,* New York, W. H. Holbrooke, 1849.

DOWNING (Ellen – 1828–1869)

One of the poets of *The Nation.* Disappointed in her love for Joseph Brenan, was to end her days in a convent. Her collections of verse are posterior to the period under discussion.

DRENNAN (William – 1754–1820)

BIOGRAPHY

The son of a Presbyterian minister, he was born in Belfast on May 23, 1754. Studied in Glasgow (M.A. 1771) then Edinburgh (qualified as a medical doctor in 1778 with a *Dissertatio ... proponens quaedam de Venoesectione in Febribus continuis*). Practised in Belfast and Newry, then in Dublin from 1789.

One of the founders of the United Irishmen, he was tried for sedition but acquitted on June 26, 1794, having been defended by J. P. Curran. He then retired from politics but nevertheless figures among the patriots that Madden wrote about (*Lives of the United*

Irishmen, 2nd. series, p. 267). He is, besides, the author of one of the most famous 'committed' poems of the day, 'The Wake of William Orr'.

Married in 1800 to a relatively wealthy Englishwoman, he had two sons who also became poets (cf. below *Glendalloch*, 1859): William Drennan, Jr. (1802–73), and John Swanwick Drennan (1809–95). He came back to live in Belfast in 1807; there, he founded 'The Belfast Academical Institution' and established *The Belfast Magazine*. He died on February 5, 1820.

BIBLIOGRAPHY

(a) Poetry:

1801. In EDKINS (Josuah): A COLLECTION OF POEMS *mostly original by several hands*. Dublin: printed for the editor by Graisberry & Co, 1801, XVI + 355 p.

The collection contains: 'A Trio' (40–5); 'Epitaph on Mrs Rainey' (46–7); 'To Ireland' (48–50); 'The Aspiration' (51); 'To a Young Lady from her Guardian Spirit' (52–7); 'Verses to a Young Lady' (58–9); 'To a Friend, written at Mallow' (60–4); 'The house and the Lady' (65–9); 'Extempore, at a music meeting' (70); 'The Lottery of Love' (71–8); 'Love-Elegy' (77–9); 'Love-Elegy imitated from Tibullus' (80–1); 'Epigram on seeing Miss C.' (82); 'To J— C—' (83); 'Lines to a young gentleman' (86); 'Imitation of Horace' (87); 'To Miss Eliza M——' (90–1); 'An original Letter from Mr L.' (92–5); 'A walk on the Bason at Newry' (96–100); 'Poem addressed to Mrs Siddons' (101–6); 'Prologue to Douglas' (111); 'To S—— S——, with Kotzebue's plays' (115); 'To S.D. with a ring' (108–9); 'The Blackbird at Cabin Hill' (175–7).

1806– In THE POETICAL REGISTER, for 1806–1807.
11. London: J. Rivington, 1811.

(7 poems, 5 appearing in Edkins, and 'Juvenal, 8th satire imitated' (128); also 'In Memory of John Campbell' (158).)

1810(?) In A SELECTION OF PSALMS AND HYMNS FOR UNITARIAN WORSHIP by Robert Aspland, Pastor of the Unitarian Church, Hackney.

(1st edition: 1810 (according to O'Donoghue)
5th edition: London, sold by Rowland Hunter, 1825, XXIV + 396 (+ supplement of 84 p.).)

Dr Drennen is given as the author of hymns n° 86, 205, 332-3-4-5, 348. But Drennan is the writer in question since the author includes them in the following volume of his works.

1815. FUGITIVE PIECES IN VERSE AND PROSE.
Belfast: printed by F. D. Finlay, and sold by R. Rees, etc., March 1815, VI + 229 p.

1817. THE ELECTRA OF SOPHOCLES.
Belfast: printed by F. D. Finlay, 1817, (preface) + 83 p.
('Electra': pp. 1–78 – poems: pp. 79–83: 'Alcaic Ode of Gray (in latin) translated in English'; 'Lines written in a copy of *Robinson Crusoe*'; 'Lines written in the posthumous volume of Cowper's works'; 'Lines written in my daughter's *Vicar of Wakefield*' (dated 1815).)

1859. GLENDALLOCH *and Other Poems* by the late Dr. Drennan. 2nd edition, with additional verses by his sons, Dublin: W. Robertson; London: Simpkin; Edinburgh & Belfast, 1859, XXII (preface, memoir, contents) + 280 p.
(From page 75, the anthology consists of poems by the sons and there is hardly anything new by W. Drennan before that. The edition of *Fugitive Pieces* is obviously considered as the 1st edition, since the preface of this anthology is given as the 'original preface'.)

1874. Certain poems (8) are reprinted in:
GASKIN (J.): IRISH VARIETIES, Dublin: W. B. Kelly, 1874, L + 446 p., illustrations, map.

(b) Prose:

1785. LETTERS OF ORELLANA, *an Irish Helot, to the Seven Northern Counties not represented in the National Assembly of Delegates, Held at Dublin, October 1784, for Obtaining a more equal representation of the People in the Parliament of Ireland.*
Originally published in the *Belfast News Letter*.
Dublin: printed by J. Chambers and T. Heery, 1785, 75 p.
(Letters in an energetic style addressed to his 'fellow-slaves'. The VIth comprises a petition to the King.)

1795. A PHILOSOPHICAL ESSAY ON THE MORAL AND POLITICAL STATE OF IRELAND, *in a letter to Earl Fitzwilliam.*

3rd edition: London: printed for R. White, 1797, 63 p. (signed and dated: January 1795).

1799. LETTER TO THE RIGHT HONOURABLE WILLIAM PITT. Dublin: printed by J. Moore, 1799, 48 p.

1806. A LETTER TO THE RIGHT HONOURABLE CHARLES JAMES FOX. Dublin: John King, 1806, 36 p.

1931. THE DRENNAN LETTERS being a selection from the correspondence which passed between W. Drennan, M.D., and his brother-in-law and sister Samuel and Martha Mc Tier, during the years 1776–1819. Edited by D. A. Chart, Litt.D., Deputy Keeper of the Records of Northern Ireland. Belfast: His Majesty's Stationery Office, 1931, XV (introduction) + 432 p. (with an index). (Portrait of Drennan (frontispiece), by Mrs Martha Mc Tier. View from Cabin Hill. 1407 complete letters, extracts, or abridged letters, and brief notes on the unpublished ones.)

DRUMMOND (Rev. William Hamilton – 1778–1865)

BIOGRAPHY

Born in Larne, and studied at the Belfast Academy and the University of Glasgow. A minister (ordained in 1800). One of the founders of the 'Belfast Literary Society' in 1801. After 1815 settled in Dublin where his interest in Celtic literature earned him election to the Royal Irish Academy. Died on October 16, 1865.

BIBLIOGRAPHY

1795. [JUVENILE POEMS. Belfast.]

1797. [HIBERNIA, a poem. Belfast. THE MAN OF AGE. Belfast, 2nd edition: 1798. 'A poem dealing with the wrongs and misgovernment of Ireland' (*Irish Book Lover*, V, 34).]

1798. [Wrote a tragedy: THE REBELS, never published.]

1806. THE BATTLE OF TRAFALGAR, a heroic poem ...
Belfast: printed by J. Smyth and D. Lyons, sold by Archer & Ward, Belfast; and J. Archer, Dublin, 1806, VIII + 124 p.

1808. [THE FIRST BOOK OF LUCRETIUS, in verse.]

1811. THE GIANT'S CAUSEWAY, a poem.
Belfast: printed by Joseph Smyth for Longman ... London ..., 1811, XXVII + 204 p. (notes from p. 103), ill.

1817. AN ELEGIAC BALLAD *on the Funeral of Princess Charlotte.*
Dublin: Graisberry & Campbell, 1817, 20 p.

1818. WHO ARE THE HAPPY? ... Dublin, ibid., 1818, 36 + 166 p.

1822. CLONTARF, a poem.
Dublin: Archer, Hodges & Mc Arthur, 1822, XVI + 83 p.
(The title poem, in blank verse, is followed, from p. 65 by 'Poetical Sketches'.)

1826. BRUCE'S INVASION OF IRELAND, a poem.
Dublin: Hodges & Mc Arthur, 1826, 114 p.

1830. ESSAY. *On the subject proposed by the Royal Irish Academy, viz to investigate* THE AUTHENTICITY OF THE POEMS OF OSSIAN *both as given in Macpherson's translation and as published in Gaelic, London, 1807, under the sanction of the highland society of London; and on the supposition of such poems not being of recent origin, to assign the probable era and country of the original poet or poets ...*

1831. Contribution to IRISH MINSTRELSY (q.v. under Hardiman (J.)).

1835. THE PLEASURES OF BENEVOLENCE.
London: Hunter; Dublin: Wakeman, Hodges & Smith, 1835, 163 p.

1840. [AUTOBIOGRAPHY OF A. H. ROWAN.]

1848. LIFE OF MICHAEL SERVETUS. London: Chapman, 1848, 16 + 198 p.

1852. ANCIENT IRISH MINSTRELSY.
Dublin: Hodges & Smith, 1852, XXVIII + 292 p.
(translations from the Irish).

?   (posth.) [THE PREACHER, a poem ... with some sermons and a biography by Rev. J. S. Porter.]

DUDLEY (M.E.)

Author of *Juvenile Researches* (prose and poetry), London, 1835, and *Emmet, the Irish Patriot*, and *Other Poems*, ibid., 1836.

DUFFERIN (Helen Selina Sheridan, later Mrs Blackwood, Lady Dufferin; later Countess of Gifford – 1807–1867)

BIOGRAPHY

Granddaughter of Richard Brinsley Sheridan (see Mrs Alicia Lefanu's family tree), and sister of Caroline Norton, married Price Blackwood who was to succeed to the title of Baron Dufferin. A widow, she complied with the wishes of the Count of Gifford who wanted to make her his wife before his death. She is particularly remembered for a few pretty little sentimental songs. Died in London, on June 13, 1867.

BIBLIOGRAPHY

1840.   THE IRISH EMIGRANT.
London: E. Hodges, printer, 1 sheet in-4°.

TERENCE'S FAREWELL.
London: Ryle & Co, printers. id.

1861.   TO MY DEAR SON ON HIS 21ST BIRTHDAY.
Clandeboye: privately printed, n.d. [1861?], in-4°.

1863.   LISPINGS FROM LOW LATITUDES.
London: Murray, 1863, 98 p., ill. (prose).

1894.   SONGS, POEMS AND VERSES edited with a Memoir and some account of the Sheridan Family, by her son The Marquis of Dufferin ...
London: Murray, 1894, X + 429 p.

(Note the re-printing of 'The Irish Emigrant' p. 105, and a comedy in 3 acts performed in 1863 in the Haymarket, *Finesse; or, A Busy Day in Messina*, p. 287.)

See:

HAMILTON (C. J.): *Notable Irishwomen* (pp. 142–153).

DUFFY (Sir Charles-Gavan – 1816–1903)

BIOGRAPHY

Born in Monahan in 1816. Studied Law (a barrister in 1842), but very early on devoted himself to journalism (*Morning Register*, Dublin, (Belfast) *Vindicator* and, in particular, *The Nation* which he founded with Thomas Davis and John Blake Dillon and edited to the end). Arrested on several occasions including 1848, he organised his defence so well that it was never possible to convict him of high treason. He thus escaped transportation. A member of Parliament in 1852, he became disenchanted with Irish politics and emigrated to Australia whose Prime Minister he was to become. Knighted in 1873. Died in the south of France, on February 8, 1903.

BIBLIOGRAPHY

To gain an idea of Duffy's productiveness, all the issues of *The Nation* should be seen; his published books give only a very feeble idea of it.

1845. THE BALLAD-POETRY OF IRELAND.
Dublin: James Duffy, 1845, XLVIII + 252 p.
(A study and anthology in which, beside numerous anonymous texts, figure pieces by Banim, Callanan, Carleton, Crofton, Croker, Curran, Davis, Ferguson, Griffin, Keegan, Lover, Mangan, Moore, Mahony (Prout), Walsh, etc.)

1848. THE CREED OF THE 'NATION'. A Profession of Confederate Principles.
Dublin: Mason, 1848, 15 p.

Among the works posterior to 1850, beside a certain number of articles in *The Contemporary Review*, note:

1880–3. YOUNG IRELAND. A Fragment of Irish History: 1840–1850.
London, Paris, New York: Cassell, Petter, Calpin & Co, 2 v. I: VIII + 778 p., 1880. II: XV + 780 p., 1883. This 2nd volume is entitled:
FOUR YEARS OF IRISH HISTORY; A Sequel to 'Young Ireland'.

1892. THOMAS DAVIS. London: Kegan Paul, Trench & Co, 6 + 398 p.

1898. MY LIFE IN TWO HEMISPHERES.
London: Fisher Unwin, 1898, 2 v.
I: XI + 325 p. II: X + 395 p.
(Recently reprinted (facsimile) by the Irish University Press with an introduction by John H. Whyte.)

EDGEWORTH (Maria – 1767–1849)

BIOGRAPHY

Richard Lovell Edgeworth's third child and first daughter by his first marriage (he would remarry three times, his fourth wife Frances Anne Beaufort being almost Maria's contemporary). Was brought up in England until her 16th year, where she attended Mrs Latuffière's school in Derby and returned to Edgeworthstown in Ireland in 1782, with her whole family. It was there that she wrote the bulk of her literary work, dividing her time between literature, the education of her younger brothers and sisters, and the management of the estate. The family atmosphere there, was one of unity and happiness, despite moments of sorrow: some deaths, the 1798 rebellion after which the Edgeworths, although loyalists, were suspected because of the attachment of their tenants, and the Great Famine. The relative remoteness of Edgeworthstown interfered neither with social events (there was a constant stream of illustrious visitors) nor travel (London in 1799, France in 1802–3). The translation of *Practical Education* having made father and daughter famous, they were received everywhere in Paris where Maria particularly appreciated the salons of Madame Delessert and Madame Récamier, and the company of Father Morelle and La Harpe. It is also in Paris that she met the Chevalier Edelcrantz, Secretary to King Gustav VI of Sweden, who asked for her hand.

Maria's refusal had chiefly to do with the obligation that she would have been under to leave Ireland for Scandinavia, but it seems that the episode held a certain nostalgia for her. 1813: in London again where the novelist receives another warm welcome, meets Lord Byron, Malthus, the Romillys, Humphry Davy. She was to return in 1817–19, while she is to be found in Paris again in 1820 and in Scotland in 1823 where she is received at Abbotsford. Scott himself was to be a guest at Edgeworthstown in August 1825 as Wordsworth would be later. 1830 sees her last stay in England, 1833 her last long tour of Ireland: she visits Connemara and stops over with the Martins of Ballynahinch. She died on May 22, 1849.

BIBLIOGRAPHY

This has been established in a complete and thorough manner by Slade (Bertha Coolidge):

Maria Edgeworth 1767–1849, A Bibliographical Tribute, with 8 plates in collotype and 4 facsimiles. London: Constable, 1937, xxxii + 253 p.

(a) Novels, tales and miscellanea, first editions:

1795.   LETTERS FROM LITERARY LADIES ...
London: J. Johnson, 1795, IV + 79 + 49 p. Reprinted: New York, Garland, 1974.

1796.   THE PARENT'S ASSISTANT; *or Stories for Children.*
London: J. Johnson, 1796, 2 v.
    I. 'The Little Dog Trusty'; 'The Orange Man'; 'Tarlton'; 'Lazy Lawrence'; 'The False Key'; 'Barring Out'. XII + 226 p.
    II. 'The Birthday Present'; 'Old Poz'; 'The Mimic'. II + 177 p.
In 1800, there was to be an enlarged edition in 6 volumes, with the following additional titles:
    II. 'Simple Susan'.
    III. 'The Bracelet'; 'The Little Merchants'.
    IV. 'Mademoiselle Panache'.
    V. 'The Basket Woman'; 'The White Pigeon'; 'The Orphans'; 'Waste not, Want not'; 'Forgive and Forget'.
    VI. 'Eton Montem'.
Certain of these stories were also included in *Early Lessons* and *Moral Tales* (q.v. below).

1798.   PRACTICAL EDUCATION.
London: J. Johnson, 1798, 2 v.

I: XII + 385 p. II: IV + pp. 387 to 794.

(An essay written in collaboration with Richard Lovell Edgeworth, Maria's father. Was to be reprinted, in 3 volumes, in a revised edition, in 1800. Also: New York, Garland, 1974.)

1799.   A RATIONAL PRIMER.

London: J. Johnson, 1799, VI + 40 + 69 p.

(An educational work, written in collaboration with R. L. Edgeworth.)

1800.   CASTLE RACKRENT, an Hibernian Tale. Taken from facts, and from the manners of Irish squires, before the year 1782.*

London: J. Johnson, 1800.

(Preface: I–XI, Advertisement to the English reader: p. XIII, Glossary: p. XV, Tale: Part I: 1–62, Part II: 63–182.

The best modern edition is by Oxford University Press (Oxford English Novels) edited with an introduction by George Watson, 1964, XXXV + 130 p.)

1801.   EARLY LESSONS.

London: J. Johnson, 1801, 10 parts

I. 'Harry and Lucy', Part I: IV + 112 p.

II. 'Harry and Lucy', Part II: IV + 119 p.

III. 'Rosamond', Part I: IV + 127 p. ('The Purple Jar'; 'The Two Plums'; 'The Injured Ass'; 'The Day of Misfortunes'.)

IV. 'Rosamond', Part II: IV + 67 p. ('Rivuletta'; 'The Thorn'; 'The Hyacinths'.)

V. 'Rosamond', Part III: IV + 95 p. ('The Story of the Rabbit'.)

VI. 'Frank', Part I: 111 p.

VII. 'Frank', Part II: 110 p.

VIII. 'Frank', Part III: 91 p.

IX. 'Frank', Part IV: IV + 95 p.

X. 'The Little Dog Trusty'; 'The Orange Man'; 'The Cherry Orchard': 106 p.

MORAL TALES FOR YOUNG PEOPLE.

London: J. Johnson, 1801, 5 v.

I. 'Forester': XI + 238 p.

II. 'Angelina'; 'The Knapsack': 197 p.

III. 'The Prussian Vase'; 'Mlle Panache': 192 p.

IV. 'The Good Aunt': 190 p.

V. 'The Good French Governess': 190 p.

BELINDA.

London: J. Johnson, 1801, 3 v.

I: 370 p. II: 387 p. III: 359 p.

'THE MENTAL THERMOMETER'

(A tale) in *The Juvenile Library*, Vol. I, pp. 378–84.

London: T. Hurst, 1801.

1802. ESSAY ON IRISH BULLS.*

London: J. Johnson, 1802, 316 p.

(A work written by father and daughter in collaboration, would be revised for the 1803 edition.)

1804. POPULAR TALES.

London: J. Johnson, 1804, 3 v.

(I. 'Lame Jervas'; 'The Will'; 'The Limerick Gloves'; 'Out of Debt, out of Danger': IV + 384 p.

II. 'The Lottery'; 'Rosanna'; 'Murad the Unlucky'; 'The Manufacturers': 367 p.

III. 'The Contrast'; 'The Grateful Negro'; 'To-Morrow': 394 p.)

1805. THE MODERN GRISELDA, a tale ...

London: J. Johnson, 1805, 170 p.

1806. LEONORA.

London: J. Johnson, 1806, 2 v., I: 291 p. II: 291 p.

1807. 'LITTLE DOMINICK; *or, The Welsh Schoolmaster*'.

(A tale) in *Wild Roses; or, Cottage Tales*, Vol. I, pp. 57–60.

London: A. Lemoine, 1807.

1809. ESSAYS ON PROFESSIONAL EDUCATION.

London: J. Johnson, 1809, VIII + 496 p.

(Published under the name of R. Lovell, actually written in collaboration.)

**1809–
12.** TALES OF FASHIONABLE LIFE.

London: J. Johnson, Vols. I, II, III, 1809;

IV, V, VI, 1812.

(I. ENNUI; *or, Memoirs of the Earl of Glenthorn** (VII + 400 p.)

II. ALMERIA (1–155); MADAME DE FLEURY (159–284); THE DUN (287–338).

III. MANŒUVRING (369 p.).

      IV. VIVIAN (IV + 460 p.).
      V. EMILIE DE COULANGES (1–199); first part of THE
ABSENTEE* (201–392).
      VI. THE ABSENTEE* (sequel) (466 p.).)

1811. In *Cottage Dialogues* (q.v. under Mary Leadbeater):
Notes and preface.

1814. CONTINUATION OF EARLY LESSONS.
London: J. Johnson & Co, 1814, 2 v.
I: XXXVI + 287 p. II: 324 p.
('Frank', 'Rosamond', 'Harry and Lucy'.)

PATRONAGE.
London: J. Johnson & Co, 1814, 4 v., I: 418 p.
II: 431 p. III: 402 p. IV: 388 p.
(A third edition of this novel, published by Hunter in 1815,
includes some changes.)

1816. READINGS ON POETRY.
London: published by R. Hunter, successor to J. Johnson,
1816, XXVIII + 213 p.
(By R. L. and M. Edgeworth. Both names appear on the
title page. An essay. The second edition of the same year is
amended.)

1817. HARRINGTON, a tale: and ORMOND*, a tale.
London: R. Hunter, Baldwin, Cradock, & Joy, 1811, 3 v.
I: Harrington: IV + 521 p. II: Ormond: 422 p. III: Ormond:
352 p. (2nd edition, revised, the same year).
(*Ormond* was reprinted in the Irish University Press Irish
Novel Series in 1972 with an introduction by A. N.
Jeffares.)

1818. Poems, in *Harmonica* Cork, (q.v. under Milliken), pp.
113–5.

1820. MEMOIRS OF RICHARD LOVELL EDGEWORTH, ESQ.
Begun by himself and Concluded by his Daughter, Maria
Edgeworth.
London: R. Hunter, etc., 1820, 2 v., I: 392 p. II : VII +
498 p.
(Corrections in the second edition (1821) and, especially,
in the third (1844). A modern re-issue 'with a critical
introduction by Desmond J. Clarke' has recently appeared
under the imprint of the Irish University Press.)

1821. ROSAMOND, A Sequel to 'Early Lessons'.
London: R. Hunter, etc., 1821, 2 v.
I: VII + 252 p. II: 272 p.

1822. FRANK, A Sequel to 'Frank' in 'Early Lessons'.
London: R. Hunter, etc., 1822, 3 v.
I: XXVI + 324 p. II: 346 p. III: 300 p.

1825. HARRY AND LUCY Concluded; Being the Last Part of
'Early Lessons'.
London: R. Hunter, etc., 1825, 4 v.
I: XVIII + 287 p. II: 340 p. III: 319 p. IV: 336 p.

1826. 'THOUGHTS ON BORES' in
Janus; or, The Edinburgh Literary Almanack.
Edinburgh: Oliver & Boyd, 1826.

1827. 'ON FRENCH OATHS' (an essay) in
Amulet, 1827.

1828– GARRY OWEN; *or, The Snow-Woman*: and
32. *Poor Bob, The Chimney-Sweeper.*
London: J. Murray, 1832, 116 p., ill.
(Had initially appeared in *The Christmas Box*, London: W.
H. Ainsworth, 1828, pp. 33–8.)

1834. HELEN, a tale.
London: R. Bentley, 1834, 3 v.
I: 336 p. II: 336 p. III: 322 p.

1848. ORLANDINO.
Edinburgh: W. & R. Chambers, 1848, 175 p. (Chambers's
Library for Young People).
(A moral tale about the benefits of temperance.)

(b) Novels, etc., complete editions:

1825. TALES AND MISCELLANEOUS PIECES.
London: R. Hunter, etc., 1825, 14 v.

1832– TALES AND NOVELS.
33. London: Baldwin, etc., 1832–3, 18 v.

1893. THE NOVELS OF M. EDGEWORTH.
London: J. M. Dent ...; New York: Dodd, Mead & Co,
1893, 12 v.

(This is the edition used by the present author, with the exception of *Castle Rackrent* for which Watson was preferred and *The Absentee* read in the edition published by Macmillan in 1910, with a preface by Anne Thackeray Ritchie.)

The Longford Edition (London, 1893 again) was recently re-issued in two photographic reprints: A.M.S. Press. New York, 1967; G. Olms, Hildesheim, West Germany, 1969.

(c) Dramatic works:

1817.   COMIC DRAMAS in 3 Acts.
London: R. Hunter, etc., 1817, 7 + 381 p.
(Contains the three following plays, which do not seem to have been performed:

LOVE AND LAW (5–136).
THE TWO GUARDIANS (137–254).
THE ROSE, THISTLE AND SHAMROCK (255 seq.).

The second is a comedy of manners set in England, the first and the third (the latter being more sentimental) are Irish plays. A second, amended edition appeared the same year.)

1827.   LITTLE PLAYS FOR CHILDREN.
London: R. Hunter, etc., 1827, VIII + 255 p.
('The Grinding Organ' (3–73); 'Dumb Andy' (97–155); 'The Dame Holiday' (159–255).)

(d) Secondary material:

Among GENERAL WORKS, that all devote space to her, the following should be mentioned (q.v. in general bibliography):

BAKER: *History of the English Novel*, Vol. VI; COLBY: *Yesterday's Woman*. pp. 86–144; FLANAGAN: *Irish Novelists*, pp. 51–106; HAMILTON: *Notable Irishwomen*, Ch. VI; HARRISON: *Irish Women Writers*, Ch. I, pp. 1, 49; KRANS, passim; LECLAIRE; MASEFIELD: *Women Novelists*, Ch. V; ROSA: *The Silver Fork School*, passim; UTTER & NEEDHAM: *Pamela's Daughters*; WHITMORE: *Woman's Work in English Fiction*, Ch. VII; etc.

Among SPECIALISED STUDIES are the following:

EDGEWORTH (Mrs F. A.): *A Memoir of M. Edgeworth with*

selections from her letters. London: privately printed, 3 v., 1867.

ZIMMERN (Helen): *Maria Edgeworth*, London: Allen, 1883, 219 p. 'Eminent Women Series'.

HARE (Augustus): *The Life and Letters of Maria Edgeworth*, London: Arnold, 1894, 2 v., I: VI + 327 p. II: 340 p.

LAWLESS (Emily): *Maria Edgeworth*, London: Macmillan, 1904, VIII + 219 p.

HILL (Constance): *Maria Edgeworth and her Circle in the Days of Buonaparte and Bourbon*, London, New York: John Lane, 1910, XVIII + 301 p., ill.

BUTLER (H. J. and H. E.): *The Black Book of Edgeworthstown and Other Edgeworth Memories (1585–1817)*, London: Faber & Gwyer, 1927, XII + 259 p.

CLARKE (Isabel C.): *Maria Edgeworth, her Family and Friends*, London: Hutchinson, 1949, 208 p.

NEWBY (Percy H.): *Maria Edgeworth*, London: A. Barker, 1950, 98 p. 'English Novelists' Series'. Reprinted: Falcroft, Penn.: Falcroft Library Editions, 1973.

HAUSERMANN (H. W.): *The Genevese Background*, London: Routledge & Kegan Paul, 1952, X + 224 p. (4: 'M. Edgeworth's Debt to Geneva and Letters', pp. 30–156).

INGLIS-JONES (Elisabeth): *The Great Maria, a Portrait of Maria Edgeworth*, London: Faber & Faber, 1959, 265 p., ill.

MC WHORTER (Oleta E.): *Maria Edgeworth's Art of Prose Fiction*, University of Arkansas, 1965, The Hague: Mouton, 1971, 258 p.

HAWTHORNE (Mark D.): *Doubt and Dogma in Maria Edgeworth*, Gainesville: University of Florida Press, 1967, 93 p.

NEWCOMER (James): *Maria Edgeworth the Novelist, 1768–1849. A Bicentennial Study*, Fort Worth: Texas Christian University Press, 1967, IX + 172 p.
Maria Edgeworth, Lewisburg: Bucknell University Press, 1973, 94 p. 'Irish Writers' Series'.

HURST (Michael): *Maria Edgeworth and the Public Scene*, London: Macmillan, 1969, 206 p.

MURRAY (Patrick): 'The Irish Novels of Maria Edgeworth', *Studies*, LIX, 1970, pp. 267–78.

COLVIN (Christina), ed.: *Maria Edgeworth: Letters from England 1813–1844.* Oxford: Clarendon Press, 1971, XLII + 649 p.

CRAIG (Charles Robert): *Maria Edgeworth and The Common Sense School.* Unpublished dissertation, University of Nebraska, 1971, *Dissertation Abstracts* (32) 913A.

LYNCH (Patricia A.): *The World of the Edgeworth Novels: The Society Aspect.* Unpublished thesis, U.C.C., 1971.

BUTLER (Marilyn): *Maria Edgeworth: a Literary Biography.* Oxford: Clarendon Press; London: Oxford University Press, 1972, 531 p.

HOWARD (W. J.): *The Genesis of the Regional Novel: A Study of Maria Edgeworth and Sir Walter Scott.* Unpublished thesis, Leeds, 1975.

There is also a work devoted to her cousin, the priest:

WOODGATE (M. V.): *The Abbé Edgeworth.* Dublin: Brown & Nolan, 1935, 14 + 237 p.

EDGEWORTH (Richard Lovell – 1744–1817)

Father of the former, a man of great philosophical and scientific learning, a politician and a critic of his daughter's works, he wrote, in collaboration with her, the following titles (q.v. under Maria Edgeworth).

1798. PRACTICAL EDUCATION.

1802. ESSAY ON IRISH BULLS.

1809. ESSAYS ON PROFESSIONAL EDUCATION.

1816. READINGS ON POETRY.

1820. MEMOIRS.

On the subject of R. L. Edgeworth, see:

CLARKE (Desmond): *The Ingenious Mr Edgeworth.* London: Oldbourne, 1965, 256 p.

EDKINS (Josuah)

Nothing is known about the editor of the three following anthologies:

1789. A COLLECTION OF POEMS MOSTLY ORIGINAL BY SEVERAL HANDS.

Dublin: printed for the editor by M. Graisberry, XXXIII + 328 p., ill.

(Authors represented, in order of appearance in the volume: Henry Headly, Dr Johnson, J. S., Thomas Spring, General Wolfe, John Kemble, the Rev. John Ball, W. Preston, Mr Pratt, W. Hayley, R. Guinness, Horace Walpole, S.W.-T.C.D., James White, G.M., Daniel Webb, M.D., a Gentleman, Stella, C. J. Fox, Samuel Whyte, H. Grattan, F. B., Mrs Barbauld, E. Burke, E. Sharkey, Dr Mc K., R. Cumberland, Th. Smith, Lord Derry, R. B. Sheridan, Gen. Conway, C. S. Williams, Peter Pindar, C. T. Emmet + anonymous).

1790. (same title).

Dublin: printed for the editor by Graisberry and Campbell, Vol. II, 1790, XI + 364 p.

(Authors represented: W. Preston, M., R., I., W. T. J., the Rev. Dean Evelyn, C. T. Emmet, J. White, A Lady, the Rev. S. Shepherd, Goldsmith, Mrs Barbauld, Henry Jones, Miss S., W. B., N., Samuel Whyte, F.B., Mrs Lefanu, Mr Headly, A., W.M., T., Rev. John Lawson, Mr Lyttleton, Sheridan, Captain T. Ford, G., U.)

1801. (same title).

Dublin: printed for the editor by Graisberry & Co, 1801, XVI + 355 p.

(Notes in the preface:

'The present volume differs from my two former, in this particular, that it is solely, and exclusively, the growth of Ireland.'

The authors represented are: W. Preston, William O'Brien Lardner, H., Normannus, W.B., William Drennan, George Robert Fitzgerald, Charles Graydon, Thomas Robertson, A Lady, J.B.)

EGAN (Pierce – 1772–1849)

BIOGRAPHY

Born of Irish parents in London or Dublin (it is not known which), initially made his reputation as a sports reporter, then became famous after the publication of his book *Life in London* (1820, etc.), illustrated by George and Robert Cruikshank, and his monthly *Pierce Egan's Life in London*. Married in 1813, he had a son (Pierce Egan the younger, 1814–80) who was to achieve a certain success in the popular novel.

BIBLIOGRAPHY

Will be found in *The Cambridge Bibliography*. Only two titles are relevant to the history of Irish–English literature:

1821. REAL LIFE IN IRELAND; *or, The Day and Night Scenes, rovings, rambles and sprees, bulls, blunders, bodderation and blarney of Brian BORU, Esq. and his elegant friend Sir Shawn O'Dogherty.* Exhibiting a real picture of characters, manners, etc., in high and low life in Dublin and various parts of Ireland. Embellished with humorous coloured engravings ... by a real Paddy.
London: Jones & Co and J. L. Marks, 1821, VII + 296 p.

1834. (21.2,Dublin) LIFE IN DUBLIN; *or, Tom, Jerry and Logic on their Travels.*
(A comedy, apparently unpublished.)

A recent study is devoted to him:

REID (J. C.): *Bucks and Bruisers: Pierce Egan and Regency England.* London: Routledge & Kegan Paul, 1971, 253 p.

EIFFE (P.)

Author of *The Battle of Clontarf, an Historical Poem; and Other Poems*, Dublin, 1831. The extremely harsh review of it printed in *The National Magazine* (II, 196) seems amply justified by the examples quoted.

ELLIS (Hercules – 1810(?)–1879)

Born in Dublin, studied at Trinity College. A lawyer, and editor of the following anthologies:

1849.   THE SONGS OF IRELAND, second series, edited by Hercules Ellis.
Dublin: Duffy; London: Simpkin, 1849, XVIII + 288 p.
(The first series was edited by M. J. Barry (q.v. 1845).)

1850.   ROMANCES AND BALLADS OF IRELAND ...
Dublin: J. Duffy, 1850, XXXI + 432 p.
(Contains many pieces inspired from the Irish and by J. C. Mangan.)

1851.   THE RHYME BOOK.
London: Longman, etc.; Dublin: Duffy, 1851, 712 p.
(A work in large format each page of which comprises illustrations drawn on the occasion of the Great Exhibition at the Crystal Palace.)

EMMET (Robert – 1778–1803)

The young Irish hero figures among the authors only on account of a few pages the two most famous of which have already been quoted in the present work. They will be found, for example in:

MADDEN (R. R.): *The Life and Times of Robert Emmet*. Dublin: J. Duffy, 1847, 343 p.

A list of secondary literature on Robert Emmet, some of which is recent (H. Landreth, L. O'Broin, etc.), and of the works that he has inspired, among which the excellent novelistic reconstruction by Gwynn (Stephen): *Robert Emmet*. London: Macmillan, 1909, VII + 332 p., would be endless.

Robert Emmet was the son of the Viceroy's private doctor. He was born in Dublin and studied at Trinity College where he gained distinction for his oratorical talents and his sense of history and formed a friendship with Thomas Moore. In 1798 he was dismissed from College on account of his nationalist ideas. In 1800, he embarked on a journey in the course of which he met Talleyrand and Napoleon. On July 23, 1803, he launched an attack against Dublin Castle. The preparation of this attack had absorbed his fortune. After his failure, he hid for a while and managed to communicate with his fiancée, Sarah Curran. Having been betrayed, he was arrested on August 25, condemned to death on September 19 and hanged the next day.

See:

BOURKE (F. S.): *The Rebellion of 1803, An Essay in Bibliography.* Dublin: Three Candles, 1933, 16 p. (Bibliographical Society of Ireland, Vol. V, n° 1).

FERGUSON (Sir Samuel – 1810–1886)

BIOGRAPHY

Born in Belfast on March 10, 1810, into a family of the Ascendancy. Studied at Trinity College. Having qualified as a lawyer in 1838, he was to occupy some important posts in this profession which he abandoned in 1867 to become an archivist at Dublin Castle.

In 1848, had married Mary Catherine Guinness and, the same year, had founded the Protestant branch of the 'Repeal Association'. However, he would very soon revert to more conservative opinions that would earn him a knighthood in 1878. This conservatism did not, however, prevent him from being, indirectly, one of the prime inspirations of Irish nationalism through the enthusiasm and competence with which he carried out his exploration of the Gaelic past, and the quality of his epic poetry. Having received an honorary doctorate from the University of Dublin in 1864 and from the University of Edinburgh in 1884, he was elected President of the Royal Irish Academy in 1882. Died at Strand Lodge, Howth, near Dublin, on August 9, 1886.

BIBLIOGRAPHY

All the works published in book form are posterior to 1850, but these are sometimes reprints of texts published in periodicals, and these contributions to magazines, particularly *Blackwood's* and the *Dublin University Magazine*, are extremely numerous in the period here under discussion.

(a) Works published in periodicals before 1850:

1832. 'THE FORGING OF THE ANCHOR' (a poem).
Blackwood's, XXXI (Feb.), p. 281.
(Reprinted in *Lays* (q.v. 1865) and separately in 1883 (q.v.).)

'THE WET WOOING, Narrative of '98'.
ibid., (April), p. 624.

'LIGHT AND DARKNESS' (a poem).
ibid., XXXII (Oct.), p. 681.

1833. 'AN IRISH GARLAND' (4 poems).
ibid., XXXIII (Jan.), p. 87.

'THE FORREST-RACE ROMANCE' (prose).
ibid., XXXIII (Feb.), p. 243.

'THE FAIRY WELL' (a poem).
ibid., XXXIII (April), p. 667.

'SONGS AFTER BÉRANGER' (4 poems).
ibid., XXXIII (May), p. 844.

'THE DEATH SONG OF REGNER LODBROG' (a poem).
ibid., XXXIII (June), p. 910.

'DON GOMEZ AND THE CID' (a poem).
Dublin University Magazine, II, 8 (Aug.), p. 143.

'NORA BOYLE' (prose).
Blackwood's, XXXIV (Sept.), p. 344.

'THE HISTORY OF PIERCE BODKIN' (prose).
Dublin University Magazine, II, 10 (Oct.), p. 456.

'WILLY AND PATE, a County Down Pastoral' (a poem).
ibid., II, 11 (Nov.), p. 575.

'THE TALE OF THE TUB' (a poem).
ibid., II, 12 (Dec.), p. 691.

'THE RETURN OF CLANEBOY' (prose).
Blackwood's, XXXIV (Dec.), p. 929.

1834. 'INAUGURAL ODE' (a poem).
Dublin University Magazine, II, 13 (Jan.), p. V.

'HILLOA, OUR FANCY'.
ibid., II, 13 (Jan.), p. 25.

'SHANE O'NEILL'S LAST ARMOUR'.
Blackwood's, XXXV (Feb.), p. 249.

'ATHENS' (sonnet).
Dublin University Magazine, III, 14 (Feb.), p. 158.
'FRAGMENTS FROM THE HISTORY OF GRANA WEAL'.
ibid., III, 14 (Feb.), p. 194.
'CAPTAIN BEY' (a poem).
ibid., III, 14 (Feb.), p. 231.
'THE SIXPENNY MANIFESTO' (a political article).
ibid., III, 15 (Mar.), p. 253.
'GRANA WEAL'S GARLAND' (3 poems).
ibid., III, 15 (Mar.), p. 292.
'THE FAIRY THORN'.
ibid., III, 15 (Mar.), p. 331.
(One of Ferguson's most successful and most famous poems, reprinted in *Lays*, 1865, like the following piece.)
'THE FORESTER'S COMPLAINT' (a poem).
ibid., III, 16 (April), p. 386.
'HARDIMAN'S IRISH MINSTRELSY'.
ibid., III, 16 (April), p. 456.
(The first number in a series of four:
    No 2: IV, 20, Aug. 1834, p. 152.
    No 3: IV, 22, Oct. 1834, p. 444.
    No 4: IV, 23, Nov. 1834, p. 514.
in which Ferguson gives his own English translations of Gaelic pieces translated in Hardiman's anthology q.v.)

No 1: 'Lord Mayo', 'The County Mayo', 'Planxty Stafford', 'Whiskey', 'Carolan's Praise of Squire Toby Peyton', 'George Brabazon', 'The Cup of O'Hara', 'Green Jack', 'Madam Crofton', 'Gentle Mable Kelly', 'Grace Nugent', 'Peggy O'Corcoran', 'Fanny Betagh', 'The Hawk of Ballyshannon', 'Mary Maguire'.

No 2: 'Uuilecan Dubh O', 'O! Mary Dear', 'Black Rose-Bud', 'Molly Astore', 'Celia Connelan', 'Ellen a Roon', 'Blooming Deirdre', 'Nora of the amber hair'.

No 3: 'Torna's Lament', 'O'Hussey's Ode to Hugh Maguire', 'Ireland and King James', 'Timoleague', 'The Fair Hills of Ireland'.

No 4: 'Torna's Lament' (2nd version), 'O'Byrne's Bard to the Clans of Wicklow', 'Agnew's Lamentation', 'Timoleague' (2nd version), 'Ode to O'Connelan', 'Molly Astore' (2nd version), 'Kitty Tyrrell', 'Mild Mable Kelly', 'Grace Nugent', 'Drimin Dhu', 'Boatman's Hymn', 'The Fair Hills of Ireland'.

Many of these pieces were reprinted in subsequent volumes.

'THE STRAY CANTO' (a poem).
Dublin University Magazine, IV, 19, July, 1834, p. 72.

'IRISH STORYISTS' (prose).
ibid., IV, 21 (Sept.), p. 298.

'FANCY, THE SCENE SHIFTER' (a poem).
ibid., IV, 21 (Sept.), p. 325.

1834– 'HIBERNIAN NIGHTS' ENTERTAINMENTS'.
36. ibid., IV, 24, Dec. 1834, p. 674, 1st night
'The Death of the Children of Usnach',
(prose, with passages in verse).
ibid., V, 25, Jan. 1835, p. 58, 2nd night
'The Captive of Killeshin'.
ibid., V, 26 (Feb.), p. 192, 3rd night
'The Rebellion of Silken Thomas'.
(This tale is continued in the 5 following numbers.)
ibid., V, 27 (Mar.) p. 293, 4th night
ibid., V, 28 (April), p. 438, 5th night
ibid., V, 30 (June), p. 705, 6th night
ibid., VI, 31 (July), p. 50, 7th night
ibid., VI, 32 (Aug.), p. 207, 8th night
ibid., VI, 33 (Sept.), p. 278, 9th night
'Corby Mac Gilmore'.
(Tale continued the two following nights.)
ibid., VI, 35 (Nov.), p. 537, 10th night
ibid., VI, 36 (Dec.), p. 640, 11th night
ibid., VII, 37, Jan. 1836, p. 96, 12th night
'Rosabell of Ross'.
(A tale, in prose interspersed with verse continued in the last three nights.)
ibid., VII, 39 (Mar.), p. 327, 13th night
ibid., VII, 40 (April), p. 380, 14th night
ibid., VII, 41 (May), p. 579, 15th night

(*The Hibernian Nights* are said to have been published in book form in 1872 in America; they definitely were in 1887 in Dublin.)

1836.   'THREE BALLADS'.
ibid., VII, 37 (Jan. 1836), p. 66.

'THE SKETCHER FOIL'D' (a poem).
ibid., VIII, 43 (July), p. 16.

'THE ATTRACTIONS OF IRELAND' (prose).
ibid., VIII, 43 (July), p. 112.
(Continued in Sept. (n° 45, p. 315) and in Dec. (n° 48, p. 658).)

'THE BREHON LAWS' (prose).
The Penny Cyclopoedia, London: C. Knight, 1836, Vol. 5, p. 382.

1837.   'CURIOSITIES OF IRISH LITERATURE' (prose).
Dublin University Magazine, IX, 51 (Mar.), p. 341.
(Continued in May (n° 53, p. 546).)

'THE SCOTIC CONTROVERSY'.
ibid., IX, 54 (June), continued in October.

'THE INVOLUNTARY EXPERIMENTALIST' (prose).
Blackwood's, XLII (Oct.), p. 487.

1838.   'FATHER TOM AND THE POPE' (prose).
ibid., XLIII (May), p. 607.

'SONNET, suggested by Mr Wall's Paintings of THE FALLS OF NIAGARA'.
ibid., XLIII (May), p. 647.

'A VISION OF ROSES' (prose).
ibid., XLIII (May), p. 648.

1839.   'G. PETRIE'.
Dublin University Magazine, XIV, 84, Dec. 1839, p. 638.

1840.   'OF THE ANTIQUITY OF THE HARP' (prose).
Ancient Music of Ireland (q.v. under Bunting).

'THE DUBLIN PENNY JOURNAL' (prose).
Dublin University Magazine, XV, 85 (Jan.), p. 112.

1844.   ''ORDNANCE MEMOIR OF IRELAND' (prose).
ibid., XXIII, 136 (April), p. 495.

'MRS. H. GRAY'S ETRURIA' (prose).
ibid, XXIV, 143 (Nov.), p. 527.

'EUGÈNE SUE' (prose).
ibid., XXIV, 144 (Dec.), p. 702.

1845. 'ROBERT BURNS' (prose).
ibid., XXV, 145 (Jan.), p. 66.
ibid., XXV, 147 (Mar.), p. 289.

'MRS. BARRETT BROWNING' (prose).
ibid., XXV, 146 (Feb.).

'BETHAM'S ETRURIA CELTICA' (prose).
Blackwood's, LVII (April), p. 474.

'PETRIE'S ROUND TOWERS' (prose).
Dublin University Magazine, XXV, 148, (April), p. 379.

'O'CONNOR'S IRISH BRIGADE'.
ibid., XXV, 148 (May).

'JERUSALEM'.
ibid., XXVI, 153 (Sept.).

'THE WELSHMEN OF TIRAWLEY' (a poem).
ibid., XXVI, 153 (Sept.), p. 308.
(reprinted in *Lays*, 1865).

'LETTER TO HALLAM: HENRI DE LONDRES'.
ibid., XXVI, 155 (Nov.).

'THE DIDACTIC IRISH NOVELISTS: CARLETON, MRS
HALL' (prose).
ibid., XXVI, 156 (Dec.), p. 737.

1847. 'THOMAS DAVIS' (an article and a poem).
ibid., XXIX, 170 (Feb.), p. 120.

'TO CLARENCE MANGAN, a poem'.
ibid., XXIX, 174 (June), p. 693.

'ARCHITECTURE IN IRELAND' (prose).
ibid., XXIX, 174 (June), p. 693.

1848. 'REEVE'S ECCLESIASTICAL ANTIQUITIES' (prose).
ibid., XXXI, 182 (Feb.).

'O'DONOVAN'S THE ANNALS OF IRELAND' (prose).
ibid., XXXI, 183 (Mar.), p. 359.
ibid., XXXI, 185 (May), p. 571.

'NINEVEH'.
ibid., XXXI, 184 (April).

1849. 'INHERITOR AND ECONOMIST' (a poem).
ibid., XXXIII, 197 (May), p. 638.

'RUSKIN'S SEVEN LAMPS OF ARCHITECTURE' (prose).
ibid., XXXIV, 199 (July).

'DUBLIN' (a poem imitated from Juvénal).
ibid., XXXIV, 199 (July), p. 102.

'FERGUSSON ON FORTIFICATION' (prose).
ibid., XXXIV, 200 (April).

'HUNGARY' (a poem).
ibid., XXXIV, 201 (Sept.), p. 292.
(reprinted in *Lays*, 1865).

'PHYSICAL GEOGRAPHY – THE AIR'.
ibid., XXXIV, 203 (Nov.).

'FALLACIES OF THE FALLACIES'.
ibid., XXXIV, 204 (Dec.).

1850. 'IRISH TOURISTS. GIRALDUS CAMBRENSIS'.
ibid., XXXV, 205, 206, 207 (Jan., Feb., Mar.).

'THE SIEGE OF DUNBEG' (a prose narrative).
Blackwood's, LXVII (Feb.), p. 153.

'RUMMAGE REVIEW'.
Dublin University Magazine, XXXVI, 215 (Dec.).

(b) Books (after 1850):

1861. THE CROMLECH ON HOWTH, a poem ... with illumina-
tions from the Books of Kells, etc.
London: Day & Son, 1861, unpaginated, in 4°.

1865. LAYS OF THE WESTERN GAEL, *and Other Poems.*
London: Bell & Dally, 1865, VI + 248 p.
('Lays of the Western Gael' (1–101)
'Ballads and Poems' (105–146)
'Versions from the Irish' (169–226)
Notes (229 seq.).)

1872. CONGAL, a poem, in five books.
Dublin: E. Ponsonby; London: Bell and Dally, 1872,
IX + 236 p.

1880. POEMS.
Dublin: W. Mc Gee; London: G. Bell & Sons, 1880, 168 p.

1883. THE FORGING OF THE ANCHOR.
London, Paris, New York: Cassell & Co, 1883, XXIV p.,
ill.

1887. HIBERNIAN NIGHTS' ENTERTAINMENTS.
Dublin: Sealy, etc.; London: Bell, 1887, 278 p.

1888. THE REMAINS OF ST PATRICK ... The Confession and
Epistle to Coroticus translated into English blank verse ...
Dublin: Sealy, Bryers & Walker; London: G. Bell & Sons,
1888, XXXI + 102 p.

1897. LAYS OF THE RED BRANCH, with an introduction by Lady
Ferguson.
London: T. Fisher Unwin; Dublin: Sealy, etc., 1897,
XXVIII + 161 p.
(A re-issue of the *Lays* of 1865 and the *Poems* of 1880, but
arranged in more logical order.)

Note also the following edition:

POEMS OF SIR SAMUEL FERGUSON with an introduction
by Alfred Perceval Graves.
Dublin: Talbot Press; London: T. Fisher Unwin, n.d.
[1918], 403 p. ('Every Irishman's Library').
(Includes a biographical notice, and a bibliography that
has been of great help to the present author in compiling
his.)

(c) Secondary material:

GENERAL WORKS:
All studies on Irish poetry, the translations (cf. Heaslip), and all the
anthologies. Note: Boyd (E. A.): *Ireland's Literary Renaissance,*
Brown (T.), Farren (R.), Graves (A. P.): *Irish Literary and
Musical Studies,* Kinsella (T.), Morton (D.): *The Renaissance of
Irish Poetry,* W. B. Yeats in Mc Carthy (*Irish Lit.*, Vol. III), etc.

SPECIALISED STUDIES:

YEATS (W. B.): Articles of 1896, etc., in *Uncollected Prose.*

O'HAGAN (J.): *The Poetry of Sir Samuel Ferguson,* Dublin: M. H.
Gill, 1887, 88 p.

FERGUSON (Lady): *Sir Samuel Ferguson in the Ireland of his Day,*
Edinburgh & London: Blackwood, 1896, 2 v.

Irish Book Lover, I, 9 (April 1910) 113–115; I, 10 (May 1910)
125–27.

DEERING (A.): *Sir Samuel Ferguson, Poet and Antiquarian,*
Philadelphia, 1931, 145 p. + index.

BROWN (Malcolm): *Sir Samuel Ferguson*, Lewisburg Bucknell University Press, 1973, 101 p., 'Irish Writers' Series'.

O'DRISCOLL (Robert): *An Ascendancy of the Heart*, Dublin, The Dolmen Press, 1976, 84 p.

FITZGERALD (Edward – 1809–1883)

Although mentioned in the course of this study, Fitzgerald will not be considered here. It is not only that his connections with Ireland are extremely tenuous, but that, with the exception of a piece here and there published in magazines, cf. *The Gem* 1830–1, *Keepsake* 1834, 1835, 1837, etc., *Athenaeum* 1831, and the *Memoir of Bernard Barton* (1849), all his works, including the famous *Rubáiyát of Omar Khayyám* (1859) are posterior to the period under discussion.

Born in Suffolk, E. Fitzgerald was of Irish parentage (Mary Fitzgerald, and John Purcell, a native of Kilkenny). There is a good recent selection of the author's works by Joanna Richardson (*Fitzgerald, Selected Works*, London: Rupert Hart-Davis, 1962, 755 p.).

FITZGERALD (Preston)

A poet and playwright, studied at Trinity College, author of:

1810. [THE SPANIARD AND SIORLAMH (a play).]

1813. SPAIN DELIVERED, a poem, in 2 cantos, *and Other Poems.* London: J. J. Stockdale & R. M. Butler, 1813, 100 p.

1819. [THE SIEGE OF CARTHAGE (a play).]

FITZSIMONS (Edward)

A lawyer, a native of Tipperary, and the object of Brenan's attacks in *The Milesian Magazine*. Author of:

1814. IRISH MINSTRELSY; A Selection of Original Melodies of Erin with characteristic words by E. Fitzsimons and symphonies and accompaniments by Mr J. Smith.
London: Goulding & Co, 1814, 54 + 2 p.

1819. (C.S.) ANZIKO AND COANZA; *or, Gratitude and Freedom*; an opera in 3 acts, music by Sir John Stevenson.
Dublin: printed by W. H. Tyrrell, 1819, XII + 49 p.

1821. LETTERS FROM FRANCE AND THE NETHERLANDS *in the Summers of 1820 and 1821*.
Dublin: printed by W. Underwood, 1821, 217 p.

FOX (George – 1809–1880(?))

Born in Belfast, studied at Trinity College, and known for a single poem 'The County of Mayo', translated from the Irish:

'On the deck of Patrick Lynch's boat I sat in woeful plight ...'

FRANKLIN (Andrew – 1760(?)–1845)

A successful playwright and a native of Cork. About 1805, was editor of *The Morning Advertiser*. Wrote the following plays:

1785. (4.1, S.A.) [THE HYPOCHONDRIAC.
(music by T. Giordani; unpublished).]

1792. (26.3, C.G.) THE MERMAID, a farce ...
London: Robinson, 1792, 33 p.

1797. (15.5, D.L.) THE WANDERING JEW; *or, Love's Masquerade*.
A comedy, in two acts ...
London: G. Cawthorn, 1797, 55 p.

(9.11, D.L.) A TRIP TO THE NORE, a musical entertainment, in 1 act ...
London: G. Cawthorn, 1797, 22 p.

1798. (16.10, D.L.) [THE OUTLAWS.
(a musical drama. Only the *Songs, etc.* from it were published the same year. Manuscript in the Larpent collection, music by Florio).]

1799. (5.8, HAY.) [GANDER HALL.
(unpublished farce. Larpent collection).]

(3.10, D.L.) [EMBARKATION.
(a musical entertainment. *Songs, etc.* printed the same year. Manuscript: Larpent collection. Music by Reeve).]

1800. (24.3, D.L.) THE EGYPTIAN FESTIVAL, an opera, in three acts ...
London: J. Ridgway, 1800.

1804. (March, D.L.) THE COUNTERFEIT, a farce, in two acts ...
London: Robinson, 1804, 47 p.

FRAZER (John De Jean – 1804 (1813(?))–1852)

A contributor to *The Nation*. Author of:

POEMS FOR THE PEOPLE, Dublin: printed by J. Browne, 1845, VIII + 112 p.

POEMS, Dublin: J. Mc Glashan, 1851, 12 + 240 p.

Yeats mentions him. Cf. *Uncollected Prose*, p. 161.

FURLONG (Thomas – 1794–1827)

BIOGRAPHY

Born at Scarawalsh, in County Wexford. Father a farmer. Apprenticed in Dublin at age of 14. Entertains the Muse at an early age and corresponds with Moore. Developed a friendship with the latter as with Maturin and Lady Morgan. Achieved publication as early as 1819 and contributed to *The New Monthly Magazine, The New Irish Magazine, The Morning Register,* and *The Dublin and*

London Magazine in particular. Although aware of O'Connell's failings, he fought for Catholic Emancipation. Towards the end of his life, concentrated on Gaelic literature of which he produced English versions for Hardiman. Ferguson had little sympathy for these translations (v. 'Hardiman's Irish Minstrelsy' n° 3, *Dublin University Magazine*, Ferguson.). Died at 33 years of age, on July 25, 1827. Buried in Drumcondra.

BIBLIOGRAPHY

1819. [THE MISANTHROPE, *and Other Poems*.
London: H. Colburn, 1819.] Dublin: Underwood, 1821, 4 + 40 p., 2nd ed.

1821. [LINES WRITTEN IN A BLANK PAGE OF LADY MORGAN'S 'ITALY'.(?)]

1824. THE PLAGUES OF IRELAND. Dublin: printed for the author, 1824, 6 + 38 p.

1825. POEMS AND MISCELLANIA 'by the author of *The Plagues of Ireland*' in: *Dublin and London Magazine*. London: Robins (cf. I. Mar. 1825, p. 46; April, p. 68, 79 (review of *Fairy Legends* by Croker); May, p. 138 ('Fancy'); July, p. 240 ('Stanzas'); Oct., p. 371 ('Tales of Low Life'); Nov., p. 398.)

1829. THE DOOM OF DERENZIE, a poem.
London: J. Robins, 1829, XII + 155 p.

1831. A translation of 'Remains of Carolan' and of a certain number of other Gaelic poems in: *Irish Minstrelsy* (q.v. under Hardiman – Note (pp. LXIX–LXXX) 'Memoir of Thomas Furlong' by the same Hardiman).

1832– Also other translations in *The Dublin Penny Journal* which
33. also devotes to the author an article: 'Memoir of Thomas Furlong' (1794–1827), Vol. I, n° 6, 4 Aug. 1832, p. 43.

GEOGHEGAN (Arthur Gerard – 1810–1889)

A contributor to *The Nation*. His collections of poetry are posterior to 1850. In 1858, the Chevalier de Châtelain translated his poem *The Monks of Kilrea* (1853).

GRADY (Thomas)

A native of Limerick from which he fled to the Continent in order to evade the fine imposed upon him as a result of the publication of *The Nose Gay* in which he took to task the banker George Evans Bruce. Died in exile. Author of the following satirical works:

1783.   [THE DANCIAD, a poem by a young gentleman.
Limerick, 1783.]

1798.   [THE VISION, a poem.
Dublin, 1798.]

1799.   THE BARRISTER, a poem. Dublin: Dorin, 1799, 4 + 14 p. in-4°.

1800.   THE WEST BRITON, being a collection of Poems on various subjects.
Dublin: printed by Graisberry & Campbell for Bernard Dorin ... 1800.
(2nd edition according to the preface, but this is no doubt a hoax.)

1815.   No 1. *Being The First Letter of* THE COUNTRY POST-BAG.
Dublin: printed by J. M'Kern for the author,
Oct. 27, 1815, 10 p.

No 2. *Being The Second Letter of the Country Post-Bag.*
Dublin: printed for the author, Nov. 4, 1815, 10 p.

No 3, *or* THE NOSEGAY; *Being The Third Letter of the Country Post-Bag*
Dublin: printed by Brett Smith, Dec. 3, 1815, 26 p.
(Dedicated to Thomas Moore.)

GRAHAM (Rev. John – 1774–1844)

Mentioned in the present study as the compiler of *The Lays of Ancient Derry*, this Orange poet is also the author of the following poems on historical subjects.

[**1820.** GOD'S REVENGE AGAINST REBELLION, Dublin.

1822. THE KING'S VISION, ibid.

1823. SIR HARCOURT'S VISION, ibid.

1828. POEMS, Belfast.]

'GRATTAN (H. P.)'
(Henry Willoughby Grattan PLUNKETT – 1808–1889)

BIOGRAPHY

Born in Dublin, wrote for *Punch* under the name 'Fusbos', author of a certain number of plays and of a short poem inspired by G. Cruikshank's anti-alcoholic sketches, lived for 23 years in the United States and died in London on December 25, 1889.

BIBLIOGRAPHY (works before 1850)

1835. (R.A.) THE DUMB CONSCRIPT; *or, a Brother's Love and a Sister's Honour*, a drama in 2 acts.
London: Dick's Standard Plays, n° 429, n.d., 11 p.

(15.7, R.V.) THE CORSAIR'S REVENGE; *or, Love and Vengeance*,
a romantic drama, ibid., n° 751, n.d., 11 p.

1836. (London) THE WHITE BOYS, a romantic drama in 3 acts.
ibid., n° 422, n.d., 20 p.

1839. (29.7, S.W.) THE GOLD SEEKERS; *or, The Outcasts of Anzasca*.
(A musical drama, apparently unpublished.)

1840. (6.1, S.W.) NORAH O'DONNELL; *or, The Sybil of the Camp*.
(An unpublished drama.)

(13.7, E.O.H.) MY UNCLE'S CARD; or, The First of April, an original farce in one act.
London: Dick's Standard Plays, n° 573, n.d., 13 p.

1842.   (–9) FAUST; or The Demon of Drachenfels, a romantic drama.
London: Dick's Standard Plays, n° 419, n.d., 13 p.

(n.d., P.W., Liverpool) THE FAIRY CIRCLE; or, Con O'Callaghan's Dream, a legendary Irish domestic drama.
ibid., n° 432, n.d., 18 p.

1848.   THE BOTTLE, a poem.
New York: Talbot Walts, 1848, unpaginated, ill.

GRIFFIN (Gerald – 1803–1840)[1]

BIOGRAPHY

Born in Limerick on December 12, 1803. Father a farmer; spent the greater part of his childhood thirty miles from his native town in a house overlooking the Shannon estuary. Studied initially under a private tutor then in Limerick and Loughill. When his parents decided to leave for the New World, Gerald was one of those who remained behind, in Ireland, with an elder brother, William, a doctor in Adare. He was then seventeen. Met John Banim and with him formed a friendship that was at times stormy. Began to take an interest in the theatre, ran a local newspaper, The General Advertiser. Bent on pursuing a literary career, he went to London, the city

> Where every brow is dark with care
> And every eye with pride.

He experienced three years of wretchedness and only escaped literally, starving to death, thanks to the unexpected success of some articles in News of Literature and Fashion. He returned to

[1] Revised and updated by John Cronin

Ireland in 1827, crossing back to England only for short stays. He wanted to go on the stage: it was the novel that made him famous and thenceforth it was to this *genre* that he devoted his time, as well as to some lyrical works fired by his platonic love for Mrs Lydia Fisher, daughter of Mary Leadbeater.

For several years, he had toyed with the idea of devoting his life to God and joined the Christian Brothers (founded by E. I. Rice in 1808), after burning all his remaining manuscripts with the exception of the play *Gisippus*. It was in the house of the Brothers in Cork (Our Lady's Mount, North Monastery) that typhoid carried him off on June 12, 1840.

BIBLIOGRAPHY

(a) Stories in prose:

1827. HOLLAND-TIDE; *or, Munster Popular Tales.**
London: W. Simpkin & R. Marshall ... 1827, 378 p.
(Consists of:
1. 'Holland-Tide', 2. 'The Aylmers of Bally-Aylmer', 3. 'The Hand and Word', 4. 'St Martin's Day', 5. 'The Brown Man', 6. 'Persecutions of Jack Edy', 7. 'The Unburied Legs', 8. 'Oweny and Owney na Peak'.)

TALES OF THE MUNSTER FESTIVALS* containing 'Card-Drawing'; 'The Half-Sir'; and 'Suil Dhuv, the Coiner' by the author of 'Holland-Tide; or, Irish Popular Tales'.
London: Saunders & Otley ... 1826, 3 v.
I: XXIII + 355 p. II: 326 p. III: 316 p.

1829. THE COLLEGIANS.*
London: Saunders and Otley, 1829, 3 v.
I: 330 p. II: 349 p. III: 322 p.
(Note, on the second page, the mention: 'A second series of Tales of the Munster Festivals'. This novel, the most famous in nineteenth-century Ireland, sometimes appeared, in later editions, under the popular title of the theatrical adaptation by Dion Boucicault (q.v.): *The Colleen Bawn* (cf. London, 1861: *The Colleen Bawn; or, The Collegian's Wife*. A tale of Garryowen originally entitled 'The Collegians'.) Modern printings prefer the original title (cf. *The Collegians* by Gerald Griffin. With an introduction by Padraic Colum, Dublin: The Talbot Press, 1953.))

The Collegians, through Boucicault, | also inspired a musician, Benedict, | who based his *Lily* | *of Killarney* on it. The facts that provided Griffin with the plot of his tale of crime have been related by W. Mac Lysaght in *Death Sails the Shannon. The Authentic Story of the Colleen Bawn*, Tralee: The Kerryman, L.T.D., 1953, 136 p. (Since reprinted (1970 is the date of the most recent edition) and revised. Anvil Books, 184 p. ill.) Mac Lysaght re-established the date of the murder as 1819 and the names of the characters: Eileen O'Connor was called Ellen Hanley, Hardress Cregan: John Scanlan, and Danny Man: Stephen Sullivan, who was not hump-backed.

THE RIVALS; TRACY'S AMBITION.*
[1st edition: 1829, according to M. Sadleir. The present author has been unable to trace that edition and has only consulted the following.]
London: Saunders & Otley, 1830, 3 v.
I: XXX (contains the poem 'The Fate of Cathleen') + 306 p. ('Rivals'). II: 321 p. 'Rivals' —sequel—, 'Tracy's' from p. 109. III: 302 p. ('Tracy's, —sequel).
(Note, before the title page, the mention: 'Tales of the Munster Festival, third series'.)
Reprinted 1978 with introduction and glossary by John Cronin, Lille: P.U.L., 'C.E.R.I.U.L. Irish and Anglo Irish Texts'.

1830. THE CHRISTIAN PHYSIOLOGIST. Tales Illustrative of the Five Senses: their mechanism, uses, and government; with moral and explanatory introductions. Addressed to a young friend.
London: E. Bull, 1830, XXVI + 376 p.
'Sight: The Kelp-Gatherer'.
'Hearing: The Day of Trial'.
'Feeling: The Voluptuary Cured'.
'Smell: The Self-Consumed' (would be republished in 1854 under the title: 'The Beautiful Queen of Leix; or, The Self-Consumed').
'Taste: The Selfish Crotarie'.
'Intellect: A Story of Psyche'.
The new title of *The Christian Physiologist* in the 1854 edition of this moralising work written for one of Mrs Fisher's sons is: *The Offering of Friendship*.

1832. THE INVASION.
London: Saunders & Otley, 1832, 4 v., I: XV + 300 p. II: 310 p. III: 312 p. IV: 347 p.
(An historical novel.)

1835. TALES OF MY NEIGHBOURHOOD.*
London: Saunders & Otley, 1835, 3 v.
I, 293 p.: ('The Barber of Bantry'; 'The Great House'.)

II, 304 p.: ('Night at Sea'; 'Touch my Honour, Touch my Life'; 'Sir Dowling O'Hartigan'; 'The Nightwalker' (poem).)

III, 334 p.: ('The Village Ruin'; 'Shamid Castle' (a poem); 'The Cavern'; 'The Force of Conscience'; 'The Sunstroke'; 'Send the Fool farther'; 'Mount Orient'; 'Orange and Green' (a poem); 'The Philanthropist'; 'The Blackbirds and Yellow Hammers'.)

1836. THE DUKE OF MONMOUTH.
London: Bentley, 1836, 3 v.
I: 303 p. II: 311 p. III: 284 p.
(An historical novel.)

1842. TALIS QUALIS; OR, TALES OF THE JURY ROOM.*
London: Maxwell & Co, 1842, 3 v.
I, III + 314 p.: 'The Jury Room'; 'Sigismund'; 'The Story Teller at Fault'; 'The Knight without Reproach'; 'The Mistake'.

II, 301 p.: 'Drink, my Brother'; 'The Swans of Lir'; 'McEneiry'; 'Tibbot O'Leary'; 'The Lame Tailor of Macel' (first instalment).

III, 297 p.: sequel to the preceding; 'Antrim Jack'; 'The Prophecy'; 'Sir Dowling O'Hartigan'; 'The Raven's Nest', this last published in 1834 in Alaric Watt's *Literary Souvenir.*

(b) Poetry and dramatic works:

Mention has already been made of certain POEMS scattered among the stories (cf. *Tales of my Neighbourhood*).

A single poetical work seems to have been the object of publication in book form prior to the complete works, about which information is given below. This is, in 1841.

THE FATE OF CATHLEEN, a Wicklow Story ...
London: E. Bull, 1841, 31 p.

As far as the THEATRE is concerned, Griffin wrote at least two plays: *Aguire* (lost) and *Gisippus* the premiere of which took place in Drury Lane on February 23, 1842. This tragedy was published the same year.

GISIPPUS, a play in 5 acts, as performed at Drury Lane, by G. Griffin, Esq.
London: Maxwell & Co ... 1842, III + 77 p.

(c) Collected works:

1842–3. THE WORKS OF G. GRIFFIN.
Vol. I: *The Life of Gerald Griffin*, by his brother* (There follows a notice that has misled even the authors of the *Cambridge Bibliography*. There were, indeed, to be 12 volumes; but only eight materialised and arranged in a different order from that originally planned.)
London: Simpkins & Marshall; Dublin: J. L. Cumming; Edinburgh: Bell and Bradfute, 1843, 484 p.

Vol. II: *Tales of the Munster Festival*, 1st series:
The Collegians.
(Second source of confusion: *The Collegians* originally constituted the 2nd series of these *Tales.*)
London: Maxwell & Co; Dublin ... Edinburgh ..., 1842, 458 p.
(Third source of confusion: volume I is later than volume II and the London publisher of 1843 is no longer the same one as in 1842.)

Vol. III: *Tales of the Munster Festival*, 2nd series:
Card Drawing, The Half Sir, and *Suil Dhuv.*
London: Maxwell & Co, etc., 1842, XIII + 478 p.

Vol. IV: *Tales of the Munster Festival*, 3rd series:
The Rivals, and Tracy's Ambition.
London: Maxwell & Co, etc., 1842, 382 p.

Vol. V: *Holland Tide* (etc.).
London: Maxwell & Co, etc., 1842, 432 p.

(Fourth source of confusion: the volume only contains five of the eight tales originally published under this title. They are: 'Holland Tide'; 'The Aylmers ...'; 'The Hand and Word'; 'The Brown Man'; and 'Owney' ... Two other tales ('The Barber of Bantry' and 'The Village Ruin') come from *Tales of my Neighbourhood*; two others again out of the nine that constitute the collection ('The Knight of the Sheep' and 'The Rock of the Candle') were not included before. The former was first published in Heath's *Book of Beauty* (1841), the latter in *The Literary Souvenir* (1829).)

Vol. VI: *The Duke of Monmouth.*
London: Maxwell & Co, etc., 1842, 423 p.

Vol. VII: *Talis Qualis; or, Tales of the Jury Room.*
London: Maxwell & Co, etc., 1842, 503 p.

Vol. VII: *The Poetical Works.*
London: Simpkin & Marshall ... 1843; Simm & M'Intyre, 1851, 6 + 276 p.

1877.   THE POETICAL AND DRAMATIC WORKS.
Dublin: J. Duffy, 1877, VIII + 397 p.
'The Fate of Cathleen'; 'The Bridal of Malahide'; 'Shanid Castle'; 'Orange and Green'; 'The Traveller and the Moon'; 'Anna Blake'.
'Lyrical Poems'.
'Sonnets'.
'Miscellaneous Poems'.
'Gisippus', a play in five acts.
This is the edition we have used, but it may be a reprint of an earlier publication. New issue, ibid., 1891.

(d) Secondary material:

All general works on Irish–English literature and the novel (Baker, Flanagan, Krans, q.v. in the general bibliography as well as Monahan).

Also:

Life, by his brother (cf. supra: 1843, *Works*).

and:

GILL (W. S.): *Gerald Griffin, Poet, Novelist, Christian Brother,*
Dublin: M. H. Gill, n.d. [1940] , 111 p.

MANNIN (Ethel) *Two Studies in Integrity: Gerald Griffin and the Rev. Francis Mahony.* London: Jarrolds, 1954, 262 p., ill. (Griffin: pp. 17–132.)

CRONIN (John): *Gerald Griffin 1803–1840: A Critical Biography.* Cambridge: Cambridge University Press, 1978, 183 p.

GROVES (Rev. Edward)

A Protestant patriot, the author of the following dramatic works.

1832? THE WARDEN OF GALWAY, a tragedy.
Dublin: A. Thom, 1876, 63 p.

[„   (n.d.) ALOMPRAH; *or, The Hunter of Burmah,* a tragedy.

THE O'DONOGHUE OF THE LAKES.

THE DONAGH]

as well as a few historical and other works:

1829. STORIES FROM THE HISTORY OF GREECE ... TO ITS FINAL CONQUEST BY THE ROMANS. Adapted to the capacities of children.
Dublin: W. F. Wakeman, 1829, 2 v., I: v + 207 p., II: v + 230 p .

1836. SUMMARY OF THE HISTORY AND STATISTICS OF IRELAND; drawn up for the seventh ed. of the *Encyclopaedia Britannica,* in-4° unpaginated, 1836.

1846. PASILOGIA, an essay towards the formation of a system of universal language ...
Dublin: J. Mc Glashan, 1846, (8) + 120 + 34 p.

HALL (Anna-Maria Fielding, Mrs S. C. Hall – 1800–1881)

BIOGRAPHY

A formidable character both on account of her literary prolificity, her wifely perfections and the energetic variety of her interests: charitable causes, anti-alcoholic campaigns, feminism, spiritualism, etc.

Born in Dublin into a family of Huguenot origin, she spent her childhood in Bannow, County Wexford. At 15, she went to London where she met Samuel Carter Hall whom she married in 1824. The rest of her life was divided between fashionable gatherings, literature and philanthropic enterprises at her husband's side. Died on January 30, 1881.

BIBLIOGRAPHY

(a) Novels, stories, miscellaneous prose before 1850.
Principal works:

1829. SKETCHES OF IRISH CHARACTER.*
London: F. Westley & A. H. Davis, 1829, 2 v.
I: IX + 224 p. II: 220 p.
I: 'Lilly O'Brien'; 'Kelly the Piper'; 'Captain Andy'; 'Independence'; 'Black Dennis'; 'Old Frank'.
II: 'The Bannow Postman'; 'Father Mike'; 'Master Ben'; 'Hospitality'; 'Peter the Prophet'.
(The collection is dedicated to Miss Mitford.)

1831. SKETCHES OF IRISH CHARACTER, Second series.
London: F. Westley & A. H. Davis, 1831, VI + 448 p.
('Mabel O'Neil's Curse'; 'Annie Leslie'; 'The Rapparee'; 'Norah Clarey's Wise Thought'; 'Kate Connor'; 'We'll see about it'; 'Jack the Shrimp'; 'Irish Settlers in an English Village'; 'Mark Connor's Wooing and Wedding'; 'Luke O'Brian'; 'Larry Moore'; 'Mary Macgoharty's Petition'; 'The Last of the Line'. The collection is dedicated to Maria Edgeworth. Several stories had already appeared in magazines.)

1830. [CHRONICLES OF A SCHOOL-ROOM.]

1832. THE BUCCANEER, a Tale.
London: R. Bentley, 1832, 3 v., I: 343 p. II: 306 p. III: 314 p. (an historical tale of 1666).

1835. THE OUTLAW.
London: R. Bentley, 1835, 3 v., I: 304 p. II: 307 p. III: 307 p.

TALES OF WOMAN'S TRIALS.
London: Houlston & Son, 1835, 471 p.

1837. UNCLE HORACE, a Novel.
London: H. Colburn, 1837, 3 v., I: 327 p. II: 319 p. III: 312 p.

1838. LIGHTS AND SHADOWS OF IRISH LIFE.*
London: H. Colburn, 1838, 3 v.
  I: VI + 335 p.: 'The Groves of Blarney'.
  II: 341 p.: 'Sketches on Irish Highways during the Autumn of 1834'.
  III: 346 p.: 'Illustrations of Irish Pride'; 'The Dispensation'; 'Old Granny'.

[1840? *Stories of the Irish Peasantry* (see 1850).]

MARIAN; *or, A Young Maid's Fortunes.*
London: H. Colburn, 1840, 3 v., I: 308 p. II: 300 p. III: 304 p.

1841. IRELAND: ITS SCENERY, CHARACTER, etc.
London: How & Parsons, 1841, 3 v.
I: XII + 435 p. II: VIII + 468 p. III: VIII + 512 p.
(Very beautiful illustrations. Written in collaboration with S. C. Hall. The volume is dedicated to Prince Albert.)

1843. A WEEK AT KILLARNEY.
London: J. How, 1843, 208 p., ill.
(Written in collaboration with S. C. Hall.)

1845. CHARACTERISTIC SKETCHES OF IRELAND AND THE IRISH by W. CARLETON, S. LOVER, and MRS HALL, with etchings by Kirkwood.
Dublin: P. D. Hardy & Sons, 1845, 288 p.
(by Mrs Hall: 'The Irish Agent' (p. 275); 'Philip Garraty; or, We'll See About it' (p. 291).)

THE WHITEBOY; *a Story of Ireland in 1822.**
London: Chapman & Hall, 1845, 2 v., I: 318 p. II: 306 p.

1848. A MIDSUMMER EVE: *a Fairy Tale of Love.*
London: Longman, etc., 1848, 270 p., ill.

1850. STORIES OF THE IRISH PEASANTRY.*
Edinburgh: W. & R. Chambers, 1850, 302 p.
(According to Brown, whom Leclaire follows, this volume appeared a first time, in London, in 1840. The present author has found no trace of this possible first edition. The

1850 publication contains: 'Too Early Wed'; 'Time Enough'; 'It's only a Drop'; 'Do you Think I'd Inform?'; 'The Landlord Abroad'; 'The Landlord at Home'; 'It's only a Bit of a Stretch'; 'Sure it Was Always So'; 'It's only the Bit and the Sup'; 'The Follower of the Family'; 'Reddy Ryland'; 'The Crock of Gold'; 'The Wrecker'; 'It's only my Time'; 'Going to Law'; 'Union is Strength'; 'Family Union'; 'Going to Service'; 'Debt and Danger'; 'The Tenant Right'.)

After 1850, only the following is worthy of mention in the present context:

1869. THE FIGHT OF FAITH.
London: Chapman & Hall, 1869, 2 v., I: 311 p. II: 326 p.
(An historical novel: the Battle of the Boyne.)

(b) Dramatic works:

1837. (20.2, ST.J.) ST PIERRE, THE REFUGEE; a burletta, in 2 acts ...
London: J. Macrone, 1837, 27 p.

(27.3, ibid.) MABEL'S CURSE; a musical drama, in 2 acts.
London: J. Duncombe, n.d., Vol. XXVIII, 24 p.

1838. (16.4, ADEL.) THE GROVES OF BLARNEY; a drama, in 3 acts ...
London: Chapman & Hall, n.d., 44 p.

1845. (16.6, QU.) JUNIPER JACK; *or, My Aunt's Hobby*, a burletta.
(Probably unpublished.)

(c) Secondary material:

See the general bibliography, in particular: Buckley, Hamilton (*Notable Irishwomen*, X, 129–141), Harrison (*Irish Women Writers*, IV, 280–306), Maginn *(Gallery)*.

HALL (Samuel Carter – 1800–1889)

BIOGRAPHY

Born on May 9, 1800, near Waterford where his father, an officer, was garrisoned. After a few years in Cork, he went to London where he studied law. It was, however, to literature that he devoted himself: he knew everyone thanks to his work as editor of several periodicals (*Amulet, Art Journal,* etc.). In addition to his personal creativity he collaborated on various works with Maria Fielding whom he married in 1824. Died at Kensington on March 16, 1889.

BIBLIOGRAPHY

Not included are the countless works that he edited and which, with a few exceptions (cf. 1844: *The Beauties of the Poet Moore*) have no connection with Ireland, and works posterior to 1850. A list of them will be found in the *D.N.B.*, etc. Note only:

1820. [THE TALENTS, Cork (a satirical poem).]

1823. LINES WRITTEN AT JERPOINT ABBEY.
London: publisher not indicated, 1823, 16 p., ill. (A description of an ancient abbey in the region of Kilkenny.)

1841. IRELAND, ITS SCENERY, CHARACTER, etc.
(q.v. under Anna Hall. Work written in collaboration).

1843. A WEEK AT KILLARNEY.
id.

1850? POEMS by S. C. Hall, F.S.A., of the Inner Temple, Barrister at Law.
(Neither place, publisher nor date: 'printed for private circulation' is the only information on this slim 8-page volume in large format, printed in 2 columns that include several short poems of Irish inspiration.)

1883. RETROSPECT OF A LONG LIFE FROM 1815 TO 1883.
London: R. Bentley, 1883, 2 v.
I: VIII + 520 p. II: 523 p.
(Includes 'Recollections of Ireland'.)

HAMILTON (Sir William Rowan – 1805–1865)

Born in Dublin on August 9, 1805, a famous astronomer, and friend of Wordsworth whose guide he was in Ireland. In his lifetime, only published poetry in magazines or anthologies, but a large number of his poems will be found in the following book:

GRAVES (R. P.): *Life of Sir W. Rowan Hamilton*, Andrews Professor of Astronomy in the University of Dublin and Royal Astronomer of Ireland ... including selections from his poems, correspondence, and miscellaneous writings.
Dublin: Hodges Figgis; London: Longmans, etc., 1882, 3 v.
I: XVIII + 698 p. II: 719 p. III: XXXV + 673 + 15 p.

HARDIMAN (James – 1790(?)–1855)

An archaeologist and medievalist, the author of works such as:

1820. THE HISTORY OF GALWAY.
Dublin: printed by W. Folds, XVI + 317 + LX p.

[**1826.** ANCIENT IRISH DEEDS ... *chiefly relating to Landed Property, from the 12th to the 17th century.*
also published in Dublin, etc.]

Owes his place in nineteenth-century Irish–English literature to his famous anthology:

1831. IRISH MINSTRELSY; *or, Bardic Remains of Ireland with English Poetical Translations.*
London: Joseph Robins, 1831, 2 v.
I: LXXX + 376 p. II: 436 p.

I: Introduction on lyrical literature in Gaelic. 'Memoir of Carolan' (XLI–LXVIII). 'Memoir of Th. Furlong' (LXIX–LXXX). 'Remains of Carolan'. 'Sentimental Songs'.

II: 'Jacobite Relics'. 'Odes, Elegies', etc.

The authors of the English versions are: D'Alton, Furlong, Lawson, Henry Grattan Curran, Drummond ...
Ferguson wrote a severe critique of the work in the *Dublin University Magazine* (April, August, October, November 1834: Vol. III and IV, n° 16, 20, 22, 23).

The Irish University Press has undertaken the reprinting of Hardiman's 2 volumes 'with a critical introduction by Maire Mac an tSaoi'.

Also published:

[**1843.** AN ACCOUNT OF THE TWO IRISH WILLS.
THE STATUTE OF KILKENNY.]
He died in Galway where he was University Librarian.

HARDY (Philip Dixon – 1794(?)–1875)

Ran several magazines including the *Dublin Penny Journal* and *The National Magazine*. Is the author of the following works and anthologies.

[**1814.** WELLINGTON, a poem in 3 cantos.

1824? BERTHA, a tale of Erin, in 6 cantos, 2nd edition, Dublin.

1826. A WREATH FROM THE EMERALD ISLE (an anthology).

1827? THE PLEASURES OF PIETY, a poem, 2nd edition, Dublin.

1831. THE HARP OF ZION (a collection of Protestant hymns.)]

1837. LEGENDS, TALES AND STORIES OF IRELAND.
Dublin: J. Cumming, 1837, 328 p.

Brown also attributes to him: *Essays and Sketches of Irish Life and Character* and *Ireland in 1846–7, considered in reference to the rapid growth of Popery*, as well as some topographical works.

HARKIN (Hugh – 1791–1854)

A Catholic journalist from the North, he wrote under several pseudonyms ('H.', 'Henry Picken', 'Unexva', etc.) and contributed to the (Belfast) *Vindicator, The Dublin Penny Journal* and *The Nation*.

His first works to have appeared in book form are his occasional poems, but note *Sacred Songs for the People*, 1849.

HAROLD (Edmond, Baron de . .)

An Irishman, author of:

POEMS OF OSSIAN lately discovered by Edmond Baron de Harold, Colonel Commander of the Regiment of Konigsfeld, Gentleman of the Bed Chamber of his most S. H. the Elector Palatin, member of the German Society of Manheim, of the Royal Antiquarian Society of London, and of the Academy of Dusseldorf.
Dusseldorf: by J. Cretien Daenzer, 1887, XVI + 176 p.
(Note 'Preface to my Country' (Ireland), p. IX and the dedication to Grattan, pp. XV–XVI.)

HAYNES (James – 1788–1851)

Born in Tipperary, studied at Trinity College, died in Norwood, near London, on January 24, 1851. Author of the three following 5-act tragedies in verse:

1821. (21.2, D.L.) CONSCIENCE; or, The Bridal Night.
London: Hurst, Robinson & Co; Edinburgh: Constable & Co, 1821, 94 p.

1823. (Nov. C.G.) DURAZZO.
ibid., 1823, 148 p.

1840. (21.2, D.L.) MARY STUART.
London: J. Ridgway, 3rd edition, 1840, 103 p.

HELY (Rev. James)

A translator, cf.:

OGYVIA; or, a Chronological Account of Irish Events ... written originally in Latin by Roderic O'Flaherty, Esq. Translated by the Rev. James Hely.
Dublin: printed by W. Mc Kenzie, 1793, 2 v., I: LXXXIII (+ IX) + 272 p. II: (II) + 419 p.

HITCHCOCK (Robert)

Official prompter at the Theatre Royal, Dublin. Author of:

AN HISTORICAL VIEW OF THE IRISH STAGE *from the earliest period down to the close of the season 1788* ...
Dublin: Marchbank, Vol. I.: (unpaginated intro.) + 315 p., 1788, Vol. II: 263 p., 1794.

Also wrote three comedies between 1773 and 1775.

HOLFORD (George Peter)

Author of:

THE CAVE OF NEPTUNE; a dramatic poem; on the Victory gained by the English Fleet, under the command of Lord Howe, in 1794.
London: printed by T. Burton, 1799, 54 p.

TRUE PATRIOTISM *or, Poverty Ennobled by Virtue*, a drama; performed for the first time on Dec. 21, 1798 at the Theatre in Louth.
Louth: printed for the author by J. Jackson, 1799, 73 + 3 p. (unpaginated epilogue).
(A play violently hostile to the Irish rebellion of 1798. J. O. Bartley speaks of it in *Teague, Shenkin and Sawney*, pp. 167–8 and in 'A Topical Play of '98', *Irish Book Lover*, Sept. 1941.)

HOWARD (Alfred – 'Paddy Kelly')

A journalist, wrote for *The Comet* and, between 1832 and 1835, ran *Paddy Kelly's Budget; or, a penny-worth of fun*, a humorous weekly of a rather alarming intellectual level, before launching in London a more ephemeral publication: *Punchinello; or, Punch and Judy.* He is the author of a play performed in Crow Street on October 14, 1840, and apparently published the same year: O'DONOGHUE OF THE LAKES; *or, The Harlequin and the Leprechaun.*

JEPHSON (Robert – 1736–1803)

BIOGRAPHY

Born in Ireland. Studied in Dublin. A military career, then in the service of the Lord Lieutenant of Ireland. Member of Parliament in 1778. A friend of Horace Walpole. Died at Blackrock, near Dublin, on May 31, 1803.

BIBLIOGRAPHY

(a) Dramatic works:

1775. (17.2, D.L.) BRAGANZA, a tragedy ...
London: T. Evans & T. Davies, 1775, 76 p.
(The action takes place in Lisbon. Blank verse.)

1779. (8.2, D.L.) THE LAW OF LOMBARDY, a tragedy ...
London: T. Evans, 1799, 72 p.
(Inspired by *Much Ado*. Blank verse.)

1781. (17.11, C.G.) THE COUNT OF NARBONNE, a tragedy ...
London: T. Cadell, 1781, 84 p.
(Based on *The Castle of Otranto* by H. Walpole and on *The Mysterious Mother*, an unpublished tragedy by the same author. Blank verse.)

1783. (May S.A.) THE HOTEL; *or, The Servant with Two Masters*,
a farce.
Dublin: printed and sold by all booksellers, 1783, 46 p.

1784. (Jan., S.A.) THE CAMPAIGN; *or, Love in the East Indies*,
a comic opera.
(*Songs, etc*, in —. London: T. Cadell, 1785, 23 p. The play was performed again at Covent Garden on March 15, 1787, in an improved version under the title *Love and War*.)

1787. (14.4, D.L.) JULIA; *or, The Italian Lover*, a tragedy.
London: Charles Dilly, 1787, 8 p. + epilogue.
(Set in Genoa. Blank verse.)

1791. (16.2, C.G.) TWO STRINGS TO YOUR BOW, a farce in two acts.
London: C. & G. Kearsley, 1791, 48 p.
(Granada.)

1796.   (15.11, D.L.) CONSPIRACY, a tragedy.
Dublin: J. Archer, 1796, 85 p.
(Rome. Based on *La Clemenza di Tito* by Metastasio.
Blank verse.)

(b) Miscellanea:

1794.   THE CONFESSIONS OF JEAN-BAPTISTE COUTEAU, *Citizen
of France*, written by himself: and translated from the
original French ...
London: J. Debrett, 1794, 2 v., I: 257 p.; II: 232 p.
(Prose. Satire on the French Revolution.)

ROMAN PORTRAITS, a poem in heroick verse ...
London: G. G. & J. Robinson, 1794, 277 p. ill.

(c) Secondary material:

PETERSON (Martin S.): *Robert Jephson* (1736–1803). *A Study of
his Life and Works*. Lincoln, Nebraska, 1930, 45 p. (University of Nebraska Studies in Language, Literature and Criticism, n° 11.)

KEEGAN (John – 1809–1849)

Poor, unhappy in marriage, and borne off by cholera, Keegan published nothing in book form during his lifetime. He had however written a lot (stories and poems) for a certain number of magazines, as follows:

The Leinster Express (1837–8, 1844).

Dublin University Magazine (cf. the unsigned pieces 'Legends and Tales of the Queen's County Peasantry': n° 1: XIV, 81, Sept. 1839, pp. 366–76 ('The Banshee'); n° 2: id., 82, Oct. 1839, pp. 487–94 ('The Bewitched Butter'); n° 3: id., 83, Nov. 1839 pp. 580–6 ('The Sheoge').

Irish Penny Journal (cf. 'Tales of My Childhood' which begin in n° 30, 23 Jan. 1841, pp. 236–40).

The Nation (poems certain of which would reappear in *The Spirit of the Nation*, 1843).

Dolman's Magazine (London).

Irish National Magazine (1846).

Irishman (1849).

His works have been collected together in the following volume:

LEGENDS AND POEMS, edited by the Late Very Rev. Canon
O'Hanlon, M.R.I.A., with memoir by D. J. O'Donoghue.
Dublin: Sealy, Bryers and Walker, 1907, XXXIV + 552 p.
(1–490: 'Legends: Tales of the Rockites; Tales of My
Childhood'; 'Legends and Tales of the Queen's County
Peasantry ...', 493, seq.: 'Poems'.)

KEIGHTLEY (Thomas – 1789–1872)

Collaborated with T. C. Croker on *Fairy Legends*. The author of
a large number of historical works on Rome, Greece, India, the
Crusades and England. Also:

THE FAIRY MYTHOLOGY,
London: W. H. Ainsworth, 1828, 2 v., I: XV + 334 p.
[II: ?]

TALES AND POPULAR FICTIONS, their resemblance and transmis-
sion from country to country. London: Whittaker & Co, 1834,
XIII + 354 p.

KENEALY (Edward – 1819–1880)

A lawyer, politician, demagogue and journalist born in Cork.
Contributed to *Fraser's, Bentley's, Punch, Ainsworth's Magazine*
and was to found *The Englishman*. Most of his works are posterior
to 1850. Note, however, the following poetical pieces: [*Brallaghan*,
London, 1845. *A New Pantomime*, London, 2nd ed., 1850. *Noah's
Ark*, 1850.]
His complete poems were published in 3 v. in London between
1875 and 1879.

KENNEDY (Patrick – 1801–1873)

With T. C. Croker, shares pride of place among nineteenth-century Irish folklorists. However, all the works by the author of *Legendary Fictions of the Irish Celts*, published in book form are posterior to 1850.

KENNEDY (William – 1799–1871)

BIOGRAPHY

Born near Dublin on December 26, 1799. Studied in Belfast where he had J. Sheridan Knowles as teacher, then in Scotland where he became acquainted with theology. An admirer of Byron, he left for Greece to serve the revolution. Returned disillusioned and settled in London where he ran several journals including *The Englishman's Magazine* from April to October 1831. Visited the United States in 1838, on the occasion of an official journey to Canada, and returned as Consul in Texas from 1841 to 1847. Died in Paris in 1871.

BIBLIOGRAPHY

1826. [MY EARLY DAYS (prose).]

1827. FITFUL FANCIES.
Edinburgh: Oliver & Boyd; London: G. B. Whittaker, 1827, VII + 191 p. (poems).

1830. [THE ARROW AND THE ROSE, *and Other Poems.*]

1831. [AN ONLY SON (prose).]
The Continental Annual and Romantic Cabinet for 1832 with illustrations by Samuel Prout, edited by W. Kennedy. London: Smith, Elder & Co, IX + 313 p.

1838. THE SIEGE OF ANTWERP, an historical play, in 5 acts. London: E. Moxon; Edinburgh: A. & C. Black, 1838, 109 p. (verse).

1841. TEXAS – *The Rise, Progress and Prospects of the Republic of Texas.*
London: R. Hastings, 1841, 2 v., I: LII + 378 p. II: 548 p.

On W. Kennedy, see:

MARSHALL (J. J.): *Irish Book Lover*, II, 11, June 1911, pp. 169–71. *Life of W. Kennedy, Poet, Journalist, and British Consul, 1799–1871.* Dungannon: Tyrone Printing Co, 1920, 57 p.

KENNEY (James – 1780–1849(?))

BIOGRAPHY

A playwright who was as prolific as, alas, he was mediocre, and who yet was extremely popular in his time, because of, among others, the play of which Byron speaks in *English Bards and Scotch Reviewers* (565):

> 'Kenney's "World" – Ah, where is Kenney's wit?
> Tires the sad gallery, lulls the listless pit'.

Born in Ireland, he very soon went to England where, after working in a bank, he devoted himself to the theatre. Married Thomas Holcroft's widow, daughter of the French critic Sebastien Mercier. Assiduously frequented the circle of Samuel Rogers. Lived for a few years in France where, according to O'Donoghue, he died on August 1, 1840, in Paris. G. C. Boase, however, claims that he was struck down by a heart attack at 22 South Terrace, Alexander Square, Brompton, on July 25, 1849. Both agree in their emphasis of the eccentricity of the author who was tormented by a nervous disease.

BIBLIOGRAPHY

(a) Poetry:

1803. SOCIETY, a poem, in 2 parts, *with Other Poems*.
London: Longman, etc., 1803, VIII + 172 p.

1820. VALDI; *or, the Libertine's Son*, a poem.
ibid., 1820, VI + 128 p.

cf. also *Gem* (1829–32), *Forget me Not* (1829–31).

(b) Dramatic works:

1803.   (5.11, C.G.) RAISING THE WIND, a farce, in 2 acts.
London: Longman, etc., 1804, IV + 46 p.

1804.   (20.11, D.L.) MATRIMONY, a petit opera, in 2 acts.
London: Longman, etc., 1804, IV + 46 p.
(also *Songs, etc. in* —, ibid., 1804, 20 p. music by M. King).
A play based on *Adolphe et Clare* by Marsollier.

1805.   (12.2, C.G.) TOO MANY COOKS, a musical farce, in 2 acts.
London: Longman, etc., 1805, 44 p.
(also *Songs, etc. in* —, ibid., 1805, 20 p. music by M. P. King).

1807.   (12.1, D.L.) FALSE ALARMS; *or, My Cousin*, a comic opera, in 3 acts.
London: Longman, etc., 1807, II + 76 p.
(also *Airs, etc., in* —, ibid., 1807, 23 p., music by King and Braham).

(19.11, D.L.) ELLA ROSENBERG, a melodrama, in 2 acts.
London: Longman, etc., 1807, 41 p. (music by King).

(1.12, C.G.) THE BLIND BOY, a melodrama, in 2 acts.
[London, 1807.]
London: Cumberland's British Theatre, n.d., Vol. XXIV, 34 p.

1808.   (31.3, D.L.) THE WORLD! a comedy, in 5 acts.
London: Longman, etc., 1808, 94 p.
(prologue in verse by M. G. Lewis).

1810.   (12.6, LYC.) OH! THIS LOVE! *or, The Masqueraders.*
(unpublished).

1812.   (25.1, LYC.) TURN OUT ! a musical farce, in 2 acts.
London: Sharpe & Hailes, 1812.

(20.11, C.G.) LOVE, LAW AND PHYSIC, a farce, in 2 acts.
[Dublin, 1821.]
London: Cumberland's British Theatre, n.d., Vol. XXIV, 41 p.

1814.   (20.4, C.G.) DEBTOR AND CREDITOR, a comedy, in 5 acts.
London: J. Miller, 1814, 48 p.

1815.   (17.5, C.G.) THE FORTUNE OF WAR.
(unpublished: the manuscript is in the Larpent Collection).

1816. (1.2, C.G.) THE PORTFOLIO; *or, The Family of Anglade,*
a drama, in 2 acts.
London: Longman, etc., 1816, 52 p.

1817. (3.5, D.L.) [THE TOUCHSTONE; *or, The World as it Goes.*
London, 1817.]

(10.5, D.L.) [A HOUSE OUT AT WINDOWS.
London, 1817. Music by Corri.]

1818. (17.12, C.G.) A WORD FOR THE LADIES.
(unpublished: the manuscript is in the Larpent Collection).

1821. (20.9, HAY.) MATCH-BREAKING; *or, The Prince's Present,*
a comedy, in 3 acts.
London: Simpkin, etc., 1821, 49 p.

1822. (3.7, HAY.) [JOHN BUZZBY; *or, a Day's Pleasure.*
London, 1822.]

1823. (7.7, HAY.) SWEETHEARTS AND WIVES, a comedy, in 2
acts.
[*Songs, etc., in —,* London: 1823, music by Whitaker,
Nathan, T. Cooke and Perry, text: Philadelphia, 1827.]
London: Webster, n.d., pp. 323–72 of *Series of Dramatic
Entertainments.*

1824. (10.8, HAY.) THE ALCAID, a comic opera, in 3 acts.
[London, 1824].
London: Cumberland's British Theatre, n.d., Vol. VIII,
58 p.

1825. (28.10, D.L.) THE WEDDING PRESENT.
(unpublished, music by Horn).

1826. (16.3, D.L.) [BENYOWSKY; *or, The Exiles of Kamschatka.*
London, 1826. Based on a play by Kotzebue, music by Sir
J. Stevenson, Cooke, Horn, Livins and Kelly.]

(28.7, HAY.) THIRTEEN TO THE DOZEN.
(unpublished).

(18.10, G.G.) THE GREEN ROOM.
(unpublished).

1827. (6.9, HAY.) SPRING AND AUTUMN; *or, Married for
Money,*
a comic drama, in 2 acts.
London: Lacy's Acting Edition, n.d., Vol. XXIV, 40 p.

(1.10, D.L.) THE ILLUSTRIOUS STRANGER; *or, Married
and Buried,*

an operatic farce, in 2 acts.
[London, 1827. Written in collaboration with J. Milligen, music by Nathan.]
London: Cumberland's British Theatre, n.d., Vol. XXIII, 36 p.

(21.11, D.L.) FORGET AND FORGIVE.
(unpublished: the play was performed again on 15.3.1828 under the title *Frolicks in France*).

1829. (21.2, C.G.) PETER THE GREAT.
(unpublished; written in collaboration with Thomas Morton, after *La Bataille du Pultawa* by Frédéric du Petit-Méré (1808); music by Cooke and Carnaby).

(4.5, D.L.) MANSANIELLO, a grand opera, in 3 acts.
London: Moxon, 1831, 55 p.
(adapted from *La Muette de Portici* by Scribe).

1831. (8.4, D.L.) [THE PLEDGE; *or, Castilian Honour*.
London, 1831, adapted from *Hernani*.]

(17.11, C.G.) THE IRISH AMBASSADOR, *a comedy, in 2 acts*.
New York: S. French, n.d. (*Minor Drama*, Vol. XXXVII), 41 p.

1832. (16.2, D.L.) THE SELF-TORMENTOR.
(unpublished).

1833. (9.12, OLYM.) FIGHTING BY PROXY, a burletta.
London: J. Miller, 1835, 20 p.

1834. (16.1, OLYM.) DANCING FOR LIFE.
(unpublished).

(17.4, C.G.) [A GOOD-LOOKING FELLOW.
London, 1834; written in collaboration with A. Bunn.]

1835. (10.1, D.L.) [THE KING'S SEAL.
London, 1835; written in collaboration with Mrs Core.]

(26.1, OLYM.) NOT A WORD.
(unpublished).

(8.6, E.O.H.) THE SPIRIT OF THE BELL.
(unpublished; music by G. H. Rodwell).

1836. (27.12, D.L.) HUSH! *or, Secrets at Court*.
(unpublished).

1838. (21.2, C.G.) MACKINTOSH AND CO.
(unpublished).

(3.11, C.G.) BARBARA; *or, The Bride of a Day.*
(unpublished).

1840. (21.9, SUR.) THE SICILIAN VESPERS, an historical
tragedy, in 5 acts.
London: J. Miller, 1840, 66 p.

1841. (23.11, HAY.) LOVE EXTEMPORE.
London: Dick's Standard Plays, n.d., n° 733, 14 p.

1844(?) (LYC.) ALADIN; *or, the Wonderful Lamp.*
(unpublished; in collaboration with A. R. Smith).

1845. (1.5, PRINC.) INFATUATION.
(unpublished).

1846. (11.5, ADEL.) UP THE FLUE; *or, What's in the Wind?*
(unpublished; original title: *Felo de Se*; in collaboration
with Dion Boucicault).

KERTLAND (William)

A Dublin tradesman and the author of a handful of poems in
Walker's Hibernian Magazine (1798, 1800, 1804) and in some
nationalist newspapers (the Belfast *Vindicator*: August 1840; *The
Nation*, December 17, 1842) and according to O'Donoghue, two
books of verse, of which the present author has located only the
first:

1822. PATRICK AND KATHLEEN, a domestic tale in verse,
Dublin: J. Cummins, 1822, (VI + 32 p.)

[n.d. THE WOES OF WHISKEY.]

also wrote for the theatre three plays which were performed but not
published:

1833. (5.1, Dublin) THE MAID OF SNOWDON.

(ibid.) MR AND MRS PRINGLE.

1835. (10.1, ibid.) SHAWN LONG AND THE FAIRIES.
(music by F. W. Southwell).

KNOWLES (James Sheridan – 1784–1862)

BIOGRAPHY

One of the rare playwrights of talent of the period, an engaging character: absent-minded, impulsive, even eccentric and hardly gifted for business matters but generous and hard-working ...

Born in Cork, on May 12, 1784. Father a teacher and lexicographer, first cousin to R. B. Sheridan, married to one of the Le Fanu girls. Followed his family to London, at the age of 9. Benefited very early on from his friendship with Hazlitt who introduced him to Leigh Hunt, Coleridge and Lamb. Practised various professions before joining a touring company. Met Kean then Macready who both encouraged him to write for the theatre where he was to have a prodigious success evidenced by his triumphal visits to Ireland and the United States in 1834–5. More or less abandoned the stage ten years later, after having been ordained in the Baptist Church. Died in Torquay on November 30, 1862.

BIBLIOGRAPHY

(a) Poetry:

1796.   ['THE WELSH HARPER' a ballad.]

1810.   A COLLECTION OF POEMS ON VARIOUS SUBJECTS. Waterford: printed by John Bull, 1810, 8 + 72 p.

1817.   [THE SENATE; *or, Social Villagers of Kentish Town*, a canto.
London (signed: 'Selim').]

1832–4. [Poems, in *Athenaeum*.]

(b) Dramatic works (in verse, individual works):

1810.   (Waterford) LEO; *or, The Gipsy*.
Various Dramatic Works, 1874 (q.v.), Vol. I.

1812.   (2.3, Belfast) BRIAM BOROME; *or, The Maid of Erin*, a drama, in 3 acts.
[New York: 1828].
Various Dramatic Works, 1874, (q.v.), Vol. I.
(also: Dick's (670), Lacy (CIX), etc.)

1815.   (13.2, Belfast) CAIUS GRACCHUS, a tragedy, in 5 acts.
Glasgow & London: Ridgway, etc., 1823, 101 p.

1820. (17.5, C.G.,) VIRGINIUS; *or, The Liberation of Rome,*
a tragedy, in 5 acts.
London: Ridgway, 1820, 85 p.

1825. (5.1, D.L.) THE FATAL DOWRY.
[London: 1825, based on a play by Massinger.]

(11.5, D.L.) WILLIAM TELL, a play, in 5 acts.
London: T. Dolby, n.d. (1825).

1828. (22.11, D.L.) THE BEGGAR'S DAUGHTER OF BETHNAL GREEN,
a comedy in 5 acts.
London: Stewart & Ridgway, etc., 1828, 92 p.

1831. (22.11, D.L.) ALFRED THE GREAT; *or, The Patriot King,*
an historical play.
London: Ridgway, 1831, 85 p.

1832. (5.4, C.G.) THE HUNCHBACK,
a play, in 5 acts.
London: E. Moxon, 1832, VIII + 118 p.

(1.10, C.G.,) A MASQUE *(The Vision of the Bard).*
London: E. Moxon, 1832, 14 p.
(in honour of W. Scott).

1833. (24.4, C.G.) THE WIFE: a Tale of Mantua,
a play, in 5 acts.
London: E. Moxon, 1833, 120 p.

1834. (19.2, R.V.) THE BEGGAR OF BETHNAL GREEN.
[London, 1834. A new version of *The Beggar's Daughter.*
Three acts instead of five.]

1836. (29.11, D.L.) THE DAUGHTER.
London: E. Moxon, 1837, 108 p.
(performed again under the title: *The Wrecker's Daughter).*

1837. (26.6, HAY.) THE BRIDAL, a tragedy, in 5 acts, adapted for
representation (with 3 original scenes by J. S. Knowles)
from *The Maid's Tragedy* of Beaumont and Fletcher.
London: Chapman & Hall, 1837, 51 p.

(9.10, HAY.) THE LOVE-CHASE, a comedy, in 5 acts.
London: E. Moxon, 1837, 111 p.

1838. (23.5, C.G.) WOMAN'S WIT; *or, Love's Disguises,*
a play, in 5 acts.
London: E. Moxon, 1838, 120 p.

(9.10, HAY.) THE MAID OF MARIENDORPT, a play, in 5 acts.
London: E. Moxon, 1838, 111 p.

1839.   (4.11, C.G.) LOVE, a play, in 5 acts.
London: E. Moxon, 1840, 116 p.

1840.   (19.9, C.G.) JOHN OF PROCIDA; or, The Bridals of Messina,
a tragedy, in 5 acts.
London: E. Moxon, 1840, 116 p.

1841.   (12.10, C.G.) OLD MAIDS,
a comedy, in 5 acts.
London: E. Moxon, 1841, 128 p.

1842.   (4.6, HAY.) THE ROSE OF ARRAGON, a play, in 5 acts.
London: E. Moxon, 1842, 120 p.

1843.   (24.4, D.L.) THE SECRETARY,
a play, in 5 acts.
London: E. Moxon, 1843, 68 p.

1866.   (21.5, STR.) ALEXINA; or, True unto Death,
a drama, in 2 acts.
London: Adams, etc., 1866, 48 p.

(c) Miscellaneous prose, individual works:

Novels or stories, works on dramatic art, and religious pamphlets.

1831?   THE ELOCUTIONIST, a Collection of Pieces in Prose and Verse, peculiarly adapted to display the art of reading, in the most comprehensive sense of the term.
Belfast: Sims & Mc Intyre, etc., 1831, 7th edition enlarged, XXXVI + 384 p.

1832.   [THE MAGDALEN and Other Tales, London.]

1846.   FORTESCUE, a novel.
London: printed for private circulation, 1846, 178 p. in-4°.

1847.   GEORGE LOVELL, a novel.
London: E. Moxon, 1847, 3 v., I: 238 p. II: 304 p. III: 320 p.

1849.   THE ROCK OF ROME; or, The Arch Heresy.
London: T. C. Newby, 1849, VIII + 280 p.
(An anti-Catholic pamphlet.)

1851. THE IDOL DEMOLISHED BY ITS OWN PRIEST, *an Answer to Cardinal Wiseman's Lectures on Transsubstantiation.*
Edinburgh: Adam & Charles Black, 1851, 308 p.

1855. [THE GOSPEL ATTRIBUTED TO MATTHEW *is the Record of the Whole Original Apostlehood*, London.]

1856. [A DEBATE UPON THE CHARACTER OF JULIUS CAESAR, Boston.]

1873. LECTURES ON DRAMATIC LITERATURE delivered by J. S. Knowles during the years 1820–1850.
London: privately printed for J. Mc Henry, 1873, 228 p., in-4°.

LECTURES ON ORATORY, GESTURE AND POETRY.
id., ibid., 1873, 243 p., in-4°.

1875. [LECTURE ON MACBETH, London.]

1876. SHERIDAN KNOWLES' CONCEPTION AND MR IRVING'S PERFORMANCE OF MACBETH.
London: Effingham Wilson, 1876, 19 p.

(d) 'Collected' or selected works:

1833–4. [SELECT WORKS OF J. S. KNOWLES. Prose Tales and Four Plays, with Memoir, Boston.]

1835. [SELECT DRAMATIC WORKS OF J. S. KNOWLES. Four plays with a memoir by R. Shelton Mackenzie, Baltimore.]

1838. THE DRAMATIC WORKS OF J. S. KNOWLES. Four plays with a memoir by R. Shelton Mackenzie.
Calcutta: W. Rushton, 1838, in-4°.
(IV + 'Virginius' (30 p.); 'The Beggar' (23 p.); 'William Tell' (32 p.); 'The Hunchback' (31 p.); 'The Wife' (26 p.); 'The Love Chase' (25 p.); 'The Daughter' (23 p.).)

1841–3. [id., London, 3 v.]

1856. THE DRAMATIC WORK OF J. S. KNOWLES, in 2 v.
London: Routledge & Co, 1856.
I: 448 p. – 'Caius Gracchus'; 'Virginius'; 'W. Tell'; 'Alfred the Great'; 'The Hunchback'; 'The Wife'; 'The Beggar'; 'The Daughter'.
II: 457 p. – 'The Love-Chase'; 'Woman's Wit'; 'The Maid of Mariendorpt'; 'Love'; 'John of Procida'; 'Old Maids'; 'The Rose of Arragon'; 'The Secretary'.

1873– [MISCELLANEOUS DRAMATIC WORKS AND POEMS.
74.   London: privately printed.]

1874. VARIOUS DRAMATIC WORKS OF J. S. KNOWLES now first collected.
London: privately printed for James Mc Henry, 1874, in-4°.

> I: 274 p. – 'Hersilia'; 'Vaccination'; 'The Storm'; 'Leo'; 'Brian Boroihme'; 'A Masque'; 'The Bridal'; 'Alexina'.

> II: 272 p. – 'The Duke of London'; Unpublished extracts and scenes from various plays; 'Guillaume Tell' (French trans. of W. Tell by Marc Monnier).

TALES AND NOVELETTES COLLECTED.
London: privately printed for J. Mc Henry, 1874, 331 p., in-4°.

1883– [THE DRAMATIC WORKS.
92.   London & New York.]

(d) Secondary material, etc.:

KAVANAGH and other general works on the theatre, Maginn (*Gallery*).

KNOWLES (R. B.): *The Life of James Sheridan Knowles by his Son.* London: J. Mc Henry, 1872, XI + 177 p.

MEEKS (Leslie H.): *Sheridan Knowles and the Theatre of his Time*, Bloomington, Indiana: The Principia Press, 1933, XL + 239 p. (an excellent study, very well documented).

KNOWLES (Richard Brinsley – 1820–1882)

Born in Glasgow, the son of the previous. A lawyer and journalist. Converted to Catholicism, the very year (1849) in which his father published: *The Rock of Rome; or, The Arch-Heresy.* Author of a biography of James Sheridan Knowles (q.v. above, 1872) and of: *The Maiden Aunt*, a five-act comedy in verse, performed at the Haymarket on 19.11.1845, published the same year in London.

LALOR (James Fintan – 1807–1849)

One of the most famous and most extremist members of 'Young Ireland', a contributor to *The Nation* then to *The Irish Felon*. A collection of his writings was published by L. Fogarty in 1918.

LANE (Denny – 1818–1895)

Under the signature 'Doinnall-na-glanna' or under his initials, contributed to *The Nation*. He was born in Cork where he was Chairman of the Gas Company.

LANIGAN (Rev. John – 1758–1828)

A Catholic priest, taught at Maynooth college from which he had to resign when suspected of Jansenism. The author of:

AN ECCLESIASTICAL HISTORY OF IRELAND ... *to the beginning of the XIIIth century ...*
    Dublin: Hodges & M'Arthur, 1822, 4 v.
etc.

LARDNER (Dionysius – 1793–1859)

A mathematician born in Dublin, the creator and animator of the famous *Lardner's Cabinet Cyclopoedia* which was to consist of 133 volumes.
Dion Boucicault (q.v.) was his natural son.

LAWSON (Edward S.)

One of Hardiman's collaborators for his *Irish Minstrelsy*, also figures in *Songs of Ireland* by H. Ellis. Had previously published, in 1815, in London, a poetical translation entitled *Relics of Melodino*.

LEADBEATER (Mary Shackleton, Mrs — – 1758–1826)

BIOGRAPHY

Born at Ballitore, County Kildare, in December 1758, into a family of Quakers. Her grandfather was the founder of a local school where Edmund Burke, and Napper Tandy studied. Stayed for a time in London: thus, in 1784, she met Burke, Sir Joshua Reynolds and Crabbe, but spent the greater part of her life in her native village of which she wrote the *Annals*. Married in 1791 and had a daughter, Lydia, who was to be Griffin's great inspirer. Died at Ballitore on June 27, 1826.

BIBLIOGRAPHY

1790. In: *A Collection of Poems* ((q.v. under J. Edkins).
Vol. II, 1790, p. 108, p. 113, p. 118.

1794. EXTRACTS AND ORIGINAL ANECDOTES FOR THE IMPROVEMENT OF YOUTH.
Dublin: Jackson, 1794, 234 p.
(miscellaneous prose, but contains a few poems).

1808. POEMS ... to which is prefixed her translation of the 13th book of the *Aeneid*; with the Latin original, written in the fifteenth century, by Maffaeus.
Dublin: M. Keene, 1808, 419 p.

1811. COTTAGE DIALOGUES AMONG THE IRISH PEASANTRY.
With notes and a preface by Maria Edgeworth.
London: J. Johnson, 1811, 343 p.
(54 dialogues take up 268 p. The rest is taken up by the glossary and notes.

A 4th edition, in 1813 (Dublin: Cumming), adds a 2nd series of 44 dialogues (140 pages + glossary). 1841 (Dublin: Kennedy) sees the appearance of a 291-page edition with a 3rd series: 20 extra dialogues.)

1813. THE LANDLORD'S FRIEND, intended as a sequel to 'Cottage Dialogues' ...
Dublin: J. Cumming, 1813, 113 p. (11 dialogues).

1814. TALES FOR COTTAGES accommodated to the present condition of the Irish Peasantry.
Dublin: J. Cumming, 1814, 227 p.
(written in collaboration with Elizabeth Shackleton; at the end, includes a play, *Honesty is the Best Policy*).

1822. COTTAGE BIOGRAPHY; being a collection of Lives of the Irish Peasantry ...
Dublin: C. Bentham, 1822, 178 p.
(contains a few poems).

MEMOIRS AND LETTERS OF RICHARD AND ELIZABETH SHACKLETON LATE OF BALLITORE, IRELAND; compiled by their daughter ... including a concise biographical sketch, and some letters, of her grandfather, Abraham Shackleton.
London: Harvey & Darton, 1822, 221 p.
(enlarged edition, 1849: London: Gilfin, 272 p.)

1823. BIOGRAPHICAL NOTICES OF MEMBERS OF THE SOCIETY OF FRIENDS, WHO WERE RESIDENT IN IRELAND.
London: Harvey & Darton, 1823, 366 p.

1826. THE PEDLARS, a Tale. Dublin: printed by Bentham and Hardy, 1826, 180 p.

1862. THE LEADBEATER PAPERS: THE ANNALS OF BALLITORE by Mary Leadbeater with a Memoir of the author, Letters from Edmund Burke ... Mrs R. Trench and Rev. George Crabbe.
London: Bell and Daldy, 1862, 2 v.
(I: 416 p. 'Memoir' – 'The Annals of Ballitore' – 1766–1824. II: 403 p. 'Correspondence'.)

(On the subject of this author, besides this 'Memoir', cf. Hamilton (*Notable Irishwomen*) and Harrison (*Irish Women Writers*).

LEDWICH (Rev. Edward – 1738(?)–1823)

A famous medievalist born in Dublin in 1737 or 38. Collaborated on Vallancey's and Walker's research (q.v.) and published: ANTIQUITIES OF IRELAND, Dublin: printed for Arthur Grueber ... 1790, 473 p. + index, numerous plates, large format. A 2nd edition (526 p.) was published in Dublin (J. Jones) in 1804.

Of his numerous monographs, it is worth mentioning those that Ledwich devoted to Dunamase and Kilkenny.

Certain views held by the author, notably about St Patrick, were the cause of disputes with John Lanigan and James Stewart. In this domain also, Ledwich was a pioneer.

LE FANU (Alicia Sheridan, Mrs – 1753–1817)

Sister of Richard Brinsley, aunt of the following (who, to facilitate matters, has the same Christian name), and grandmother of Joseph Sheridan Le Fanu. An outline of the family tree is of assistance here:

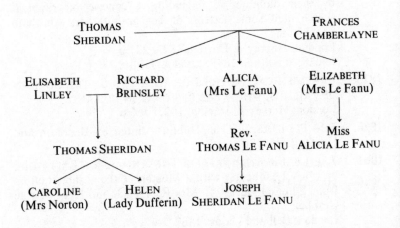

Author of:

THE SONS DE ERIN; *or, The Modern Sentiments*, a comedy in 5 acts performed at the Lyceum Theatre, by Mrs Le Fanu. London: J. Ridgway, 1812, v + 90 + 4 p.

LE FANU (Alicia, Miss)

Niece of Richard Brinsley and of the former. The author of the following poems, novels and miscellanea, barring false attributions.

1809. THE FLOWERS; *or, The Sylphid Queen,* a fairy tale in verse.
London: J. Harris, 1809, 52 p.

1812. ROSARA'S CHAIN; *or, The Choice of Life,* a poem.
London: M. J. Godwin, 1812, 108 p.

1816. STRATHALLAN.
London: Sherwood, Neely & Jones, 1816, 4 v.: I: 536 p.
II: 363 p. III: 344 p. IV: 306 p.

1819. LEOLIN ABBEY, a novel.
London: Longman, etc., 1819, 3 v. I: 395 p.
II: 286 p. III: 276 p.

1823. DON JUAN DE LAS SIERRAS, a romance.
London: Newman & Co, 1823, 3 v., I: IV + 210 p.
II: 212 p. III: 298 p.

1824. TALES OF A TOURIST.
London: Newman & Co, 1824, 4 v., I: 257 p. II: 268 p. III: 257 p. IV: 250 p.

MEMOIRS OF THE LIFE AND WRITINGS OF MRS SHERIDAN, MOTHER OF THE LATE RT. HON. R. B. SHERIDAN ... with remarks upon a late life of the Rt. Hon. R. B. Sheridan; and also criticisms and selections from the works of Mrs Sheridan; and biographical anecdotes of her family and contemporaries. By her grand-daughter, Alicia Le Fanu.
London: G. & W. B. Whittaker, 1824, XI + 435 p.

1826. HENRY THE FOURTH OF FRANCE, a romance.
London: Newman & Co, 1826, 4 v., I: 231 p.
II: 229 p., III: 240 p., IV: 226 p.

LE FANU (Joseph Sheridan – 1814–1873)[1]

BIOGRAPHY

Born in Dublin on August 28, 1814, was R. B. Sheridan's great-nephew on his mother's side, and descended from a Huguenot family on his father's side. Studied initially at home under his father's direction, then at Trinity College, Dublin. Intended to become a lawyer but never practised.

Contributed very early to the *Dublin University Magazine* and joined the staff in 1837 before becoming editor from 1861 to 1869 or 72. Until 1844, the date of his marriage, Le Fanu wrote tales, short stories and poems. From 1844 to 1858 was particularly occupied with journalism: as early as 1839, out of the 3 papers that he had taken over, he made a daily, *The Evening Mail* and a monthly, *The Warder*. From 1858, the year in which his wife died, he wrote, in retirement, his longest novels which are dominated by themes of terror, death and diabolism. Died in Dublin on February 7, 1873.

Was one of the major authors of nineteenth-century Ireland.

BIBLIOGRAPHY

(a) **Before 1850,** Le Fanu only published 2 works:

1845.   THE COCK AND ANCHOR being a chronicle of Old Dublin City.*
Dublin: W. Curry, Jun. and Co ... 1845, 3 v.
I: 347 p. II: 327 p. III: 346 p.
(In the edition published in 1873 by Chapman & Hall (London, 418 p.), this novel has the title *Morley Court*. A modern edition, with the original title, was published in London, in 1967, by Cassell (The First Novel Library) with an introduction by Herbert Van Thal.)

1847.   THE FORTUNES OF COLONEL TORLOGH O'BRIEN. A Tale of the Wars of King James. With illustrations by Hablot K. Browne.
Dublin: James Mc Glashan ... 1847, 342 p.

Numerous, however, before this date, are the contributions to the *Dublin University Magazine* that would reappear, in their original

[1] Updated by Jean Lozès.

form, in later volumes or that are the outlines, the rough drafts, of future novels. These details are given as the bibliography proceeds.

1838. (Jan.) – 'THE GHOST AND THE BONE-SETTER': XI, 61, p. 50.
(This text and the ten that follow were republished in *The Purcell Papers* by the late Joseph Sheridan Le Fanu ... with a memoir by Alfred Perceval Graves. London: Bentley, 1880, 3 v., I: XXXI + 236 p. II: 273 p. III: 289 p.)

(Mar.) – 'THE FORTUNES OF SIR ROBERT ARDOGH': XI, 63, p. 313. (Will become 'The Haunted Baronet' in *Belgravia*, 1870, and appear under this 2nd title in Vols. I and II of *Chronicles of Golden Friars*. London: Bentley, 1871, 3 v., I: VIII + 303 p. II: 328 p. III: 298 p.)

(June) – 'THE LAST HEIR OF CASTLE CONNOR': XI, 66, p. 713.

(Aug.) – 'THE DRUNKARD'S DREAM': XII, 68, p. 151.

(Nov.) – 'PASSAGE IN THE SECRET HISTORY OF AN IRISH COUNTESS': XII, 71, p. 502.
(Reprinted in another form and under the title 'The Murdered Cousin' in GHOST STORIES AND TALES OF MYSTERY with Illustrations by 'Phiz'. Dublin: J. Mc Glashan, 1851, 304 p.
3rd form (very much amplified) 'Maud Ruthyn': *Dublin University Magazine*, 1864. Then, the same year, in volume form under the title: *Uncle Silas, a Tale of Bartram Haugh*. London: R. Bentley ..., 1864, 3 v., I: XI + 325 p. II: IV + 315 p. III: IV + 324 p.)

1839. (April) – 'THE BRIDAL OF CARRIGUARAH': XIII, 76, 405 p.

(May) – 'SCHALKEN THE PAINTER'': XIII, 74, p. 579.
(Reprinted in *Ghost Stories* (1851) before reappearing in *The Purcell Papers*.)

(June) – 'SCRAPS OF HIBERNIAN BALLADS': XIII, 78, p. 752.

(July) – 'JIM SULIVAN'S ADVENTURES IN THE GREAT SNOW'; XIV, 79, p. 103.

(Oct.) – 'A CHAPTER IN THE HISTORY OF A TYRONE FAMILY': XIV, 82, p. 398.

(Enlarged, it became: *The Wyvern Mystery,* London: Tinsley Brothers, 1869, 3 v., I: VIII + 275 p. II: VI + 264 p. III: VI + 277 p.)

1840.   (Feb.) – 'AN ADVENTURE OF HARDRESS FITZGERALD, A ROYALIST CAPTAIN': XV, 86, p. 145.

(Oct.) – 'THE QUARE GANDER': XVI, 94, p. 390.

1846.   (Jan., Feb., June) – 'MISCELLANEA MYSTICA' (attrib. made by M. Sadleir): XXVII, 157; 158, p. 155; 162, p. 691.

1847.   (Nov.) – 'THE WATCHER' from the reminiscences of a bachelor: XXX, 179, p. 526.
(Reprinted in 1851 in *Ghost Stories.*)

(Dec.) – 'FIRESIDE HORRORS FOR CHRISTMAS'; XXX, 180, p. 631. (The present author's attribution).

1848.   (Jan.) – 'THE FATAL BRIDE', 2nd contribution from the reminiscences of a bachelor: XXXI, 181, p. 15.

(passim, series:) – 'EVENINGS WITH THE WITCHFINDERS'. (The present author again suggests that this be attributed to Le Fanu.)

(April, June) – 'SOME ACCOUNT OF THE LATTER DAYS OF THE HON. RICHARD MARSTON OF DUNORAN'.
(2nd form: 'The Evil Guest' (*Ghost Stories,* 1851).
3rd form: *A Lost Name,* London: R. Bentley, 1868, 3 v., I: IV + 314 p. II: IV + 309 p. III: IV + 299 p.)

(June) – 'THE STATE PROSECUTIONS' (editorial): XXXI, 186, p. 785.

(July) – 'THE IRISH LEAGUE' (id.): XXXIII, 187, p. 115.

1850.   (Jan., Feb.) – ' THE MYSTERIOUS LODGER'.

(June) – 'BILLY MALOWNEY'S TASTE OF LOVE AND GLORY': XXXV, 210, p. 692.

(July) – 'SHAMUS O'BRIEN', a ballad: XXXVI, 211, p. 109.
(This poem, famous particularly in the United States where Samuel Lover recited it with an ending of his own invention, is reprinted, along with the 'Hibernian Ballads' of June 1839 and Le Fanu's later plays in verse in:
The Poems of Joseph Sheridan Le Fanu, edited by Alfred Perceval Graves, with a portrait ...
London, Downey ..., 1896, XXVIII + 164 p.

C. V. Stanford made an opera of it, published in 1896 (London: Boosey & Co).

(b) Chronological summary and later works (in book form):

1845. THE COCK AND ANCHOR.

1847. THE FORTUNES OF COLONEL TORLOGH O'BRIEN.

1851. GHOST STORIES.

1863. THE HOUSE BY THE CHURCHYARD*. London: Tinsley, 3 v.

1864. UNCLE SILAS.
WYLDER'S HAND. London: Bentley, 3 v.

1865. THE PRELUDE (pamphlet). Dublin: Herbert.
GUY DEVERELL. London: Bentley, 3 v.

1866. ALL IN THE DARK. London: Bentley, 2 v.

1867. THE TENANTS OF MALORY. London: Tinsley, 3 v.
THE POEM OF SHAMUS O'BRIEN. Manchester: Heywood.

1868. HAUNTED LIVES. London: Tinsley, 3 v.
A LOST NAME. London: Bentley, 3 v.

1869. THE WYVERN MYSTERY. London: Tinsley, 3 v.

1871. CHECKMATE. London: Hurst and Blackett, 3 v.
CHRONICLES OF GOLDEN FRIARS. London: Bentley, 3 v.
THE ROSE AND THE KEY. London: Chapman & Hall, 3 v.

1872. IN A GLASS DARKLY. London: Bentley, 3 v.

1873. WILLING TO DIE. London: Hurst and Blackett, 3 v.

1880. THE PURCELL PAPERS,* reprinted Sank City, Wis.: Arkham House, 1975.

1893. THE POEMS.

1923. MADAME CROWL'S GHOST, etc. London: Bell.

1976. THE COLLECTED WORKS. ed. Sir Devendra P. Varma. New York: Arno Press, 52 v.

Also at different times various paperbacks with varying titles.

(c) Secondary material:

ELLIS (S. M.): *Wilkie Collins, Le Fanu and Others*, pp. 140–91, London: Constable, 1931, 1951 (detailed bibliography).

BOWEN (E.): Introduction to *Uncle Silas*, London: The Cresset Press, 1947, and to *The House by the Churchyard*, London: Anthony Blond, 1968.

PRITCHETT (V. S.): Introduction to *In a Glass Darkly*, London: John Lehman, 1947 (Chiltern Library).

BROWNE (N.): *Sheridan Le Fanu*, London: Arthur Barker, 1951, 135 p. ('The English Novelists Series').

PENDZOLT (P.): *The Supernatural in Fiction* (q.v. in general bibliography), pp. 67, seq.

COOLEY (Leo Patrick): *Joseph Sheridan Le Fanu: The Struggle of an Irish Imagination.* Unpublished dissertation, New York University, 1969. *Dissertation Abstracts* (30) 3453A–4A.

BEGNAL (Michael): *Sheridan Le Fanu*, Lewisburg: Bucknell University Press, 1971, 87 p. ('Irish Writers Series').

SULLIVAN (Kevin): '*The House By the Churchyard* : James Joyce & Sheridan Le Fanu' in: Porter, R. J. & Brophy, J. D., eds: *Modern Irish Literature*, New York, Twayne, 1972, 315–34.

BYRNE (Patrick, F.): 'Joseph Sheridan Le Fanu: A Centenary Memoir', *Dublin Historical Record*, XXVI, 3, 1973, 80–92.

also various recent articles:

MCCORMACK (W. J.) in *Long Room*, 1971, etc.

SULLIVAN (Kevin) in *Irish University Review*, II, 1, Spring 1972, 5–19.

DENHAM (Peter) in *Eire–Ireland* IX, 3, Aug. 1974, 152–8.

LOZÈS (Jean) in *Caliban* (Toulouse) XI, 1974, 153–64, etc.

LEVER (Charles – 1806–1872)

BIOGRAPHY

The most prolific and most famous of nineteenth-century Irish novelists. Born in Dublin on August 31, 1806 (the date adopted by L. Stevenson, the author of the most recent printed biography, and not 1809 as will be found in a certain number of other works), into a family of English origin. Attended classes in various schools in the capital before enrolling at Trinity College (B.A.: 1827) where he showed himself to be more gifted for practical jokes than for medicine which he made his profession, practising from 1831 to 1836 in various provincial market-towns. It was in this period that, under the influence of W. H. Maxwell (q.v.) he began to write. He is to be found in Brussels in 1837 as doctor to the British legation, a post that he abandoned in the face of his increasing literary success. From 1841 to 1845, in Dublin, he was editor of *The Dublin University Magazine*. In his house at Templeogue, he received numerous celebrities including W. M. Thackeray. He took to the road again in 1845: Brussels once more, Germany, Switzerland, Italy; he settled in Florence in 1847, then in Spezia. He was not to leave Italy except for brief visits to London and Dublin. Was British consul in Trieste in 1867. Died there on May 31, 1872.

BIBLIOGRAPHY

(a) Works before 1850:

1837– THE CONFESSIONS OF HARRY LORREQUER.
40. (*Dublin University Magazine*; Feb. 1837, IX, 50, p. 145 to Feb. 1840, XV, 86, pp. 159–70, 20 instalments, 53 chapters.)
Volume: _____ illustrated by Phiz.
Dublin: W. Curry, June & Co.; Edinburgh: Fraser and Crawford, 1839, XV + 344 p.

1839– 'CONTINENTAL GOSSIPINGS by Harry Lorrequer'.
47. (*Dublin University Magazine:*
Ch. 1: XIII, 76, April 1839, p. 426.
Ch. 2, 3: XIII, 77, May 1839, p. 565.
Ch. 4, 5, 6: XIV, 79, July 1839, p. 23.
'A Chapter of Continental Gossip': XXIX, 173, May 1847, p. 541.)

1840– CHARLES O'MALLEY, THE IRISH DRAGOON.
41. (*Dublin University Magazine*: Mar. 1840, XV, 87, p. 345, to Dec. 1841, XVIII, 108, pp. 643–78, 22 instalments, 122 chapters.)
Volume: _____ edited by Harry Lorrequer, with illustrations by Phiz. Dublin: W. Curry, etc., 1841, 2 v. I: IX + 648 p. II: VII + 336 p.

1842– NUTS AND NUTCRACKERS.
45.   (*Dublin University Magazine:* Jan. 1842, XIX, 109, p. 111, to May 1844, XXIII, 137, pp. 530–3, 12 issues.)
Volume: _____ London: Orr; Dublin: Curry, 1845, 8 + 232 p.

1842– OUR MESS; JACK HINTON, THE GUARDSMAN.
43.   (*Dublin University Magazine:* Mar. 1842, XIX, 111, p. 293, to Dec. 1842, XX, 120, pp. 635–58, 11 instalments, 62 chapters.)
Volume: _____ Dublin: W. Curry, etc., 1843, X + 396 p.

1843. ARTHUR O'LEARY.
(*Dublin University Magazine:* 'Loiterings of Arthur O'Leary, by the editor': Jan. 1843, XXI, 121, p. 1, to Dec. 1843, XXII, pp. 635–54, 10 instalments, 14 sections).
Volume: _____ : *His Wanderings and Ponderings in many lands*, edited by his friend, Harry Lorrequer, illustrated by G. Cruikshank.
London: Colburn, 1844, 3 v., I: 290 p. II: 320 p. III: 328 p.

1844. (OUR MESS, II:) TOM BURKE OF 'OURS'.
Dublin: W. Curry, etc., 1844, 2 v.
(Volume I contains *Jack Hinton* (cf. *supra*). Volumes II (xi + 372 p.) and III (x + 290 p.) *Tom Burke*.)

1845. TALES OF THE TRAINS; being some chapters of railroad romance, by Tilbury Tramp, Queen's messenger.
(*Dublin University Magazine:* Jan. 1845, XXV, 145, p. 1, to May 1845, XXV, 149, pp. 519–27, 5 instalments, 5 parts.)
Volume: _____ London: Orr; Dublin: Curry, 1845, VIII + 356 p.

THE O'DONOGHUE, a Tale of Ireland Fifty Years Ago, illustrated by H. K. Browne.
Dublin: W. Curry, etc., 1845, XI + 410 p.

ST PATRICK'S EVE, illustrated by Phiz.
London: Chapman & Hall, 1845, 203 p.

1846 THE KNIGHT OF GWYNNE, a Tale of the Time of the Union.
–47.   (Monthly instalments: Jan. 1846–July 1847.)
Volume: _____ London: Chapman & Hall, 1847, 628 p., illustrations by Phiz.

[**1848.** HORACE TEMPLETON.
(The undated edition seen by the present author:
Philadelphia: T. B. Peterson, carries this title and is
subtitled, *an autobiography.* According to L. Stevenson,
the first edition: London: Chapman and Hall, 1848, 2 v., is
entitled:
Diary and Notes of Horace Templeton, Esq., Late
Secretary of Legation at   .)]

1848   ROLAND CASHEL.
–50.   (Monthly instalments: May 1848, November 1849.)
Volume: _____ with illustrations by Phiz.
London: Chapman & Hall, 1850, VIII + 627 p.

1850? CONFESSIONS OF CON GREGAN, THE IRISH GIL BLAS.
with illustrations ... by H. K. Browne.
London: W. S. Orr & Co., n.d., [1849? 1850?]
(After its appearance in monthly instalments also
undated.)

1850– MAURICE TIERNAY, THE SOLDIER OF FORTUNE.
5?   (Began to appear in *Dublin University Magazine:* XXXV,
208, p. 411, and ran until Dec. 1851. Published in book
form in 1852 says Brown, with no other details.
London: Hodgson, n.d. [1855 according to the catalogue in
the British Museum.]

(b) Works after 1850:

1852. THE DALTONS; *or, Three Roads in Life.*
London: Chapman & Hall, 1852, 2 v.

1852– SIR JASPER CAREW, *his Life and Experiences.*
55.   *Dublin University Magazine:* July 1852 – June 1854.
London: T. Hodgson, n.d., [1855?].

1852– THE DODD FAMILY ABROAD.
54.   Instalments: Sept. 1852–April 1854.
London: Chapman & Hall, 1854.

1854– THE MARTINS OF CRO' MARTIN.
56.   Instalments: Dec. 1854–June 1856.
London: Chapman & Hall, 1856.

1855– THE FORTUNES OF GLENCORE.
57.   *Dublin University Magazine:* Aug. 1855–April 1857.
London: Chapman & Hall, 1857, 3 v.

1857– DAVENPORT DUNN, a *Man of Our Day*.
59.   Instalments: July 1857–April 1859.
           London: Chapman & Hall, 1859.

1858–? GERALD FITZGERALD, '*The Chevalier*'.
           Dublin University Magazine: Jan. 1858–July 1859.
           New York: Harper, n.d.

1859– ONE OF THEM.
61.   Instalments: Dec. 1859–Jan. 1861.
           London: Chapman & Hall, 1861.

1860– A DAY'S RIDE, a *Life's Romance*.
62.   *All the Year Round:* 18 August 1860 to 23 Mar. 1861.
           London: Chapman & Hall, 1862.

1862– BARRINGTON.
63.   Instalments: Feb. 1862 to Jan. 1863.
           London: Chapman & Hall, 1863.

1863   TONY BUTLER.
65.   *Blackwood's Magazine:* Oct. 1863–Jan. 1865.
           Edinburgh & London: Blackwood, 1865.

           LUTTRELL OF ARAN.
           Instalments: Dec. 1863 to Feb. 1865.
           London: Chapman & Hall, 1865.

1864– CORNELIUS O'DOWD.
72.   *Blackwood's:* Feb. 1864–May 1872.
           Edinburgh & London: Blackwood, 3 v.
           I: 1864; II, III: 1865.

1865– SIR BROOK FOSSBROOKE.
66.   *Blackwood's:* May 1865–Nov. 1866.
           Edinburgh & London: Blackwood, 1866, 3 v.

1867– THE BRAMLEIGHS OF BISHOP'S FOLLY.
68.   *Cornhill Magazine:* June 1867–Oct. 1868.
           London: Smith, Elder & Co, 1868, 3 v.

1868. PAUL GOSLETT'S CONFESSIONS.
           St Paul's Magazine: Mar.–May 1868.
           London: Virtue, 1868.

1868– THAT BOY OF NORCOTT'S.
69.   *Cornhill:* Nov. 1868–Mar. 1869.
           London: Smith, Elder & Co, 1869.

1869. A RENT IN A CLOUD.
           London: Chapman & Hall, 1869.

1869– 'SHAMROCKIANA'.
70. *Cornhill:* Dec. 1869–Mar. 1870.

1870– LORD KILGOBLIN: A Tale of Ireland in Our Own Time.
72. *Cornhill:* Oct. 1870–Mar. 1872.
London: Smith, Elder & Co, 1872, 3 v.

The complete works appeared in 34 v. in 1876–4, in 37 v. in 1897–9, and in 32 v. in Boston in 1902.

(c) Secondary material, etc.:

General studies, particularly: Baker (E.A.): *The History of the English Novel*, Vol. VII, pp. 49–61, Buckley, (M.) q.v. in the general bibliography.

Specialised studies:

POE (Edgar A.): 'Essay on "Charles O'Malley" ', *Collected Works* (J. H. Ingram, ed.), 1875, Vol. IV.

FITZPATRICK (W. J.): *The Life of Charles Lever*, London: Ward, Lock & Co., 1879, 1884 (revised), XII + 392 p.

DOWNEY (E.): *Charles Lever: His Life in his Letters*, Edinburgh & London: W. Blackwood and Sons, 1906, 2 v. I: XII + 395 p. II: 414 p.

WALDMANN (K.): *Charles Lever*, University of Marburg, 1913.

DICKENS (Charles): *Letters to Charles Lever*, edited by F. V. Livingston, Cambridge, Massachussetts, 1933.

STEVENSON (Lionel): *Dr Quicksilver, The Life of Charles Lever*, London: Chapman & Hall, 1939, VII + 308 p., reprinted 1969.

ABERNETHY (Dermot): *Charles Lever, Irish Novelist*, unpublished B. Litt. thesis: Trinity College, Dublin, Oct. 1954, 314 + XXV p.

O'KEEFE (Thomas P.): *Charles Lever. A Study of 19th Century Anglo–Irish Fiction*, unpublished thesis, U.C.D., 1972.

JEFFARES (A. N.): 'Lever's Lord Kilgoblin', *Essays and Studies*, 1975.

LOVER (Samuel – 1797–1868)

BIOGRAPHY

A poet, novelist, playwright, illustrator and musician, this talented Jack-of-all-trades unfortunately did not manage to become really great in any *genre.*

Born in Dublin on February 24, 1797. Father a broker. Attempted to join the paternal firm but very soon abandoned it for the fine arts and then for literature. Settled in London in 1835, he frequented Lady Blessington's circle.

Dickens's partner in launching *Bentley's Miscellany* and, in a general way, an important figure in the world of letters. His success was heightened further from 1844 onwards after he started his famous 'Irish evenings' at which he sang, recited or acted works of his own authorship. America received him with enthusiasm in 1846. Died in the course of a trip to Jersey, on July 6, 1868.

BIBLIOGRAPHY

(a) Miscellaneous prose:

1831– LEGENDS AND STORIES OF IRELAND.
34. 1st SERIES: Dublin: Wakeman, 2nd edition, 1832, XXIII + 254 p. with 6 etchings by the author (the 1st edition may date from 1831).
It contains:
'King O'Toole and St Kevin'; 'Lough Corrib'; 'Ms. from the Cabinet of Mrs —'; 'The White Trout'; 'The Battle of the Berrins'; 'Father Roach'; 'The Priest's Story'; 'The King and the Bishop'; 'A Legend of Clonmacnoise'; 'An Essay on Fools'; 'The Catastrophe'; 'The Devil's Mill'; 'The Gridiron'; 'Paddy the Piper'; 'The Priest's Ghost'; 'New Potatoes'; 'Paddy the Sport'; 'Ballad and Ballad Singers'.

2nd SERIES: London: Baldwin, 1834, X + 324 p.
This time the illustrations are not all by the author, W. Harvey contributed. The volume is dedicated to Th. Moore.
Contains:
'Barny O'Reirdon, the Navigator'; (had appeared in the *Dublin University Magazine:* I, 1, Jan. 1833, p. 17, 2, Feb. p. 127.); 'The Burial of the Tithe'; 'The White Horse of the Peppers'; 'The Curse of Kishogue'; 'The Fairy Finder';

'The Leprechaun and the Genius'; 'The Spanish Boar and the Irish Bull'; 'Little Fairy' (*Dublin University Magazine*, I, 4 April 1833); 'Judy of Roundwood'.
In his 1889 re-issue, D. J. O'Donoghue adds to the 2 volumes that he prefaced, a 3rd volume constituting a 3rd SERIES: Westminster: A. Constable, 1889, XXVIII + 219 p. under the title *Further Stories of Ireland, Miscellaneous Stories, Sketches, etc* ... consisting of:
'St Patrick & the Serpent'; 'It's Mighty Improvin' '; 'The Irish Post Boy'; 'Dublin Porters, Carmen and Waiters'; 'The Irish Brigade'; 'Paddy at Sea'; 'Illustrations of National Proverbs' (these had appeared in 1833 in *The Irish Penny Magazine*, the first of them in Volume I, n° 5, p. 37); 'The Happy Man' (1839, q.v. dramatic works).)

1834. POPULAR TALES AND LEGENDS OF THE IRISH PEASANTRY.
Dublin: W. F. Wakeman, 1834, 404 p.
(In placing this anthology among Lover's prose works an (unfortunate) tradition is being followed since, it seems, only the illustrations are by him, the text being by Carleton (2 items), Mrs Hall (1 item), D. O'Donoho (sic?), etc.).

1837. RORY O'MORE, a National Romance.
London: Bentley and Sons, 1837, 3 v.
I: 300 p. II: 300 p. III: 315 p. (Ill. by the author).

1842. HANDY ANDY, a Tale of Irish Life.
London: F. Lover, 1842, IV + 380 p., with 24 ill. by the author.
(Note the modern edition: 'with an introduction by John D. Sheridan', London: Dent, 1954, (Everyman's n° 178).)

1844. TREASURE TROVE ... a series of Accounts of Irish Heirs, being a romantic Irish tale of the last century ... with 26 ill. on steel by the author.
London: F. Lover, 1844, IV + 411 p.
(The cover of the monthly instalments that preceded the publication in book form bore the title *£–S–D; or, Accounts of Irish Heirs*, furnished to the public monthly by Samuel Lover, accountant for Irish inheritances.
London: F. Lover & R. Groombridge.)

1845. CHARACTERISTIC SKETCHES OF IRELAND AND THE IRISH ... with etchings by Kirkwood.
Dublin: P. D. Hardy & Sons, 1845, 288 p.
(Also contains stories by Carleton and Mrs Hall.
Those by Lover are:
'Paddy Mullonney's Travels in France' (211); 'A Legend of Clonmacnoise' (225); 'Ballads and Ballad singers', these last two had already appeared in *Legends and Stories*.)

(b) Poetry:

1831. THE PARSON'S HORN BOOK.
Dublin: printed and sold at the office of *The Comet*, 1831, 136 p., ill.
(The illustrations are by Lover as, doubtless, are part of the satirical verses.)

1839. SONGS AND BALLADS.
London: Chapman & Hall, 1839, XII + 135 p.
(Divided into 2 parts:
'Songs of the Superstitions of Ireland' (cf. 'Rory O'More', p. 7), 12 titles.
'Legendary Ballads and Miscellaneous Songs', 64 titles.)

1840. ENGLISH BIJOU ALMANACK FOR 1840 poetically illustrated by S. Lover.
London: A. Schloss, in-64°.

1844. MR LOVER'S IRISH EVENINGS: THE IRISH BRIGADE.
London: Johnson, 1844, 12 p.

1858. THE LYRICS OF IRELAND edited and annotated by S. Lover.
London: Houlston & Wright, 1858, XXV + 360 p.
(An anthology of various poets, it contains a certain number of pieces by Lover.)

1859. RIVAL RHYMES, IN HONOUR OF BURNS; with curious illustrative matter.
Collected and edited by Ben Trovato.
London: Routledge, etc., 1859, 144 p.
(pastiches).

1860. METRICAL TALES *and Other Poems.*
London: Houlston & Wright, 1860, 127 p., ill.
('The Fisherman'; 'Father Roach'; 'The Blacksmith'; 'The Dew-Drop'; 'The Crooked Stick'; 'To Mary'; 'The Flooded Hut of the Mississipi'; 'Nymph of Niagara'; 'The Flower of Night'; 'The Forsaken'; 'Yearning'; 'Love and Death'.)

1861. ORIGINAL SONGS FOR THE RIFLE VOLUNTEERS.
London: C. H. Clarke, VIII + 101 p.
(In collaboration with Charles Mackay and Thomas Miller.)

? THE POETICAL WORKS OF SAMUEL LOVER.
London & New York: Routledge & Sons, XXIV + 506 p., ill.
(Contains: Preface; 'Songs of the Superstitions of Ireland'; 'Legendary and Traditional Ballads'; 'Songs of the Rifle Volunteers'; 'American Subjects'; 'Miscellaneous Songs'; 'Metrical Tales and Miscellaneous Poems'; 'Imitations of Some Popular Authors'.)

(c) Theatrical works:

1835. (9.11, OLYM.) THE BEAU IDEAL.
(unpublished).

(26.12, OLYM.) THE OLYMPIC PICNIC.
(unpublished).

1837. (25.9, ADEL.) RORY O'MORE, a comic drama, in 3 acts.
London: Dick's Standard Plays, n° 356, 23 p.

1838. (26.5, HAY.) THE WHITE HORSE OF THE PEPPERS,
a comic drama, in 2 acts.
London: Acting National Drama, Vol. V, 35 p.

1839. (20.5, HAY.) THE HAPPY MAN, an extravaganza, in 1 act.
ibid., Vol. VII, 20 p.

(26.7, E.O.H.) THE HALL PORTER, a comic drama, in 2 acts.
ibid., Vol. VII, 31 p.

1840. (29.9, C.G.) THE GREEK BOY,
a musical drama, in 2 acts.
ibid., Vol. IX, 33 p.

1841.   (22.4, E.O.H.) IL PADDY WHACK IN ITALIA,
an operetta, in 1 act.
London: Duncombe's British Theatre, Vol. XLIV, 30 p.

1850.   (Nov., N.N.T.) BARNEY THE BARON, a farce, in 1 act.
London: Dicks Standard Plays, n° 328.

1854.   (18.11, HAY.) THE SENTINEL OF THE ALMA.
-(unpublished).

1861.   (1.4, LYC.) MAC CARTHY MORE; or, *Possession Nine Points of the Law*,
a comic drama, in 2 acts.
London: Lacy, Vol. LI.
(d) Secondary material, etc.:

General works (on the novel, poetry, the theatre) *D.N.B., Cambridge*, etc. Also:

BERNARD (W. B.): *The Life of S. Lover, R.H.A., Artistic, Literary and Musical*, with selections from his unpublished papers and correspondence.
London: H. S. King, 1874, 2 v.

SYMINGTON (A. J.): *Samuel Lover*, a Bibliographical Sketch with Selections from his Writings and Correspondence.
London: Blackie & Son, 1880, X + 256 p.

LUTTRELL (Henry – 1765(?)–1851)

BIOGRAPHY

Born in Dublin between 1765 and 1767, the natural son of Lord Carhampton. Was a member of the Irish parliament in 1798 and, after the Union, settled in London where he enjoyed a high reputation as a man of wit in fashionable circles and was friendly with the glories of the day: Campbell, Macaulay, Moore (who speaks of him in his diary), etc. Died there in 1851.

BIBLIOGRAPHY

Luttrell contributed to *The Times* in 1826–7 and *Keepsake* in 1829. His works in book form are:

1819. LINES WRITTEN AT AMPTHILL PARK IN THE AUTUMN
OF 1818.
London: J. Murray, 1819, 46 p.

1820. ADVICE TO JULIA, a letter in rhyme.
London: J. Murray, 1820, 236 p. (good manners, in verse).

1822? LETTERS TO JULIA in Rhyme – To which are added *Lines
Written at Ampthill Park.*
London: J. Murray, 1822, third edition, XX + 265 p.

1827. CROCKFORD HOUSE, a rhapsody, in two cantos; *A
Rhymer in Rome.*
London: J. Murray, 1827, 147 p.

and, perhaps, the same year, the following work that is also
attributed to Croly:

> MAY FAIR, in four cantos.
> London: Ainsworth, 1827, 194 p.

Two ARTICLES on the author should be pointed out:

DOBSON (A.): 'A Forgotten Poet of Society', *St James's Magazine,*
XXXIII, 1878.

CROSSE (A.): 'An Old Society Wit', *Temple Bar*, CIV, 1895.

LYNCH (Patrick – 1757–?)

The present author has not been able to establish beyond doubt
whether Bunting's collaborator and the intriguing character here in
question are really one and the same person.

Born in Quin, County Clare, developed very early a fascination
for the classics and mnemonic methods, cf. these two titles of 1817:

> [THE CLASSICAL STUDENT'S METRICAL MNEMONICS,
> containing, in familiar verse, all the necessary definitions
> and rules of the English, Latin, Greek and Hebrew
> languages ...

and

AN EASY INTRODUCTION TO PRACTICAL ASTRONOMY,
And the Use of the Globes, including in mnemonic verses
and rhymic couplets, as the most effectual means hitherto
invented for assisting the memory – the necessary axioms,
definitions, and rules of Chronology, Algebra and
Trigonometry, with the prognostics of the weather ...]

He had previously published, in 1815:

[AN INTRODUCTION TO THE KNOWLEDGE OF THE IRISH
LANGUAGE.]

One reference work holds that he died in 1818, another attributes to
him a *Life of St Patrick* (1828) and claims that he died about 1830.

LYSAGHT (Edward – 1763–1810(?))

Born in Brickhill, County Clare, on December 21, 1763. Studied
at Trinity. A lawyer, a man of wit and the godfather of Lady
Morgan. Died in 1810 or 1811. Published a single volume in which
there are some extremely pleasant pieces.

1811.   POEMS, by the late Edward Lysaght, Esq. Barrister at
Law ...
Dublin: Gilbert & Hodges, 1811, XXII + 110 p.

Mc BRIDE (John)

Author of the following poetical collections:

1828.   [THE AGITATOR, Dublin.

1832.   THE ANTI-UNION MELODIST, Dublin.

?   THE IRISH VOLUNTEERS, Dublin, 3rd ed., 1833.

?   THE O'CONNELLITE; *or, Patriot's Companion.*

1839.   VICTORIA REGINA, Belfast.]

Mc CANN (Michael Joseph – 1824(?)–1883)

A contributor to *The Nation* (cf. 'The Clanconnel War Song', January 28, 1843, etc.).

Mc CARTHY (Denis Florence – 1817–1882)

BIOGRAPHY

Born in Dublin on May 1817 into a Catholic family. Studied at Maynooth, but abandoned the idea of the priesthood as he was later to abandon Law to which he had devoted himself on leaving the seminary, and became a professor of English literature in the new Catholic university. A partisan of Repeal, he contributed to *The Nation* and took part in the Young Ireland movement. A talented translator. Died at Blackrock on April 7, 1882.

BIBLIOGRAPHY

The volumes of translations, particularly from the Spanish (Calderon) are omitted.

1843. Several poems previously published in *The Nation*, etc., are collected in:

THE SPIRIT OF THE NATION (q.v. in the list of periodicals under the name of the paper). Also, 1894: THE NEW SPIRIT OF THE NATION (q.v. ibid.)

1846. THE POETS AND DRAMATISTS OF IRELAND with an introduction on the early religion and literature of the Irish people.
Dublin: J. Duffy, 1846, XII + 252 p.
(An anthology of 18th-century authors edited by D. F. Mc Carthy.)

THE BOOK OF IRISH BALLADS edited by D. F. Mc Carthy. Dublin: J. Duffy; London: Simpkin & Marshall, 1846, IX + 252 p.
(The anthology dedicated to Samuel Ferguson, comprises the following subdivisions:
'Ballads illustrative of Fairy Mythology and Traditions'.

'Ballads illustrative of Superstitions and Customs of Ireland'.
'Historical Ballads'.
'Descriptive Ballads'.
'Legendary Ballads'.
'Ballads of the Affections'.
'Political Ballads'.
'Miscellaneous'.
The large majority of the poems bears the signature of well-known Irish writers of the time.)

1847–
49.   in The *Dublin University Magazine:*
'THE FORAY OF O'DONNELL, A.D. 1495'.
XXX, 172, April 1847, p. 488 (a long narrative poem).

'THE BELL-FOUNDER'.
XXX, 177, Sept. 1847, p. 279 (id.)

'THE VOYAGE OF ST BRENDAN'.
XXXI, 181, Jan. 1848, p. 89, (id.).

'THE BRIDAL OF THE YEAR; SUMMER LONGINGS'.
XXXI, 185, May 1848, p. 642, (poems).

'SCENES AND STORIES FROM THE SPANISH STAGE: THE SECRET IN WORDS'.
XXXII, 187, July 1848, p. 1.

'THE ANGEL OF TOIL'.
XXXII, 188, Aug. 1848, p. 119 (a story).

'SCENES AND STORIES FROM THE SPANISH STAGE, II'.
XXXII, 191, Nov. 1848, p. 518.

'SOUNDS AND ECHOES'.
XXXII, 192, Dec. 1848, p. 648 (translated poems).

'SCENES AND STORIES FROM THE SPANISH STAGE, III'.
XXXIV, 200, Aug. 1849, p. 139.

'A SEPTEMBER GARLAND'.
XXXIV, 201, Sept. 1849, p. 305 (translated poems).

'MOORISH ROMANCES AND GERMAN BALLADS'.
XXXIV, 203, Nov. 1849, p. 541 (translated poems).

1850.   BALLADS, POEMS AND LYRICS, original and translated.
Dublin: J. M'Glashan, 1850, X + 388 p.

(Contains the three long narrative poems that head this list of contributions by Mc Carthy to the *Dublin University Magazine*, then: 'Ballads and Lyrics' (11–164); 'National Poems & Songs' (167–203); 'Miscellaneous Poems, Translations'.)

Note, after 1850:

1857.   UNDER-GLIMPSE, *and Other Poems.*
London: D. Bogue, 1857.

THE BELL-FOUNDER *and Other Poems.*
ibid., 1857 (re-titled *Irish Legends and Lyrics* in the Dublin edition of 1858).

1872.   SHELLEY'S EARLY LIFE.
London: J. C. Hotten, 1872 (a biography).

1879.   THE CENTENARY OF MOORE, an Ode.
London: privately printed, 1879.

1882.   POEMS.
Dublin: Gill & Son, 1882.

Mac DONNELL (Æneas – 1783–1858)

Born in Westport, County Mayo, a lawyer and defender of Catholic interests for which he wrote countless pamphlets. The author of a novel set in his native district:

THE HERMIT OF GLENCONELLA, a tale.
London: G. Cowie & Co, 1820, VI + 293 p.

Mc GEE (Thomas D'Arcy – 1825–1868)

BIOGRAPHY

Born in Carlingford, County Louth, into a family of Ulster origin. Studied in Wexford. Went to America in 1842, ran the *Boston Pilot* there and was correspondent of *The Freeman's Journal*. Contributed to *The Nation* and, back in Ireland, became secretary of the committee of the Irish Confederation in 1847. After the 1848 uprising, fled to the New World, first to the United

States where he headed The New York *Nation* (1848) and *The American Celt* (1850), then to Montreal where he launched *The New Era*, became a member of Parliament in 1857 and played an increasingly important part in the political life of Canada. A revolutionary turned conservative and considered a traitor to the Fenian cause, he was murdered in the streets of Ottawa on April 7, 1868.

BIBLIOGRAPHY

This has been established by J. COLEMAN: 'Bibliography of T. d'Arcy Mc Gee', *Bibliographical Society of Ireland Publications*, vol. II, n° 7, 1925, pp. 135–9.

Before 1850, there are no poems published in book form although numerous pieces had appeared in periodicals prior to this date. There are, on the other hand:

1844. HISTORICAL SKETCHES OF O'CONNELL AND HIS FRIENDS, including ... Th. Moore ... Th. Furlong, R. L. Shiel ... Th. A. Emmet ... etc., with a glance at the future destiny of Ireland.
Boston: Donahoe & Rohan, 1844, 208 p.

[EVA MC DONALD, a Tale of the United Irishmen, 1844.]

1846. GALLERY OF IRISH WRITERS: *The Irish Writers of the XVIIth Century.*
Dublin: Duffy, 1846, X + 252 p.

1847. A MEMOIR OF THE LIFE AND CONQUEST OF ART MC MURROGH *King of Leinster, from A.D. 1377 to A.D. 1417.* With some notices of the Leinster wars of the fourteenth-century.
Dublin: Duffy, 1847, XXIII + 204 p.

1849. MEMOIR OF CHARLES GAVAN DUFFY.
Dublin: W. Hogan, 1849, 32 p.

After 1850, note the following titles:

1852. POEMS.
Dublin: reprinted for *The Nation*, 1852.

1853. A HISTORY OF THE ATTEMPTS TO ESTABLISH THE PROTESTANT REFORMATION IN IRELAND ...
Boston, 1853.

1858. CANADIAN BALLADS AND OCCASIONAL VERSES.
Montreal: Lovel, 1858.

1862. A POPULAR HISTORY OF IRELAND.
Glasgow: Cameron & Ferguson, 1862.

1869. THE POEMS OF THOMAS D'ARCY MC GEE.
London, New York, Montreal: Sadleir & Co, 1869,
XII + 612 p.
(Contains a biography and the complete poetical works,
rich in nationalistic material.)

More on account of his political influence than his writings,
numerous Studies, etc., have been devoted to the author. Cf. within
the limits of the twentieth-century:

HARVEY (D. C.): *Thomas D'Arcy Mc Gee, The Prophet of
Canadian Nationality*, University of Manitoba, 1923, 30 p.

SKELTON (I. M.): *The Life of Thomas D'Arcy Mc Gee*, Garden-
vale (Canada): Garden City Press, 1925, VI + 554 p.

BRADY (A.): *Thomas D'Arcy Mc Gee*, Toronto: Macmillan, 1925,
182 p.

PHELAN (J.): *The Ardent Exile: The Life and Times of Thomas
D'Arcy Mc Gee*, Toronto: Macmillan, 1951, X + 317 p.

Mc GREGOR (Patrick)

Author of:

THE GENUINE REMAINS OF OSSIAN literally translated; with a
preliminary dissertation ... Published under the patronage of
the Highland Society of London.
London: Smith, Elder & Co, etc., 1841, VII + 537 p.

Mc HENRY (James – 1785–1845)

BIOGRAPHY

Born in Larne on December 20, 1785. Studied in Dublin and
Glasgow where he obtained a medical degree. Emigrated
immediately to the United States where, in Philadelphia, he was

editor of *The American Monthly Magazine*. Was nominated
United States consul in Derry in 1842, and died in his native town
on June 21, 1845.

BIBLIOGRAPHY

(a) Poetical and dramatic works:

It is particularly as a novelist that Mc Henry is known. However,
he figures prominently in D. J. O'Donoghue for the quantity if not
the quality of his poetical writings, cf.:

1808. THE BARD OF ERIN *and Other Poems,*
Belfast: printed by Smyth, 1808, 8 + 80 p.

1810. [PATRICK, a poetical tale of 1798, Glasgow.

1822. THE PLEASURES OF FRIENDSHIP, Philadelphia; reprinted
in London in 1825 under the title: *The Blessings of
Friendship.* The present author has only seen an edition
bearing the original title published in Philadelphia in 1834
by Grigg and Elliot (200 p.)

1823. WALTHAM, an American Revolutionary Tale in 3 Cantos,
New York.

1829. THE JACKSON WREATH.

1830. THE FEELINGS OF AGE: THE STAR OF LOVE, Philadelphia.

1839. BRITANNIA, an Ode, London.

THE ANTEDILUVIANS; *or, The World Destroyed,* a poem
in ten books, London.]

And the author of *The Poets of Ireland* also attributes to him the
following plays:

[WHICH SHALL I MARRY? (a musical comedy).

GERTRUDE OF WYOMING (a drama).

GENIUS (a comedy).

THE USURPER (an historical tragedy performed in 1827,
published in Philadelphia in 1829).]

(b) Novels:

1823. [THE WILDERNESS, New York.]

1824.   O'HALLORAN; *or, The Insurgent Chief*, Philadelphia.
(The edition that the present author has read (Belfast:
Henderson, 480 p.) is of 1847. This novel was also
published under the title:
THE INSURGENT CHIEF; *or, The Pikemen of 1798* (cf.
National Library, Dublin, Ir 82379 M 1).)

1825.   THE HEARTS OF STEEL, an Irish historical romance of the
last century.
The edition consulted by the present author, that is
obviously not the first, is the undated edition by Cameron
and Ferguson, Glasgow (149 p.).

1831.   [MEREDITH.]
The first and last titles are taken from Brian Cleeve.

Mac KENZIE (Andrew – 1780–1839)

Born in Dunover, County Down, the author of poems published
in the Belfast papers and of two collections:

1810.   POEMS AND SONGS ON DIFFERENT SUBJECTS.
Belfast: printed by Alexander Mackay, 1810, 10 + (14) +
37 + 184 p.

[1823.   (according to F. J. Bigger in *The Irish Book Lover.* III,
n° 2, July 1912: 'The Bard of Dunover', pp. 197–9).

or

1832.   (according to O'Donoghue):
THE MASONIC CHAPLET *and Other Poems*, Belfast.]

MACLISE (Daniel – 1806–1870)

The most famous Irish artist of the time, born in Cork, a
contributor to *Fraser's Magazine*, and the illustrator of numerous
novels, etc., under his real name or the pseudonym 'Alfred Croquis'.
Also wrote at least one poem, the humorous 'Merry Xmas in the
Baron's Hall' (*Fraser's*, May 1838).

Mac NEVIN (Thomas – 1810–1848)

A nationalist historian, born near Galway, died in Bristol. The author of the following works:

1831. GERALD, a national dramatic poem, in 3 acts, founded on the invasion of Ireland by Henry III.
Dublin: printed by J. Blundell, 1831, 24 p.

1844. THE LEADING STATE TRIALS OF IRELAND *from the year 1784 to 1803 ...*
Dublin: Duffy, 1844, 598 p.

1845? THE HISTORY OF THE VOLUNTEERS OF 1782.
Dublin: Duffy, 1845, 4th edition, VI + 250 p.

1846. CHARACTERS OF GREAT MEN AND THE DUTIES OF PATRIOTISM.
Dublin: J. M'Glashan, 1846, 34 p.

THE CONFISCATION OF ULSTER IN THE REIGN OF JAMES I *commonly called the Ulster Plantation.*
Dublin: Duffy; London: Simpkin, Marshall & Co, 1846, VIII + 260 p.

THE LIVES AND TRIALS OF H. ROWAN, THE REV. W. JACKSON, THE DEFENDERS, W. ORR, FINNERTY, etc.
Dublin: Duffy, 1846, 598 p.

MACREADY (William – 1755(?)–1829)

BIOGRAPHY

Born in Dublin. Father an upholsterer. A professional actor, he first worked in a touring company then in Smock Alley, Dublin, before leaving for Liverpool and Manchester on the recommendation of Macklin. In Manchester, he married Christina Ann Birch on June 18, 1786. From this union came the famous actor, one of the greatest of the nineteenth-century, William Charles Macready (1792–1873). For 12 years, starting from September 1786, W. Macready acted at Covent Garden. He then became manager of provincial theatres and this quite regularly led him to bankruptcy. He is the author of three plays.

BIBLIOGRAPHY

1787. (28.8, HAY.) THE VILLAGE LAWYER, a farce, in two
acts ...
(Nicoll gives 1795 as the date of publication. The present
author has been able to consult only the 5th edition of this
play inspired by *La Farce de Maître Patelin*: Dublin: P.
Byrne, 1801, 24 p.)

1792. (21.4, C.G.) THE IRISHMAN IN LONDON; *or, The Happy
African*, a farce, in two acts ...
London: T. N. Longman, 1793, 37 p.
(Based on *The Intriguing Footman*, a play by J. Whiteley,
Sheffield, 1791.)

1795. (1.5, C.G.) THE BANK NOTE; *or, Lessons for Ladies*, a
comedy, in five acts ...
London: T. N. Longman, 1795, 84 p.
(inspired by *The Artful Husband* by W. Taverner.)

On the author, besides Bartley (*Teague*), Duggan (*Stage Irishman*)
and Kavanagh (*The Irish Theatre*), q.v. in the general bibliography,
see:

DOWNER (Alan S.): *The Eminent Tragedian William Charles
Macready*, Cambridge, Mas.: Harvard University Press, 1966,
XIV + 392 p., ill.
(Although, as the title indicates, the work deals with the son,
there are also some extremely interesting glimpses of the
father's career, his familial and financial difficulties, etc.)

MACREADY (William Ch.): *The Journal of William Charles
Macready, 1832–1851* abridged and edited by J. C. Trewin,
London: Longmans,1967, 315 p.

MADDEN (Richard Robert – 1798–1886)

An indefatigable character in his role of doctor, magistrate,
defender of the oppressed in Jamaica, Havana, Australia and
Ireland, and also writer of many works among which those
following may be mentioned:

1846. LITERARY REMAINS OF THE UNITED IRISHMEN OF 1798.

(The edition from which the present author has worked is the following:
Dublin: J. Duffy, 1887, xix + 360 p.).

1847.   THE LIFE AND TIMES OF ROBERT EMMET ESQ.
Dublin: J. Duffy, 1847, 343 p.

1867.   THE HISTORY OF IRISH PERIODICAL LITERATURE *from the end of the XVIIth century to the middle of the XIXth century. Its origin, progress, and results.*
London: T. C. Newby, 1867, 2 v., I: VII + 338 p., II: 531 p.

MAGINN (William – 1794–1842)

BIOGRAPHY

Born in Cork, son of the headmaster of a school in Marlboro Street, an original and remarkable teacher. Entered Trinity College, Dublin, in 1806, several years younger than the requisite age. Showed himself to be extraordinarily gifted for languages. At 19, succeeded his father in the Marlboro Street school where he was headmaster for ten years, during which he also prepared himself for the ministry, and qualified as a lawyer at 25. He took an active part in the literary contests of Cork, 'The Athens of the South', in the course of which he made a bitter enemy of Samuel Carter Hall.

He then contributed to *The Advertiser* and the Cork *Freeholder*, the London *Literary Gazette* and *Blackwood's* in which his writings testify to the incredible variety of his genius. In 1823, he married Ellen Bullen, left for London, then Paris, at the end of 1824, as correspondent for *The Representative*. When he returned to the British capital, it was to carve out an important place in the world of journalism. In 1827, he became editor of *The Standard*. He later became the editor of *Fraser's*.

Despite a fairly considerable income for the time, Maginn was regularly in debt and escaped neither prison nor the slums nor the boisterous interventions of creditors. His emotional life was complicated by an unhappy episode in the course of his platonic relations with Letitia Landon, which hastened the disintegration of his character. There was a brief return to journalism in Liverpool in 1839 (*Lancaster Herald*). In 1842 he was again arrested for debt (some £10,000). His friends, (among whom was Thackeray) came to his aid once more, but his health was irreversibly damaged and he died of tuberculosis, four months after his release, on August 21, 1842 at Walton-on-Thames.

BIBLIOGRAPHY

(The catalogue in the British Museum attributes to Maginn the following works:

1828. MEMOIRS OF VIDOCQ, translated from the French,
London: Hunt & Clarke, 1828, 4 v., I: XXII + 237 p. II: XI + 266 p. III: XII + 251 p. IV: XII + 275 p.

1829. TALES OF MILITARY LIFE.
London: H. Colburn; 1829, 3 v., I: VII + 335 p. II: 322 p. III: 331 p.

1830. MEMOIRS OF MADAME DU BARRI, translated from the French,
London: Whittaker, 1830, 4 v., I: XXXIV + 357 p. II: XII + 348 p. III: XII + 347 p. IV: XI + 343 p.

and names the author as having collaborated on:

1832. FISHER'S DRAWING ROOM SCRAP BOOK with poetical illustrations by L(etitia) E(lizabeth) L(andon). London: Fisher, 1832.)

Works of certain authorship are:

1827. WHITEHALL; *or, The Days of George IV.*
London: W. Marsh, 1827, VI + 330 p. (a novel).

1841. MAGAZINE MISCELLANIES.
(no information regarding date or publisher), 160 p.
(Comprises reprintings from *Blackwood's* including a sort of autobiography: 'The Tobias Correspondence' that had originally appeared in July (XLIII, pp. 52–63) and August 1840 (205–14), and poems and stories from *Fraser's.*)

1844. JOHN MANESTY, THE LIVERPOOL MERCHANT by the late William Maginn, LL.D., with illustrations by George Cruikshank.
London: J. Mortimer, 1844, 2 v.
I: VII + 291 p. II: IV + 295 p. (a novel).

1849. MAXIMS OF SIR MORGAN O'DOHERTY, Bart.
Edinburgh & London: W. Blackwood & Sons, 1849, 138 p.

(142 maxims. 1st appearance in collaboration with Lockhart (n° I, II, III) and W. H. Forbes (III) in *Blackwood's:*
n° I: XV, 24 May, 597–605; n° II: XV, 24 June, 632–642; n° III: XVI, 24 Sept., 334–349.
O'Doherty, moreover, served as Maginn's pen name for numerous other articles in this magazine and *Fraser's.*)

1850. HOMERIC BALLADS with translations and notes by the late William Maginn, LL.D.
London: John W. Parker, 1850, XII + 300 p.
(Preface by John Churchill. Greek text opposite the translations originally published in *Fraser's* (XI, 582; XVII, 1, 251, 359, 506, 648, 728; XVIII, 71, 209, 367, 489, 621, 739; XXII, 383; XXV, 521; XXVI, 61, 439)).)

1854. NOCTES AMBROSIANÆ* by John Wilson ..., Wm. Maginn, LL.D., J. G. Lockhart, James Hogg and others, New York: 1854.
Revised edition with memoirs and notes by R. Skelton Mackenzie, New York: W. J. Middleton, 1863–6, 5 v.
(Vol. I, 1866: XXXII + 486 p.; II, 1863: XXXVI + 432 p.; III, 1866: XVI + 469 p.; IV, 1866: XXII + 468 p.; V, 1863: XXII (Memoir of W. Maginn) + portr. + 465 p.
The *Noctes* were originally published in *Blackwood's.*)

1855–   MISCELLANEOUS WRITINGS OF THE LATE DR MAG-
57.   INN, Edited by Dr Shelton Mackenzie.
New York: Redfield, 1855–7, 5 v.
(Vol. I, 1855: VIII + 374 p.: 'The O'Doherty Papers'.
II, 1855: VI + 383 p.: 'The O'Doherty Papers'.
III, 1856: 353 p.: 'The Shakespeare Papers'.
IV, 1856: 342 p.: 'Homeric Ballads and Translations and Comedies of Lucian.'
(The translations of Lucian had appeared in *Fraser's* like the pieces in the next volume: XIX, 89, 215, 470, 630, 732; XX, 300; XXI, 32.)
V, 1857: CX + 358 p.: 'The Fraserian Papers'.)

1857–   PHOTOGRAPHIC SIMILES OF THE ANTIQUE GEMS
59.   FORMERLY POSSESSED BY THE LATE PRINCE PONIA-
TOWSKI, accompanied by a description and poetical illustrations of each subject, carefully selected from classical authors, together with an essay on ancient gems and

gem-engraving by James Prendeville ... assisted by the
late Dr Maginn.
London: Longman, etc., 1st series, 1857, XXXIV + 126 (+
243) + X. 2nd series, 1859, 127 + 261 + XI + XXI p.

1859.   SHAKESPEARE PAPERS. Pictures Grave and Gay ...
London: R. Bentley, 1859, 368 p.
(cf. above. A new edition was issued in 1860).

1873.   A GALLERY OF ILLUSTRIOUS LITERARY CHARACTERS
(1830–1838), drawn by the late Daniel Maclise, R.A. and
accompanied by notices chiefly by the late William
Maginn, LL.D. (Republished from *Fraser's Magazine*)
edited by William Bates ...
London: Chatto & Windus, n.d. [1873], X + 239 p.

1885.   MISCELLANIES PROSE AND VERSE edited by R. W.
Montagu.
London: Sampson Low, etc., 1885, 2 v.
I: XIX + 373 p. II: VI + 384 p. (a very bad edition).

ON MAGINN, SEE:

OLIPHANT (Mrs): *Annals of a Publishing House.* SAINTSBURY
(G.): *History of English Prosody.* MONAHAN (M.): *Nova
Hibernia.*

Also:

THRALL (M.): *Rebellious Fraser's* (Ch. VIII to XI + Appendix 6:
300–6) in which will be found a list of Maginn's publications
in this magazine.

HOUGTON (W. E.) in *The Wellesley Index* gives the articles in
Blackwood's starting from 1824.

(For all these titles cf.: the general bibliography; also: general
studies, anthologies, *D.N.B.*)

MAHONY (Rev. Francis Sylvester, 'Father PROUT'
– 1804–1866)

BIOGRAPHY

Born in Cork in 1804 into the old Irish family of the O'Mahonys,
native of Kerry, his father was a prosperous wool merchant. In 1815

entered Clongowes Wood Jesuit College, continued his studies at St Acheul in Amiens then at the novitiate of the Society of Jesus in Paris, rue de Sèvres, and completed his secondary education in Rome in 1823–5. Then returned to Ireland by way of Genoa not without having received a good measure of advice to abandon a vocation that did not seem to suit him. Mahony, however, stood fast. He reappears as Vice-Principal at Clongowes, a post that he lost as the result of a racy escapade that his pupil John Sheehan has recounted, then immediately afterwards in Fribourg, Switzerland and, once again, in Rome where he completed his theology and was ordained priest, but *not* in the Society of Jesus which had dismissed him. In 1832, while cholera was raging, he practised his ministry in his native town. But he quarrelled with the bishop, went to London and, without actually being defrocked, received the status of free priest and, while remaining faithful to the promises of his ordination, abandoned priestly duties for journalism and literature. In England's capital, he frequented all circles including Lady Blessington's; from 1834, he was on the staff of *Fraser's* which he left in 1837 to join *Bentley's*. That same year saw him travelling throughout Europe, an occupation that he pursued for some nine years. In 1846 he was the Rome correspondent for *The Daily News* and exchanged his pseudonym for that of 'Don Jeremy Savonarola'. His last journalistic post was that of Paris correspondent for *The Globe* and his last *bête noire* the newspaper *L'Univers* (his former victims were individuals: Moore, O'Connell, Ainsworth, Kenealy). It was in Paris, on May 18, 1866, that this singular and endearing figure of nineteenth-century Irish–English literature died.

BIBLIOGRAPHY

1836. THE RELIQUES OF FATHER PROUT *late P.P. of Water-grasshill in the County of Cork, Ireland*. Collected and arranged by Oliver Yorke, Esq. Illustrated by Alfred Croquis, Esq. London: James Fraser, 1836, 2 v., I: XV + 324 p., II: 323 p.

(Oliver Yorke, like Father Prout, is obviously none other than F. Mahony in person who, in the preamble, praises his work and deplores his own death. Alfred Croquis is Daniel Maclise's pseudonym. The writings collected here had appeared in *Fraser's* in the two previous years. They are:

Vol. I: 'Father Prout's Apology for Lent' (1); 'A Plea for Pilgrimages'; 'Sir W. Scott's Visit to the Blarney Stone' (47); 'The Groves of Blarney' (90); 'The Watergrasshill Carousal' (97); 'Dean Swift's Madness' (162); 'The Rogueries of Tom Moore' (211); 'Literature and the Jesuits' (265); 'Vert-Vert, a poem, by Gresset' (304).

Vol. II: 'The Songs of France', I: 'Wine and War' (1); II: 'Women and Wooden Shoes' (52); III: 'Philosophy' (94). 'The Songs of Italy', I: (193); II: (237). 'Jerome Vida's Silkworm': (292).)

1837. THE TOUR OF ... M. DE LA BOULLAYE LE GOUZ.
(q.v. under T. Crofton Croker).

1847. FACTS AND FIGURES FROM ITALY *by Don Jeremy Savanarola, Benedictine Monk,* addressed during the last two winters to Charles Dickens, Esq. being an appendix to his 'Pictures'.
London: R. Bentley, 1847, 309 p.
(Deals with the close of Gregory XVI's reign and the beginning of Pius IX's.)

1873. A GALLERY OF ILLUSTRIOUS LITERARY CHARACTERS.
(q.v. under Maginn.) F. S. Mahony wrote the following articles in it: 'Miss Landon', pp. 111–114 (orig. pub. *Fraser's* VIII, 433), 'Béranger', pp. 152–156 (XI, 300), 'H. O'Brien', pp. 165–6 (XII, 154).

1876. THE FINAL RELIQUES OF FATHER PROUT (the Rev. Francis Mahony), collected and edited by Blanchard Jerrold.
London: Chatto & Windus, 1876, XV + 532 p.
(This is not, strictly speaking, one of Mahony's works but a biography written by Jerrold, in which the author relates memories of, and inserts passages from Prout which were not published or not collected in book form.)

1881. THE WORKS OF FATHER PROUT edited with a biographical introduction and notes by Charles Kent.
London: G. Routledge & Sons, 1881, XXXIX + 502 p.
(Comprises: *The Reliques* and 'Miscellaneous Pieces' but not *Facts and Figures* nor certain unpublished pieces that figure in Jerrold's edition.)

On F. S. Mahony, see:

MONAHAN (M.): *Nova Hibernia*, THRALL (M.): *Rebellious Fraser.*

> (q.v. in the general bibliography as well as general studies, anthologies. *D.N.B.*, etc.).

Also:

CLEMEN (C.): 'A Neglected Humorist: Father Prout', *Catholic World*, CXXXVII, 1933, pp. 706–10.

MANNIN (Ethel): *Two Studies in Integrity. Gerald Griffin and the Rev. Francis Mahony ('Father Prout').*
London: Jarrolds, 1954, 271 p., ill.
(the part concerning this author – the best biography that exists – will be found on pp. 134–262).

MALTON (James – ?–1803)

An English architect settled in Dublin. Author of the famous and admirable book:

A PICTURESQUE AND DESCRIPTIVE VIEW OF THE CITY OF DUBLIN (1794? 1799? The first date for this work, the plates of which were drawn in 1791, was given by the Irish University Press when announcing the book's reprinting 'with a critical introduction by the Hon. Desmond Guinness' (oblong folio II + 64 p.); the second, by the catalogue of the British Museum whose copy (1899, n. 16) is neither dated nor paginated).

MANDEVILLE (Edward M. – ?–1801)

A poet. Contributed to *Walker's Hibernian Magazine.*

Author of:

MISCELLANEOUS POEMS. Waterford: printed by John Veacock, 1798, 20 + 196 p.

MANGAN (James, 'Clarence' – 1803–1849)[1]

BIOGRAPHY

Born in Dublin on May 1, 1803. His father, a small tradesman not gifted for business and fairly irresponsible as well, was soon ruined and the young James, having received a sound education which was too soon interrupted, was obliged to take employment as clerk to a lawyer. He nevertheless knew how to palliate his cultural insufficiencies by a constant perusal of books, particularly of foreign literature (and notably German and Oriental literature), and books on mysticism and magic ...

Sickly, puny, disappointed by his family, broken by an impossible love and over-indulging sometimes in opium and always in alcohol, he led a miserable life, moving from lodging to lodging, working as a copyist, in his spare time writing multitudes of poems which were published through the agency of his many friends, priests or laymen. The man was, however, fairly unsociable, shy to the point of eccentricity, and for ever short of money, an extraordinary polyglot who was versed in the most incongruous sciences but who was incapable of running his own life. Struck down by the cholera epidemic, he died in a Dublin hospital on June 20, 1849, not long after the downfall of the 'Young Ireland' that he had supported with all his might.

BIBLIOGRAPHY

(a) Works published in periodicals:

1818– Contributions to various almanacs (*Grant's, New*
26.   *Ladies'*).

1830. **The National Magazine.**
          'SCHILLER'S ADDRESS TO HIS FRIENDS'. (J. M.)
          I, Oct., p. 354.

1832. **The Comet.**
etc.   – 1832: — 'SONNETS BY AN ARISTOCRAT'. (J.C.M.)
                   II, 61, 24 June, p. 70.

          — 'TO MY NATIVE LAND'. (id.)
          II, 64, 15 July, p. 94.

          'THE DYING ENTHUSIAST TO HIS FRIEND'. (id.)
          II, 67, 5 Aug., p. 119.

[1] Revised and updated by Jacques Chuto.

'GOETHE'S BALLAD OF THE FISHERMAN'. (id.)
II, 70, 26 Aug., p. 142.

'To' ... ('The charm that gilded life is over').
(Clarence.) II, 86, 16 Dec., p. 270.

'THE ASSEMBLY'. (id.)
II, 87, 23 Dec., p. 278.

– **1833:** 'CHILDHOOD' (id.)
II, 91, 20 Jan., p. 310.
also in this number, and concluded in the next, the
story in prose: 'AN EXTRAORDINARY ADVEN-
TURE IN THE SHADES'.

'TRIN. COL. DUB. CON. MAG.' (id.)
II, 92, 27 Jan., p. 315.

'VERSES TO A FRIEND'. (id.)
ibid., p. 318.

'ELEGIAC VERSES'. (id.)
II, 94, 10 Feb. p. 334.

'VERY INTERESTING SONNETS TO CAROLINE'.
(id.) II, 95, 17 Feb., p. 343.
also in this number, continued in number 98 (10
March) and concluded in number 99 (17 March)
a humorous essay (prose):

'A TREATISE ON A PAIR OF TONGS'.

'TRANSLATION: HOPE'. (id.)
II, 96, 24 Feb., p. 351.

'VERY ELEGANT SONNETS: A FAST KEEPER.
SYMPTOMS OF DISEASE OF THE HEART'. (id.)
II, 99, 17 Mar., p. 375.

'BROKEN HEARTED LAYS'. (id.)
III, 112, 16 June, p. 475.

'A GRAND AND TRANSCENDENT ODE AND
ACROSTIC, WRITTEN FOR THE PURPOSE OF
GIVING GLORY TO THE COMET'. (id.)
III, 114, 30 June, p. 494.

'MY MAUSOLEUM'. (id.)
III, 115, 7 July, p. 503.

'LIFE IS THE DESERT AND THE SOLITUDE'. (id.)
III, 117, 21 July, p. 517.

1832. **The Dublin Penny Journal.**

etc. **– 1832:** 'SONETTO DI FILICAJA'. (C. Clarence St., Liverpool)
I, 20, 10 Nov., p. 160.

'WHERE IS THINE ARM, ITALIA'. (Unsigned) I, 23, 1st Dec., p. 184.

'SONETTO DI PETRARCA' (C. Clarence St., Liverpool)
I, 32, 2 Feb., p. 253.

'FILICAJA: ON THE EARTHQUAKES OF SICILY'. (C.)
I, 36, 2 Mar., p. 288.

'THE SEPARATION'. (From the German of Klopstock) (Clarence)
I, 41, 6 April, p. 325.

'THE ONE MYSTERY'. (id.)
I, 46, 11 May, p. 368.

'VERSES FROM THE GERMAN OF HOLTY'. (id.)
I, 50, 8 June, p. 397.

'THE TWO SORTS OF HUMAN GREATNESS, by Blumauer'.
(id.), ibid., p. 400.

'THE NEW-YEAR'S NIGHT OF AN UNFORTUNATE MAN'. (From the prose of J. P. Richter.)
I, 51, 15 June, p. 403.

'ENTHUSIASM'. (id.)
II, 54, 13 July, p. 10.

'SCHILLER'S LAMENT OF CERES'. (id.)
II, 55, 20 July, p. 19.

1833. **The Dublin Satirist.**

etc. **– 1833:** 'THE MAIDEN'S LAMENT', from the German of Schiller (Clarence) I, 10, 24 Aug., p. 75.

'THE OPENING OF THE NEW CENTURY', from Schiller's poems, (id.) I, 12, 7 Sept., p. 91.

'POMPEII'. (id.)
I, 14, 21 Sept., p. 107.

'ENIGMA', from Schiller ('It whirls thee') (id.)
I, 16, 5 Oct., p. 123.

'MY TRANSFORMATION, A WONDERFUL TALE'
(prose) (id.) I, 18, 19 Oct., p. 141.

'SONG' ('The Summer sun hath often thrown a
beam') (id.) I, 19, 26 Oct., p. 147.

– **1834:** 'ENIGMA', from Schiller ('In one wide meadow')
(id.) I, 33, 1 Feb., p. 259.

'ENIGMA', from Schiller ('Knowest thou that
image') (id.) I, 34, 8 Feb., p. 267.

'TO A FRIEND', from Rosenkranz (id.)
I, 35, 15 Feb., p. 275.

'THE WRANGLING WIFE', from Weiss (id.)
I, 36, 22 Feb., p. 282.

'THE EXILE', from Lubeck von Schmidt (id.)
I, 37, 1 Mar., p. 290.

'THE LITTLE COTTAGE', from Weiss (id.)
I, 38, 8 Mar., p. 298.

'THE MAID OF ORLEANS', from Schiller (id.)
I, 39, 15 Mar., p. 306.

'SONNET BY M. LANGIER DE PORCHÈRES' (id.)
I, 40, 22 Mar., p. 314.

'THE DYING FATHER', from Gellert (id.)
I, 42, 5 Apr., p. 330.

'THE CUCKOO', from Gellert (id.)
I, 44, 19 Apr., p. 346.

'STANZAS', from Gœthe ('Say, dost thou know the
land') (id.) I, 44, 19 Apr., p. 346.

'THE PILGRIM', from Schiller (reprinted from
Dublin University Magazine) (id.)
I, 50, 31 May, p. 399.

The Weekly Dublin Satirist.

'A DIALOGUE IN THE SHADES'
II, 53, 21 June, p. 3.
(includes a poem entitled 'Lamentation for the
death of Joe King, late angler & fisher' signed
'Clarence').

'SONG FOR PUNCH DRINKERS', from Schiller
(Clarence) II, 54, 28 June, p. 10.

(The present author has been unable to consult n° 55 which the National Library of Ireland does not possess.)

'COVETOUSNESS', from Rabner (id.)
II, 56, 12 July, p. 26.

'SONNET: TO LAURA IN HEAVEN', from the Italian of Petrarch (id.) II, 57, 19 June, p. 34.

'SONNET FROM THE FRENCH OF JEAN PAS-SERAT' (id.) II, 58, 26 July, p. 42.

'TO THE MEN' from the German of Johann von Kalchberg (id.) II, 59, 2 Aug., p. 50.

'WRITTEN ON GOOD FRIDAY', Sonnet from Petrarch (id.) II, 61, 16 Aug., p. 66.

'THE OLD MAN', from Gellert (id.)
II, 62, 23 Aug., p. 74.

'LINES TO ...' tr. from the French (id.)
(«Vous désirez que sur ma lire ...»
'Oh! Ask me not for other lays')
II, 66, 20 Sept., p. 106.

'SONNET FROM THE PORTUGUESE OF CAMOENS' (id.) ('O Vain desires ...') II, 67, 27 Sept., p. 114.

'PAGANINI', a sonnet from the Italian of Moscati (id.) II, 68, 4 Oct., p. 122.

'GUIDE TO VIRTUE', from the German of Kolom-bus (id.) II, 69, 11 Oct., p. 130.

'THE TRIUMPH OF VIRTUE', from the Dutch of Otto van Veen (id.) II, 70, 18 Oct., p. 138.

'SONNET FROM THE PORTUGUESE OF CAMOENS' ('What now should bind me to this world of blindness') (id.) II, 71, 25 Oct., p. 146.

'BYRON', from the French of Lamartine (id.)
(«Toi dont la terre encor ignore le vrai nom»
'Thou whose true name the earth as yet can scarcely tell'), II, 72, 1 Nov., p. 154.

'THE KING OF THULE' from the German of Gœthe (id.) II, 73, 8 Nov., p. 162.

'THE TWO EPOCHS' after the manner of Coleridge (id.) II, 80, 27 Dec., p. 218.

(The present author has been unable to consult nº 81 which the National Library of Ireland does not possess.)

- **1835:** 'A RAILWAY OF RHYME' (id.)
II, 82, 10 Jan. 1835, p. 234.

? ('To —' ('How long since we two parted')(C) II, 91, 14 Mar., p. 306.)

? ('THE SWEETS OF SOLITUDE' (id.)
III, 113, 13 Aug., p. 66.)

? ('THE GAME-KEEPER'S DAUGHTER' (id.)
III, 115, 29 Aug., p. 82.)

'A SONG FOR CLOUD-BLOWERS' (Clarence)
III, 115, 28 Nov., p. 186.

'LINES TO ——' ('I knew that disaster/
Would shadow thy morning') (id.)
III, 129, 5 Dec., p. 194.

'HUMANUM EST ERRARE' (id.)
III, 131, 19 Dec., p. 210.

'VERSUS-VERSES' (id.)
III, 132, 26 Dec., p. 218.

1833.   **Irish Penny Magazine.**

etc.   - **1833:** ('LAMENT FOR MACLEAN OF AROS' (trans. from the Gaelic) (unsigned).
I, 42, 19 Oct. 1833, p. 336.)

- **1842:** ('AN ANCIENT LAMENT:
Ye Mighty Chiefs that guard our coast'. (M.)
II (New series), 1, 1 Jan. 1842, p. 7.)
(Two attributions for which the present author bears responsibility.)

1834.   It is from this year onwards that date Mangan's con-
etc.   tributions to
The Dublin University Magazine.

- **1834:** 'THE LITERARY LADY'. (trans. from Schiller)
(C.)
III, 13 (Jan.), pp. 43–5.

'THE GODS OF ANCIENT GREECE'. (id.)
III, 14 (Feb.), pp. 113–6.

'ANNA' (Fitz Adam)
III, 18 (June), p. 671.

'THE PILGRIM'. (id.) (Clarence).
III, 18 (June), p. 694.

'THE STORY OF CONSTANCY'. (trans. from Bürger) (C.)
IV, 19 (July), pp. 29–32.

'CURIOSITY', (translation from Schiller) (Clarence)
IV, 20 (Aug.), p. 191.

'TO MY FRIENDS'. (id.) (J. C. Mangan)
IV, 22 (Oct.), p. 368.

'THE OPENING OF THE NEW CENTURY' (id.)
ibid., p. 425.

'THE BALLAD OF LEONORE'. (trans. from Bürger) (id.) IV, 23 (Nov.), pp. 509–13.

'THE ROMANCE OF DON GAYSEROS'. (trans. from La Motte Fouqué) (id.)
IV, 24 (Dec.), p. 622–4.

'SONG PARAPHRASED FROM THE GERMAN OF HÖLTY'. (id.)
ibid., p. 673.

'TO THE BELOVED ONE'. (trans. from Heine) (id.) ibid., p. 703.

– **1835:** 'ANTHOLOGIA GERMANICA Nº 1: THE LYRICAL AND SMALLER POEMS OF SCHILLER' (unsigned).
V, 25 (Jan.), pp. 39–57.

'ANTHOLOGIA GERMANICA Nº II: SCHILLER'S LAY OF THE BELL AND MESSAGE TO THE IRON FOUNDRY' (id.).
V, 26 (Feb.), pp. 140–54.

'ANTHOLOGIA GERMANICA Nº III: MISCELLANEOUS POEMS AND METRICAL TALES' (various poets) (id.).
V, 28 (April), pp. 393–407.

'THE DIVER' (trans. from Schiller) (J.C.M.)
V, 29 (May), pp. 590–593.

'STANZAS' (unsigned).
V, 30 (June), p. 723.

'SONNET' ('Bird, that discoursest') unsigned, attributed to Mangan by D. J. O'Donoghue.
V, 30 (June), p. 724.

'THE DEMON-YAGER' (trans. from Bürger) (J.C.M.)
VI, 31 (July), pp. 20–24.

'SONNETS' (id.) (4 from various languages, 2 original ones (p. 296): 'Life', 'Love'.) VI, 33 (Sept.), pp. 295–6.

'ANTHOLOGIA GERMANICA Nº IV' (MATTHISON, SALIS), (unsigned).
VI, 34 (Oct.), pp. 403–19.

'MAN' (trans. from Lamartine) (J.C.M.)
VI, 35 (Dec.), pp. 696–701.

– 1836: 'ANTHOLOGIA GERMANICA Nº V: FAUST AND THE MINOR POEMS OF GOETHE' (unsigned).
VII, 39, (Mar.), pp. 278–302.

'ANTHOLOGIA GERMANICA Nº VI: THE GERMAN FABULISTS'. (id.)
VII, 41 (May), pp. 518–33.

'SAINT-GEORGE'S KNIGHT. A Spanish Legend. Translated from Uhland' (J.C.M.)
VII, 42 (June), pp. 674–5.

'ANTHOLOGIA GERMANICA, Nº VII: KERNER'S LYRICAL POEMS. STRAY LEAFLETS FROM THE GERMAN OAK'. (unsigned).
VIII, 44 (Aug.), pp. 143–63.

'ANTHOLOGIA GERMANICA Nº VIII: SCHILLER'S DRAMA OF WALLENSTEIN'S CAMP' (id.).
VIII, 48 (Dec.), pp. 721–37.

–1837: 'ANTHOLOGIA GERMANICA Nº IX' (id.), 2nd part.
IX, 49 (Jan.), pp. 33–46.

'ANTHOLOGIA GERMANICA Nº X: TIECK AND THE OTHER SONG-SINGERS OF GERMANY' (unsigned).
IX, 51 (Mar.), pp. 271–88.

'NIGHT THOUGHTS OF SIN AND SORROW' (unsigned).
IX, 54 (June), pp. 727–8.

'THE 24TH OF FEBRUARY. A Tragedy in 1 act translated from the German of ... Werner' (by the author of *Anthologia Germanica*).
X, 55 (July), pp. 26–53.

'LITERÆ ORIENTALES. PERSIAN AND TURKISH POETRY' (unsigned). X, 57 (Sept.), pp. 274–92.

'ANTHOLOGIA GERMANICA Nº XI. MISCELLANEOUS POEMS' (id.).
X, 60 (Dec.), pp. 651–65.

– 1838: 'LITERAE ORIENTALES, II, TURKISH POETRY' (id.).
XI, 64 (Mar.), pp. 291–312.

'ANTHOLOGIA GERMANICA Nº XII. THE LESS TRANSLATABLE POEMS OF SCHILLER' (id.).
XII, 67 (July), pp. 46–64.

'ANTHOLOGIA GERMANICA Nº XIII. M KLAUER KLATTOWSKI'S PUBLICATIONS' (id.).
XII, 68 (Aug.), pp. 167–83.

'LITERAE ORIENTALES, III, TURKISH POETRY' (id.).
XII, 69 (Sept.), pp. 328–46.

'THE THIRTY FLASKS' ('The Out and Outer') (attributed by D. J. O'Donoghue relying on O'Daly) (prose).
Part I: XII, 70 (Oct.), pp. 408–24.
Part II: XII, 72 (Dec.), pp. 666–86.

'THE MAN IN THE CLOAK, a very German story' (signed B.A.M., attributed by O'Donoghue) (prose).
XII, 71 (Nov.), pp. 552–68.

– 1839: 'ANTHOLOGIA GERMANICA Nº XIV: GELLERT'S TALES AND FABLES' (signed: 'The Out-and-Outer').
XIII, 73 (Jan.), pp. 44–59.

'A SIXTY-DROP DOSE OF LAUDANUM' ('The Out and Outer') (prose).
XIII, 75 (Mar.), pp. 267–78.

'A POLYGLOTT ANTHOLOGY' ('The Out-and-Outer').
XIII, 76 (April), pp. 483–501.

'A MIDSUMMER ANTHOLOGY'. (2 of the poems are by Mangan: 'The Lover's Farewell' (672), 'Stanzas' (J.C.M.) (672–3).) XIII, 78 (June).

'ANTHOLOGIA GERMANICA N° XV. WETZEL'S POEMS' (unsigned).
XIV, 79 (July), pp. 69–84.

– 1840: 'LITERAE ORIENTALES, IV, ARABIAN, PERSIAN AND TURKISH POETRY' (unsigned).
XV, 88 (April), pp. 377–94.

'STRAY LEAFLETS FROM THE GERMAN OAK, SECOND DRIFT (J.C.M.)'. XV, 90 (June), pp. 625–34.

– 1841: 'THE ROMANTIC AND LYRIC POETRY OF SPAIN' (by the contributor of the *Anthologia Germanica*).
XVII, 97 (Jan.), pp. 17–33.

'DOCTOR EISENBART' (from the German) (unsigned).
XVII, 101 (May), p. 627.

'ANTHOLOGIA GERMANICA N° XVI. BALLADS AND MISCELLANEOUS POEMS' (J.C.M.).
XVIII, 103 (July), pp. 19–36.

– 1842: 'CHAPTERS ON GHOSTCRAFT'. Part I (Ch. I–XI) (signed 'The Out-and-Outer') (prose).
XIX, 109 (Jan.), pp. 1–17.

'ANTHOLOGIA GERMANICA N° XVII. BALLADS AND ROMANCES' (unsigned).
XIX, 110 (Feb.), pp. 201–16.

'STRAY LEAFLETS FROM THE GERMAN OAK, THIRD DRIFT' (J.C.M.).
XIX, 114 (June), pp. 772–80.

'STRAY LEAFLETS FROM THE GERMAN OAK, FOURTH DRIFT' (unsigned), XX, 116 (Aug.), pp. 149–54.

'THE THREE HALF-CROWNS' (poetical transla-

tions from the Italian attributed to Mangan by O'Donoghue, unsigned).
XX, 120 (Dec.), pp. 682–93.

– **1843:** 'ANTHOLOGIA GERMANICA Nº XVIII. FREILI-GRATH'S POEMS' (unsigned).
XXI, 121 (Jan.), pp. 29–42.

– **1844:** 'STRAY LEAFLETS FROM THE GERMAN OAK, FIFTH DRIFT' (J.C.M.)
XXIII, 134, (Feb.), pp. 171–82.

'LITERÆ ORIENTALES, V. OTTOMAN POETRY' (unsigned).
XXIII, 137 (May), pp. 535–50.

– **1845:** 'ANTHOLOGIA GERMANICA Nº XIX. MISCEL-LANEOUS POEMS' (id.).
XXV, 145 (Jan.), pp. 95–111.

'STRAY LEAFLETS FROM THE GERMAN OAK, SIXTH DRIFT' (id.).
XXV, 146 (Feb.), pp. 179–86.

'ANTHOLOGIA GERMANICA Nº XX. SIMROCK'S POEMS' (id.).
XXVI, 151 (July), pp. 30–45.

'STRAY LEAFLETS FROM THE GERMAN OAK, SEVENTH DRIFT' (J.C.M.).
XXVI, 152 (Aug.), pp. 145–152.

'KHIDDER' (unsigned), XXVI, 152 (Aug.), pp. 236–9.

'ANTHOLOGIA GERMANICA Nº XXI. THE LATER GERMAN POETS' (id.).
XXVI, 153 (Sept.), pp. 283–97.

– **1846:** 'LITERÆ ORIENTALES, VI. OTTOMAN POETRY' (id.).
XXVII, 157 (Jan.), pp. 43–57.

'STRAY LEAFLETS FROM THE OAK OF GERMAN POETRY. A FRESH GATHERING. FIRST GARLAND. POEMS BY JOSEPH CHRISTIAN BARON VON ZEDLITZ' (id.).
XXVII, 159 (Mar.), pp. 293–303.

'ANTHOLOGIA GERMANICA N° XXII. UHLAND'S BALLADS' (id.).
XXVII, 162 (June), pp. 675–90.

'STRAY LEAFLETS FROM THE OAK OF GERMAN POETRY. A FRESH GATHERING. SECOND GARLAND' (id.).
XXVIII, 164 (Aug.), pp. 164–78.

'LOVE, DESPAIR, DEATH', a ballad from the Swedish (J.C.M.).
XXVIII, 167 (Nov.), p. 623.

'POEMS FROM THE NORTH AND THE EAST' (J.C.M.).
XXVIII, 168 (Dec.), pp. 656–67.

– **1847:** 'ANTHOLOGIA HIBERNICA N° I' (J.C.M.) (translations from the Irish).
XXIX, 170 (Feb.), pp. 239–50.

'ANTHOLOGIA HIBERNICA N° II' (unsigned).
XXIX, 173 (May), pp. 624–33.

'ANTHOLOGIA HIBERNICA N° III' (id.).
XXX, 175 (July), pp. 66–80.

'THE DEATH-CHANT OF KING REGNER LODBROK'. (trans. from the Danish, unsigned, attributed to Mangan by O'Donoghue).
XXX, 176 (Aug.), pp. 214–23.

'LAYS OF MANY LANDS' (J.C.M.)
XXX, 177 (Sept.), pp. 314–325.

'LAYS OF MANY LANDS II' (id.).
XXX, 178 (Oct.), pp. 398–411.

'THE MARVELLOUS BELL' (from the Bohemian, J.C.M.)
XXX, 178 (Oct.), pp. 439–41.

'STRAY LEAFLETS ... IV' (J.C.M.) (N° III appears nowhere in the magazine).
XXX, 179 (Nov.), pp. 546–59.

'LAYS OF MANY LANDS III' (id.).
XXX, 180 (Dec.), pp. 657–70.

– **1848:** 'LAYS OF MANY LANDS, IV' (id.).
XXXI, 181 (Jan.), pp. 45–56.
(Three poems, with no generic title.) (J.C.M.)

'HUSH-A-BY BABY' (from the Irish).
A translation from the Hungarian: 'UNREST IN THE GRAVE'.
'LAMENT OF SEANCHAN FOR THE DEATH OF DALLAN' (from the Irish).
XXXI, 182 (Feb.), pp. 247–51.

'THE EVE OF ST SILVESTER, from the Russian of Tzobovsk' (J.C.M.).
XXXI, 186 (June), pp. 781–5.

'LAYS OF MANY LANDS. VI'.
XXXII, 187 (July) pp. 104–115.

'AN ODE OF HAFIZ' (unsigned).
XXXII, 191 (Nov.), p. 539.

'LAYS OF MANY LANDS. VI'.
XXXII, 191 (Nov.), pp. 540–45.

– 1849: 'LAYS OF MANY LANDS. VI'.
XXXIII, 193 (Jan.), pp. 91–101.

'GASPARO BANDOLO, an anecdote of the South of Italy, 1820' (J.C.M.).
XXXIII, 197 (May), pp. 650–52.

1839. **The Vindicator, Belfast.**

etc. **– 1839?:**('I HEAR A SOFT MUSIC MINGLING WITH THE WIND ...' (J.C.) I, 18, 29 June, p. 4.)

? ('A DESPAIRING SONNET' (F.C.M.)
('For once I dreamed that mutual love was more ...') I, 19, 3 July, p. 4.)

'A FAST KEEPER' (J.C.M.)
('My friend, Tom Bentley, borrowed from me lately') I, 21, 10 July, p. 4.

'THE PHILOSOPHER AND THE CHILD' (id.)
('I met a venerable man ...')
I, 51, 23 Oct., p. 4.

– 1840: 'HOPE' (id.)
('Over all that breathes on earth')
II, 130, 25 July, p. 4.

'SIGHS OF AN UNLOVED ONE' from the German of Bürger (id.) ('Love is each living creature's lot')
II, 142, 5 Sept., p. 4.

'SONNET – THE DEPARTURE OF LOVE' (id.)
('Spirit of wordless love …')
II, 157, 28 Oct. p. 4.

? ('SONG' (M.)
('Go – Court the glance of every eye')
II, 173, 23 Dec., p. 4.)

– 1841: ('THE FICKLE ONE' (id.)

–? II, 176, 2 Jan., p. 4.)

'HOFER, THE PATRIOT OF TYROL' by James C.
Mangen (sic), Esq.
('Victory! Victory! Innspruck's taken')
II, 177, 6 Jan., p. 4.

? ('CLONTARF' (J.)
('I gazed, Clontarf, upon the waves')
II, 204, 10 Apr., p. 4.)

'PERSIAN DRINKING SONG' by James C. Mangan, Esq. ('Summer yet lingers, yet blushes and
blesses') III, 216, 22 May, p. 4.

'PATHETIC HYPOTHETICS' (id.)
('Were hope …')
III, 237, 4 Aug., p. 4.

'AN ELEGY ON THE ULSTER PRINCES BURIED AT
ROME' (id.).
('O, Woman of the piercing wail …')
III, 260, 23 Oct., p. 4.

1840–1. The Irish Penny Journal.

– 1840: 'THE WORLD'S CHANGES' (M.).
I, 1, 4 July, p. 7.

'APOLOGUES AND FABLES in Prose and Verse
from the German and other languages.
I: THE DISCONTENTED STONES' (prose,
unsigned).
I, 2, 11 July, pp. 14–5.

'ALEXANDER AND THE TREE' (M.).
I, 4, 25 July, p. 28.

'APOLOGUES … II: THE THREE RINGS' (prose,
id.).
I, 4, 25 July, pp. 28–30.

'LIFE AND ITS ILLUSIONS' (id.).
I, 8, 22 Aug., p. 60.

'THE WOMAN OF THREE COWS' (id.).
I, 9, 29 Aug., p. 69.

'APOLOGUES ... III: THE STORY OF THE OLD
WOLF' (prose, id.).
I, 10, 5 Sept., pp. 76–8.

'THE DIVORCED. A Translation from the
Moldavian' (id.).
I, 11, 12 Sept., p. 84.

'AN ELEGY ON THE TIRONIAN AND TIRCON-
NELLIAN PRINCES BURIED AT ROME^e' (id.).
(='O Woman of the piercing wail', trans. from
the Irish.)
I, 16, 17 Oct., pp. 123–5.

'SONNET: THE DEPARTURE OF LOVE' (id.).
I, 17, 24 Oct., p. 133.

'APOLOGUES ... IV: THE EAGLE AND THE DOVE'
(id.) (a verse translation from Gœthe).
I, 18, 31 Oct., p. 144.

'THE FIELD OF KUNNERSDORF. From the German of Tiedge' (id.).
I, 20, 14 Nov., p. 159.

'APOLOGUES ... V: THE OLD MAN AND THE
YOUTHS. From the French of La Fontaine' (id.)
(verse).
I, 26, 26 Dec., p. 206.

– 1841: 'APOLOGUES ... VI: THE REMORSE OF A NIGHT'
(id.) (prose).
I, 27, 2 Jan., pp. 213–4.

'LAMENTATIONS OF MAC LIAG FOR KINCORA'
(id.) (trans. from the Irish).
I, 28, 9 Jan., pp. 220–1.

'KATHALEEN-NY-HOULAHAN' (id.) (trans. from
the Irish.)
I, 29, 16 Jan., pp. 228–9.

1842–9. The Nation.

– 1842: 'OUR FIRST NUMBER' (unsigned).
I, 1, 15 Oct. p. 9.

Mangan reappears in 1842 and 1843 in the columns of the paper, but for short pieces (epigrams, etc., signed 'Hi-Hum', 'Terrae Filius', 'Vacuus'), devoid of interest. His important contributions date from 1846.

– 1846: 'THE WARNING VOICE' (J.C.M.).
IV, 176, 21 Feb., p. 297.

'FREEDOM AND RIGHT' (from the German of Freiligrath) (id.).
IV, 182, 4 April, p. 393.

'FIRE AND LIGHT' (from the German of Herweg) (id.).
IV, 183, 11 April, p. 411.

'SIBERIA' (Clarence Mangan).
IV, 184, 18 April, p. 425.

'THE PEAL OF ANOTHER TRUMPET' (J.C.M.).
IV, 186, 2 May, p. 457.

'ECHOES OF FOREIGN SONG: CONSTANTINE' (from the Greek) (id.).
IV, 187, 9 May, p. 473.

'THE DREAM OF JOHN MAC DONNELL' (from the Irish) (id.).
IV, 188, 16 May, p. 489.

'DARK ROSALEEN' (from the Irish) (id.).
IV, 190, 30 May, p. 521.

'THE STRICKEN BROTHERS' (from the German of Dr J. Kerner) (id.).
IV, 193, 20 June, p. 569.

'AN INVITATION' (a Yankee).
IV, 195, 4 July, p. 601.

'A VISION OF CONNAUGHT IN THE XIIITH CENTURY' (Clarence Mangan).
IV, 196, 11 July, p. 619.

'LAMENT OVER THE RUINS OF THE ABBEY OF TEACH MOLAGA' (from the original Irish of John O'Cullen) (id.).
IV, 200, 8 Aug., p. 681.

'NOT AT HOME' (from the German of Dr J. Kerner) (J.C.M.).
ibid., p. 683.

'A LAMENTATION FOR THE DEATH OF SIR MAURICE FITZGERALD, KNIGHT OF KERRY' (an abridged translation from the Irish of Pierce Ferriter) (id.).
IV, 203, 29 Aug., p. 729.

'THE SAW-MILL' (a Mourner).
IV, 205, 12 Sept., p. 763.

'REMINISCENCES OF DISTANT LANDS, Nº 1: THE LURLAY OF THE RHINE' (J.C.M.).
IV, 206, 19 Sept., p. 779.

'COUNSEL TO THE WORLDLY WISE' (id.).
IV, 208, 3 Oct., p. 811.

'SARSFIELD' (from the Irish) (id.).
V, 211, 24 Oct., p. 41.

'A CRY FOR IRELAND' (id.).
V, 212, 31 Oct., p. 57.

'FAR, FAR, STILL SO FAR' ('Oh! darkly it looms') (id.).
V, 216, 28 Nov., p. 120.

'THE SORROWS OF INISFAIL' (from the Irish) (id.).
V, 217, 5 Dec., p. 137.

– 1847: 'THE GLAIVE SONG' (from the German of C. T. Körner) (id.).
V, 237, 24 April, p. 457.

'A TALE OF A COFFIN' (Clarence Mangan).
V, 239, 8 May, p. 491.

'THE DAWNING OF THE DAY' (from the Irish) (J.C.M.).
V, 245, 12 June, p. 571.

'SONG OF THE ALBANIAN, 1826' (id.).
V, 254, 15 Aug., p. 714.

'IRELAND'S RESURRECTION' (id.).
V, 265, 30 Oct., p. 888.

'THE TESTAMENT OF CATHAEIR MOR' (from the Irish) (id.).
V, 267, 13 Nov., p. 921.

– **1848:** 'A VOICE OF ENCOURAGEMENT: A NEW YEAR'S LAY' (id.).
VI, 274, 1st Jan., p. 9.

'THE WRONGS AND WOES OF ERIN' (from the Irish of David Bruoder) (id.).
VI, 277, 22 Jan., p. 57.
VI, 278, 29 Jan., p. 73.

'FAREWELL TO MY COUNTRY' (from the French of A. de Lamartine) (id.).
VI, 280, 12 Feb., p. 105.

– **1849:** Numbers 2, 8 Sept., pp. 26–7, and 3, 15 Sept., p. 43 of Vol. VII (new series) devote a somewhat condescending article to Mangan who has just died. The following poems are quoted:
'THE RIDE ROUND THE PARAPET' (Rueckert); 'THE CARAMANIAN EXILE'; 'HERE WE MEET, WE THREE, AT LENGTH'; 'SIBERIA'; 'THE WARNING VOICE'; 'AN INVITATION'; 'THE LOVELY LAND'; 'A FAST KEEPER'.

'CURTAIN THE LAMP' (C.M.).
VII, 4, 22 Sept., p. 58.

Nº 10, 3 Nov., p. 155, presents: 'THE POETS AND POETRY OF MUNSTER'.

1845–6. The Irish Union Magazine.
The Irish Monthly Magazine.
(The translations from the German in Vol. 1 (March to August 1845) which bear the first title, may be by Mangan. He is, however, only mentioned by name from Vol. 2 onwards (Sept. 1845, etc.: *Irish Monthly Magazine*.))

– **1845?:**('M. DE LAMARTINE: HARMONY FIRST' ('Thou at whose prompting soars the lark upborne',) unsigned translation: O'Donoghue suggests that Mangan is the author.
II, 7 Sept. 1845, pp. 10–3.)

('GLEANINGS FROM THE GERMAN. SHEAF THE FIRST: Jean-Paul Richter' (prose. unsigned), id., pp. 39–42.)

? ('M. DE LAMARTINE: HARMONY TWELFTH'
('The voice of days gone by e'er Ossian came',
unsigned.)
II, 8 (Oct.), pp. 90–6

? ('GLEANINGS FROM THE GERMAN. SHEAF THE
SECOND: Jean-Paul Richter' (id.).
id., pp. 127–9.)

'LOOSE LEAVES FROM AN ODD VOLUME' N° 1.
Trans. from Friedrick Rueckert by James Clarence
Mangan ('Restraint Essential to Exertion'. 'A
Mystery'. 'Try again'. 'Large Development of
Cautiousness'. 'Counsel of a Cosmopolitan'. 'The
Quietest Place'. 'The Fires of 1837'. 'Death in
Life'. 'The Divining Rod'. 'An Evening Fantasy'.
'The Unit Must Lead'. 'The Poet also an Artist'.
'Cheer up'. 'The Night is Falling in Chill Decem-
ber'. 'Strike the Balance'. 'Wisdom & Folly'. 'Rest
only in the Grave'. 'The Golden Age').
id., pp. 152–6.

? ('GLEANINGS FROM THE GERMAN. SHEAF THE
THIRD: Goethe' (prose. unsigned).
id., pp. 171–4).

? ('M. DE LAMARTINE: HYMN OF THE NIGHT'
('Oh, earth! the day declines along the hill' ...
unsigned).
id., pp. 191–3.)

? ('THE THREEFOLD PREDICTION', a psychological
narrative (attributed by D. J. O'Donoghue).
id., pp. 194–213.)

'LOOSE LEAVES FROM AN ODD VOLUME' BY J.
C. MANGAN, N° II.
Part I. Poetry (translated).
'The Retributive Gift' (E. Moerike). 'Lines
Written in a Nunnery Chapel' (T. Creizenach).
'The Burial of Alaric I' (Count Platen-Haller-
mund). 'The Last of the True Believers' (A.
Schnezler). 'The Musician & his Audience' (F.
Rueckert). 'The Tree of Life' (id.).

Part II. Prose (original)

'Fate of the Poet'. 'Take a Right View of the Matter'. 'The Spiritual Sun'. 'Greatness'. 'Time'. id., pp. 228–35.

? ('M. DE LAMARTINE: HYMN OF THE MORNING' (C.).
II, 10 (Dec.), pp. 251–6.)

– 1846: ('GLEANINGS FROM THE GERMAN, SHEAF THE FOURTH: Novalis' (prose, unsigned).
II, 11 (Jan. 1846), pp. 372–5.)

'LOOSE LEAVES FROM AN ODD VOLUME, N⁰ III'. By J. C. Mangan.

(Part I. Poetry (translated)
'The Picture Bible' (F. Freiligrath). 'The Miller's Daughter' (Eichendorff). 'Definitions'. – 'A Warning' – 'Another Warning' (Heine). 'Young Germanists & Old' (G. Herwegh).

Part II. Prose (original): no titles.)
id., pp. 390–4.

? (M. DE LAMARTINE: 5TH HARMONY ('Whence, Lord! this peace that all my soul o'erflows') (C.)
II, 12 (Feb.), pp. 426–30.)

1847–8. Duffy's Irish Catholic Magazine.

– 1847: 'THE HYMN "TE DEUM LAUDAMUS" rendered into English' (J.C.M.).
I, 1 (Feb.), p. 9.

'DAVID LAMENTH (sic) SAUL AND JONATHAN' (id.).
I, 2 (Mar.), p. 44.

? ('THE HYMN "STABAT MATER DOLOROSA" rendered into English', unsigned, attributed – wrongly, in the present author's opinion – to Mangan by O'Donoghue.)
I, 3 (April), p. 62.)

'LAMENTATION OF JEREMIAS OVER JERUSALEM' (J.C.M.) ibid., pp. 69–71.

'THE DEATH AND BURIAL OF RED HUGH O'DONNELL (A.D. 1602)' (id.).
I, 4 (May), pp. 91–3.

'FATHER KLAUS OF UNTERWOLDEN, a Swiss Tradition' (id.).
I, 7 (Aug.), pp. 178–9.

? ('THE HYMN OF PIO NONO' (M.). This translation from the Italian could be by Mangan.
I, 10 (Nov.), p. 268.)

– 1848: 'ST PATRICK'S HYMN BEFORE TARAH' (from the original Irish) (J.C.M.)
II, 13 (Feb.), pp. 6–7.

'LOCHLAN O'DALY ON THE SUPPRESSION OF THE MONASTERIES' (from the Irish) (id.).
II, 14 (Mar.), pp. 32–3.

'ST COLUMBA'S HYMN TO ST BRIDGET' (from the Liber Hymnorum) (id.).
II, 15 (April), p. 84.

'SACRED IRISH POETRY' (from the Irish by John Murphy). ('Holy are the works of Mary's blessed son') (id.).
II, 16 (May), pp. 107–8.

'LAMENT OF FERGHAILL OG MAC AN BHAIRD FOR HIS VISIT TO SCOTLAND' (from the original Irish) (id.).
II, 18 (July) p. 157.

1848. The United Irishman.

'A VISION, A.D. 1848' (J.C.M.).
N° 3, 26 Feb., p. 43.

'THE MARSEILLAISE' (id.).
N° 6, 18 Mar., p. 89.

'LETTER' from J. C. Mangan to Mitchel to assure him of his support at the time of his prosecution.
N° 7, 25 Mar., p. 106.

'IRISH NATIONAL HYMN' (James Clarence Mangan).
N° 14, 13 May, p. 211.

1848. The Irish Tribune.

'THE TRIBUNE'S HYMN FOR PENTECOST' (James Clarence Mangan).
N° 2, 17 June, p. 24.

1849–50. The Irishman.

– 1849: 'LOOK FORWARD' (J.C.M.).
I, 2, 13 Jan., p. 25.

'PANEGYRIC OF THOMAS DUBA BUTLER, EARL OF ORMOND' (from the Irish) (id.) p. 29.

'THE VISION OF EGAN O'REILLY' (from the Irish of Egan O'Rahilly) (id.) I, 4, 27 Jan., p. 59.

'DUHALLOW' (from the Irish of Ch. Boy M'Quillan) (id.) I, 8, 24 Feb., p. 122.

'MARCH FORTH, EIGHTEEN FORTY NINE' (id.).
I, 10, 10 Mar., p. 155.

'THE BARD, CATHAL O'DALY'S KEEN FOR OWEN ROE O'NEILL' (from the original Irish) (id.).
I, 12, 24 Mar., p. 187.

'SKETCHES AND REMINISCENCES OF IRISH WRITERS. N° I: C. R. Maturin' (James Clarence Mangan) (the first in a series of critical articles in prose).
id., p. 187.

'THE FUNERALS' (J.C.M.).
I, 13, 31 Mar., p. 204.

'THE VOICE OF FERGHALL MAC WARD FROM ALBA TO IRELAND' (from the Irish) (id.).
I, 14, 7 April, p. 217.

'SKETCHES ... N° II: DR. PETRIE' (James Clarence Mangan).
id., p. 218.

'SKETCHES ... N° III: JOHN ANSTER' (id.).
I, 16, 21 April, p. 251.

'FOR SOUL AND COUNTRY' (J.C.M.).
I, 17, 28 April, p. 267.

'BEAR UP' (id.).
I, 19, 12 May, p. 299.

'SKETCHES ... N° IV: THE REV. C. P. MEEHAN'
(James Clarence Mangan).
id., same page.

'GHAZEL' (from the Arabic) (J.C.M.).
I, 20, 19 May, p. 315.

'THE SIEGE OF MAYNOOTH' (id.).
I, 21, 26 May, p. 331.

'WORDS OF ENCOURAGEMENT' (from the
Swedish) (id.) id., ibid.

'SKETCHES ... N° V: MISS EDGEWORTH' (James
Clarence Mangan).
id., ibid.

'A WORD IN REPLY TO JOSEPH BRENAN'
(J.C.M.).
I, 22, 2 June, p. 347.
The poem answers another poem (signed J.B.,
appearing on p. 331 of the previous number and
entitled 'A Word to James Clarence Mangan') the
last two lines of which were:

> One thing remains – but one – Herr Mangan, hear!
> To live thy poetry – to act thy rhyme.

'LET NOT THE GAEL DESPAIR' (from the Irish of
David O'Bruoder') (id.).
I, 23, 9 June, p. 363.

'THE FAMINE'. (id.)
ibid.

'SKETCHES ... N° VI: G. GRIFFIN' (James
Clarence Mangan).
I, 24, 16 June, p. 379.

N° 25 (23 June) includes, on p. 393, an obituary of
Mangan and, in a black rectangle, quotes on p.
395:
'Lays of Younger Years:
 Genius: a Fragment,
 The False and the True Glory'.
The next two numbers each include a poem 'in
memoriam', one by J. Brenan (408), the other
signed 'Shamrock' (427).

'SKETCHES ... Nº VII: REV. DR TODD' (James Clarence Mangan).
I, 26, 30 June, p. 411.

'WATCH THE CLOCK' (id.).
I, 28, 14 July, p. 443.

'SKETCHES ... Nº VIII: JOHN O'DONOVAN' (id.).
ibid.

'SKETCHES ... Nº IX: W. MAGINN' (id.).
I, 30, 28 July, p. 470.

'STILL A NATION' (id.).
I, 36, 8 Sept., p. 571.

'Unpublished Poems of James Clarence Mangan: THE EXPEDITION AND DEATH OF KING DATY' (from the Irish of Owen John O'Hennessy).
I, 37, 15 Sept., p. 587.

'Unpublished Poems ...: MOREEN CULLENAN' (from the Irish of John O'Tuomy).
I, 42, 20 Oct., p. 667.

'Unpublished Poems ...: THE NAMELESS ONE'.
I, 43, 27 Oct., p. 683.

'Unpublished Poems ...: MILER MAGRATH'S APOSTACY' (from the Irish of Bonaventure O'Hussey).
I, 44, 3 Nov., p. 699.

'Unpublished Poems ...: HAVE HOPE' (to a suffering patriot friend).
I, 45, 10 Nov., p. 715.

'Unpublished Poems ...: THE LAST WORDS OF THEODORE KORNER' (from the German).
I, 47, 24 Nov., p. 747.

'Unpublished Poems ...: THE BARRIER' (from the Persian).
I, 48, 31 Nov., p. 763.

– 1850: 'Unpublished Poems ...: CONSOLATION AND COUNSEL'.
II, I, 5 Jan., p. 11.

'Unpublished Poems ...: THE ONE OLD SER-

PENT' (from the German of De La Motte
Fouqué).
II, 3, 19 Jan., p. 43.

'Unpublished Poems ...: WHEN HEARTS WERE
TRUMPS'.
II, 4, 26 Jan., p. 59.

'Unpublished Poems ...: THE CROPPY'S GHOST'.
New series, n° 2 (17 Aug.), p. 27.

'SKETCHES ... (n° X): J. C. MANGAN' (self
portrait signed E.W.).
ibid., pp. 27–8.

(b) Works published in book form:

1843. in: THE SPIRIT OF THE NATION
by the writers of the *Nation* Newspaper.
Dublin: J. Duffy, 1843, VIII + 76 p.
id. Part II, ibid., 1843, id.

1845. id. complete edition, with music, ibid., 1845, VI + 437 p., in
4°.
in: Duffy (C. G.): THE BALLAD-POETRY OF IRELAND.
Dublin: J. Duffy, 1845, XLVIII + 252 p.

ANTHOLOGIA GERMANICA: GERMAN ANTHOLOGY: a
series of translations from the most popular of the German
Poets by J. C. Mangan, in 2 v.
Dublin: W. Curry, Jun. & Co.; London: Longmans, Brown
& Co, 1845, I: VIII + 208 p. II: VIII + 223 p.
There is a preface by the author in which it is said that, but
for one exception, the poems contained in this volume have
all appeared in the *Dublin University Magazine.* However,
not all the poems appearing under the same title in this
magazine are reprinted in the anthology.
    Father Meehan re-published this volume in 1884
(Dublin: Duffy), without the author's preface but with a
23-page introduction. The 1884 edition comprises twenty
extra poems.

1846. In: Montgomery (H. S.): SPECIMENS OF THE EARLY
NATIVE POETRY OF IRELAND.
Dublin: J. M'Glashan, etc., 1846, VIII + 223 p.

(6 poems by Mangan including the famous 'Ode to the Maguire', p. 137).
Enlarged edition: Dublin: Hodges Figgis, 1892, XV + 311 p.

in: Mac Carthy (D. F.): THE BOOK OF IRISH BALLADS. Dublin: J. Duffy ... 1846, IX + 252 p.

1849. THE POETS AND POETRY OF MUNSTER: a selection of Irish songs by the poets of last century, with poetical translations by the late James Clarence Mangan, now for the first time published. With the original music, and biographical sketches of the authors by John O'Daly.
Dublin: John O'Daly, 1849, XVI + 269 p.
2nd edition: 1850 (+ 3 poems)
3rd edition: 1884 (by Father Meehan, with a preface, and an autobiographical fragment by Mangan).
4th edition: 1925 (with an intro. by J. P. Dalton).

1850. in: Ellis (H.): ROMANCES AND BALLADS OF IRELAND. Dublin: J. Duffy, 1850, XXXI + 432 p.

1851. in: MISCELLANY.
Dublin: Celtic Society, 1849 (pub.: 1851), 16 p.:
'The Testament of Cathaeir Mor', a revised version of the poem which appeared under this title in *The Nation*, V, 267, 13 Nov. 1847, p. 921.

1852. THE TRIBES OF IRELAND: a satire, by Aenghus O'Daly with poetical translations by the late J. C. Mangan; together with an historical account of the Family of O'Daly; and an introduction to the history of satire in Ireland by John O'Donovan.
Dublin: J. O'Daly ..., 1852, 112 p. Reprinted: Cork, Tower Books, 1976.

POEMS ORIGINAL AND TRANSLATED BY JAMES CLARENCE MANGAN, being a selection from his contributions to Irish periodicals. Ed. by M. R. Leyne.
Supplement to *The Nation*, Sat. Dec. 25, 1852, 16 p. (including an introduction).

1859. POEMS BY JAMES CLARENCE MANGAN; with biographical introduction by John Mitchel.
New York: P. M. Haverty ..., 1859, 460 p.
(The introduction by Mitchel runs from pages 7 to 31.)

1884. ESSAYS IN PROSE AND VERSE edited by C. P. Meehan.
Dublin: Duffy, 1884, XV + 320 p.

1886. IRISH AND OTHER POEMS with a selection from his translations. Dublin: M. H. Gill, 1886, 144 p.

1897. JAMES CLARENCE MANGAN: HIS SELECTED POEMS.
with a study by the editor: Louise Imogen Guiney.
Boston, New York: Lawson Wolffe & Co; London: John Lane, 1897, 342 p.

1903. POEMS OF JAMES CLARENCE MANGAN.
(Many hitherto uncollected) Centenary Edition edited, with preface and notes, by D. J. O'Donoghue. Introduction by John Mitchel.
Dublin: M. H. Gill, 1903, 1910, XLVII + 332 p., ill.

1904. PROSE WRITINGS OF JAMES CLARENCE MANGAN.
(Centenary edition) edited by J. O'Donoghue.
With an essay by Lionel Johnson.
Dublin: O'Donoghue & Co ..., M. H. Gill ...; London: A. H. Bullen, 1904, XV + 331 p.

1969. THE AUTOBIOGRAPHY OF JAMES CLARENCE MANGAN ed. by James Kilroy.
Dublin: Dolmen Press, 1969, 36 p.

Selected Poems, edited by Michael Smith, foreword by A. Cronin.
Dublin: The Gallery Press, 1973, 96 p.

(c) Secondary literature:

(1) General Studies:

Nearly all works dealing with Irish–English literature, poetry and translations from the Gaelic; anthologies. Cf. particularly (q.v. in the general bibliography): Auden (W. H.), Blacam (A. de), Boyd (E. A.), Brooke (S. A.), Corkery (D.), Crone (J. S.), Farren (R.), Graves (A. P.), Greene (D. H.), Heaslip (K. W.), Kinsella (T.), Mc Carthy (J.), Mac Donagh (D.), Mac Donagh (T.), Monahan (M.), O'Connor (Frank), Read (Ch.), Ryan (D.), Taylor (G.), etc.

Sean O'Casey speaks of Mangan in his autobiography: *Drums Under the Windows* (1945, Macmillan Paperbacks: I, 617).

W. B. Yeats has devoted several pages to him. Cf. in Vol. III of *Irish Literature* by Mac Carthy, in *Poetry and Ireland* (1908), and *Uncollected Prose*, passim.

(2) Studies on the author:

Besides the introductions, etc., already mentioned in connection with the works published in book form, see:

THOMPSON, (Francis): 'James Clarence Mangan', *Academy*, 25 Sept. 1897. Also 'A Bewildered Poet', id., 16 May 1903; 'Mangan the Unhappy', id., 15 Aug. 1903.

O'DONOGHUE (D. J.): *The Life and Writings of James Clarence Mangan*, Edinburgh: P. Geddes; Dublin: Gill, etc., 1897, XXIV + 250 p., ill.

JOHNSON (Lionel): 'James Clarence Mangan', *Academy*, 5 Feb. 1898, pp. 142 seq., reprinted in *Post Liminium*, London: E. Matthews, 1911, pp. 218 seq.

JOYCE (James): *James Clarence Mangan*, London: Ulysses Bookshop, 1902, 1930, 16 p. (Had originally appeared in: *St Stephens, A Record of University Life*, I, 6 May, 1902, pp. 115–7.)

CAIN (Henry E.): *James Clarence Mangan and the Poe-Mangan Question*, Washington, D.C. (publisher not mentioned, prob.: the Catholic University of America), 1929, XI + 83 p. (an enticing title but no solution is offered to the problem raised).

COLUM (Padraic): 'James Clarence Mangan', *Dublin Magazine*, VIII, n° 2, April–June 1933, pp. 32–40.

SHERIDAN (John D.): *James Clarence Mangan*, London: Duckworth; Dublin: Talbot Press, 1937, 128 p. ('Noted Irish Lives Series').

D'ALTON (Louis): 'The Man in the Cloak', *Two Irish Plays*. London: Macmillan, 1938.

O'HEGARTY (P. S.): *A Bibliography of J. C. Mangan*, Dublin: privately printed by Alex Thom & Co, 1941, 8 p. (a reprint from the *Dublin Magazine*).

BROPHY (Liam): 'Poe and Mangan: Twin Souls', *Ave Maria* (Notre-Dame, Indiana), 16 July 1949, pp. 71–5.

THOMPSON (F. J.): 'Poe and Mangan', *Dublin Magazine*, Jan. 1950. 'Mangan in America', id., July 1952, pp. 30–41.

JEFFARES (A. N.): 'Tribute to a Dublin Poet and Writer: James Clarence Mangan', *Envoy*, IV, n° 14, Jan. 1951, pp. 23–32.

HOLZAPFEL (Rudolph. P.): 'Mangan's Poetry in the *Dublin University Magazine*: a bibliography', *Hermathena*, CV, 1967, pp.40–54.

James Clarence Mangan: a Check-list of Printed and Other Sources, Dublin: Scepter Publishers, 1969, 88 p.

KILROY (James): Preface to *The Autobiography of James Clarence Mangan*, q.v. above 1969.
James Clarence Mangan, Lewisburg: Bucknell University Press, 1970, 74 p. ('Irish Writers Series').

CHUTO (Jacques): 'Mangan's "Antique Deposit" in T.C.D. Library', *Long Room*, 2, Autumn–Winter 1970, pp. 38–39.

'A Further Glance at Mangan and the Library', *Long Room*, 5, Spring 1972, pp. 8–10.

'Mangan, Petrie, O'Donovan, and A Few Others: The Poet and the Scholars', *Irish University Review*, VI, 2, Autumn 1976, pp. 169–187.

'James Clarence Mangan: In Exile at Home', *Etudes Irlandaises*, new series 1, 1976, pp. 35–50.

OUCHI (Giichi): 'On James Clarence Mangan', *General Studies* (Waseda University, Tokyo), Feb. 1973, pp. 47–61.

DONAGHY (Henry J.): *James Clarence Mangan*, New York: Twayne, 1974, 141 p.

WELCH (Robert): ' "In Wreathed Swell": J. C. Mangan, Translator from the Irish', *Eire-Ireland*, XI, 2, Summer 1976, pp. 36–55.

MARTIN (Harriet Letitia – 1801–1891)

Author of the two following novels:

1835. CANVASSING.
in: *The Mayor of Windgap* (and *Canvassing*),
by the O'Hara Family (= Banim) in 3 v.
London: Saunders & Otley, 1835.
(to be found in volume III: 316 p.).

1848. THE CHANGELING
London: Saunders & Otley, 1848, 3 v.
I: 315 p. II: 350 p. III: 414 p.

MARTIN (James – 1783–1860)

Born in Millbrook, County Meath, a mediocre and prolific poet. The author of:

TRANSLATIONS FROM ANCIENT IRISH MSS *and Other Poems.* London: Sherwood, Neely & Jones ... 1811, VIII + 112 p.

[In O'Donoghue, mention will also be found of the following works:

1813. POEMS. Cavan.

1816. POEMS ON VARIOUS SUBJECTS, ibid.

1823. MAN'S FINAL END.

1824– COTTAGE MINSTRELSY. Kells.
41.   Second series, ibid., 1841.

1831. A POETICAL LETTER *Addressed to the Independent Electors of the Co. of Meath.*

1838. REFORMATION THE THIRD ... and THE PERVERTS OF ATHBOY. Dublin.

1841. THE WOUNDED SOLDIER.
         THE MEDAL AND GLASS. Kells.

1842. THE TRUTH-TELLER. Kells.

1844. THE REPEALER. Cavan.

1845. A DIALOGUE BETWEEN JOHN BULL AND GRANU-WAILE. Kells.

1849. EDMUND AND MARCELLA. Kells.

1853. THE MASS.

1855. JOHN AND MARY. Trim. (prose)

and, with no date: *Death and the Poet, Dialogue between an Irish Agent and his Tenant, The Dirge of Erin, Imitation of Dean Swift, The Irish Bard, Miscellaneous Verse, Paddy the Politician, Poem on the Immaculate Conception.*]

MARTIN (Mary Letitia – 1815–1850)

Daughter of Richard Martin, 'Humanity Dick', founder of the Society for the Protection of Animals and ... famous for his duels, a friend of George IV and the proprietor of the immense estate of Ballynahinch, Connemara, where his daughter was born. The latter, who was to become the heroine of Charles Lever's novel, *The Martins of Cro'Martin*, and whom in her days of splendour everyone called 'The Princess of Connemara', had a short and difficult life. Ruined, married to a poor man, she died in childbirth shortly after having arrived in New York as an emigrant. She was the author of a novel, undated, and entitled: *St Etienne*, a tale of the Vendean War. She also wrote, based on her own experience: JULIA HOWARD, a romance, 1850.

MATURIN (Charles-Robert – 1780–1824)[1]

BIOGRAPHY

Little enough is known of the life of Ireland's most famous Romantic novelist. He was born in 1780 in Dublin where his father worked in the Post Office. His family had emigrated from France at the Revocation of the Edict of Nantes. Studied theology. Was ordained. Curate of Loughrea then St Peter's, Dublin. Married very young, he seems to have known poverty throughout his life despite the success of this or that literary work. Died on October 30, 1824, subsequent to an accidental poisoning.

BIBLIOGRAPHY

(a) Novels:

1807.   THE FATAL REVENGE; *or, The Family of Montorio*,
a romance, by Dennis Jasper Murphy.
London: Longman, Hurst, Rees & Orme, 1807, 3 v.
I: VIII + 400 p. II: 518 p. III: 493 p.
Reprinted: New York, Arno Press, 1974. Foreword by Henry D. Hicks, introduction by M. Levy. 3 v.

[1] Revised and updated by Claude Fiérobe.

1808. THE WILD IRISH BOY.*
London: Longman, etc., 1808, 3 v.
I: VII + 276 p. II: 342 p. III: 406 p.
Reprinted: New York, Arno Press, 1977, with an introduction by E. F. Bleider. 3 vols.

1812. THE MILESIAN CHIEF, a romance.*
London: H. Colburn, 1812, 4 v., I: VI + 228 p.
II: 218 p. III: 239 p. IV: 204 p.

1818. WOMEN; or, Pour et Contre.*
Edinburgh: Constable; London: Longman, 1818, 3 v.
I: V + 275 p. II: 276 p. III: 408 p.

1820. MELMOTH, THE WANDERER, a tale.
Edinburgh: Constable; London: Hurst & Robinson, 1820, 4 v.
I: XII + 341 p. II: 321 p. III: 368 p. IV: 453 p.
(Three other editions deserve a mention: one dating from the end of the nineteenth century:
London: Bentley & Son, 1892, 3 v., 'with a memoir and bibliography of Maturin's works'.
Two recent ones:
Lincoln: University of Nebraska Press, 1961, introd. by W. F. Axton.
London: Oxford University Press, 1968, D. Grant, ed.).

1824. THE ALBIGENSES, a romance.
London: Hurst, Robinson & Co, 1824, 4 v., I: 438 p.
II: 366 p. III: 335 p. IV: 277 p.
Reprinted: New York, Arno Press, 1974, with a foreword by J. Gray and an introduction by Dale Kramer. 4 v.

1825. LEIXLIP CASTLE, an Irish Family Legend. In: *The Literary Souvenir; or, Cabinet of Poetry and Romance.*
London: Hurst and Robinson, 1825.
Reprinted in: *The Grimoire and Other Supernatural Stories*, collected by Montague Summers, Fortune Press, 1936, pp. 23–27.

(b) Dramatic works:

1816. (9.5, D.L.) BERTRAM; or, *The Castle of St Aldobrand*, a tragedy, in 5 acts.
London: J. Murray, 1816, 1 + 94 p.

1817. (8.3, D.L.) MANUEL,
a tragedy, in 5 acts.
London: J. Murray, 1817, VIII + 1 + 34 + 2 p.

1819. (12.5, C.G.) FREDOLPHO, a tragedy, in 5 acts.
London: A. Constable, etc., 1819, 1 + 114 p.

1826. THE SIBYL'S PROPHECY, a dramatic fragment in *The Literary Souvenir; or, Cabinet of Poetry and Romance,* 1826, Vol. 2, pp. 128–36.

1830. (30.3, C.S.) OSMYN THE RENEGADE; *or, The Siege of Salerno.*
(Unpublished, and the manuscript lost, but extracts from it are to be found in *The Irish Quarterly Review,* II, March 1852, pp. 166–9.)

(c) Miscellanea:

1816. LINES ON THE BATTLE OF WATERLOO, by John Shee, Esq. (i.e. C.R.M.), Undergraduate, T.C.D.
Dublin: printed for R. Milliken, Grafton Street, 56 p. (a poem).

'OH SWEET IS THE FEELING', 'STRANGER TO THE TREE', 'STRANGER TO THE STREAM' (poems) in *A Select Collection of Melodies* ... collected and arranged by Alexander Campbell, Edinburgh: Oliver & Boyd, 1816, Vol. 2.

1819. SERMONS.
Edinburgh: Constable; London: Hurst & Robinson, 1819, XII + 475 p. (2nd edition 1821).

1824. FIVE SERMONS ON THE ERRORS OF THE ROMAN CATHOLIC CHURCH preached in St Peter's Church, Dublin ...
Dublin: W. Folds & Son, 1824, 163 p. (2nd edition 1826).

1937. THE CORRESPONDENCE OF SIR WALTER SCOTT AND CHARLES ROBERT MATURIN. ed. by F. Ratchford and W. H. Mc Carthy.
Austin, Texas: University of Texas Press, 1937, X + 128 p.

N.B. – A poetical work published under Maturin's name but author of which he is not, has deliberately been omitted from

'miscellanea'. It was the Rev. J. Willis (q.v.) who wrote it, authorising his colleague to publish it in his name:
The Universe, a poem. London: H. Colburn, 1821, 108 p.

(d) Secondary material:

All works dealing with the Gothic novel give a place to Maturin. Birkhead *(Tale of Terror)*, Killen (*Le Roman 'Terrifiant'*), Lévy *(Le Roman 'Gothique')*, Railo *(The Haunted Castle)*, Summers *(The Gothic Quest)*, Varma *(The Gothic Flame)*. Also: Praz *(Romantic Agony)*, Cambridge Bibliography, *D.N.B.*, etc.
Besides these, see:

IDMAN (N.): *C. R. Maturin, His Life and Works*, London: Constable, 1923, 326 p.

SCHOLTEN (W.): *C. R. Maturin, The Terror-Novelist*, Amsterdam: H. J. Paris, 1933, 197 p.

LAYMAN (B. J.): *C. R. Maturin and the Romance of Terror.* Unpublished thesis, University of Virginia, 1943, v + 161 p.

BRETON (A.): Preface to the French translation of *Melmoth*, Paris: Pauvert, 1954 (the preface is unpaginated).

HINCK (H. W.): *Three Studies in Maturin.* Unpublished thesis, University of Iowa, 1954, 197 p.

RUFF (M. A.): 'Maturin et les Romantiques Français', introduction to *Bertram*. Paris: Corti, 1956 (also includes a bibliography).

HARRIS (J. B.): *Charles Robert Maturin, a study.* Unpublished dissertation, Wayne State University, 1965, *Dissertation Abstracts* (30) 282A.

MAYOUX (J. J.): 'La grande création satanique du Rév. Maturin (Baudelaire)'. *Etudes Anglaises*, XXII, 4, Oct.–Dec. 1969, pp. 393–6.

FIEROBE (Claude): 'L'Univers Fantastique de *Melmoth the Wanderer*' in: *La Raison et l'Imaginaire, S.A.E.S., Actes du Congrès de Rennes, 1970.* Paris: Didier, n.d., pp. 105–116.

Charles Robert Maturin (1780–1824), L'homme et l'oeuvre, Lille, P.U.L.: Paris: Editions Universitaires, 1974, 748 p.

'A propos de Maturin: ni vrai ni faux, mais fantastique', *Etudes Irlandaises*, I, 3, 1974, pp. 23–8.

'France in the Novels of Charles Robert Maturin' in P. Rafroidi et al.: *France–Ireland, Literary Relations*, 1974, pp. 119–131.

'Quelques images de la nature irlandaise dans l'oeuvre de C. R. Maturin' *S.A.E.S., Actes du Congrés de St Etienne, 1975*, Paris: Didier, 1977, pp. 117–124.

'Transgression et écriture: Maturin et le roman gothique', *Cahier du Centre du Romantisme Anglais*, Clermont-Ferrand, 1976.

KRAMER (Dale): *Charles Robert Maturin*, New York: Twayne, 1974, 166 p.

LOUGY (Robert): *Charles Robert Maturin*, Lewisburg: Bucknell University Press, 1975 ('Irish Writers' Series').

BRIHAULT (J.): 'Joyce et Maturin. L'héritage gothique de *A Portrait*', *Cahiers du Centre d'Etudes Anglo–Irlandaises*, Rennes, 1, 1976, pp. 51–60.

MATURIN (Edward – 1812–1881)

BIOGRAPHY

The son of the preceding, born in Dublin, studied at Trinity College (B.A.: 1832). Settled in the United States where he taught Latin and Greek. Died in New York on May 28, 1881.

BIBLIOGRAPHY

1848. [THE IRISH CHIEFTAIN; *or, The Isles of Life and Death*. Glasgow, 1848, 316 p. (a novel).]

1850. LYRICS OF SPAIN AND ERIN.
Boston: Ticknor, Reed & Fields, 1850, 208 p.

1852. BIANCA, a tale of Erin and Italy.
New York: Harper & Brothers, 1852, 395 p. (a novel)

MAXWELL (Rev. William Hamilton – 1792–1850)

BIOGRAPHY

The author of 'military' novels, his biographers have sent him, contrary to all likelihood, to Waterloo and other places. It is true that a Captain Hamilton Maxwell really existed, a Scotsman related to the novelist by marriage, but who did not write novels.

Born in Newry in 1792. Studied at Trinity College, Dublin; was ordained in 1813, and immediately took up his duties as curate in County Down where he lived until his marriage in 1817. The parish in which he then lived in Connemara possessed a scanty flock of faithful but put at his disposal abundant stocks of game, and he divided his time between hunting and literature. A friend of Charles Lever whom he launched. Died in Scotland on December 29, 1850.

BIBLIOGRAPHY

1825. O'HARA; or, 1798.*
London: J. Andrews, 1825, 2 v., I: XL + 264 p.
II: 294 p. (a novel, published anonymously).

1829. STORIES OF WATERLOO, and Other Tales.
London: H. Colburn, 1829, 3 v., I: 336 p. II: 279 p.
III: 296 p. (again anonymous).

1832. WILD SPORTS OF THE WEST, with Legendary Tales and Local Sketches by the author of 'Stories of Waterloo'.
London: R. Bentley, 1832, 2 v., I: XVI + 327 p.
II: VII + 343 p.

1833. THE FIELD BOOK ; or, Sports and Pastimes of the United Kingdom.
London: Effingham Wilson, 1833, VIII + 616 p.

1834. THE DARK LADY OF DOONA.
London: Smith, Elder & Co, 1834, 306 p.
(Library of Romance, Vol. IX).

1835. MY LIFE.
London: R. Bentley, 1835, 3 v., I: XVI + 288 p. II: 300 p.
III: 340 p.
(Later published under the title: Adventures of Captain Blake; or, My Life.)

1837. THE BIVOUAC; or, Stories of the Peninsular War.

London: R. Bentley, 1837, 3 v., I: 304 p.
II: 292 p. III: 272 p.

1838. Contributions to
Sporting ... edited by Nimrod.
London: A. H. Baily & Co, 1838, VIII + 144 p., ill.
(By Maxwell: 'DEER STALKING IN THE IRISH HIGHLANDS'
(108); 'RECOLLECTIONS OF A GROUSE SHOOTER' (126).)

1839. THE VICTORIES OF THE BRITISH ARMIES ...
London: R. Bentley, 1839, 2 v., I: XI + 406 p.
II: X + 402 p., ill.

1841. 'THE EXPEDITION OF MAJOR AP OWEN *to the Lakes of
Killarney, and the reason why he returned before he got
there*' in: *The Pic-Nic Papers* edited by C[harles] D[ickens],
Part I, London: Ward, Lock & Tyler, 1841, 120 p.
(pp. 87–95.)

LIFE OF FIELD-MARSHAL HIS GRACE THE DUKE OF
WELLINGTON.
London: A. H. Baily, 1841, 3 v., I. XIII + 576 p. II: XII +
512 p. III: XVI + 512 p., ill.

1842. RAMBLING RECOLLECTIONS OF A SOLDIER OF FORTUNE.
Dublin: W. Curry, Jun. & Co, 1842, XII + 296 p.
(later republished under the title: *Flood and Field*).

1843. THE FORTUNES OF HECTOR O'HALLORAN AND HIS MAN
MARK ANTONY O'TOOLE.*
London: R. Bentley, n.d. [1843?], 412 p., ill.

1844. WANDERINGS IN THE HIGHLANDS AND ISLANDS.
with Sketches taken on the Scottish Border; being a sequel
to 'Wild Sports of the West'.
London: A. H. Baily, 1844, 2 v.
I: XII + 334 p. II: VIII + 354 p.

1845. HINTS TO A SOLDIER ON SERVICE.
London: T. C. Newby, 1845, 2 v., I: 291 p. II: 319 p.

HISTORY OF THE IRISH REBELLION IN 1798, *with
memoirs of the Union and Emmett's insurrection in
1803* ... with illustrations by G. Cruikshank.
London: Baily Brothers, Cornhill, 1845, VII + 477 p.

PENINSULAR SKETCHES BY ACTORS ON THE SCENE
edited by ...
London: H. Colburn, 1845, 2 v., I: VIII + 389 p.
II: IV + 388 p.

1846. CAPTAIN O'SULLIVAN; *or, Adventures, Civil, Military, and Matrimonial, of a Gentleman on Half-Pay.*
London: H. Colburn, 1846, 3 v., I: 303 p. II: 298 p.
III: 314 p.

1847. HILL-SIDE AND BORDER SKETCHES *with Legends of the Cheviots and the Lammermuir.*
London: R. Bentley, 1847, 2 v., I: 342 p. II: 338 p.

1848. BRIAN O'LINN; *or, Luck is Everything.*
London: R. Bentley, 1848, 3 v., I: 312 p. II: 318 p.
III: 333 p.

THE IRISH MOVEMENTS: *Their Rise, Progress and Certain Termination; with a few broad hints to Patriots and Pikemen.*
London: Baily Brothers, 1848, 66 p.

1859. ERIN GO BRAGH; *or, Irish Life Pictures ...* *
with a biographical sketch by Dr. Maginn.
London: R. Bentley, 1859, 2 v., I: XII + 358 p.
II: 368 p.

'TERENCE O'SHAUGHNESSY'S FIRST ATTEMPT TO GET MARRIED', 30 p. in:
Tales from 'Bentley', Part I, London: R. Bentley, 1859.

MEAGHER (Thomas Francis – 1823–1867)

One of the influential members of Young Ireland. Born in Waterford, died in the United States where he ran several newspapers. The author of *Speeches on the Legislative Independence of Ireland*, 1853, and of a few poems certain of which had appeared, in 1849, in *Echoes from Parnassus*, Cork.

MEEHAN (Alexander S.)

A contributor to *The Nation* (his pseudonym was 'Astroea'), the author of *Lays of Modern Derry*, 1848.

MEEHAN (Rev. Patrick – 1812–1890)

A Catholic priest and friend of Mangan, and a contributor to *The Nation* ('Clericus', 'C.P.M.', 'D.M'L.', etc.), translator of:

THE GERALDINES from the original latin of D. de Rosario O'Daly. Dublin: J. Duffy, 1847, 12 + 238 p.

and the author of several historical works posterior to 1850:

THE CONFEDERATION OF KILKENNY, 1860.

THE FATES AND FORTUNES OF HUGH O'NEILL, 1868.

THE RISE AND FALL OF THE IRISH FRANCISCAN MONASTERIES, 1869, etc.

MILLIKEN (or MILIKIN, Richard Alfred – 1767–1815)

BIOGRAPHY

Born in Castlemartyr, County Cork, on September 8, 1767. A lawyer blessed with many talents: those of musician, painter, playwright and poet. His first literary efforts appeared in Cork, in 1795, in the *Monthly Miscellany*, then, in 1797–8, in *The Casket; or, Hesperian Magazine* of which he was the founder. Said to have taken an active part in the repression of the 1798 rebellion. Died on December 16, 1815.

BIBLIOGRAPHY

If 'The Groves of Blarney', the poem that made Milliken famous (it is a pastiche of a popular ballad that would in turn be arranged by Mahony) is found in all anthologies, most of Milliken's other works have shown themselves to be elusive.

(a) **Dramatic works:**

The following titles are attributed to him: *Dungourney in Egypt* (1805), *Darby in Arms* (1810), *Macha*, a tragedy, and *The Anachonda*.

(b) Poetry:

Beside *Dermid* and *The Geraldine* (dates ?) we owe him:

1807. THE RIVERSIDE, a poem in 3 books. Cork: printed by J. Connor, 1807, 147 p. in-4°.

He also figures abundantly in:

1818. HARMONICA; *or, Elegant Extracts of English, Scotch and Irish Melodies from the Most Approved, Popular and Modern Authors.* With a Preface. Cork: J. Bolster, Patrick Street, 1818, 240 + XIII p.

(Other Irish authors represented in this interesting poetical anthology: E. S. Barrett, A. Cherry, J. W. Croker, Thomas Dermody, Maria Edgeworth, Thomas Moore, J. O'Keeffe, Mrs Tighe.)

And there is a posthumous collection:

1823. POETICAL FRAGMENTS OF THE LATE RICHARD ALFRED MILLIKEN, with memoir. London: Longman, 1823, 38 + 82 p. (H.K.)

(c) Miscellanea:

1810. THE SLAVE OF SURINAM (a story in prose), Cork: printed by Mathews, 1810, 2 + 143 p.

MILLINGEN (John Gideon – 1782–1862)

A doctor and man of letters born in Westminster. Irish and Dutch origins. The author of:

(a) Dramatic works:

1811. (19.1, LYC.) THE BEE-HIVE, a musical farce, in 2 acts ... Music ... by Mr Horn.
London: W. N. Wyatt, 1811, 43 p.

1819. (7.8, HAY.) LADIES AT HOME; *or, Gentlemen, We can Do Without You.*
A female interlude, in 1 act.
London: Lacy's Acting Edition, Vol. X, n.d., 15 p.

1827. (4.10, D.L.) THE ILLUSTRIOUS STRANGER; *or, Married &*
Buried.
A farce in 1 act.
id., ibid., Vol. LII, 30 p.

1834. (22.7, R.V.) WHO'LL LEND ME A WIFE?
A farce, in 2 acts.
London: Duncombe, Vol. XVIII, n.d., 32 p.

1835. (24.2, D.L.) THE MISER'S DAUGHTER, a drama, in 2 acts.
London: J. Miller, 1835, v + 25 p.

1836. (27.2, QU.) BORROWED FEATHERS,
A farce, in 1 act.
London: Duncombe, Vol. XX, n.d. 28 p.

(b) Miscellaneous prose:

1826. SKETCHES OF ANCIENT AND MODERN BOULOGNE.
Boulogne: Le Roy-Berger, 1826, III + 197 p.

1830. ADVENTURES OF AN IRISH GENTLEMAN.
London: H. Colburn & R. Bentley, 1830, 3 v.
I: XV + 229 p. II: 308 p. III: 297 p.

1839. STORIES OF TORRES VEDRAS, *Sketches of a Soldier's*
Wandering Life.
London: R. Bentley, 1839, 3 v., I: XV + 317 p.
II: 319 p. III: 342 p.

1841. THE HISTORY OF DUELLING ...
London: R. Bentley, 1841, 2 v., I: XII + 399 p.
II: XII + 428 p.

1845. JACK HORNET *or, The March of Intellect.*
London: R. Bentley, 1845, 3 v., I: 315 p. II: 296 p.
III: 322 p. (a novel)

1848. RECOLLECTIONS OF REPUBLICAN FRANCE FROM 1790
TO 1801.
London: H. Colburn, 1848, 2 v.

MITCHEL (John – 1815–1875)

BIOGRAPHY

Born in County Derry in 1815. Studied in Newry, then at Trinity College, Dublin. A lawyer, called to the bar in 1840. Became a member of the Repeal Association in 1843 and started contributing to *The Nation* where he would take the place of his friend Davis on the latter's death. The leader of Young Ireland's most advanced wing, he hastened the break with O'Connell and eventually left the Irish Confederation and his paper to put into action the revolutionary principles that he displayed in a new organ *The United Irishman*. This led to his arrest and condemnation for high treason with fourteen years of hard labour, even before the beginning of the 1848 Rising. He escaped to the United States where he ran several papers and adopted a regrettable and unexpected political attitude: he in fact supported slavery. He returned to Ireland in 1872 and was elected member for Tipperary in 1875. He died in Newry the same year.

BIBLIOGRAPHY

A man of action and a very talented polemist. In the period under discussion, Mitchel chiefly published pamphlets and articles (cf. for the latter: *The Nation*: September 9, 1843; March 2, May 27, 1844; regularly between November 1845 and the beginning of December 1847; January 8, 1848 (Letter to Duffy); February 2, 1850 (Letter to Lalor). *The United Irishman*: every week between February 12 and May 27, 1848).

Among the WORKS PUBLISHED IN BOOK FORM, note the following:

1846. THE LIFE AND TIMES OF AODH O'NEILL, PRINCE OF ULSTER, *called by the English, Hugh, Earl of Tyrone* ...
Dublin: Duffy, 1846, VII + 252 p.

1854. JAIL JOURNAL; *or, Five Years in British Prisons.*
[New York: office of *The Citizen*, 1854].
New York: P. M. Haverty, 1868, VIII + 370 p.
Dublin: M. H. Gill & Son, 1913, XLVII + 453 p.

1860. THE LAST CONQUEST OF IRELAND (PERHAPS).
[New York, 1861.]
Dublin: *The Irishman Office*, 1861, 14 + 326 p.

STUDIES concerning Mitchel are numerous. Besides all historical works dealing with 1848, see:

DILLON (W.): *Life of J. Mitchel*, London: Kegan Paul, Trench & Co, 1888, 2 v., I: XX + 343 p. II: VIII + 312 p.

S (P.A.): *The Life of J. Mitchel, with an historical sketch of the '48 movement in Ireland*, Dublin: Duffy & Co, 1889, XVIII + 285 p.

MONTEGUT (E.): *J. Mitchel: A Study of Irish Nationalism*, translated and edited by J. M. Hone, Dublin and London: Maunsel & Co, 1915, 61 p.

O'HEGARTY (P. S.): *J. Mitchel: An Appreciation, with some account of Young Ireland*, Dublin and London: Maunsel & Co, 1917, VII + 136 p.

WALSH (L. J.): *J. Mitchel*, Dublin and Cork: Talbot Press, 1934, 110 p.

MAC CALL (S.): *Irish Mitchel: A Bibliography*, London: T. Nelson & Sons, 1938, 391 p.

See also *The Irish Book Lover*: VII, n° 4, Nov. 1915, pp. 57–8; VIII, n° 5, Dec. 1915, pp. 86–8 (bibliography by J. M. Douglas).

MONTGOMERY (Henry Riddell – 1818–1904)

Author of:

1840. AN ESSAY *Towards Investigating the Causes that Have Retarded the Progress of Literature in Ireland.*
Belfast: Phillips, 1840, 108 p.

1846. SPECIMENS OF THE EARLY NATIVE POETRY OF IRELAND in *English Metrical Translations*, by Miss Brooke, Dr. Drummond, S. Ferguson, J. C. Mangan, T. Furlong, H. Grattan Curran, Ed. Walsh, J. D'Alton and J. Anster, etc. With historical and biographical notices by H. R. Montgomery.
Dublin: J. M'Glashan; London: W. S. Orr & Co, 1846, VIII + 223 p.
(Enlarged edition: Dublin: Hodges Figgis, 1892, XV + 311 p.)

Also:

1860. THOMAS MOORE, HIS LIFE, WRITING, AND CONTEM-
PORARIES.
London: T. Cautley, 1860.

1865. MEMOIRS OF THE LIFE AND WRITINGS OF SIR R.
STEELE.
Edinburgh: W. P. Nimmo, 1865, 2 v.

1884. FAMOUS LITERARY IMPOSTURES.
London: E. W. Allen, 1884.

and see: *Irish Book Lover.*
I, pp. 100–1; IX, 7, 8, Feb.–Mar. 1918, pp. 71–2.

MOORE (George)

Mentioned in the present work as a contributor to *The Dublin Magazine* in 1800, is probably the man who published the following works cited by O'Donoghue:

[1799. OBSERVATIONS OF THE UNION, Dublin.

1804. MONTBARD; *or, The Buccaneer*, a tragedy, London.

1826. THE MINSTREL'S TALE *and Other Poems*, London.]

MOORE (Thomas – 1779–1852)[1]

BIOGRAPHY

Born in Dublin at 12 Aungier Street on May 28th 1779. Son of a tea-merchant and grocer. Catholic family. Studied at the school run by Samuel Whyte and at Trinity College (B.A.: 1799), where Robert Emmet was his contemporary and friend. Soon gave all his time to poetry and took up residence in England. After a brilliant entry into high society, he experienced a growing literary success, enhanced by his gifts as a singer. The darling of Whig circles whose cause was served by his satirical pen, the friend of Byron and of nearly all the writers and artists of his time, was the most involved

[1] Revised and updated by Thérèse Tessier.

of all Irish writers in the Romantic movement. His *Irish Melodies* which genuinely tried to revive the musical heritage of his native land then won him a European reputation. Held responsible for a major act of embezzlement done by his substitute in a post he once occupied in Bermuda, he had to flee England and remained for two years in Continental exile in Paris.

From 1825 onwards he produced long prose works including biographies (Sheridan, Byron, Lord Edward Fitzgerald), religious controversy, Irish history, etc. His family life, enriched by the tender love of his wife Bessy, was overshadowed by the tragedies of constant poverty and the death of his five children. He died in 1852 after a ten-year period of silence due to illness.

BIBLIOGRAPHY

(a) Poetical works:

1793– in *Anthologia Hibernica* (q.v. under periodicals): II, Oct.
94. 1793, p. 299: 'To Zelia on her charging the author with writing too much on love'; 'A Pastoral Ballad'; Dec., p. 451; 'On the Loss of a Favourite Bird'; III, Feb. 1794, p. 137: 'A Paraphrase of Anacreon's 5th Ode'; Mar., p. 223: 'To Samuel Whyte, Esq.'.

1798. in the *Dublin Magazine and Irish Monthly Register*, I, Sept. 1798, p. 203: 'Imitation of Anacreon's 1st Ode'.

1800. ODES OF ANACREON.
London: J. Stockdale, 1800, VIII + 255 p.

1801. THE POETICAL WORKS OF THE LATE THOMAS LITTLE.
London: J. & T. Carpenter, 1801, XIX + 175 p.

1802. A certain number of songs with words, and sometimes
etc. music, by Moore, appear on sheets.
cf. 1802: 'O Lady Fair'.
1805: 'A Canadian Boat Song', etc.
they are not mentioned here. The publishers of these are R. Rhames, Dublin, J. T. Carpenter, London, etc. The latter published 7 of them in 1804 under the title SONGS AND GLEES.

1806. EPISTLES, ODES AND OTHER POEMS.
London: J. Carpenter, 1806, XI + 341 p.

1808. CORRUPTION AND INTOLERANCE.
London: J. Carpenter, 1808, X + 55 p.

1808– IRISH MELODIES.
34.   — *A Selection of Irish Melodies with symphonies and accompaniments by Sir John Stevenson and characteristic words by Thomas Moore, Esq.*
London: J. Power.

1ST SERIES:
    1ST NUMBER, 1808   (but the preface is signed Feb. 1807) 51 p. folio.

    2ND NUMBER, 1808
    3RD NUMBER, 1810
    4TH NUMBER, 1811
    5TH NUMBER, 1813
    6TH NUMBER, 1815

2ND SERIES:
    7TH NUMBER, 1818
    8TH NUMBER, 1821   (with symphonies and accompaniments by Henry R. Bishop)
    9TH NUMBER, 1825
    10TH NUMBER, 1834   „   „
    SUPPLEMENT, 1834   „   „

They are to be found in 2 volumes and 5 books at the British Museum (H. 1391):

Volume I, Book n⁰ 1 and 2, 102 p.; 2: n° 3 and 4, 109 p.; 3: n° 5 and 6, 113 p.

Volume II, Book 4: n° 7 and 8, 136 p.; 5: n° 9 and 10, Sup., 145 p.

The later editions generally respect the initial order of the poems. Note, however, that the 1st piece in n° 2 'St Sesanus and the Lady' afterwards figures at the beginning of n° 8; and that the 2nd and 3rd pieces in n° 7 are reversed.

The most recent text of the original words and music is the 1963 reprinting of an edition dating from 1879, by Gill & Son, Dublin, 262 p. (*Moore's Irish Melodies*).

1809.   THE SCEPTIC, a philosophical satire.
London: J. Carpenter, 1809, 26 p.

1813.   INTERCEPTED LETTERS; *or, The Two-Penny Post Bag.*
[1st ed., London: J. Carr, 1813]
8th ed., ibid., 1813, VII + 101 p.

1816. SACRED SONGS, first number.
(published separately in London by J. Power, 78 + 3 p., and in Dublin by W. Power.
2nd number: 1824).

LINES ON THE DEATH OF SHERIDAN from *The Morning Chronicle* of Monday, Aug. 5, 1816 ...
London: W. Hone, 1816, 8 p.

1817. LALLA ROOKH, An Oriental Romance.
London: Longman, Hurst, Rees, Orme & Browne, 1817, 405 p.

1818. NATIONAL AIRS, first number.
etc.
[London and Dublin: Power, 1818.]
(2nd number: 1820, ibid., 3rd number: 1821, 4th number: 1822, 5th number: 1826, 6th number: 1827, London only.)

THE FUDGE FAMILY IN PARIS.
[1st ed. London: Longman, etc., 1818]
2nd ed. ibid., 1818, VIII + 168 p.

MELODIES, SONGS AND SACRED SONGS.
New York: Goodrich & Co, 1818, 225 p.

Numerous poems in: *Harmonica* (Cork) (q.v. under Milliken).

1819. TOM CRIB'S MEMORIAL TO CONGRESS ... by One of the Fancy.
London: Longman, etc., 1819, XXXI + 88 p.

THE WORKS OF THOMAS MOORE.
Paris: Galignani, 1819, 6 v., 1 703 p.

1823. THE LOVES OF THE ANGELS, a poem.
London: Longman, etc., 1823, XIV + 198 p.

FABLES FOR THE HOLY ALLIANCE; RHYMES ON THE ROAD, etc.
London: Longman, etc., 1823, XIV + 198 p.

1826. EVENINGS IN GREECE,
etc.   ['First Evening'. London: J. Power, 1826.
'Second Evening', ibid., 1832.]

Evenings in Greece, First and Second Evenings, the Poetry by Th. Moore, the Music Composed and Selected by H. R. Bishop. With the music.
London: J. Power, n.d., 210 p., folio.

1827.   A SET OF GLEES.
[London: J. Power, 1827.]

1828.   ODES UPON CASH, CORN, CATHOLICS, AND OTHER MATTERS.
Selected from the columns of the 'Times' Journal.
London: Longman, etc., 1828, 183 p.

LEGENDARY BALLADS, with the music (H. R. Bishop).
London: J. Power, 1828, 81 p.

1831.   THE SUMMER FÊTE, a poem with songs. With the music (H. R. Bishop, Moore).
London: J. Power, 1831, 108 p.

1834.   VOCAL MISCELLANY.
[First number: London: J. Power, 1834.
2nd number: ibid., 1835.]

1835.   THE FUDGES IN ENGLAND, being a sequel to 'The Fudge Family in Paris'.
London: Longman, etc., 1835, VII + 312 p.

1839.   ALCIPHRON, a poem.
[London: J. Macrone, 1839.]
(an unfinished poetical version of *The Epicurean*, q.v. prose).

1840–   THE POETICAL WORKS COLLECTED BY HIMSELF.
41.   London: Longman, etc., 1840–1, 10 v.

1849.   SONGS, BALLADS, AND SACRED SONGS.
London: Longman, etc., 1849, 284 p.

(b) Dramatic works:

1801.   (24.7, HAY.) THE GYPSY PRINCE, a comic opera, in 2 acts. Composed and selected by Michael Kelly ...
London: Printed for M. Kelly, to be had at his Music Warehouse, n.d., 68 p.

1811.   (9.9, LYC.) M.P.; *or, The Blue Stocking*, a comic opera, in 3 acts ... the music composed and selected by the author of the piece. The overture and arrangements for the orchestra by Mr Horn ...

London: J. Power, 1811, VII + 94 p.
(Anonymous, but Moore signed his preface.)

(c) Miscellaneous prose:

1807. THE LIFE OF SALLUST in: *The Works of Sallust*, trans: Arthur Murphy, London: J. Carpenter, 1807.

1810. A LETTER TO THE ROMAN CATHOLICS OF DUBLIN.
1st ed.: London: Carpenter, 1810, 40 p.
2nd ed.: Dublin: Gilbert & Hodges, 1810, (2) + 37 p.

1814– 34. Articles in *The Edinburgh Review*.
'LORD THURLOW'S POEMS': XXIII, Sept. 1814, p. 411.
'BOYD'S TRANSL. FROM THE FATHERS': XXIV, Nov. 1814, p. 58.
'FRENCH NOVELS': XXXIV, Nov. 1820, p. 372.
'FRENCH ROMANCES': XL, Mar. 1824, p. 158.
'IRISH NOVELS': XLIII, Feb. 1826, p. 356.
'FRENCH OFFICIAL LIFE': XLIV, June 1826, p. 156.
'ANN BOLEYN': XLV, Mar. 1827, p. 321.
'PRIVATE THEATRICALS': XLVI, Oct. 1827, p. 368.
'PROTESTANTISM IN GERMANY' (in collaboration with R. H. Brabant): LIV, Sept. 1831, p. 238.
'FRENCH LITERATURE: RECENT NOVELISTS': LVII, July 1833, p. 330.
'OVERTON'S PORTRAITURE OF THE CHURCH': LVIII, Oct. 1833, p. 31.
'O'BRIEN'S ROUND TOWERS OF IRELAND': LIX, April 1834, p. 143.
(This list is taken from the *Wellesley Index*, with the omission of the 3rd item: 'Coleridge's Christabel'; it is now proven not only that Moore was not its author, but also that he strongly disapproved of it.)

1824. MEMOIRS OF CAPTAIN ROCK, THE CELEBRATED IRISH CHIEFTAIN, with some account of his ancestors written by himself.
[1st ed.: London: Longman, etc., 1824.]
4th ed.: London: Longman, etc., 1824, XIV + 376 p.

1825. MEMOIRS OF THE LIFE OF THE RIGHT HONOURABLE BRINSLEY SHERIDAN.
London: Longman, etc., 1825, XII + 719 p.

1827. THE EPICUREAN, a tale.
London: Longman, etc., VIII + 332 p.

1830. LETTERS AND JOURNALS OF LORD BYRON with notices of his Life by Thomas Moore.
London: J. Murray, 1830, 2 v., I: VIII + 670 p. II: 823 p.

1831. THE LIFE AND DEATH OF LORD EDWARD FITZGERALD.
London: Longman, etc., 1831, 2 v., I: XI + 307 p. II: 305 p.

1833. TRAVELS OF AN IRISH GENTLEMAN IN SEARCH OF A RELIGION.
London: Longman, etc., 1833, 2 v., I: XII + 335 p. II: VII + 354 p.

1835– THE HISTORY OF IRELAND.
  45. London: Longman, etc., 4 v. ('The Cabinet Cyclopoedia')
(I: 1835, XII + 321 p. II: 1837, XV + 345 p. III: 1840, XIX + 327 p. IV: 1845, XX + 313 p.)

(d) Posthumous memoirs, correspondence, collections, etc.:

1853. MEMOIRS, JOURNAL, AND CORRESPONDENCE edited by Ld J. Russell.
London: Longman, etc., 1853, 8 v.

1878. PROSE AND VERSE, HUMOROUS, SATIRICAL AND SENTIMENTAL, with suppressed passages from the Memoirs of Lord Byron ..., introd. by R. H. Shepherd.
London: Chatto & Windus, 1878, X + 444 p.

1910. POETICAL WORKS, Oxford.

1925. TOM MOORE'S DIARY, a selection edited with an introduction, by J. B. Priestley.
Cambridge: University Press, 1925, XV + 218 p.

1964. THE LETTERS OF THOMAS MOORE, edited by Wilfred S. Dowden.
Oxford: Clarendon Press; London: Oxford University Press, 1964, 2 v., (I: 1793–1818 II: 1818–1847) 989 p.
Journal 1818–1841 (Selection), edited by P. C. Quennell.
London, 1964, XV + 256 p.

(e) Selected secondary material:

All works on Irish–English poetry. Also: Brandes (*Main Currents*), Courthope (*History of English Poetry*), Maginn (*Gal-*

lery), Monahan (*Nova Hibernia*), Saintsbury (*History of English Prosody*), Symons (*The Romantic Movement in English Poetry*), etc. (q.v. in general bibliography).

Beside the above, see:

POE (E. A.): *The Poetic Principle*, 1848.

VALLAT (G.): *Thomas Moore, sa Vie et ses Œuvres*, Paris: A. Rousseau; London: Asher; Dublin: Hodges Figgis, 1886, XX + 293 p.

GWYNN (S.): *Thomas Moore*, London: Macmillan, 1904, 203 p. ('English Men of Letters').

THOMAS (A. B.): *Moore en France*, Paris: Champion, 1911, XII + 173 p.

STOCKLEY (W. F. P.): *Essays in Irish Biography*, Cork University Press, 1933, 191 p. ('Moore and Ireland': 1–34; 'The Religion of Thomas Moore': 34–92.)

MAC MANUS (M. J.): *A Bibliographical Hand-List of the First Editions of Thomas Moore*, Dublin: reprinted from the 'Dublin Magazine' for private circulation, 1934.

MAC CALL (S.): *Thomas Moore*, London: G. Duckworth; Dublin: Talbot Press, 1935, 132 p.

STRONG (L. A. G.): *The Minstrel Boy. A Portrait of Tom Moore*, London: Hodder & Stoughton, 1937, XII + 317 p.

JONES (H. M.): *The Harp that Once, A Chronicle of the Life of Thomas Moore*, New York: Henry Holt & Co, 1937, XVI + 365 p.

JORDAN (Hoover H.): 'Thomas Moore' in *The English Romantic Poets and Essayists* edited by C. W. and L. H. Houtchens, New York M.L.A., 1957, 1966, (pp. 199–220).
Bolt Upright: The Life of Thomas Moore. Salzburg Studies in English Literature, Salzburg, 1975, 2 v, VI + 666 p.

de FORD (Miriam A.): *Thomas Moore*, New York: Twayne, 1967, 128 p. ('Twayne's English Author Series').

TESSIER (Thérèse): *La Poésie lyrique de Thomas Moore (1779–1852)*, Paris: Didier, 1975, XIV + 498 p. ('Etudes Anglaises').

WHITE (TERENCE DE VERE —): *Tom Moore, the Irish Poet*, London: Hamish Hamilton, 1977, XIV + 281 p.

MORGAN (Sydney Owenson, Lady – 1776–1859)

BIOGRAPHY

Born in 1776, as it has finally been possible to establish in spite of the concealments and repeated lies of the interested party, on Christmas Day, on a boat that was crossing the Irish Sea. Her father Mac Owen was a Catholic from Connaught who had abandoned his religion, anglicised his name and adopted the acting profession; he was to become distinguished in this field. Her mother, *née* Jane Hill, died in 1789. Sydney Owenson studied at Mrs Terson's school in Clontarf then in humbler Dublin boarding schools and had eventually to interrupt her schooling when the successive bankruptcies of the theatres that her father directed made the family's financial situation almost desperate. The young girl began to write and took a job as governess first near Dublin, then with the Crawfords in Northern Ireland. With literary fame, her worldly life developed and, in the course of a stay with some titled friends, she met a doctor, Charles Morgan, who became her husband. At the request of Sydney who was hardly eager to link her future to that of a commoner, the Duke of Richmond kindly had him knighted. Lady Morgan divided the rest of her life between England, Ireland (where she defended the cause of the Emancipation) and France. She visited that country three times, in 1816, in 1818–19 when she was the guest of La Fayette and opened a literary and political salon in Paris, and in 1828–30 when Stendhal was among her friends. She died in 1859, on April 13, in London.

BIBLIOGRAPHY
(a) Poetical and dramatic works:

1801. POEMS.
Dublin: Printed by Alex Stewart ... and Mr. Phillips, London, 1801, 157 p.

1805. TWELVE ORIGINAL HIBERNIAN MELODIES; with English Words, Imitated and Translated from the Works of the Ancient Irish Bards.
London: Preston, n.d. [1805], 23 p. folio.
(The musical arrangements are by Hook.
Contents: 'Ned of the Hills'; 'Cathleen Nolan'; 'The Mountain Sprite'; 'Shelah na Conolan'; 'Drimenduath'; 'Dha Vecca's un Choolen'; 'Away with the tear'; 'Open the door 'tis your true love'; 'O let me hush thy tender fears'; 'Oh Gracey once I thought thee mine').

1807. THE LAY OF AN IRISH HARP; *or, Metrical Fragments.*
London: R. Phillips, 1807, XV + 199 p.

(4.3, C.S.) THE FIRST ATTEMPT; *or, The Whim of the Moment,* a comic opera.
[London, 1807, folio.] (Music by T. S. Cooke).

1818. [VERSES TO MARIANNE HOWARD.
(according to O'Donoghue).]

(b) Novels:

1803. ST CLAIR; *or, the Heiress of Desmond.*
London: Harding, etc.; Dublin: J. Archer, 1803,
VI + 248 p.

1805. THE NOVICE OF ST DOMINICK.
London: R. Phillips, 1806, 4 v., I: 364 p. II: 379 p. III: 393 p. IV: 395 p.

1806. THE WILD IRISH GIRL.*
[1st ed.: London: Phillips, 1806, 4 v.]
London: H. Colburn, 1846, XLII + 421 p. (revised edition).

1809. WOMAN, *or, Ida of Athens.*
London: Longman, etc., 1809, 4 v. I: XXVIII + 223 p. II: 272 p.

1811. THE MISSIONARY, an Indian Tale.
London: J. J. Stockdale, 1811, 3 v. I: 228 p. II: 255 p. III: 222 p.
(republished under the title *Luxima, the Prophetess* (revised), cf. London: C. Westerton, 1859, IV + 330 p.).

1814. O'DONNEL, a National Tale.*
London: H. Colburn, 1814, 3 v. I: XII + 295 p. II: 331 p. III: 339 p.
(Revised edition: ibid., 1836, XVI + 442 p.)

1818. FLORENCE MACARTHY, an Irish Tale.*
[1st edition, London: H. Colburn, 1818, 4 v.]
N. York: D. and J. Sadleir & Co, n.d., 588 p.

1827. THE O'BRIENS AND THE O'FLAHERTYS, a National Tale.*
London: H. Colburn, 1827, 4 v. I: XI + 295 p. II: 340 p. III: 332 p. IV: 362 p.

1835.   THE PRINCESS *or, The Beguine.*
London: R. Bentley, 1835, 3 v., I: 340 p. II: 332 p. III: 383 p.

(c) Miscellaneous prose:

1804.   A FEW REFLECTIONS, *Occasioned by the Perusal of a Work, entitled 'Familiar Epistles to F. J(ones), Esq.'*
Dublin: printed by J. Parry, 1804, V + 77 p.

1817.   FRANCE.[1]
[1st ed.: London: Colburn, 1817, 2 v.]

4 ed., with additional notes, ibid., 1818, 2 v.
I: XVI + 428 p. II: VII + 415 + CLXXI p.
(The appearance of this work was followed by a multitude of replies, beginning with:
Defauconpret (A. J. B.): *Observation sur l'Ouvrage intitulé «La France»,* Paris: H. Nicolle, 1817, 138 p.
also:
Dupin (Baron F.P.C.): *Lettre, a Mylady Morgan,* Paris, 1818.
Playfair (W.): *France As it Is, not Lady Morgan's France,* 1819. Etc.)

1821.   ITALY.
London: H. Colburn, 1821, 2 v., I: XI + 356 p. II: IX + 482 + 28 p.

[LETTERS TO THE REVIEWERS OF 'ITALY'.
London: H. Colburn, 1821.]

1822.   THE MOHAWKS: A SATIRICAL POEM. (Written in collaboration with Sir Charles Morgan.)

1824.   THE LIFE AND TIMES OF SALVATOR ROSA.
London: H. Colburn, 1824, 2 v., I: XVI + 405 p. II: VIII + 379 p.

1825.   ABSENTEEISM.
London: H. Colburn, 1825, XIX + 160 p.

1829.   THE BOOK OF THE BOUDOIR.
London: H. Colburn, 1829, 2 v., I: XII + 339 p. II: IV + 323 p.

---

[1] Note the recent anthology by: Suddaby (Elizabeth) and Yarrow (P. J.), eds.: *Lady Morgan in France.* Newcastle upon Tyne: Oriel Press, 1971, 399 p.

1830. FRANCE IN 1829–30. (See footnote on previous page.)
London: Saunders & Otley, 1830, 2 v., I: IX + 527 p. II: IV + 559 p.

1833. DRAMATIC SCENES FROM REAL LIFE.*
London: Saunders & Otley, 1833, 2 v., I: XX + 329 p. II: 316 p.
(Three stories written in dialogue that are classified here under 'miscellaneous' rather than under novels on account of that particular form: They are 'Manor Sackville'; 'The Easter Recess'; 'Temper'.)

1840. WOMAN AND HER MASTER.
London: H. Colburn, 1840, 2 v., I: VIII + 334 p. II: IV + 416 p.
(Women through the ages.)

1841. THE BOOK WITHOUT A NAME.
London: H. Colburn, 1841, 2 v., I: VI + 355 p. II: 357 p.
(Written in collaboration with Sir Charles Morgan; items by Lady Morgan are:
I: 'Le Cordon Bleu'; 'Milton's House'; 'St Alban's Abbey'; 'Memoirs of the Macaw of a Lady of Quality'.
II: 'The Hong Merchant's Widow'; 'Pimlico'; 'The Hotel de Carnavalet'; 'Irish Historians'; 'A Walk in the Snow'; 'Malahide Castle'; 'Puck of the Pale'.)

1851. LETTER TO CARDINAL WISEMAN.
London: Westerton, 1851, 39 p.

1859. PASSAGES IN MY AUTOBIOGRAPHY, an Odd Volume.
London: R. Bentley, 1859, XI + 339 p.

1862. LADY MORGAN'S MEMOIRS. DIARIES AND CORRESPONDENCE, collected by W. H. Dixon.
London: W. H. Allen & Co, 1862, 2 v., I: VIII + 532 p. II: 559 p.

(d) Secondary material:

GENERAL WORKS: (q. v. in the general bibliography):
Baker (*History of the English Novel*, Vol. 7), Chorley (*The Authors of England*), Flanagan (*The Irish Novelists 1800–50* (pp. 107–164)), Hamilton (*Notable Irishwomen*, Ch. VII), Harrison (*Irish Women Writers*, Ch. III, pp. 110–279), Krans (*Irish Life in Irish Fiction*, passim), Leclaire (*Bibliography*, 19–21), Maginn (*Gallery*), Paston (*Little Memoirs of the XIXth Century*), Rosa

(*The Silver Fork School*, passim), Utter and Needham (*Pamela's Daughters*, passim), Whitmore (*Woman's Work in English Fiction*, Ch. VII).

Also the MEMOIRS, etc., of Croker (J. W.), Hall (S. C.), Scott (W.), etc.

Monographs, etc.:

FITZPATRICK (W. J.): *Friends, Foes and Adventures of Lady Morgan*, Dublin: W. B. Kelly; London: Simpkin & Marshall, 1859, 144 p.

> *Lady Morgan, her Career, Literary and Personal, with a glimpse of her friends, and a word to her calumniators.*
> London: C. J. Skeet, 1860, XII + 308 p.

STEVENSON (Lionel): 'Vanity Fair and Lady Morgan', *P.M.L.A.*, XLVIII, 1933, pp. 547–551.

> *The Wild Irish Girl: The Life of Sydney Owenson, Lady Morgan, 1776–1859.*
> London: Chapman & Hall, 1936, 330 p., reprinted 1969.

MORAUD (Marcel I.): *Une Irlandaise libérale en France sous la Restauration, Lady Morgan, 1775–1859*, Paris: M. Didier, 1954, 205 p. («Etudes de Littérature Etrangère et Comparée» 25.)

NEWCOMER, (James): ' "Manor Sackville": Lady Morgan's Study of Ireland's Perilous Case', *Eire–Ireland*, X, 3, Autumn 1975, pp. 11–17.

JEFFARES (A. Norman): 'Early Efforts of the Wild Irish Girl', pp. 293–305 in *Le Romantisme anglo-américain*, Mélanges offerts à Louis Bonnerot. Paris, Didier, 1971 («Etudes Anglaises» 39).

MULCHINOCK (William P. – 1820–1864)

A poet born in Tralee. Contributed to the Cork *Southern Reporter* (cf. *Echoes from Parnassus*) and to *The Nation* (cf. *The Spirit of the Nation*). Resided in the United States from 1849 to 1855. There, he ran *The Irish Advocate* and published a collection *Ballads and Songs*, New York, 1851.

MUSGRAVE (Sir Richard – 1757(?)–1818)

Author of: *Letter on the Present Situation of Public Affairs*, 1795, *Memoir of the Different Rebellions in Ireland*, 1801.

NORTON (Caroline E. S. Sheridan, Mrs —, 1808–1877)

BIOGRAPHY

Granddaughter of Richard Brinsley Sheridan (see the family tree of Mrs Alicia Le Fanu), and daughter of Lady Dufferin whose beauty and intelligence she is said to have shared. Born in London in 1808. Her first marriage (1829–69) seems to have been unhappy. She remarried again in 1877, the year of her death. Her second husband was Sir W. Stirling-Maxwell.

BIBLIOGRAPHY

(a) Poetry:

1829. THE SORROWS OF ROSALIE, a tale, *and Other Poems.*
London: J. Ebers & Co, 1829, 136 p.
(The author's name is not indicated.)

1830. THE UNDYING ONE, *and Other Poems.*
London: H. Colburn, 1830, VIII + 272 p.

1833. POEMS.
Boston: Allen & Ticknor, 1833, IV + 148 p.

1836. A VOICE FROM THE FACTORIES, in serious verse.
London: J. Murray, 1836, IX + 40 p.

1840. THE DREAM, *and Other Poems.*
London: H. Colburn, 1840, X + IV + 301 p.

LINES (*on the Young Queen Victoria*, etc.)
London: Saunders & Otley, 1840, 4 p.

1845. THE CHILD OF THE ISLANDS, a poem.
London: Chapman & Hall, 1845, XVI + 238 p.

1847. FISHER'S DRAWING-ROOM SCRAPBOOK with poetical illustrations by Mrs Norton. London: The Caxton Press, 84 p.

AUNT CARRY'S BALLADS FOR CHILDREN ..., *Adventures of a Wood Sprite, the Story of Blanche and Brutikin.*
London: J. Cundoll, 1847, 53 p., in-4°, ill.

1849. [THE MARTYR, a tragedy, in verse, London.]

1850. [TALES AND SKETCHES in prose and verse, London.]

1859. THE CENTENARY FESTIVAL, Verses on R. Burns.
London: reprinted from the *Daily Scotsman*, 1859, 8 p., in-4°.

1862. THE LADY OF LA GARAYE, a poem.
Cambridge: Macmillan & Co, 1862, XIX + 128 p.

1888. [BINGEN ON THE RHINE, a poem.
London: J. Walker & Co, 1888.]

1892. SELECTED POEMS in *The Poets and the Poetry of the Century*, edited by A. H. Miles. London: Hutchinson, Vol. VII, 1892.

(b) Miscellaneous prose:

Beside a certain number of pamphlets on matrimonial legislation, the custody of children, etc.

1841? LETTERS, JUNE 1836–JULY 1841.
London: privately printed, VI + 51 + 66 p.

1848. LETTERS TO THE MOB by Libertas, reprinted from the *Morning Chronicle.*
London: T. Bosworth, 1848, 21 p.

1851. STUART OF DUNLEATH, a Story of Modern Times.
London: H. Colburn, 1851, 3 v. I: XI + 290 p. II: 299 p. III: 345 p.

1861. Contribution to *Macmillan's Magazine.*
etc.

1863. [LOST AND SAVED, a novel.
London: Hurst & Blackett, 1863, 3 v.]

1868. OLD SIR DOUGLAS, a novel, London, ibid., 3 v. I: VII + 308 p. II: 307 p. III: 308 p.

1934. SOME UNRECORDED LETTERS OF C. NORTON in the Altschul Collection of the Yale University Library, edited by Bertha Coolidge.
Boston: privately printed, 1934, 25 p.

(c) Secondary material:

HECTOR (A. F.) (i.e.: Mrs Alexander): *Women Novelists of Queen Victoria's Reign, A Book of Appreciations.*
London: Hurst & Blackett, 1897, pp. 275–90.

PERKINS (J. G.): *The Life of Mrs Norton,* London: J. Murray, 1909, XIV + 312 p.

ACLAND (Alice): *Caroline Norton,* London: Constable, 1948, 235 p.

O'BRIEN (Fitz-James – 1828–1862)

BIOGRAPHY

Born in Cork in 1828 to James O'Brien and Eliza O'Driscoll ... After having inherited, on coming of age, the substantial fortune of his maternal grandfather, left Ireland for London where he quickly squandered his riches.

Emigrated to the U.S.A. about 1852. There, he was to become a distinguished figure in the literary bohemia of New York and experience success as a journalist, playwright and short story writer: his horror stories ('The Diamond Lens' (1858), 'What was It' (1859), 'The Wondersmith', 'id.)) are among the most remarkable ever written. Died from a wound in 1862 during the American Civil War.

BIBLIOGRAPHY

This has been established in detail by Francis Wolle (q. v. below) whose work gives, beside other things, details on

(a) Poems published in periodicals:

1845–7. *The Nation* (seven pieces)

1848. *The Cork Magazine* (ten pieces)

1849. *The Irishman*

1850. *The Family Friend*

1851. *The Parlour Magazine*
The Dublin University Magazine

Household Words
1852. *The Lantern.*
(From then on, O'Brien's name appeared in *The American Whig Review, The New York Daily Times, Harper's New Monthly Magazine*, etc.)

(b) Tales or short stories also published in magazines.

but none of which is anterior to 1850.

(c) Plays

of which the first 4 and the last were performed at Wallack's Theatre, the 6th at Laura Keene's Theatre – the others were not performed.

1852. 25.12. MY CHRISTMAS DINNER, a farce.

1854. 11.12. A GENTLEMAN FROM IRELAND. A comedy, in two acts.

27.12. THE SISTERS. A drama, in two acts.

1856. 4.2. DUKE HUMPHREY'S DINNER. A dramatic sketch.

THE CUP AND THE LIP.

1860. 2.7. THE TYCOON; *or, Young America in Japan.* A Burlesque.

? BLOOD WILL TELL.

? THE TWO OPHELIAS.

? SAMSON.

1863. 30.9. ROSEDALE.

(d) Publications in book form:

The Poems and Stories of Fitz-James O'Brien. Collected and edited, with a Sketch of the Author, by William Winter, Boston: J. R. Osgood & Co, 1881.
The Fantastic Tales of Fitz-James O'Brien. Edited with an introduction by Michael Hayes, London: J. Calder, 1977.

Secondary material:

WOLLE (Francis): *Fitz-James O'Brien, a Literary Bohemian of the Eighteen-Fifties.* Boulder, Colorado, 1944, XI + 309 p.

('University of Colorado Studies'. Series B. Studies in the Humanities. Vol. 2, n° 2).

O'BRIEN (Henry – 1800–1835)

An Irish archaeologist and author of *The Round Towers of Ireland* (London: Whittaker, 1833; 2nd edition, Dublin: J. Cumming, 1834, 36 + 524 p.) in which he expounded the thesis of the oriental origin of these towers. O'Brien accused Moore of having plagiarised him in his *History of Ireland* and a quarrel followed, F. S. Mahony vigorously siding against Moore.

O'BRIEN (William Smith – 1803–1864)

One of the greatest politicians of nineteenth-century Ireland and leader of the hapless rebellion of 1848. Condemned to death then reprieved, he was subjected to hard labour until 1854.

Has left no strictly speaking 'literary' work but a certain number of speeches, pamphlets (cf.: *Plan for the Relief of the Poor in Ireland*, London: J. M. Richardson, 1830, 59 p.) and one larger work:

PRINCIPLES OF GOVERNMENT; *or, Meditations in Exile*. Dublin: J. Duffy, 1856, 2 v., I: VIII + 388 p. II: 380 p.

O'CALLAGHAN (John Cornelius – 1805–1883)

A lawyer born in Dublin, a contributor to *The Nation* and author of *History of the Irish Brigades in the Service of France*, Glasgow, 1869, reprinted in 1970 by the Irish University Press.

O'CONNELL (Daniel – 1775-1847)

The 'Liberator', whose life has been written countless times from W. J. O'Neill's *Personal Recollections* (q.v.) to Angus Macintyre's recent work (*The Liberator*, London: Hamish Hamilton, 1965, 348 p.) not forgetting Seán O'Faolain's *King of the Beggars* (1938), was not a man of letters, although, in 1843, he tried his hand at history with *A Memoir of Ireland, Native and Saxon, 1772-1860*, London: Dolman.

His speeches, letters, journal, etc, have nevertheless been collected several times, cf.:

THE LIFE AND SPEECHES (J. O'Connell).
Dublin: J. Duffy, 1846, 2 v.

THE SPEECHES & PUBLIC LETTERS (M. F. Cusack).
Dublin: M'Glashan & Gill, 1875.

CORRESPONDENCE (W. J. Fitzpatrick).
London: J. Murray, 1888, 2 v.

DANIEL O'CONNELL: HIS EARLY LIFE AND JOURNAL (A. Houston).
London: Sir Isaac Pitman, 1906.

etc.

And in the catalogues of the British Museum and the National Library of Ireland, a number of pamphlets written by Daniel O'Connell will also be found.

O'CURRY (Eugene – 1796-1862)

Born in Dunaha, County Clare in 1796. Until 1815 worked on his father's farm. In 1834, after various posts, he found work on the staff of the Ordnance Survey of Ireland and then as an archivist specialising in Gaelic manuscripts (he established the British Museum catalogue in this field). In 1858 the chair of Irish History and Archaeology at the Catholic University was to reward the labours of this tireless self-taught man.

His influence had made itself felt well before 1850; his great works published in book form are posterior to this date, critical editions with translations such as:

THE SICK BED OF CUCHULAINN & THE ONLY JEALOUSY OF EMER. THE 'TRI THRUAIGHE NA SCÉALAIGHEACHTA': *The Three Most Sorrowful Tales of Erinn.* Dublin: J. F. Fowles, 1858.

studies like:

LECTURES ON THE MANUSCRIPT MATERIALS OF ANCIENT IRISH HISTORY, Dublin: J. Duffy, 1861.

ON THE MANNERS & CUSTOMS OF THE ANCIENT IRISH. London: Williams & Norgate; Dublin: W. B. Kelly; New York: Scribner, 1873, 3 v.

The centenary of the death of the great scholar was celebrated in 1962, cf. the articles by Micheál O hAodha in *The Irish Times.* See also D. Ryan: *The Sword of Light.*

O'DALY (John – 1800–1878)

Born in Farnane, County Waterford, was educated in the 'hedge-schools', he himself taught Irish at Kilkenny then came to set himself up as bookseller in Dublin. There, he was to work with Mangan and Walsh and do much for the development of Gaelic. His principal works are:

1844. RELIQUES OF IRISH JACOBITE POETRY (q.v. under Walsh, E.)

1846. SELF-INSTRUCTION IN IRISH. Dublin: J. Daly, 1846, 56 p.

1847. [O DUBHAGAIN (Seán): THE KINGS OF THE RACE OF EIBHEAR ... edited by J. Daly with a translation by M. Kearney. Dublin, 1847.]

1849. THE POETS & POETRY OF MUNSTER (q.v. under Mangan, J. C.).

After 1850, note among others the edition of the *Fenian Poems* for the Ossianic Society of Dublin: 1st series, 1859, XXXII + 320 p.; 2nd series, 1861, XVI + 224 p.

O'DONOVAN (John – 1809–1861)

Born in Attateemore, County Kilkenny; the 'fifth master' worked at the Irish archives from 1826 then, after 1829, at the Ordnance Survey. There he met O'Curry whose sister he married.

In the impressive list of his publications mention will be made of:

1842. THE BANQUET OF DUN NA N-GEDH, *and* THE BATTLE OF MAG RATH ... with a translation and notes.
Dublin: Irish Archaeological Society, 1842, XXIII + 360 p., in-4°.

1843. THE TRIBES AND CUSTOMS OF HY-MANY ... with a translation and notes, ibid., 1843, 212 p., in-4°.

1844. THE GENEALOGIES, TRIBES & CUSTOMS OF HY-FIACHRACH ... id., ibid., 1844.

1845. A GRAMMAR OF THE IRISH LANGUAGE.
Dublin: Hodges, 1845, 88 + 460 p.

But there are also:

IRISH CHARTERS IN THE 'BOOK OF KELLS' (1846)

LEABHAR NA gCEART (1847).

THE GENEALOGY OF CORCA LAIDHE (1849)

and the author's most formidable compilation:

ANNALA RIOGHACTA EIREANN, *Annals of the Kingdom of Ireland by the Four Masters*

which he published in 7 volumes, in Dublin: Hodges, Smith & Co. between 1848 and 1851.

In 1840, O'Donovan, with O'Curry, founded the Archaeological Society. In 1850, he was appointed to the chair of Celtic studies at the University of Belfast. He died in Dublin in 1861.

His correspondence was collected between 1924 and 1932 by Father O'Flanagan (50 volumes) and he figures in nearly all works devoted to Ireland (see, among others, D. Ryan: *The Sword of Light*).

O'FLANAGAN (Theophilus – 1762–1814)

Born near Tulla (Clare); studied at Trinity College; a teacher by profession. An important translator to whom we owe the English text of the following works:

1795. CAMBRESIS REFUTED (John Lynch)
Dublin: printed by J. Hill, 1795, 16 + 63 + 48 p.

1808. 'ADVICE TO A PRINCE' (T. Mac Brody); 'DEIRDRE; *or, The Lamentable Fate of the Sons of Usnach'.*
Transactions of the Gaelic Society, Vol. I, 28 + 40 + 54 + 240 + 36 p.
Dublin: printed by J. Barlow, 1808.

1822. THE ANNALS OF INNISFALLEN.
Dublin: printed by J. Christie, 1822, 34 + 30 p.

OGLE (Rt Hon. George – 1742(?)–1814)

Born in County Wexford, a conservative politician, hostile to Catholic Emancipation, member for Wexford then Dublin, and author of a few famous songs including 'Banna's Banks' and 'Molly Asthore'. His name appears in the following volumes:

1775. [POETICAL AMUSEMENTS AT A VILLA NEAR BATH.]

1839. THE POPULAR SONGS OF IRELAND (q.v. under Croker (T. C.)).

1849. THE SONGS OF IRELAND (q.v. under Ellis (H.)).

O'HAGAN (John – 1822–1890)

Born in Newry. Studied at Trinity College. A barrister, later a judge. A member of the Young Ireland party, he contributed to *The Nation* under the pseudonym 'Sliabh Cuilinn'. Several poems by him will be found in *The Spirit of the Nation.* His other publications (cf. 1880: *The Song of Roland*; 1887: *The Poetry of Samuel Ferguson*; 1890: *The Children's Ballad Rosary*) as may be seen, are all posterior to the period under discussion.

O'HALLORAN (Sylvester – 1728–1807)

A medical man and archaeologist who dealt with many a subject, from gangrene to the following:

1770.   INSULA SACRA.
Limerick, printed by T. Welsh, 1770, 35 p.

1772.   AN INTRODUCTION TO THE STUDY OF THE HISTORY AND ANTIQUITIES OF IRELAND. Dublin: printed by T. Ewing, 1772, (8) + 20 + 384 p.

1774.   IERNE DEFENDED.
Dublin: printed by T. Ewing, 1774, 36 p.

1778.   A GENERAL HISTORY OF IRELAND.
[London, 1778, 2 v.]
Dublin: printed by H. Fitz-Patrick, 1803, 3 v. (the first consisting of the 2nd title in this list). We know that this work would later on decide Standish O'Grady's vocation.

1789.   'An Introductory Discourse to the Poem of "CONLOCH" ' in *Reliques of Irish Poetry*, (q.v. under Ch. Brooke.)

O'KEEFFE (John – 1747–1833)

BIOGRAPHY

John O'Keeffe (whose name is often spelt O'Keefe) was born on June 24, 1747, in Dublin (Abbey Street) to an Irish father and mother (his mother was an O'Connor and came from County Wexford).

He studied in the Irish capital with Father Austin of the Society of Jesus, then at the Dublin School of Design where he devoted himself for a time to the fine arts. His theatrical vocation had, however, been precociously awakened, Farquhar's plays had been a revelation to him, and he soon became an actor in Mossop's company. Married in 1774 to Mary Heaphy, daughter of the manager of the Dublin Theatre Royal, his marriage proved unhappy. John and Mary separated in 1781, he went to live in England and, in spite of his profound love for his native country, never returned to Ireland. Mary's name was never again mentioned in the family, O'Keeffe's daughter Adelaide tells us, except on the day in 1814 when the author learnt that he was a widower.

John O'Keeffe had three children from his marriage: a son who died in infancy, John Tottenham (1775–1803) and Adelaide (1776–1855), her father's companion, secretary and editor. With the exception of four plays which are juvenilia, it was during O'Keeffe's period in London (1781–1815) – or at least during the first part of this period, since he stopped writing for the theatre in 1798 – that his dramatic works were composed. In 1815, he was living in Chichester, and in 1830, in Southampton. It was there that on February 4, 1833, died he whom Hazlitt (*Lectures on the English Comic Writers.* VIII) would call 'The English Molière' and Lady Morgan (*O'Keeffe's Legacy*, p. xi) 'The Béranger of Ireland', he whom Scott recalled in one of the *Tales of My Landlord* and in *St Ronan's Well*, and he of whom Thomas Lawrenson painted a very beautiful portrait which is in the National Portrait Gallery in London.

The most prolific of the authors of musical comedies of the late XVIIIth century, and too prolific to have had the time to worry about the quality, he nevertheless remains an interesting character with the contrast of his forced gaiety and – in private – his reserve, his severity, even his melancholy, with the ironies and adversities of his life: a Jacobite, he was, in fact, paid by the House of Brunswick; a patriot, he was an exile; a countryman, he found himself a townsman in spite of himself; a Catholic, he had a son who became a Protestant minister; a painter, he went almost blind in the last years of his life.

BIBLIOGRAPHY

(a) Poetry:

1795. OATLANDS; OR, THE TRANSFER OF THE LAUREL, a poem. London: H. Debrett, 1795, 10 p.
(An occasional poem devoid of interest.)

1800. in: *The Dublin Magazine and Irish Monthly Register:*

'Lines': 'The sun shone forth in radiance bright': Vol. IV. Feb. 1800, pp. 115–6.

'SIMON THE PAUPER', a ballad in 3 parts: 'At twilight, 'twas bleak, for the winds whistled round'. Vol. IV, May 1800, pp. 305–6.

'THE CITY BRANIM': 'Jack Bonzum was of gentle mind'. (That nothing oriental be sought in this ... vegetarian poem.) Vol. V, July 1800, pp. 57–9.

'THE SHEPHERD AND THE SURVEYOR, on the inclosing of the commons': 'A Hillock green where many there were not', Vol. V, Oct. 1800, pp. 249–53.

1818. HER MOUTH WITH A SMILE in *Harmonica*, Cork, (q.v. under Milliken.)

1826. (see also *Recollections*, below).

1834. O'KEEFFE'S LEGACY TO HIS DAUGHTER *being The Poetical Works of the Late John O'Keeffe, Esq., the dramatic author.*
London: Whittaker, 1834 (posth.), XXVIII + 396 p.
(The work is edited by Adelaide O'Keeffe.
I-X subscribers; XI-XXVIII: memoir; passim: poems including:
'WAR AND PEACE' (anti-war poem) (pp. 5–111).
'MY LAMENTATION' (to the tune 'Erin go Bra') (pp. 162–64).
'PATRICK'S DAY IN THE MORNING' (p. 167).
'BONA THE RAKE' ... (4 cantos on Napoleon) (pp. 179–263).
'MY SIX DELIGHTFUL STORIES' (tales) (pp. 272–321).
'REVOLUTIONS IN EUROPE' (pp. 347–389).)

(b) Prose:

O'Keeffe did some journalism (in *The Morning Herald* according to O'Donoghue, in *The Morning Chronicle* in which he signed himself as 'The Seer', according to Adelaide O'Keeffe).

1826. RECOLLECTIONS OF THE LIFE OF JOHN O'KEEFFE, written by himself, in 2 volumes, London: H. Colburn, 1826, portr. I: XII + 407 p. II: VIII + 427 p.

(c) Dramatic works: plays published complete or in part:

1767. (14.1, S.A.) THE SHE GALLANT; *or, Square-Toes Outwitted*, a new comedy in two acts.
London: T. Lowndes & J. Williams, 1767, 36 p.
(*The She Gallant* would be revived, with alterations under the title *The Positive Man*.)

1778. (2.7, HAY.) TONY LUMPKIN IN TOWN, a farce.
London: T. Cadell, 1780, 37 p.

(The work is dedicated to G. Colman who wrote the prologue.)

1779. (14.8, HAY.) THE SON IN LAW, a comic opera, in 2 acts. London: B. Bladon and H. Lowndes, 1792, 32 p. (Also figures in *Cumberland's British Theatre*, with comments, engraving, etc., Vol. 31, 36 p.)

1781. (16.6, HAY.) THE DEAD ALIVE, a comic opera, in 2 acts. Dublin, sold by the booksellers, 1783, 34 p. (Unauthorised edition, the composer's name not given. The play is entitled *Edward and Caroline* in the manuscript in the Larpent collection.)

(3.9, HAY.) THE AGREEABLE SURPRISE, a comic opera, in 2 acts. The music composed by Dr Arnold. Dublin, 1783, 52p.; Newry: printed by R. Stevenson, 1783, 36 p. (It is in this play that the poem

> 'Amo, amas
> I love a lass'.

is found. For a more reliable version see the 1829 edition of *Cumberland's British Theatre*, Vol. 31, 39 p. with remarks, notes on the costumes, etc ...)

(28.11, C.G.) THE BANDITTI; *or, Love's Labyrinth*, a comic opera, music by Dr Arnold. (No complete text exists (the manuscript is in the Larpent collection) but only: *Songs, Duets, Trios, Choruses, etc ... in the Comic Opera of The Banditti*, London: T. Cadell, 1781, 27 p. The play was recast under the title *The Castle of Andalusia*.)

1782. (C.G.) THE POSITIVE MAN, in 2 acts, the music by Michael Arne. (This operetta is a revised version of the comedy *The She Gallant* and was published for the first time in *The Dramatic Works*, 1798, Vol. II, p. 425–462.)

(17.8, HAY.) HARLEQUIN TEAGUE; *or, The Giant's Causeway*. Only the *Songs*, etc., have been published, London: 1782. Text in the Larpent collection.

(2.11, C.G.) THE CASTLE OF ANDALUSIA, in 3 acts, the music by Dr Arnold.

(The same year, there is also:
[*Songs, Duets, Trios, etc ... in the Comic Opera of The Castle of Andalusia.*]
The British Museum possesses the 2nd edition of these '*Songs, Duets, etc ...*' (without music), London: T. Cadell, 1782, 27 p.
Text: Cork: pr. by J. Sullivan, 1783, (2) + 72 p.
        Dublin: G. Burnet, 1794, (4) + 67 p.

In *Cumberland's British Theatre* (XXXI), it appears with an attractive engraving by Spado.
It seems that *The Castle of Andalusia* is a recasting of *The Banditti.*

(25.11, C.G.) *Lord Mayor's Day; or, a Flight from Lapland,* a pantomime.
(Unpublished text, to be found in the Larpent collection.
Songs, Duets, etc. ... in Lord Mayor's Day, London: T. Cadell, 1782, 19 p. (the composer who is not indicated in this edition, was W. Shield).)

1783. (15.2, C.G.) THE MAID THE MISTRESS.
[Only the *Songs, etc. ...* have been published, London, 1783.]
(Text in the Larpent manuscripts under the title *The Servant Mistress.*
O'Keeffe's play is based on *La Serva Padrona,* Naples, 1733, by G. A. Federico.)

(26.7, HAY.) THE YOUNG QUAKER, a comedy,
Dublin, printed for the booksellers, 1784, 36 p.
(An unauthorised edition of a play then performed in the Smock Alley theatre.)

(12.8, HAY.) THE BIRTH-DAY,
a dramatic piece with songs, in 2 acts.
London: T. Cadell, 1783, 38 p.
(The musical arrangements are by Dr Arnold.)

(28.8, HAY.) GRETNA GREEN, by Ch. Stuart with alterations and additional songs by O'Keeffe.
[Published in Dublin in 1791]

(4.11, C.G.) THE POOR SOLDIER, a comic opera, in 2 acts ... A new edition, improved, and carefully corrected.
Dublin: M. Doyle, 1784, 32 p.

(The present author has been unable to find a trace of the hypothetical 1st edition of this play the musical score of which was published in London, with no date, probably in 1783 (and not in 1782, as the catalogue in the British Museum indicates) by J. Bland (30 p.) We might point out that *The Poor Soldier*, John O'Keeffe's most popular comedy, was revived in Lille on March 13, 1963. The present author established the text, and the music which was partly inspired by the Irish bard Turlough O'Carolan and partly composed by William Shield (1748–1829) was arranged for the Lille revival by Rupert Sutton. The production was by John D. Edwards.)

1784. (6.9, HAY.) PEEPING TOM OF COVENTRY, a musical farce, in 2 acts.
in *Collection of Farces* II pr. by J. Smith, Dublin, 1785, 38 p.
Dublin: Colles, 1786, (4) + 43 p.
(The play does not figure in *The Dramatic Works* of 1798. On the other hand, see *Cumberland's British Theatre*, XXXI, in which there is an edition with biographical and critical comments, by D. G.; notes on the costumes and an engraving, 36 p.)

(16.11, C.G.) FONTAINEBLEAU; *or, Our Way in France*, in 3 acts.
Dublin: W. Wilson, 1785, (10) + 75 p. (Another edition of the same year, 'sold by the booksellers', 71 p. The music of the play is by Shield.)

1785. (7.2, C.G.) THE BLACKSMITH OF ANTWERP, in 2 acts.
(Does not appear in print, it seems, before the *Dramatic Works* of 1798 (Vol. II, pp. 377–423). In this, O'Keeffe dates it to 1788(?). A non-musical comedy, it was afterwards arranged to music; cf. the London edition of 1818, in 8° (altered): *Songs, etc. ... in the Blacksmith of Antwerp*.)

(16.6, HAY.) A BEGGAR ON HORSEBACK, in 2 acts.
(Published probably for the first time in *The Dramatic Works*, 1798 (Vol. III, pp. 427–68).)

(20.12, C.G.) OMAI; *or, a Trip round the World*.
[Songs and Synopsis, London, 1785.]
(Unpublished text, to be found in the Larpent manuscripts. Music by W. Shield.)

1786. (17.2, C.G.) PATRICK IN PRUSSIA; *or, Love in a Camp*, a comic opera in 2 acts ... being a sequel to *The Poor Soldier*, Dublin, printed for the Booksellers, 1786, 34 p. (unauthorised edition, music by Shield).

This play also figures with the title reversed: *Love in a Camp; or, Patrick in Prussia*, in *The Dramatic Works*, Vol. IV, pp. 403–55 with the (erroneous ?) date of 1785.

(12.8, HAY.) THE SIEGE OF CURZOLA.

[*Songs etc. ... in The Siege of Curzola*, London, 1786, in-8°.]

(For the text, see the manuscript in the Larpent collection.)

1787. (27.1, C.G.) THE MAN-MILLINER, in 2 acts.

(Probably published only in 1798 in *The Dramatic Works*. Vol. IV, pp. 317–62.)

(31.10) THE FARMER, a comic opera, in 2 acts,

Dublin: printed by T. M'Donnell, 1788, 36 p. (unauthorised edition).

(In 1787 there had appeared in London (in-8°) *Songs, etc. ... in The Farmer*. Music by Shield.)

1788. (1.3, C.G.) TANTARA-RARA, ROGUES ALL, in 2 acts, founded on the French.

(Probably not published before *The Dramatic Works* in 1798, Vol. III, pp. 349–90.

Later entitled: *Tantara-Rara, Rogues All; or, Honesty the Best Policy*.)

(2.7, HAY.) THE PRISONER AT LARGE, a comedy, in 2 acts.

London: G. C. J. and J. Robinson, 1788, 35 p.

(6.11, C.G.) THE HIGHLAND REEL, in 3 acts, music by Mr Shield.

Dublin: (unauthorised edition), pr. by T. M'Donnel, 1789, 72 p.

1789. (3.2, C.G.) THE TOY; *or, The Lie of the Day*, in 5 acts.

(Probably published for the first time in *The Dramatic Works*, 1798, Vol. III, pp. 1–108.

The play was revised and performed again on March 9, 1796 at Covent Garden, under the title: *The Lie of the Day*.)

(14.4, C.G.) THE LITTLE HUNCH-BACK; *or, a Frolic in Bagdad*, a farce, in 2 acts.

London: J. Debrett, 1789, 35 p.

(O'Keeffe in *The Dramatic Works* gives 1787 as the date of performance.)

1790. (8.3, C.G.) THE CZAR PETER, in 3 acts, the music by Mr Shield.

(Apparently no edition of the text before *The Dramatic Works*, 1798, Vol. III, pp. 109–208. The *Songs, etc. ...* on the other hand, were published in London in 1790.

The play *The Fugitive* is a revival of this one.)

(4.9) THE BASKET-MAKER, a musical piece, in 2 acts.

[1st edition of *Songs, etc. ... in The Basket-Maker*, London: T. Cadell, 1790.]

(Text: the edition of *The Dramatic Works*, 1798, Vol. II, pp. 335–76. Music by Dr Arnold.)

1791. (14.3, C.G.) MODERN ANTIQUES; *or, The Merry Mourners,*

a farce, in 2 acts.

1st edition: according to *The Cambridge Bibliography*: Dublin, 1791, according to Nicoll: 1792 and the British Museum edition is dated 1792.

Dublin: printed by P. Byrne, 1792, 35 p.

(16.4, C.G.) WILD OATS; *or, The Strolling Gentlemen,*

a comedy, in 5 acts.

Dublin: printed for the booksellers, 1791, 76 p.

(unauthorised edition).

1793. (11.5, C.G.) SPRIGS OF LAUREL, a comic opera, in 2 acts.

London: printed for T. N. Longman, 1793, 47 p.

(Music by W. Shield. The play *The Rival Soldiers* is a revival of this one.)

(29.6, HAY.) THE LONDON HERMIT; *or, Rambles in Dorsetshire,*

a comedy, in 3 acts, prologue by G. Colman Jun.

London: J. Debrett, 1793, 103 p.

(23.11, C.G.) THE WORLD IN A VILLAGE, a comedy in 5 acts.

London: J. Debrett, n.d. [1795], 75 p.

(Prologue by John Taylor.)

1795. (19.3, C.G.) LIFE'S VAGARIES, a comedy, in 5 acts.

London: T. N. Longman, 1795, 95 p.

(This is the first title in Vol. I of *The Dramatic Works* of 1798 with *The Neglected Son* as subtitle. According to Nicoll, it is the most 'classical' (so to speak) of O'Keeffe's plays.)

(25.4, C.G.) THE IRISH MIMIC; *or, Blunders at Brighton,* a musical entertainment in 2 acts.
London: T. N. Longman, 1895, 54 p.
(Also the same year: *Songs, etc. ... in The Irish Mimic,* London. Music by W. Shield).

(21.12, C.G.) MERRY SHERWOOD; *or, Harlequin Forrester,* an operatical pantomime.
(Unpublished text, see the Larpent manuscript. *Airs, Duets and Chorusses in Merry Sherwood* ... (without indication as to author), London: T. N. Longman, 1795, 20 p. It is in this play that occurs the song 'The Friar of Orders Gray' quoted in the *Oxford Book of Irish Verse.*)

1796. (13.4, C.G.) THE WICKLOW GOLD MINE; *or, The Lad of the Hills,* an opera.
(Under this title of the 1st version of *The Wicklow Mountains,* there is:
Airs, Duets, Glees, Choruses, etc. ... in The Wicklow Gold Mine, London: T. N. Longman, 1796, 40 p.
(The names of the people differ in the revised edition.)
a Dublin edition of 1801, pr. by Folingsby, 36 p. Music by Shield.)

(23.4, C.G.) THE DELDRUM; *or 1803,* in 2 acts.
(Probably published for the 1st time in *The Dramatic Works,* 1798, Vol. IV, pp. 457–511.)

(22.6, HAY.) ALFRED; *or, The Magic Banner,* a drama in 3 acts.
[Dublin, 1796.]

(17.10, C.G.) THE WICKLOW MOUNTAINS, in 3 acts.
Music by Mr Shield.
(A new version of *The Wicklow Gold Mine.*
O'Keeffe, in *The Dramatic Works,* gives 1795 as the date of performance (?).)
Dublin: printed by J. Whitworth, 1797, 47 p.

1797. (17.5, C.G.) THE RIVAL SOLDIERS.
[London, 1798.]
(A new version of *Sprigs of Laurel.*)

(d) The so-called complete edition of the works:

1798. THE DRAMATIC WORKS OF JOHN O'KEEFFE, ESQ.
Published under the gracious patronage of His Royal
Highness the Prince of Wales. Prepared for the Press by
the author. In four volumes.
London: printed by T. Woodfall, 1798, I: 406 p. II: 462 p.
III: 468 p. IV: 511 p.
The collection comprises 29 plays. The following works,
that have already been mentioned, do not appear in the
edition of *The Dramatic Works: Agreeable Surprise, Dead
Alive, Gretna Green* (which is only partly by O'Keeffe),
*Harlequin Teague, Lord Mayor's Day, The Maid The
Mistress (or The Servant Mistress), Merry Sherwood,
Omai, Peeping Tom, Siege of Curzola, Son in Law, Young
Quaker.* It also lacks the plays that appear below under
(d).
As we have seen, it is here that the plays already mentioned for their incomplete editions appear in full for
the first time, with: *The Grenadier,* in 3 parts: a play
whose performance was banned (Covent Garden, 1789) –
it was Shield who wrote the music – and which figures here
in Vol. I, pp. 185–223.[1]

(e) Dramatic works in manuscript:

1777. (15.4, C.S.) THE SHAMROCK; *or, St Patrick's Day.*
(Larpent collection.)

1783. (23.12, C.G.) FRIAR BACON; *or, Harlequin's Adventures in
Lilliput, Brobdingnag, etc.*
(Larpent ms., Music published in London, 1784.)

1788. (26.12, C.G.) ALADDIN; *or, The Wonderful Lamp.*
(Larpent ms., Music by W. Shield.)

1789. (4.4, C.G.) FARO TABLE.
(Adaptation of *The Gamester* by Mrs Centlivre. Larpent
ms.)

1790. (4.11, C.G.) THE FUGITIVE.
(A new version of *The Czar,* Larpent ms.)

[1] *The Dramatic Works* have recently been reprinted by Georg Holms, West
Germany.

1794. JENNY'S WHIM; or, *The Roasted Emperor.*
(Was to be performed at the Haymarket on 1.9.1794, but the performance was banned. Larpent ms.)

1796. (5.11, C.G.) OLYMPUS IN AN UPROAR; or, *The Descent of the Deities.*
(Adapted from the play by Kane O'Hara: *The Golden Pippin*, Larpent ms.)

1797. (19.12, C.G.) OUR WOODEN WALLS.
(Larpent ms.)

1798. (19.5, D.L.) SHE'S ELOPED.
(Nicoll gives no indication either as to publication or manuscript. Yet the play is in the British Museum: manuscript n° 25.928 (19 May 1798): 'Ms. presented by Coventry Patmore, Esq., Nov. 1864'. It contains first a quotation from *Recollections* (Vol. 2, pp. 353–4) in a different hand (this quotation concerns the play). The manuscript itself, written in a good, perfectly legible hand, comprises 137 pages (minus the four pages of the quotation). The comedy, which is non-musical in spite of a song that was to be inserted on page 121 (blank in the manuscript) is in 5 acts.
Characters: Lord Villure, Sir Ch. Hyacinth, Major Blenner, Plodden, Mrs Egerton, etc.)

(5.6, D.L.) THE ELEVENTH OF JUNE; or, *The Daggerwoods at Dunstable.*
(Sequel to *Sylvester Daggerwood* by G. Colman, Larpent ms.)

(6.6, D.L.) A NOSEGAY OF WEEDS; or, *Old Servants in New Places.* (Larpent ms.)

(f) Secondary material:

For the bibliography, besides the *D.N.B.*, the two volumes of the *Recollections*, and the 'Memoir' in *O'Keeffe's Legacy*, see:

[ROBINSON (John): *William Shield*, Newcastle, 1891.]

BABBOCK (R. W.): 'Adelaide O'Keeffe' in *Times Literary Supplement*, 9 Jan. 1937.

For a critique of his work:

HAZLITT (W.): *Lectures on the English Comic Writers*, VIII, 1819.

HUNT (Leigh): *Wit and Humour,* 1846.

BESSET (Julian): *John O'Keeffe and William Shield.* A thesis written under the supervision of the present author. University of Lille III, 1972, IV + 364 p. (typewritten).

Also

Bartley (*Teague*: pp. 179–81), Duggan (pp. 142–54), Kavanagh (pp. 348–61), Nicoll, Symons (pp. 34–6).

O'REILLY (Edward – 1770(?)–1829)

A lexicographer and author of the following works:

1817. SANAS GAOIDHILGE-SAGSBHEARLA, *An Irish–English Dictionary.*
Dublin: printed by John Barlow, 1817, unpaginated.
(republished with corrections, by J. O'Donovan, in 1864 and 1877).

1820. TRANSACTIONS ... *for 1820 ... containing.*
A CHRONICAL ACCOUNT OF NEARLY 400 IRISH WRITERS. *Commencing with the Earliest Account of Irish History and Carried Down to the Year 1750.*
Dublin: Iberno Celtic Society, 1820.
(Has recently been reprinted by the Irish University Press.)

1824. AN ESSAY ON THE ... BREHON LAWS.
Dublin: Graisberry, 1824, 88 p.

1828. ESSAY ON THE AUTHENTICITY OF THE POEMS OF
etc. OSSIAN.
Dublin: Royal Irish Academy, *Transactions* XVI, 1828–30.

ORR (James – 1770–1816)

BIOGRAPHY

Born in Broad Island, County Antrim. A member of the United Irishmen and a contributor to *The Northern Star*, he took part in the 1798 conflict and had to flee to the United States. Back in Ireland, in Ballycarry, he practised his trade as a weaver. The success of his poems seems to have affected his balance and the last years of his life betrayed a third love, a love for the bottle.

BIBLIOGRAPHY

1804.   [POEMS ON VARIOUS SUBJECTS, Belfast.]

1817.   [POEMS, Belfast, printed by F. D. Finlay.
(With a biography by A. McDowell, also published separately the same year.)]

1846.   in:
LITERARY REMAINS OF THE UNITED IRISHMEN.
(q.v. under R. R. Madden).

Figures in the *D.N.B.*, in Hewitt and in O'Donoghue. See also: Fitzpatrick (W. J.): 'James Orr, the Patriot Poet of Ballycarry', *Irish Weekly*, 4 April, 1970, p. 6.

O'SULLIVAN (Michael John – 1794–1845)

Born in Cork, studied with Dr Maginn before taking his law examinations and working as a journalist. Wrote two unpublished PLAYS:

1814.   (C.S.) THE CORSAIR; *or, The Pirate's Isle.*
(music by J. Blewitt).

1818.   (4.6, C.S.) THE PRINCE OF THE LAKE.
(music by C. Horn).

and two COLLECTIONS OF POETRY:

1815.   THE PRINCE OF THE LAKE.
Cork: J. Bolster, 1815, 120 p.

1846.   A FASCICULUS OF LYRIC VERSE.
Cork: W. Scraggs, 1846, 84 p.

O'SULLIVAN (Mortimer – 1791–1859)

A Protestant theologian and contributor to *Blackwood's* and the *Quarterly Review.* An enemy of Thomas Moore whom he attacked in *Captain Rock Detected* (1824) and *Guide to an Irish Gentleman in Search of a Religion* (1833), he is also known for his *Digest of Evidence on the State of Ireland* (1826).

O'SULLIVAN (Samuel – 1790–1851)

The author of numerous articles in *Blackwood's.*

OTWAY (Rev. Cæsar – 1780–1842)

BIOGRAPHY

Born in 1780 in County Tipperary. Anglo–Irish family. Studied at Trinity College, Dublin (B.A.: 1801). Was ordained. Practised his ministry in the country for 17 years then in Dublin where his preaching attracted attention. In 1825 founded *The Christian Examiner* in which he launched his protégé, William Carleton. He subsequently wrote in *The Dublin Penny Journal* and *The Dublin University Magazine*, often under the pseudonym 'Terence O'Toole'. It was in Dublin that, on March 16, 1842, the death occurred of this interesting character of the Irish literary world, who was never famous, however, for his tolerance of Catholics.

BIBLIOGRAPHY

1814. A LETTER TO THE ROMAN CATHOLIC PRIESTS OF IRELAND ...
Dublin: Coyne, 1814, LVII p.

1823. A LECTURE ON MIRACLES ... with appendices.
(Wherein are detailed some of the manifold absurdities and impostures which the Roman Church has given birth to, in consequence of her ambitious and self-seeking assumption of miraculous power.)
Dublin: R. M. Tims, 1823, II + 58 p.

1827. SKETCHES IN IRELAND, *descriptive of interesting and hitherto unnoticed districts, in the North and South.*
Dublin: W. Curry, Jun. & Co, 1827, VI + 411 p.
(2nd edition corrected, ibid., 1839).

1839. A TOUR IN CONNAUGHT, *comprising sketches of Clonmacnoise, Joyce Country and Achill.*
Dublin: W. Curry, Jun. & Co, 1839, X + 422 p.

1841. SKETCHES IN ERRIS AND TYRAWLY.
Dublin: W. Curry, Jun. & Co, 1841, XV + 418 p.

OULTON (Walley Chamberlain – 1760(?)–1820(?))

BIOGRAPHY

Born in Dublin at a date unknown to the present author but which must be at least ten years before 1770 (the year suggested by the *D.N.B.*). Settled in London in 1786. The following year, tried his hand at journalism and continued to write for the theatre. Was also interested in German literature, and the work of Kotzebue in particular, and this led him to collaborate on Sheridan's *Pizarro.* Died in England about 1820.

BIBLIOGRAPHY

(a) Dramatic works:

1783. (18.12, CAP.S.) THE HAUNTED CASTLE.
(music by T. Giordani, unpublished).

1784. (7.1, CAP.S.) THE HAPPY DISGUISE; *or, Love in a Meadow.*
(unpublished).

(14.1, ibid.) THE NEW WONDER: A WOMAN HOLDS HER TONGUE.
(id.).

(5.5, ibid.) THE MAD HOUSE.
Dublin: R. Marchbank, 1786 (music by T. Giordani).

1785. (C.S.) POOR MARIA.

(20.1, S.A.) A NEW WAY TO KEEP A WIFE AT HOME.

Dublin: pr. by H. Chamberlaine, 1786, 24 p. (adaptation from *The Letter Writers* by Fielding).

(F.S.) THE RECRUITING MANAGER.
(unpublished).

1786. (27.3, S.A.) CURIOSITY; *or, A Peep through the Keyhole.*
(id.).

1787. (3.7, ROY.) HOBSON'S CHOICE; *or, Thespis in Distress.*
(id.).

1789. (12.3, C.S.) PERSEVERANCE; *or, The Third Time the Best.*
(id., but it exists in manuscript in the Larpent collection.
Music by T. Giordani).

(2.6, HAY.) AS IT SHOULD BE, a dramatic entertainment,
in 1 act.
London: W. Lowndes, 1789, 30 p.

WHAT'S THE MATTER?
[London, 1789].

1792. (7.7, HAY.) ALL IN GOOD HUMOUR, a dramatic piece, in
1 act.
London: J. Debrett, 1792, 22 p.

1797. (24.8, HAY.) THE IRISH TAR; *or, Which is the Girl?*
(unpublished but in Larpent).

1798. (8.5, C.G.) BOTHERATION; *or, A Ten Years' Blunder,*
a farce, in 2 acts.
London: G. Cawthorn, 1798, 46 p.

(Birmingham) PYRAMUS AND THISBE.

(Birmingham) THE TWO APPRENTICES; *or, Industry and
Idleness Rewarded.*

1802. (28.7, HAY.) THE SIXTY-THIRD LETTER, a musical farce,
in 2 acts ...
the Overture and music by Dr Arnold.
London: Barker & Son, 1802, 44 p.

1804. (16.4, D.L.) THE MIDDLE DISH; *or, The Irishman in
Turkey.*
(unpublished).

1810. THE FARTHING RUSHLIGHT.
(id.).

THE FORTUNATE TARS.
(id.).

1812. (15.6, HAY.) THE SLEEP-WALKER; *or, Which is the Lady?*
a farce, in 2 acts ...
London: J. Roach, 1812, 44 p.

1816. (10.8, HAY.) MY LANDLADY'S GOWN, a farce, in 2
acts ...
London: W. Simpkin & R. Marshall, 1816, 47 p.

1817. (27.2, D.L.) FRIGHTENED TO DEATH, a musical farce, in 2
acts ...
the music composed and selected by Mr T. Cooke.
London: W. Simpkin & R. Marshall, 1817, 46 p.

(b) Miscellanea:

1787– THE BUSY BODY, a collection of periodical essays,
89. moral, whimsical, comic, and sentimental ...
London: C. Stalker, n.d. [1789], 2 v.
I: 239 p. II: 239 p.
(reprintings of articles from a tri-weekly publication of the
same name which appeared between 2 January and 26
February 1787).

1796. HISTORY OF THE THEATRES OF LONDON, 1771–1795.
London: Martin & Bain, 1796, 2 v., I: VI + 196 p. II: VI +
217 p.

1800. 'AN OCCASIONAL ADDRESS spoken by Mr Macready on
opening the Birmingham Theatre, June the 4th, written by
Mr Oulton'.
Dublin Magazine and Monthly Irish Register.
V (Sept. 1800, p. 188.)

THE BEAUTIES OF KOTZEBUE containing the most
interesting scenes, sentiments, speeches, etc., in all his
admired dramas. Freely translated; connected and digested
under appropriate heads, alphabetically arranged. With
biographical anecdotes of the author, a summary of his
dramatic fables and cursory remarks ...

'Wild is the Garden, but the soil is good'.

London: Crosby & Letterman, 1800, XXXVIII + 402 p.

1811. THE DEATH OF ABEL, a poem, in 5 cantos, from the
German of S. Gessner.
London: Hogg & Co, 1811, VIII + 279 p.

1818. [HISTORY OF THE THEATRES OF LONDON FROM 1795 TO 1817.
London, 1818, 3 v.]

On the author, besides the *D.N.B.* and O'Donoghue, see Duggan, Kavanagh, Nicoll, q.v. in the general bibliography.

PARKER (Sarah – 1824–80)

BIOGRAPHY

Born in Newry, County Down, into an extremely poor family. Settled very soon in Scotland, in Ayr, where she lived all her life except for one visit to her native country. She contributed to *The Ayr Advertiser* and *Chambers's Journal* and is the author of two collections of poetry.

BIBLIOGRAPHY

1846. THE OPENING OF THE SIXTH SEAL, *and Other Poems.*
Ayr: M'Cormick & Gemmell, 1846, x + 122 p.

1856? MISCELLANEOUS POEMS, by Sarah Parker, The 'Irish Girl'.
Glasgow: Bowie & Glen, 2nd edition, 1856, x + 235 p.

PEARCE (William)

Seems to have been Irish (cf. the characters in *Netley Abbey*, and the interest in druidism noted by Snyder in his only collection of poetry:

THE HAUNTS OF SHAKESPEARE, London: D. Browne, 1778, 26 p.)

but this volume and his plays are all that is known about the author:

1785. (12.4, C.G.) THE NUNNERY, a comic opera in 2 acts, the music by Mr Shield.
[London, 1785]

The Words of the Songs, etc., in —— , London: T. & J. Egerton, 1785, 19 p.

1792.   (3.11, C.G.) HARTFORD BRIDGE; *or, The Skirts of the Camp,*
an operatic farce, in 2 acts ...
London: T. N. Longman, 1793, 41 p.
(W. Shield collaborated again on the music of this play as well as on that of the two following.)

1793.   (25.2, C.G.) THE MIDNIGHT WANDERERS, a comic opera, in 2 acts.
London: T. N. Longman, 1893, 45 p.

1794.   (10.4, C.G.) NETLEY ABBEY, an operatic farce, in 2 acts.
London: T. N. Longman, 1794, 37 p.

(30.10, C.G.) ARRIVED AT PORTSMOUTH, an operatic drama, in 2 acts ...
London: T. N. Longman, 1794, 43 p.

1795.   (6.4, C.G.) WINDSOR CASTLE *or, The Fair Maid of Kent,*
an opera ...
London: T. N. Longman, 1795, 40 p.

PEPPER (George)

An Irish emigrant to the U.S.A. where he worked as a journalist (cf. *The Irish Shield*) and wrote for the theatre: he is the author of *Kathleen O'Neill,* 1829.

PERCIVAL (Margaret)

1847.   ROSA, THE WORK-GIRL.
Dublin: J. Robertson, 1847, IV + 81 p.

1849.   THE IRISH DOVE; *or Faults on Both Sides.*
Dublin: J. Robertson, 1849, 8 + 306 p.

PETRIE (George – 1790–1866)

A painter, musicologist and archaeologist of great talent, one of the men of the Ordnance Survey, editor of the all too fleeting *Irish Penny Journal,* and the author of numerous articles and books, beginning with his famous essay:

THE ROUND TOWERS OF IRELAND. 1833, reprinted in *The Ecclesiastical Architecture of Ireland* (cf. below).

Among Petrie's works, note especially:

1839. ON THE HISTORY & ANTIQUITIES OF TARA HILL.
Dublin: pr. by R. Graisberry, 1839.
Transactions of the Royal Irish Academy, Vol. XVIII, pt II.

1843. [ILLUSTRATIONS OF THE LANDSCAPE AND COAST SCENERY OF IRELAND. Dublin: W. F. Wakeman, 1843.]

1845. THE ECCLESIASTICAL ARCHITECTURE OF IRELAND.
Dublin: Hodges & Smith, 1845, 22 + 520 p.
(A new edition in 1849 recently reproduced by the Irish University Press.)

1855. THE PETRIE COLLECTION OF THE ANCIENT MUSIC
etc. OF IRELAND.
Dublin: University Press, 1855–82, 2 v., I: 24 + 196 p., II: 48 p.
(C. V. Stanford edited a 3rd volume in the collection, of 34 + 398 p., published for the Literary Society in London, by Boosey, between 1902 and 1905.)

1872– CHRISTIAN INSCRIPTIONS IN THE IRISH LANGUAGE.
78. Dublin: printed at the University Press for the Royal Historical & Archaeological Association of Ireland, 1872–8, 2 v., I: II + 88 p., II: II + 190 p. Has also recently been reprinted by the Irish University Press.

On the author see:

DILLON (Myles): 'George Petrie (1789–1866)', *Studies,* Autumn 1967, pp. 266–76.

PIKE (Richard)

Probably the pseudonym of an Irish nationalist concealing his true character, like the (false) information which follows his name in the manuscript below, presented to the British Museum (Additional Manuscripts, 25.930) by Coventry Patmore in November 1864:

> THE CONSPIRACY; *or, the Wicklow Mountains*, a tregady (sic for 'tragedy') by R. Pike, member of Philomathic Society at Exeter. Instituted April 4th 1798.
> (42 pages folio).

(See Duggan).

PILGRIM (James)

The author of the following plays:

1836. (22.4, S.W.) PADDY MILES, THE LIMERICK BOY, a farce, in 1 act.
[1st ed.?]—
New edition, revised: London: Lacy's Acting Edition, n.d., Vol. XCV, 16 p.

1850. (1.9, City of London) THE WILD IRISH GIRL.
[New York: S. French, n.d.]

? EVELEEN WILSON, THE FLOWER OF ERIN, an original drama,
in 3 acts.
[ibid., id.].

? PADDY THE PIPER, a comic drama, in 1 act.
[ibid., id.].

? ROBERT EMMET, THE MARTYR OF IRISH LIBERTY
an historical drama, in 3 acts.
New York: Samuel French, n.d., 28 p. ('French's Standard Drama' CCXXV).

? SHANDY MAGUIRE; *or, The Bould Boy of the Mountain*, a drama, in 2 acts.
(ibid., id.].

POWER (William Grattan, alias Tyrone – 1797–1841)

BIOGRAPHY

One of the greatest Irish actors of the nineteenth-century, born in Kilmacthomas, County Waterford, on November 2, 1797. At fourteen, had already joined a touring company. Career in London and in the United States. Drowned in March 1841, while returning from America, in the shipwreck of the 'President'.

BIBLIOGRAPHY

(a) Miscellaneous prose:

The first three volumes mentioned are novels:

1830. THE LOST HEIR AND THE PREDICTION.
London: E. Bull, 1830, 3 v.
I: 313 p. II: 316 p. III: 305 p.

1831. [THE GIPSY OF THE ABRUZZIO.]

? THE KING'S SECRET.
London: E. Bull, 1831, 2nd ed., 3 v.
I: 318 p. II: 308 p. III: 377 p.

1836. IMPRESSIONS OF AMERICA DURING THE YEARS 1833, 1834 AND 1835.
London: R. Bentley, 1836, 2 v.
I: XV + 440 p. II: VI + 408 p., ill.

(b) Dramatic works:

1831. (2.2, C.G.) MARRIED LOVERS, a petite comedy, in 2 acts.
London: E. Bull, 1831, 58 p.

1832. (17.3, C.G.) BORN TO GOOD LUCK; *or, The Irishman's Fortune,*
a farce, in 2 acts, adapted from '*False and True*'.
London: Lacy's Acting Edition, n.d., Vol. II, 26 p.

(24.11, D.L.) ST PATRICK'S EVE; *or, The Order of the Day,*
a drama, in 3 acts.
London: Acting National Drama, n.d., Vol. II, 36 p.

1833. (29.5, C.G.) PADDY CARREY; *or, The Boy of Clogheen,*
a farce, in 1 act.
London: Lacy's Acting Edition, n.d., Vol. XXVI, 21 p.

1836.   (24.4, C.G.) O'FLANNIGAN AND THE FAIRIES. (unpublished).

(16.5, C.G.) ETIQUETTE; *or, A Wife for a Blunder.* (id.).

1840.   (2.4, HAY.) HOW TO PAY THE RENT, a farce, in 1 act. London: Acting National Drama, n.d., Vol. IX, 24 p.

The Dublin University Magazine devoted a long article to the author in 1852 (Vol. XL).

PRESTON (William – 1753–1807)

BIOGRAPHY

Born in Dublin in 1753. Studied at Trinity College and at the Middle Temple. A barrister, then a judge in the Court of Appeal. Also secretary of the Royal Irish Academy from 1786 until his death. Contributed to the *Transactions* of this academy and to various periodicals including *The Sentimental and Masonic Magazine* and published numerous books. A strong partisan of the established order, Preston was nevertheless not incapable of good sense and liberalism: he was hostile to the Union and favoured the Emancipation of Catholics. He died in Dublin on February 2, 1807.

BIBLIOGRAPHY

Prior to 1789 note the following titles, mentioned by O'Donoghue:

[**1776.**   *A Congratulary Poem on the Last Successes of the British Arms,* Dublin.

An Heroic Epistle to Mr Twiss, Dublin.

The Court Mirrors; or, The Age of Loyalty, an historical panegyric, Dublin.

1777.   *1777; or, A Picture of the Manners and Characters of the Age,* Dublin.

1778.   *Heroic epistle from Mr Manly.*

1779.   *The Female Congress; or, The Temple of Cottyto.*

1780.   *The Contract,* a poem.

1781.   *Poems on Several Occasions.*]

The works posterior to 1789 are the following:

1789.   in: *A Collection of Poems* (q.v. under Edkins, J., Vol. I):
'ODE TO SINCERITY'; 'THE BRUNETTE'; 'ELEGY, WRITTEN
IN THE COUNTRY'; 'ON THE APPROACH OF SPRING';
'SHADE OF ANACREON'; 'IRREGULAR ODE TO THE
MOON'.

1790.   ibid., Vol. II: 'MYRRHA'; 'ABSENCE'; 'ELIZA; AN ELEGY';
'TO A LADY WHO HAD A SCAR ON HER BREAST'; 'HOPE
AND FEAR'; 'ON THE RETURN OF SPRING'; 'ADVICE TO A
LADY'; 'ELEGY'; 'THE DELPHIC FIRE'.

1791.   OFFA AND ETHELBERT; *or, The Saxon Princes*, a tragedy.
Dublin: J. Archer, 1791, 78 p.

1792.   (12.1, C.S.) MESSENE FREED; *or, The Cruel Virtue*, a
tragedy.
[Dublin: 1793. Separately?]
in *Poetical Works*, q.v. below, 1793.

1793.   (June C.S.) DEMOCRATIC RAGE; *or, Louis the Unfortunate*, a tragedy.
London: printed for the author, 1793, 102 p.

ROSAMUNDA; *or, The Daughter's Revenge*, a tragedy.
[Dublin, 1793. Separately?]
in *Poetical Works*, q.v. infra, 1793.

THE POETICAL WORKS.
Dublin: J. Archer, 1793, 2 v., I: XIX + 417 p. II: III + 399 p.
   (I: preface, satirical and anacreontic pieces, sonnets,
elegies, love poems, ill., total of 89 poems.
   II: 'Thoughts on Lyric Poetry', odes, 'Offa and
Ethelbert', 'Messene Freed','Rosamunda'.)

1794.   THE SIEGE OF ISMAIL; *or, A Prospect of War*, an historical tragedy.
Dublin: printed by Graisberry & Campbell, 1794, XX +
102 p.

1801.   in: *A Collection of Poems* (q.v. under Edkins, J., Vol. III)
(32 poems which would all reappear in the *Posthumous
Poems* of 1809, without, unfortunately, any notice having
been taken of the author's handwritten corrections as they
may be seen, for example, in the copy of Edkins III in the
British Museum, dedicated by Preston to Dr Anderson.)

REFLECTIONS ON THE PECULIARITIES OF STYLE AND MANNER IN THE LATE GERMAN WRITERS *whose works have appeared in English, and on the tendency of their productions.*
Dublin: G. Bonham, printer to the Royal Irish Academy, 1801, 67 p.
N.B.: the copy in the British Museum comprises another, undated, essay by the author:
SOME CONSIDERATIONS ON THE HISTORY OF ANCIENT AMATORY WRITERS, 34 p.

1803. [THE ARGONOTICS, translated into English verse, with notes.]

1806. [EPISTLE TO ROBERT ANDERSON, M.D. Edinburgh.]

1809. THE POSTHUMOUS POEMS OF WILLIAM PRESTON, ESQ. Late One of the Judges of Appeal ...
Dublin: printed by Wilkinson & Courtney, 1809, XXII + 276 p. (a total of 59 poems).

1811. in: *Poetical Register and Repository of Fugitive Poetry for 1806–7* (published in 1811):
'PROPERTIUS, two elegies'; 'LINES TO MISS STEWART'; 'LINES TO FRANCES PRESTON'.

1849. in: *The Songs of Ireland* (q.v. under Ellis, H.).

PROBY (John Joshua —, 1st Earl of Carysfort – 1751–1828)

BIOGRAPHY

Born on August 12, 1751. Was British ambassador to Berlin in 1800 and St Petersburg in 1801. Member of the Irish House of Lords. Died in April 1828. The author of political tracts, poems and tragedies that seem never to have been performed.

BIBLIOGRAPHY

1786. [THE REVENGE OF GWENDOLEN, a poem. privately printed (12 copies).]

1798. POLYXENA, a tragedy, in 5 acts and in verse.

(the 1st page is missing from the edition in the British Museum, the place of publication and publisher are thus unknown to the present author), 1798, 92 p.

1810. DRAMATIC AND NARRATIVE POEMS.
London: J. Mackinlay, 1810, 2 v.
I: 393 p. II: 336 p.
   (I: 'Caius Gracchus'; 'Monimia'; 'The Fall of Carthage'; 'Polyxena' (revised).
   II: (Poems): 'The Revenge of Gwendolen'; 'The Bower of Melissa'; 'The Statues'.)

REILLY (Thomas Devin – 1824–1854)

One of the leaders of Young Ireland, a contributor to *The Nation* and to several American papers. Had to go into exile in 1849 after his imprisonment.

ROBINSON (Thomas Romney – 1792–1882)

BIOGRAPHY

His father, Thomas, who died in 1810, was a talented painter. Thomas Romney spent his childhood in Belfast and district where Percy granted him his patronage. After studying at the Belfast Academy and Trinity College, he was to distinguish himself as an author of scientific studies and the director of the Armagh observatory. He died on February 28, 1882.

BIBLIOGRAPHY

1806. JUVENILE POEMS ... to which is prefixed a short account of the author ...
Belfast: printed by J. Smyth & D. Lyons, 1806, XXX + 106 p.

[? THE TRIUMPH OF COMMERCE, Belfast.]

(See *D.N.B.*, O'Donoghue, Hewitt.)

ROCHE (Regina Maria Dalton, Mrs — 1764(?)-1845)

BIOGRAPHY

Next to nothing is known about the life of this novelist who was extremely popular in her day. Born in the south of Ireland, she died in Waterford on May 17, 1845.

BIBLIOGRAPHY

1789.   THE VICAR OF LANSDOWNE; *or, Country Quarters*, a tale.
London: J. Johnson, 1789, 2 v., I: 298 p. II: 295 p.

1793?   THE MAID OF THE HAMLET, a tale.
[1st edition, according to the *Cambridge Bibliography*, London, 1793.]
Dublin: G. Burnett, 1802, 273 p.
(No indication in this volume of an earlier edition.)

1796.   THE CHILDREN OF THE ABBEY, a tale.
[1st edition, according to the *Cambridge Bibliography*, London, 1796.]
London: W. Lane, 1797, 2nd edition, 4 v.
I: 324 p. II: 343 p. III: 286 p. IV: 307 p.

1798.   CLERMONT, a tale.
London: W. Lane, 1798, 4 v., I: 246 p. II: 218 p. III: 235 p.
IV: 339 p.
(This novel has been republished in *The Northanger Set of Jane Austen Horrid Novels* edited by Devendra P. Varma. *Clermont* is the 6th of these tales:
London: Folio Society, 1968, 373 p.)

1800.   [THE NOCTURNAL VISIT, a tale in 4 volumes. London: W. Lane, Minerva Press].

1807.   [ALVONDOWN VICARAGE, 2 v.]

THE DISCARDED SON; *or, Haunts of the Banditti*, a tale.
London: Lane, Newman & Co, 1807, 5 v., I: 315 p. II: 317 p. III: 320 p. IV: 64 p. V: 350 p.

1810.   THE HOUSE OF OSMA AND ALMERIA; *or, The Convent of St Ildefonso*, a tale.
London: A. K. Newman, 1810, 3 v., I: 208 p. II: 257 p. III: 270 p.

(?   THE MONASTERY OF ST COLOMB; *or, The Atonement*.

(M. Lévy (*Le Roman «Gothique»*) describes an edition of 1813 in 5 v. – London: A. K. Newman & Co, Minerva Press – but this cannot be the first since the novel was translated into French in 1810.))

1813. [TRECOTHIEK BOWER; *or, The Lady of the West Country,* 3 v.]

1814. LONDON TALES; *or, Reflective Portraits.*
London: J. Booth, 1814, 2 v. I: 138 p. II: 159 p.
(The first volume consists of a series of short tales; in the second, are to be found 'Vilencio' and 'Perdinand'.)

1819?
or
1820. THE MUNSTER COTTAGE BOY, a tale.
London: A. K. Newman, 1820, 4 v., I: 283 p. II: 327 p. III: 303 p. IV: 282 p.

1823. THE BRIDAL OF DUNAMORE; and LOST AND WON, two tales.
London: A. K. Newman, 1823, 3 v.
I: 306 p. II: 282 p. III: 300 p.
(The first tale fills the first two volumes; the second is to be found in volume III.)

1824. THE TRADITION OF THE CASTLE; *or, Scenes in the Emerald Isle.*
London: A. K. Newman, 1824, 4 v., I: 386 p. II: 364 p. III: 342 p. IV: 322 p.

1825. THE CASTLE CHAPEL, a romantic tale.
London: A. K. Newman, 1825, 3 v., I: 212 p. II: 307 p. III: 284 p.

1828. CONTRAST.
London: A. K. Newman, 1828, 3 v., I: XXIV + 372 p. II: 358 p. III: 326 p.

1834? (According to the *Cambridge Bibliography*).
or
1836. THE NUN'S PICTURE, a tale.
London: A. K. Newman, 1836, 3 v., I: 312 p. II: 308 p. III: 291 p.

1819? (According to the *Cambridge Bibliography*.)

RYVES (Elizabeth – 1750(?)–1797)

BIOGRAPHY

Born in Ireland, lost her fortune and had to try and live by her pen. Went to settle in London with this in view. There wrote some poems, a play that was never performed and a relatively famous novel, and translated some French works, including Rousseau's *Contrat social.* She died in utter destitution.

BIBLIOGRAPHY

1777.   POEMS ON SEVERAL OCCASIONS.
London: J. Dodsley, 1777, 176 p.
(Contains a comic opera: *The Prude.*)

1784.   AN EPISTLE TO ... LORD JOHN CAVENDISH.
London: J. Dodsley, 1784, 17 p.

DIALOGUE IN THE ELYSIAN FIELDS BETWEEN CAESAR AND CATO.
London: R. Faulder, 1784, 23 p.

1785.   THE HASTINIAD, an heroic poem, in 3 cantos.
London: J. Debrett, 1785.
(The copy in the British Museum comprises only one canto: 21 p.)

1787.   ODE TO ... LORD MELTON.
London: printed for the author, 1787, 16 p.

1790.   THE HERMIT OF SNOWDEN; *or, Memoirs of Albert and Lavinia,* taken from a faithful copy of the original manuscript which was found in the hermitage by the late Rev. Dr L —— and Mr —— in the year 17—.
Dublin: printed by H. Colbert, 1790, XXIII + 246 p.

SAVAGE (John – 1828–1888)

BIOGRAPHY

Born in Dublin on December 13, 1828. Studied art, but took to journalism, first in Ireland, where he fought in 1848, then in the

United States (*New York Tribune*). Died in New York on October 9, 1888.

BIBLIOGRAPHY

1850. LAYS OF THE FATHERLAND.
New York: J. S. Redfield, 1850, VI + 120 p.

1870? POEMS, LYRICAL, DRAMATIC & ROMANTIC, Second Collected edition. New York: T. W. Strong, 1870, 322 p.

Also:

FENIAN HEROES AND MARTYRS, Boston: P. Donahoe, 1868, 461 p.

? '98 AND '48. *The Modern Revolutionary History and Literature of Ireland.*
4th ed. New York: John B. Alden, 1884, XX + 402 p.

SAVAGE (Marmion W. – 1805–1872)

BIOGRAPHY

A novelist born in Dublin. Studied at Trinity College, then took a post in government. In 1856, settled in London. Had contributed to the *Dublin University Magazine* and would contribute to the *Annual Register* and *The Examiner*. Died in Torquay on May 1, 1872.

BIBLIOGRAPHY

Three extremely entertaining novels by the author are prior to 1850:

1845. THE FALCON FAMILY; *or, Young Ireland.*
London: Chapman & Hall, 1845, 348 p.

1847. THE BACHELOR OF THE ALBANY.
London: Chapman & Hall, 1847, XII + 299 p.
(dedicated to Lady Morgan).

1849. MY UNCLE THE CURATE.
London: Chapman & Hall, 1849, 3 v.
I: 382 p. II: 304 p. III: 326 p.

After 1850, Savage also wrote:

1852. [REUBEN MEDLICOTT; *or, The Coming Man*, 3 v.

1856. CLOVER COTTAGE adapted for the stage as:
Nine Points of the Law, a comedy.

1870. THE WOMAN OF BUSINESS; *or, The Lady and the Lawyer*,
3 v.]

SEYMOUR (Aaron Crossley Hobart – 1789–1870)

Mentioned in the present work as the author of the 'Memoir' at
the beginning of the 1816 edition of Charlotte Brooke's *Reliques*;
also wrote: *Vital Christianity*, 1810.

SHANNON (Edward N. – 1795(?)–1860)

A contributor to *The Nation*, the author of the following works:

1821. [GIUSEPPINO, an occidental story in verse, after the style of
Byron's 'Beppo'.

1826. THE CRAZED MAID OF VENICE *and Other Poems*, London.

1836. A TRANSLATION OF DANTE, etc., London.

1842. TALES OLD AND NEW *and Other Poems*.]

Shannon was at one time editor of *The Galway Vindicator*.

SHAW (Rev. William)

A GALIC AND ENGLISH DICTIONARY. London: printed for the
author by W. & A. Straham and sold by J. Murray, etc.,
1780, 2 v., unpaginated.

SHEA (John Augustus – 1802–1845)

BIOGRAPHY

Born in Cork in November 1802. Began his literary career in his native town by contributing to *The Mercantile Reporter* and *Bolster's Quarterly Magazine.* In 1827 emigrated to the United States where he worked as a journalist. Died in New York on August 15, 1845.

BIBLIOGRAPHY

1826. RUDEKKI, a tale of the 7th Century, THE LAMENT OF HELLAS, *and Other Poems.*
London: Longman, etc., 1826, 160 p.
(dedicated to Th. Moore).

1827–9. Various pòems in *Bolster's Quarterly Magazine* (Cork).
cf. II (July 1827), 'DEARDRA, a free translation of an Irish popular tale', p. 256.
III (Dec. 1829), 'THE OCEAN', p. 233.

1831. [ADOLPH, *and other Poems,* New York.]

1836. [PARNASSIAN WILD FLOWERS, Georgetown.]

1843. CLONTARF; *or, The Field of the Green Banner.* an historical romance, *and Other Poems,* New York: D. Appleton & Co, 1843, (X)+156 p.

1846. POEMS BY THE LATE JOHN AUGUSTUS SHEA,
collected by his son.
New York: for sale at the principal booksellers, 1846, 204 p.

SHEARES (John – 1776–1798)

One of* the influential members of the society of United Irishmen, was executed, with his brother Henry, on July 14, 1798. He contributed to *The Press* (q.v. in periodicals), and figures in *A Collection of Poems* by J. Edkins (I) and in *Literary Remains of the United Irishmen* by R. R. Madden (q.v.).

SHEEHAN (John – 1812(?)–1882)

One of the contributors to *The Comet* and *The Parson's Horn Book* which this newspaper published. A friend of Francis Mahony whom he had as a (whimsical) master at Clongowes College, and of Thackeray, he wrote for *Bentley's Miscellany* and was at one time Paris correspondent for *The Constitutional*.

SHEIL (Richard Lalor – 1791–1851)

BIOGRAPHY

Better known as a politician and speaker – he took an active part in the battles for Catholic Emancipation and in the 'Repeal Association'; also wrote some essays and plays. He was born in Drumdowney, County Kilkenny, on August 17, 1791, and studied in England at first, then, after having abandoned the idea of the priesthood, at Trinity College, Dublin. A barrister in 1814. A member of Parliament in 1831. Master of the Mint between 1846 and 1850. Ambassador to Florence where he died on May 28, 1851.

BIBLIOGRAPHY

(a) Dramatic works:

1814. (19.2, C.S.) ADELAIDE; *or, The Emigrants,*
a tragedy in 5 acts, and in verse.
Dublin: Coyne, 1814, VII + 74 p.

1817. (3.5, C.G.) THE APOSTATE, a tragedy in 5 acts, and in verse.
London: J. Murray, 1817, 3rd edition (there were 4 editions in the same year), X + 83 + 2 p.

1818. (22.4, C.G.) BELLAMIRA; *or, The Fall of Tunis,* a tragedy, in 5 acts, and in verse.
London: J. Murray, 1818, XII + 76 p.

1819. (10.2, C.G.) EVADNE; *or, The Statue,* a tragedy, in 5 acts, and in verse.
London: J. Murray, 1819, VI + 86 p.

1820. (3.5, C.G.) MONTONI; *or, The Phantom*
(unpublished).

1821.   (28.5, C.G.) Collaboration on DAMON AND PYTHIAS by J. Banim
(q.v. under the latter).

1822.   (11.12, C.G.) THE HUGUENOT
(unpublished).

(b) Miscellanea:

1823?   [SKETCHES OF THE IRISH BAR, probable date of the 1st edition of the book indicated below as of 1854–55.]

1825.   AN IRREGULAR ODE FOR THE DRAWING-ROOM.
3 p. in 4° (with no further information).

1840?   SHEIL'S NOCTURNAL VISIT
(a poem in 8 stanzas, with no further information).

1845.   THE SPEECHES OF THE RT HON. R. L. SHEIL, M.P.
with a memoir ... edited by Thomas Mac Nevin.
Dublin: Duffy, 1845, LXLI + 378 p.

1854-5. SKETCHES OF THE IRISH BAR ... with memoir and notes by R. S. Mackenzie.
New York: W. J. Middleton, 1854, 2 v. (2nd edition?).

SKETCHES, LEGAL AND POLITICAL, edited with notes, by M. W. Savage.
London: H. Colburn, 1855, 2 v., I: VIII + 411 p. II: 3 + 374 p.

In addition to the memoirs of Mac Nevin, Mackenzie and Marmion Savage, note:

Mc CULLAGH (W. T.): *Memoirs of the Rt Hon. R. L. Sheil,*
London: H. Colburn, 1855, 2 v., I: XII + 387 p. II: VIII + 443 p.

SHERIDAN (Richard Brinsley – 1751–1816)

BIOGRAPHY

Born on October 30, 1751, in Dublin where his grandfather was a friend of Swift and his father manager of the Theatre Royal. His mother, *née* Frances Chamberlaine, was a clergyman's daughter. It was in Dublin that he began his schooling, with Samuel Whyte but, his parents having emigrated to London, he joined them in 1760.

He was introduced to Garrick and a few other celebrities before going on to Harrow where he was able to stay thanks to an uncle's generosity: his father, after going bankrupt, had to move to the Continent, accompanied by his wife who died in exile in 1766.

In 1769, Richard Brinsley was re-united with his father in London, followed him to Bath in the following year, and from there he eloped with Elizabeth Linley, daughter of the famous composer (F. F. Moore's novel: *A Nest of Linnets*, relates the episode), and married her secretly in Calais, and then, after various imbroglios, duels, etc., at Saint Marylebone, on April 13, 1773, with the parents' blessing. He tried his hand at Law and a few other projects before embracing a theatrical career after the success of his first play, *The Rivals* (1775). One year later, he was manager of Drury Lane, a position that gave him the opportunity to write his most important play, *The School for Scandal* (1777) and establish himself in the best London society and in politics where he sided with the Whigs.

He entered Parliament towards the end of 1780. There, through his eloquence, he won a position of great importance and the gratitude of the Irish who forgave him for creating Sir Lucius O'Trigger on account of the vigour of his position in favour of their independence and of Catholic Emancipation.

Widowed in 1792, Sheridan in 1795 was re-married to Esther Jane Ogle, daughter of the Dean of Winchester. His last years brought him trouble: Drury Lane, of which he was a co-owner, had been destroyed by fire on February 24, 1809, he lacked the money to stand again for Parliament in 1812 and it was a man harried by his creditors who passed away in London on July 7, 1816.

BIBLIOGRAPHY

(a) Dramatic works prior to 1789:

Most of Sheridan's works are anterior to the period under discussion:

1775. (17.1, C.G.) THE RIVALS, a comedy. London, 1775.

(2.5, ibid.) ST PATRICK'S DAY; *or, The Scheming Lieutenant.*
Dublin, 1788.

(21.11, ibid.) THE DUENNA.

Dublin, 1777 (under the title *The Governess*),
London, 1794.

1777. (24.2, D.L.) A TRIP TO SCARBOROUGH.
London and Dublin, 1781.

(8.5, ibid.) THE SCHOOL FOR SCANDAL.
Dublin, 1780 (pirated edition), 1799.

(15.10) THE CAMP, *an Entertainment*
(in collaboration).

1779. (30.10, ibid.) THE CRITIC; *or, a Tragedy Rehearsed*.
London, 1781.

1781. (29.1) ROBINSON CRUSOE; *or, Harlequin Friday*
(unpublished).

(b) Dramatic works after 1789:

There are only a few minor titles and a single published play.

1794. (2.7, D.L.) THE GLORIOUS FIRST OF JUNE, an entertainment.
(text in Larpent Ms; *Songs, etc.*, 1794).

1797. (Mar., ibid.) CAPE ST VINCENT; *or, British Valour
Triumphant*.
(a rearrangement of the preceding. *Songs, etc.*, 1797).

1799. (24.5, ibid.) PIZZARO, a tragedy, in 5 acts, taken from the
German drama of Kotzebue.
Dublin: printed for Burnet, 1799, (6) + 78 p.

1806. (8.4, ibid.) THE FORTY THIEVES, a grand romantic drama,
in 2 acts (scenario by Sheridan, dialogue by Ch. Ward,
revised by Colman the younger. *Songs, etc.* ... 1806).

According to Walter Sichel (*Life of Sheridan*, 1909), whom
Peter Kavanagh follows (*The Irish Theatre*), the author at his
death left several unfinished works including a '*King Arthur*, a
fairy opera ...'.

(c) Miscellanea:

Sheridan wrote some POETRY, cf.:

[**1771.** THE LOVE EPISTLES OF ARISTENAETUS.

CLIO'S PROTEST.

1775.   THE GENERAL FAST, a lyric ode.]

three titles taken from O'Donoghue. cf. also:

1789, 1790.   EDKINS: *Collection* (q.v.)

[?   AN ODE TO SCANDAL & STANZAS ON FIRE.
       2nd ed. London, 1819.]

His SPEECHES were collected in 5 v. in 1816, and there are several modern editions of the WORKS (cf. R. Crompton Rhodes, Oxford: Blackwell, 1928).

(d) Secondary material:

Sheridan as an Irish author has not yet inspired the work that he deserves. One can only therefore refer to the biography by Moore (q.v.) and mention a work of comparative literature:

SINKO (G.): *Sheridan and Kotzebue.* Prace Wroclawskiego Naukowego. Ser. A n° 27, 1949.

and a fairly recent French study:

DULCK (Jean): *Les Comédies de R. B. Sheridan*, Paris: Didier, 1962, 611 p.

SNOW (Joseph)

The author of some mediocre poems and religious works.

1819.   MISANTHROPY *and Other Poems.*
       London: J. Miller, 1819, VII + 132 p.

1828.   MINOR POEMS.
       London: Longman, etc., 1828, XII + 178 p.

1831.   FORMS OF PRAYER adapted to the use of schools and families consisting of young persons. Also *Poems on Religious Subjects.*
       London: Hatchard & Son, 1831, VIII + 206 p.

       SKETCHES AND MINOR POEMS.
       London: Hatchard & Son, 1831, XII + 178 p.

1835.   PRAYERS ... *with Original Poems on Religious Subjects.*
       London: Hatchard & Son, 1835, VIII + 206 p.

1845. LIGHT IN DARKNESS; *or, Sermons in Stones; Churchyard Thoughts in verse.*
London: J. Murray, 1845, unpaginated.

1847? LYRA MEMORIALIS. *Original Epitaphs and Churchyard Thoughts in verse.* With an essay by W. Wordsworth.
London: G. Bell, 1847, 2nd edition, unpaginated.

STARKEY (Digby P. 'Advena' – 1806–1880(?))

BIOGRAPHY

Digby Pilot Starkey (or Sharkey), a lawyer born in Dublin, was one of the most faithful contributors to the *Dublin University Magazine* in which his numerous poems are signed 'Advena'. Another of his pseudonyms was 'Menenius'. He also wrote for *Chambers's Journal.*

BIBLIOGRAPHY

1843. JUDAS, a tragic mystery.
Dublin: W. Curry, Jun. & Co, 1843, XXI + 230 p.
(blank verse).

1847. THEORIA.
Dublin: J. M'Glashan, 1847, X + 228 p.
(a collection of poems, dedicated to Maria Edgeworth).

His other publications are posterior to 1850.

[1853. AN ODE COMMEMORATIVE OF HER MAJESTY'S VISIT TO THE GREAT INDUSTRIAL EXHIBITION IN DUBLIN, Dublin.
(signed 'Menenius').

1858. ANASTASIA, a poem.

1866. THE DOLE OF MALAGA, an episode of history dramatised, in 5 acts, and in verse, London.

1869. JOHN TWILLER (a novel).]

STOTT (Thomas – 1755–1829)

One of the authors of the Dromore group gathered around Percy, a republican at first, then a conservative, a move which, with his literary mediocrity, would draw down on him Byron's wrath in *English Bards and Scotch Reviewers.*

Born in Hillsborough, County Down, on April 25, 1755. A rich craftsman. Died in Dromore on April 22, 1829. His work consists of pieces that appeared in various periodicals (*Hibernian Magazine*; *Northern Star*, *Belfast News-Letter*, *Morning Post*; *Poetical Register* (1806), etc.) under his own name or the pseudonym 'Hafiz'.

Only one collection of poetry is known: THE SONGS OF DEARDRA, *and Other Pieces*, London, Ridgway, 1825, 16 + 232 p.

See Hewitt, O'Donoghue.

STUART (Charles)

A playwright of the period immediately anterior to 1789–1850. (cf. *The Cobbler of Castlebury*, 1779; *Gretna Green*, 1783; *The Distressed Baronet*, 1787; *The Stone Eater*, 1788.) Only one of the author's farces is posterior to 1789:

THE IRISHMAN IN SPAIN. London: J. Ridgway, 1791, 31 p. (1st performance: 13.8.1791).

STUART (James – 1764–1840(?))

BIOGRAPHY

Born in Armagh. Studied in his native town and at Trinity College (B.A., 1789). A member of the Bar, he never practised. Contributed to *The Hibernian Magazine, The Newry Telegraph, The Newry Magazine* of which he was editor, *The Belfast Guardian*, etc.

O'Donoghue gives September 28, 1840, as the date of his death; the *D.N.B.* opts for 1842.

BIBLIOGRAPHY

1784. Early poems in *The Hibernian Magazine*.
(Cf. p. 479 (Aug.): 'A POEM ON THE EARL OF BRISTOL'.
p. 607 (Oct.): 'A POEM; WRITTEN IN THE RUINS OF AN ANCIENT ABBEY'.
p. 735: 'ON HEARING MISS ——SING'.)

1811. POEMS ON VARIOUS SUBJECTS.
Belfast: printed by Joseph Smyth, 1811, 191 p.

1819. HISTORICAL MEMOIRS OF THE CITY OF ARMAGH, *for a period of 1373 years, comprising a considerable portion of the general history of Ireland; a refutation of the opinions of Dr Ledwich, respecting the non-existence of St Patrick; and an appendix on the learning, antiquities, and religion of the Irish nation.*
Newry: printed by Alexander Wilkinson, Telegraph Office, 1819, 631 p.
(adapted in 1900 by Father Ambrose Coleman, O.P.).

SULLIVAN (William Francis – 1756(?)–1830(?))

BIOGRAPHY

Born in Ireland about 1756, his studies at Trinity College were interrupted; a naval officer from 1776 to 1783. Then settled in England where he lived by his pen and his dramatic readings. It is to be hoped that the latter were of a better quality than the former.

BIBLIOGRAPHY

1791–2. [THE RIGHTS OF MAN
(a satirical play performed in 1791, printed in *The Thespian Magazine*, Vol. I, of 1792).]

1792. THE FLIGHTS OF FANCY, being a miscellaneous collection of original poems, epigrams, prologues, songs, etc.
Leeds: printed for the author, 1792, 52 p.

1797? THE TEST OF UNION AND LOYALTY ON THE LONG-THREATENED FRENCH INVASION.

4th edition, written and spoken by W. F. Sullivan, A.S.
London: J. Hatchard, 1803, VIII + 24 p.

1816. THE HISTORY OF MR RIGHTWAY AND HIS PUPILS; an entertaining and instructive lesson for young gentlemen ...
London: W. Darton, Jun., 1816, 85 p.

n.d. PLEASANT STORIES; *or, The Histories of Ben, the Sailor, and Ned, the Soldier.*
London: Dean & Munday, n.d., 58 p.

(These last two titles are stories in prose, for adolescents.)

TAAFFE (John – 1787–1862)

BIOGRAPHY

Born in County Louth. Sojourned for some time in Edinburgh where he met Jeffrey and Scott. A friend of Byron, who did not hesitate to laugh at his poetry but, in common with Shelley, admired his knowledge of Dante, he was, for the author of *Childe Harold*, a cumbersome companion in Pisa. Died in 1862.

BIBLIOGRAPHY

1816. [PADILLA, a tale of Palestine, a poem. London.]

1822. A COMMENT ON THE 'DIVINE COMEDY' OF DANTE.
London: J. Murray, 1822, 2 v., I: XXXI + 499 p.
(II: the present author has been unable to consult it.)

1852. ADELAIS, a poem.
London: privately printed, 1852, 2 v.
I: 283 p. II: 179 + LXXXII p.

[THE HISTORY OF THE ... ORDER OF ST JOHN OF JERUSALEM, London, 4 v.]

See:

Irish Book Lover:

GOGARTY (Thomas): 'John Taaffe', V, 5, Dec. 1913, pp. 73–5.

MC GOVERN (J. B.): 'John Taaffe as a Dantist', V, 6, Jan. 1914, pp. 95–7.

THOM(P)SON (C. Pelham)

A playwright born in Belfast, according to Kavanagh. The author of the following plays:

1814.   [ROKEBY; *or, The Buccaneer's Revenge*.
Dublin, 1814].
(A dramatic version of the poem by W. Scott.)

1828.   (14.7, SUR.) JACK ROBINSON AND HIS MONKEY, a melodrama, in 2 acts.
London: Duncombe, n.d., Vol. XXVII, 24 p.

1829.   (5.8, HAY.) NOTHING SUPERFLUOUS, an operatic farce, in 1 act.
London: Duncombe, n.d., Vol. V, 22 p.

(22.8, SUR.) THE SHADE; *or, Blood for Blood*, a drama, in 2 acts.
London: Duncombe, n.d., Vol. VI, 28 p.

1830.   (5.7, COB.) THE DUMB SAVOYARD.
ibid., id.

1835.   (26.10, ADEL.) THE KING'S COMMAND, a farce, in 2 acts.
London: Duncombe, n.d., Vol. XIX, 26 p.

TIGHE (Mary Blachford, Mrs – 1772–1810)

BIOGRAPHY

Born in Dublin on October 9, 1772. Daughter of the Reverend William Blachford. Her marriage to the member of Parliament Henry Tighe seems to have been unhappy. Very much of a success in the literary society of her time; died of tuberculosis on March 24, 1810.

BIBLIOGRAPHY

1805.   PSYCHE; *or, The Legend of Love*.
London: privately printed, 1805, VIII + 214 p.
(6 cantos in spenserian stanzas; the theme is taken from Apuleius.

The Quarterly Review of May 1811 gave a very favourable review, after the 2nd edition, and this reflected the general opinion of the time.)

1811.   PSYCHE, *with Other Poems.*
London: Longman, etc., 1811, IV + 314 p.

MARY, a Series of Reflections during 20 years,
edited by William Tighe.
Neither the place nor the publisher are indicated, 1811, 31 p.

1818.   Poems in *Harmonica*, Cork, (q.v. under Milliken).

See:

MC. C. DIX (E. R.): 'The First Edition of Mrs Tighe's *Psyche*', *Irish Book Lover*, III, 9, April 1912, p. 141.

HENCHY (Patrick): *The Works of Mary Tighe, published and unpublished.* Dublin: At the Sign of the Three Candles, 1957, *The Bibliographical Society of Ireland Publications*, Vol. VI, n° 6.

also, on the author's possible influence upon Keats:

WELLER (E. V.): *Keats and Mary Tighe. The Poems of M. Tighe; with Parallel Passages from the Works of J. Keats.*
New York: Century Co, 1928, XXIV + XV + 333 p.

TONE (Theobald Wolfe – 1763–1798)

The republican hero's writings were collected by his son:

LIFE OF THEOBALD WOLFE TONE ... WRITTEN BY HIMSELF *and continued by his son; with his Political Writing, and ... Diary, ... Narrative of his Trial; Defence before the Court Martial and Death.* Edited by his son William Theobald Wolfe Tone.
Washington: printed by Gales & Seaton, 1826, 2 v., I: VII + 566 p. II: 674 p.

There is a modern edition:

The Autobiography of Theobald Wolfe Tone abridged and edited by Seán O'Faolain.
London: Nelson, 1937, XXXI (introd.) + 307 p.

See:

MAC DERMOT (Frank): *Theobald Wolfe Tone and his Times.*
London: Macmillan, 1939; Tralee: Anvil Books, 1968 rev.
(XIV) + 306 p.

RIVOALLAN (Anatole): «Un Patriote irlandais: T. W. Tone
(1763–1798)», *Annales de Bretagne*, LXXIV, 1967,
pp. 279–97.

TRENCH (Right Reverend Richard Chenevix – 1807–1886)

BIOGRAPHY

Born in Dublin; studied at Harrow and Cambridge; ordained in
1829; Dean of Westminster in 1856. From 1864 to 1884, the year
of his retirement, was Anglican Archbishop of Dublin. Died in
London on March 28, 1886. Had written works of theology and on
the history of language, and some poems.

BIBLIOGRAPHY

1835. THE STORY OF JUSTIN MARTYR *and Other Poems.*
London: E. Moxon, 1835, V + 185 p.

1838. SABBATION; HONOR NEALE, *and Other Poems.*
ibid., 1838, VII + 187 p.

1841. POEMS.
London: Bradbury & Evans, 1841, IV + 53 p.

1842. GENOVEVA, a poem.
London: E. Moxon, 1842, 60 p.

POEMS FROM EASTERN SOURCES, THE STEADFAST
PRINCE & *Other Poems.*
ibid., 1842, VIII + 237 p.

1843. ELEGIAC POEMS.
ibid., 1843, IV + 71 p.

1849. [SACRED LATIN POETRY. London.]

1854–5. [(according to O'Donoghue).
POEMS WRITTEN DURING THE RUSSIAN WAR.

(doubtless the pieces that were to be re-printed by Kegan Paul, in London, in 1900, under the title: *In Time of War*, pp. X + 41).]

1855. [(from the same source and also for the following title) ALMA AND OTHER POEMS, London.]

1856. [LIFE'S DREAM.]
POEMS.
New York: Redfield, 1856, 336 p.

1881. [TIMOLEON, a poem.]

1885. [POEMS. London, 2 v.]

VALLANCEY (Colonel Charles – 1724–1812)

A colonel of French origin.
One of the first specialists in Irish antiquities whose learning was not always reliable but whose enthusiasm was beyond question. We owe him, among other things:

1763. A VINDICATION OF THE ANCIENT HISTORY OF IRELAND.
Dublin: L. White, 1763, 62 + 552 + 16 p., ill.

1770– [COLLECTANEA DE REBUS HIBERNICIS.
1804. 6 v.]

1772. AN ESSAY ON THE PRIMITIVE INHABITANTS OF GREAT BRITAIN.
Dublin: S. Powell, 1772, 12 + 64 p.

1773. A GRAMMAR OF THE IBERNO-CELTIC OR IRISH LANGUAGE.
Dublin: printed by R. Marchbank for G. Faulkner, etc. 1773, (8) + 52 + 192 p., ill.

1807. AN ESSAY ON THE PRIMITIVE INHABITANTS OF GREAT BRITAIN AND IRELAND.
Dublin: printed by Graisberry & Campbell, 1807, 18 + 220 p.

WALKER (Joseph Cooper – 1762(?)–1810)

Another pioneer in Irish antiquities, a friend of the preceding with whom he worked on *Collectanea*, and the author of numerous works the first of which is deservedly the most renowned:

1786.   HISTORICAL MEMOIRS OF THE IRISH BARDS *interspersed with anecdotes of, and occasional observations on the music of Ireland. Also, an historical & descriptive account of the musical instruments of the ancient Irish, and an appendix containing several biographical and other papers, with select Irish Melodies.* London: printed for T. Payne & Son at the Mews-Gate and G.G.J. and J. Robinson, Pater-Noster-Row, 1786, XIII + 166 + 124 + 6 p. in-4°.

1788.   HISTORICAL ESSAY ON THE DRESS OF THE ANCIENT & MODERN IRISH, *to which is subjoined a Memoir on the Armour and Weapons of the Irish.*
Dublin: J. Grierson, 1788, 12 + 182 p. in-4°.

1789.   [AN HISTORICAL ESSAY ON THE IRISH STAGE.]

1799.   [AN HISTORICAL MEMOIR ON ITALIAN TRAGEDY.]
(Health troubles had made it necessary for Walker to stay in Italy frequently and for long periods.)

1805.   AN HISTORICAL & CRITICAL ESSAY ON THE REVIVAL OF THE DRAMA IN ITALY.
Edinburgh: Mundell, 1805, 18 + 272 + 40 + 8 p.

1806.   AN ESSAY ON THE ORIGIN OF ROMANTIC FABLING IN IRELAND.
Dublin: Graisberry & Campbell, 1806, 21 p. (*Transactions of the Royal Irish Academy X*).

1815.   [MEMOIRS OF ALESSANDRO TASSONI
with a memoir of J. C. Walker by his brother S. Walker.]

WALLER (John Francis – 1809–1894)

All of this author's literary works (cf. THE SLINGSBY PAPERS, Dublin, M'Glashan, 1852, 144 p.; OCCASIONAL ODES, Dublin, Hodges, Smith & Co, 1864, 23 p.) as well as his compilations (cf. IMPERIAL DICTIONARY OF UNIVERSAL BIOGRAPHY, Glasgow, 1857–63) are posterior to the period under discussion. His is nevertheless an important name in the 1830's, 1840's and 1850's: under the pseudonyms 'Iota' and 'Jonathan Freke Slingsby' he was in fact one of the most important contributors to *The Dublin University Magazine* of which he was to become the editor.

Born in Limerick, was a member of the Irish Bar, honorary secretary of the Royal Dublin Society and vice-president (1864) of the Royal Irish Academy, he settled in England where he died.

See: Webb (Th. E.) in *The Dublin University Magazine*, March 1874.

WALSH (Edward – 1805–1850)

BIOGRAPHY

Born in Derry where his father, whose regiment was stationed there, was a sergeant in the Cork militia; got a 'hedge-school' education which gave him an opportunity for learning Irish and later translating it with talent. Spent some time in prison for having taken part in the Tithe war; thereafter earned his living by teaching, journalism (*The Dublin Journal of Temperance, Science and literature; The Irish Penny Journal; The Nation*) and publishing the two anthologies mentioned below. Died in Cork.

BIBLIOGRAPHY

Besides the pieces published in the newspapers:

1844.   RELIQUES OF IRISH JACOBITE POETRY; *with biographical sketches of the authors, interlineal literal translations and historical illustrative notes* by John Daly; *together with metrical versions* by E. Walsh.
Dublin: Samuel J. Machen, 1844, VIII + 120 p.
(But the copy in the British Museum consulted by the present author (11 595 f 10) is obviously incomplete.)

1847.   IRISH POPULAR SONGS; *with English metrical translations and introductory remarks and notes* by E. Walsh.
Dublin: J. M'Glashan; London: W. S. Orr & Co, 1847, 171 p.

All those who have studied the translations (Farren, Heaslip, Ryan) speak of Walsh in a laudatory manner. Cf. also:

KICKHAM (Charles J.): 'E. Walsh, a memoir' in Maher (J.): *The Valley near Slievanamon, a Kickham Anthology*, part 7.

YEATS (W. B.): in the Preface to the *Book of Irish Verse.*

WEST (Rev. Matthew – 1749–1814)

A minister of the Church of Ireland, the author of the following works:

1769. ETHELINDA, a tragedy (see below: *Poems*).

1799. PIZZARO, id. (probably unpublished).

1800? POEMS ON SEVERAL OCCASIONS.
Dublin: printed by John Exshaw, n.d. (The British Museum catalogue suggests 1800), 184 p.
(pp. 57–184: *Ethelinda; or, Love and Duty*, a tragedy – 5 acts, blank verse.)

1803. FEMALE HEROISM, a tragedy, in 5 acts, founded on revolutionary events that have occurred in France in the summer and autumn of 1793.
Dublin: printed by W. Porter, 1803, VII + 55 p.
(blank verse). (The play was probably written in 1793; it was performed in Crow Street on May 19, 1804.)

It is obviously in error that this Matthew West has been attributed a compilation of 1830: *West's Charm of Melody.*

WHITTY (Michael James – 1795–1873)

BIOGRAPHY

Born in Wexford, intended to become a priest but took up journalism (*Dublin and London Magazine; Liverpool Journal; Liverpool Daily Post*) and commanded the police force of the great port on the River Mersey. Died in 1873.

BIBLIOGRAPHY

1824.   TALES OF IRISH LIFE *illustrative of the Manners, Customs, and Conditions or the People*; with designs by G. Cruikshank.
London: J. Robins, 1824, 2 v.: I: IV + 242 p. II: 249 p.

1825, Numerous articles, tales, poems, etc., under his
etc.   initials or the pseudonym 'Rory O'Rourke' in the *Dublin and London Magazine*.
cf. the series: 'R. EMMET AND HIS CONTEMPORARIES', I, April, 1825, p. 71, etc.: 'THE WHITEBOY' II, Feb. 1826, p. 71, etc.; 'THE ORANGEMAN', III, Feb. 1827, p. 195, etc.

1870.   (Reprinted from the *Dublin & London Magazine*).
ROBERT EMMET.
Liverpool: Longmans, 1870, (2) + 10 + 276 p.

WILDE (Jane Francesca, Lady —, 'Speranza' – 1820–1896)[1]

The Madame Récamier of Chelsea, the extraordinary mother of a still more extraordinary son, before 1850 hardly published anything except in the columns of magazines, *The Nation* at first: her name appears at the beginning of 1846 as a translator; in 1847 there follow some original poems beginning with 'The Stricken Land' (V, 224, January 23, 1847, p. 249) prior to the famous revolutionary editorials of 1848: 'The Hour of Destiny' and 'Jacta Alea Est', the latter (VI, 276, July 29, 1848) being responsible for the suppression of the paper; then the *Dublin University Magazine*, for which she wrote 2 poems in 1849 while her future husband was beginning the series 'Irish Popular Superstitions'.

Note, however, a translation published in book form in 1849:

SIDONIA, THE SORCERESS (Wilhelm Heinhold, 1797–1851). London: Simms & Mc Intyre, 1849, 2 v., I: XI + 286 p., II: 292 p.

followed by:

PICTURES OF THE FIRST FRENCH REVOLUTION (a translation of Lamartine's *Histoire des Girondins*), ibid., 1850, 288 p.

[1] Revised and updated by Godeleine Carpentier and Christian Parent.

THE WANDERER AND HIS HOME (*Nouvelles Confidences* of the same), ibid., 1851, 252 p.

THE GLACIER LAND (A. Dumas's *Impressions de Voyage en Suisse*), ibid., 1852, VIII + 272 p.

and, in her later production, the collection of 1864 that includes a number of pieces published before 1850.

POEMS, Dublin: Duffy, 1864, VII + 233 p. Reprinted: Glasgow 1871, Dublin (Gill's) 1907.

Lady Wilde would also publish:

ANCIENT LEGENDS, MYSTIC CHARMS AND SUPERSTITIONS OF IRELAND *with sketches of the Irish Past* to which is appended a chapter on *The Ancient Races of Ireland* by the late Sir William Wilde. London: Ward & Downey, 1887, 2 v. I: XI + 280 p., II: VIII + 370 p. Reprinted: Galway: O'Gorman, 1971.

ANCIENT CURES, CHARMS AND USAGES OF IRELAND, ibid., 1890, XI + 256 p.

Lady Wilde has had a number of biographers, e.g.:

de BREMONT (Anna): *Oscar Wilde and his Mother.* London: Everett & Co, 1911, 200 p.

WYNDHAM (Horace): *Speranza.* London: T.V. Boardman & Co, 1951, 247 p.

LAMBERT (Eric): *Mad With Much Heart.* London: Muller, 1967, IX + 165 p.

WHITE (Terence de Vere): *The Parents of Oscar Wilde.* London: Hodder & Stoughton, 1967, 303 p.

WILLIAMS (Richard D'Alton, 'Shamrock' – 1822–1862)

One of the contributors to *The Nation* (under various signatures including 'Shamrock') and to a few other papers of the 1840's (*The Irish Tribune*, etc.). His poems were collected, cf.:

THE POEMS OF RICHARD D'ALTON WILLIAMS. Dublin: T. D. Sullivan, 4th ed., 1883, XVI + 184 p.

and, under the same title:

London: Duffy, 1894, XXIV + 334 p.

He died in the United States where he practised medicine.

WILLS (Rev. James – 1790–1868)

BIOGRAPHY

Born in Roscommon on January 1, 1790. Studied at Trinity College. A minister of the Church of Ireland where C. R. Maturin was his colleague and friend. Contributed to numerous magazines including the *Dublin University Magazine, The Dublin Penny Journal* and *The Irish Penny Journal.* (His signature was often J.U.U.). Had equally talented children: the Rev. F. C. Wills and the painter and novelist William Gorman Wills (1828–1891). Died in November 1868.

BIBLIOGRAPHY

(a) **Prose:**

A certain number of religious works, sermons, etc. Also:

1839–   LIVES OF ILLUSTRIOUS AND DISTINGUISHED IRISH-
47.   MEN.
         Dublin: Macgregor & Co, 6 v.

(b) **Poetry:**

1821.   THE UNIVERSE, a poem.
        London: H. Colburn, 1821, 108 p. (dedicated to Coleridge, published under Maturin's name for the latter's benefit).

1831.   THE DISEMBODIED *with Other Poems.*
        London: Longman, Rees & Co.; Dublin: Hodges Figgis, 1831, 255 p.

1845.   DRAMATIC SKETCHES *and Other Poems.*
        Dublin: W. Curry, Jun. & Co, 1845, XII + 345 p.
        (dedicated to John Anster).

1846.   [MORAL AND DESCRIPTIVE EPISTLES. Dublin.]

1868.   [THE IDOLATRESS *and Other Poems,* London.]

WILSON (Charles Henry – 1756(?)–1808)

Born in Bailieborough, Cavan, where his father was Protestant minister. Studied law at Trinity. Died on May 12, 1808.

It is mainly for two volumes of poetic translations from the Irish that Ch. H. Wilson continues to arouse interest. These works that have been described in detail by Seamus O'Casaide in: 'A Rare Book of Irish & Scottish Gaelic Verse'. *The Bibliographical Society of Ireland Publications*, Vol. III, N° 6, 1928, pp. 59–70, appear as follows:

1782. [POEMS TRANSLATED FROM THE IRISH LANGUAGE INTO THE ENGLISH. 48 p. in-4°.]

1790? [SELECTED IRISH POEMS TRANSLATED INTO ENGLISH.]

He also wrote two comedies:

1799. [POVERTY AND WEALTH.]

1811. [THE IRISH VALET.]

as well as the following compilations. cf.:

[A COMPLEAT COLLECTION OF THE RESOLUTIONS OF THE VOLUNTEERS ...
Dublin, 1782.

BEAUTIES OF EDMUND BURKE.
London, 1798, 2 v.

BROOKIANA.
London, 1804.]

WOLFE (Rev. Charles – 1791–1823)

BIOGRAPHY

Agreement does not seem to have been reached on the Reverend's birthplace: Dublin? County Kildare? He began his studies in Winchester, and continued them at Trinity College, Dublin. Was ordained in the Church of Ireland in 1817. Died of tuberculosis on February 21, 1823, his end being hastened by an unhappy love affair. For posterity he remains as the author of 'The Burial of Sir John Moore' published in 1815 in *Carrick's Morning Post*, reprinted in the Newry *Telegraph* of April 19, 1817, and pastiched on countless occasions.

BIBLIOGRAPHY

1825. THE BURIAL OF SIR JOHN MOORE; *with Other Poems.*
London: T. Wilson, 1825, 11 p.

[REMAINS OF THE REV. CH. WOLFE ... *with a brief memoir of his life* by the Rev. J. A. Russel.
Dublin, 1825, 2 v.]

Later editions:

THE BURIAL OF SIR JOHN MOORE *and Other Poems* ...
with memoir by C. L. Falkner.
London: Sidgwick & Jackson, 1909, XXXVIII + 61 p.

See:

HAMILTON (Walter): *Parodies.* London: Reeves & Turner, 1884.
Vol. I, 192 p.

SMALL (H. A.): *The Field of his Fame.* University of California
publications, 1953, 49 p., (English Studies n° 5).

YOUNG (Matthew)

Author of:

ANCIENT GAELIC POEMS RESPECTING THE RACE OF THE FIANS
collected in the Highlands of Scotland in the year 1784.
Dublin: Royal Irish Academy Transactions, 1786, in-4°. Vol.
I, p. 3, pp. 43–119.

YOUNG (Robert – 1800–?)

An Orange poet, the author of the following collections:

[**1832.** THE ORANGE MINSTREL, *or, Ulster Melodist,* Derry.

1840. THE ULSTER HARMONIST, ibid.

1854. POEMS AND SONGS, ibid.

1863. POETICAL WORKS, ibid.]

3

IRISH AUTHORS (1789–1850), PRINCIPAL FRENCH TRANSLATIONS

N.B. The authors' names are arranged alphabetically. The translations are given in chronological order of appearance in
French. The French title is normally followed by the English
title in italics.

The name appearing under the French title is that of the
translator. This name is given in full, each time that it has
been established, including cases in which the translation is
anonymous or signed only with initials.

BANIM (John and Michael)

(M.) CROHOORE NA BILHOGE, *ou les*   *(Crohoore of the*
Whiteboys.   *Bill-Hook)*
    A. J. B. Defauconpret, Paris: Gosselin, 1828, 3 v.

(J.) L'ANGLO-IRLANDAIS DU XIXe   *(The Anglo-Irish of*
SIÈCLE.   *the XIXth Century)*
    A. J. B. Defauconpret, Paris: Gosselin, 1829, 4 v.

(J.) L'APOSTAT, *ou la Famille*   *(The Nowlans)*
Nowlan.
    A. J. B. Defauconpret, Paris: Gosselin, 1829, 4 v.

(J.) LA BATAILLE DE LA BOYNE, *ou*   *(The Boyne Water)*
Jacques II en Irlande.
    A. J. B. Defauconpret, Paris: Gosselin, 1829, 4 v.

(J. &   JOHN DOE, *ou le Chef des*   *(John Doe)*
M.)   *rebelles.*
    A. J. B. Defauconpret, Paris: Gosselin, 1829, 2 v.

(J. &   PADRÉ NA-MOULH, *ou le Men-*   *(Peter of the Castle)*
M.)   *diant des ruines.*
    A. J. B. Defauconpret, Paris: Gosselin, 1829, 2 v.

(M.)   LES CROPPYS, épisode de l'histoire   *(The Croppy)*
    de la rébellion d'Irlande en 1798.
    A. J. B. Defauconpret, Paris: Gosselin, 1832, 4 v.

(M.)   LE CHASSEUR DE SPECTRES ET   *(The Ghost Hunter)*
    SA FAMILLE.
    A. Pichard, Paris: Levasseur, 1833, 2 v.

LE CANDIDAT.   *(Canvassing)*
(although published in France, in 1836, as being by Banim
– without further details – this translation is given here in
its place, under Martin (H. L.)

BLESSINGTON (Lady)

CONVERSATIONS DE LORD BYRON AVEC LA   *(Conversations of
COMTESSE DE BLESSINGTON.   Lord Byron)*
Ch. M. Le Tellier, Paris: H. Fournier jeune, 1833.

MAXIMES, PENSÉES ET RÉFLEXIONS.   *(Desultory Thoughts
                                          and Reflexions)*

L. X. Eyma, Paris: Librairie universelle, 1840.

BOUCICAULT (Dionysius Lardner)

LE LAC DE GLENASTON.   *(The Colleen Bawn)*
Paris: M. Lévy, 1861.
(The play had been performed at the Ambigu
Comique on 17 October of the same year.)

JEAN LA POSTE.   *(Arrah na Pogue)*
Eugène Nus, Paris: Petite Librairie dramatique, 1866
(Performed on 20.6.1866 at the Théâtre de la Gaité.)

BURKE (Edmund)

RÉFLEXIONS SUR LA RÉVOLUTION
DE FRANCE.
Londres, Paris, 1790, 36 p.

*(Reflexions on the
Revolution in France)*

LETTRE DE M.BURKE A UN MEMBRE
DE L'ASSEMBLÉE NATIONALE DE FRANCE.
Paris, 1791, 99 p., 1792, 116 p.

*(Letter to a Member
of the National
Assembly)*

Also:

ŒUVRES POSTHUMES SUR LA RÉVOLUTION
FRANÇAISE, Londres, 1799.

RECHERCHES PHILOSOPHIQUES SUR
L'ORIGINE DE NOS IDÉES DU SUBLIME ET
DU BEAU. avec un précis de la vie de l'auteur.
E. Lagentie de Lavaïsse, Paris: Pichon, 1803.

*(A Philosophical
Enquiry ...)*

CARLETON (William)

LES CHRONIQUES DE CHATEAU
CUMBER.
L. de Wailly, Paris: *L'Univers,* 1845.

(Valentine Mc Clutchy)

ROMANS IRLANDAIS; *scènes de la vie cham-
pêtre.*
L. de Wailly, Paris: E. Dentu, 1861.

*(3 stories from
Traits & Stories)*

LE MAUVAIS ŒIL, *ou le Spectre noir;*
suivi de *Cela seulement ...*
Tournai: H. Casterman, 1865.

(The Evil Eye)

CROLY (Rev. George)

SALATHIEL *ou le Juif errant,* histoire
du présent, du passé et de l'avenir.
J. Cohen, Paris: Mame et Delaunay-Vallée, 1828, 5 v.

(Salathiel)

CROWE (Eyre Evans)

LES CARDEURS, *ou Patriotisme et Vengeance.* roman irlandais. A. J. B. Defauconpret, Paris: Gosselin, 1830, 3 v.

('The Carders' like the following, is an extract from *To Day in Ireland*)

LE CONNEMARA, *ou une élection en Irlande.* A. J. B. Defauconpret, Paris: Gosselin, 1830, 3 v.

('Connemara')

EDGEWORTH (Maria)

Texts first translated:

Extract from *The Parent's Assistant* (which was to appear in volume form in Geneva (Paschoud) in 1826 under the name of the same translator, C. Pictet, and, in Paris (H. Fournier jeune) in 1832 – the 1826 edition is entitled *L'Ami des Parens,* that of 1832, *Le Livre des familles*) in: *Bibliothèque Britannique,* Geneva, 1798–9.

The same periodical published in 1802: 'Traits remarquables des moeurs des Irlandais' extracts from the glossary of *Castle Rackrent,* as well as some pages taken from the *Essay on Irish Bulls* and the first translations of the Moral Tales, 'Contes Moraux', which it will continue to publish until 1822. The present author has not chronicled the immense success of these tales collected in various anthologies throughout the nineteenth-century, including the *Bibliothèque Rose* (1859). This would have meant devoting pages to works of negligible literary interest (cf. the catalogue of the Bibliothèque nationale and, for the publications of the *Bibliothèque Britannique,* Haüserman's work mentioned in the English bibliography of Maria Edgeworth). Similar considerations have led the present author to treat in an identical manner the translations of *Practical Education* ('L'Education Pratique') the first of which also figures in the *Bibliothèque Britannique* of 1798–9 (12 numbers), and the other works or fragments of works that, strictly speaking, are didactic in character.

BÉLINDE, *conte moral.*   (*Belinda*)
Octave Ségur, Paris: Maradan, 1802, 4 v.

LÉONORA.   *(Leonora)*
C. Chenel, Paris: Dentu, 1807, 3 v.

LA MÈRE INTRIGANTE.   *(Manœuvring)*
J. Joly, Paris: Galignani, 1812, 3 v.

L'ENNUI, *ou Mémoires du Comte de*   *(Ennui)*
Glenthorn.
Mme E. de Bon, Paris: Galignani, 1812, 3 v.
subsequently re-published, cf. 1823.

LE CHATEAU DE RACKRENT.   *(Castle Rackrent)*
[Paris: Nicole, 1813–14]
Pierre Leyris has produced a recent translation, under the title of
Château Rackrent, Paris: Mercure de France, 1964.

under the generic title of:

SCÈNES DE LA VIE DU GRAND   *(Tales of Fashionable Life)*
MONDE.
P. L. Dubuc, Paris: Nicole, 1813–14.

    L'ABSENT, 3 v.   *(The Absentee)*

    EMILIE DE COULANGES.   *(Emilie de Coulanges)*

    VIVIAN, *ou l'homme sans caractère.*   *(Vivian)*

LES PROTECTEURS ET LES PROTÉGÉS.   *(Patronage)*
J. Cohen, Paris: Ledoux et Teuré, 5 v.
subsequently re-published, cf. 1823.

HARRINGTON.   *(Harrington)*
C. A. Defauconpret, Paris: Gide et Nicolle, 1817, 2 v.

ORMOND.   *(Ormond)*
A. J. B. Defauconpret, Paris: Gide et Nicolle, 1817, 3 v.

HÉLÈNE.   *(Helen)*
Mme L. Sw. Belloc, Paris: A. Guyot, 1834, 3 v.
the first volume of this translation was reprinted, also in 1834, by
Abel Ledoux.

FERGUSON (Sir Samuel)

ADIEU TO BRITTANY
(an offprint from *Revue de Bretagne et de Vendée.* Introduction by
Hersart de la Villemarqué to whom is dedicated the poem given

here with its English text and French translation. 21 stanzas, 15 p.
Nantes, 1864).

ADIEUX A LA BRETAGNE.
(the same, with no introduction).
St-Brieuc: imprimerie Guyon Francisque, 1867.

GRIFFIN (Gerald)

LA FILLE DU CORDIER, *Scènes de la vie*   *(The Collegians)*
irlandaise.
Thérèse Alphonse Karr, Paris: Didier, 1872.

JEPHSON (Robert)

LE COMTE DE NARBONNE.   *(The Count of Narbonne)*
Baronne de Vasse, Paris: Vve Ballard & fils, 1784.

KNOWLES (James Sheridan)

GUILLAUME TELL.   *(William Tell)*
Paris: Vergne, 1828.
London: Marc Monnier, 1874.
VIRGINIUS.   *(Virginius)*
Paris: Vergne, 1828.
Paris: Blondeau, 1844 (bilingual.)
LE BOSSU.   *(The Hunchback)*
Paris: Lance, 1833.

LE FANU (Joseph Sheridan)[1]

MON ONCLE SILAS.   *(Uncle Silas)*
Paris: C. Lévy, 1877 («Bibliothèque
contemporaine».) Re-published ibid. in 1883.

CARMILLA, etc.   *('Carmilla')*
A. Derimieux et E. Gille.
Paris: Denoël, 1960, («Présence du Futur» n° 42.)

CARMILLA.   *(id.)*
Jacques Papy, Paris: E. Losfeld, 1961.

LES CRÉATURES DU MIROIR.   *(In a Glass Darkly)*
Michel Arnaud, Paris: Le Terrain Vague, 1967.

Also:

— *L'Angleterre Fantastique de Defoe à Wells*, textes réunis et présentés par Jacques Van Herp, Paris, André Gérard, Marabout, 1974 (contains: La Main Fantôme, translated by Claude Boland-Maskens).

— *Le Hobereau Maudit et autres contes*, Traduction de Jean-Louis Degaudenzi, Préface de Roland Stragliati, Collection 'Les Chefs d'Oeuvre de la Science Fiction et du Fantastique', Paris, Cercle Européen du Livre, 1975, 451 p. (contains: Le Hobereau Maudit, Le Chat Blanc de Drumgunniol, Le Marché de Sir Dominick, Le Destin de Sir Robert Ardagh, Le Testament du Squire Toby, Le Fantôme de Madame Crowl, Le Défunt Sonneur de Cloches, Histoires de Spectres à Tiled House, Manifestations Etranges dans la rue Aungier, Ultor de Lacy).

LEVER (Charles)

AVENTURES D'HARRY LORREQUER.   *(Harry Lorrequer)*
Aristide Baudéan, Paris: Hachette, 1858, 2 v.

L'HOMME DU JOUR.
Aristide Baudéan, Paris: Hachette, 1861.

O'DONOGHUE, *histoire d'une famille*   *(The O'Donoghue)*
irlandaise.

---

[1] Updated by Jean Lozès.

Charles-Bernard Derosne, Paris: Hetzel et Lacroix, 1864, 2 v.

LOVER (Samuel)

L'ENTERREMENT DE LA DÎME, LE COMBAT   *(Handy Andy)*
DES FUNÉRAILLES.
A. Nettement, Paris: M. Gautier, n.d.

Mc HENRY (James)

LES CŒURS D'ACIER.   *(Hearts of Steel)*
Paris: Gosselin, 1831.

MARTIN (Harriet Letitia)

LE CANDIDAT, *mœurs irlandaises.*   *(Canvassing)*
Baronne de Los Vallès.
Paris: A. Dupont, 1836, 2 v.
(attributed in France to Banim).

MATURIN (Charles-Robert)

— EVA, *ou Amour et Religion.*   *(Woman; or, Pour et*
Paris: J. G. Dentu, 1818, 4 v.   *Contre)*

LES FEMMES, *ou Rien de trop.*   *(id.)*
Mme E. de Bon, Paris: Grandin, 1820, 3 v.

— BERTRAM, *ou le Château de St Aldobrand,*   *(Bertram)*
tragédie en 5 actes.
MM. Taylor et Charles Nodier, Paris: Gide et Ladvocat, 1821.
(This is the translation reissued in 1956 by Marcel A. Ruff (Paris:
Corti).

The next year, 1822, the two translators produced a freer version entitled *Bertram, ou le Pirate*, performed on 26 November at the Théâtre du Panorama Dramatique, published by Quoy.)

BERTRAM *(id.)*
With text and translation facing: Paris: Lance, 1832.

BERTRAM *(id.)*
Michel de M'Uzan, Paris: *Théâtre Populaire*, 1954, n° 9.

— L'HOMME DU MYSTÈRE, *ou Histoire de* *(Melmoth the*
Melmoth le voyageur. *Wanderer)*
Mme Emile Béguin, Paris: Librairie
Nationale et Etrangère, 1821, 3 v.

MELMOTH *ou l'Homme errant* *(id.)*
J. Cohen, Paris: G. C. Hubert, 1821, 6 v.
(This is the very free translation reissued in 1954 by Pauvert, with a preface by André Breton.)

MELMOTH, *l'Homme errant* *(id.)*
Maria de Fos, Paris: Librairie internationale, 1867.
(Translation reissued by Marabout in 1967.)

MELMOTH, *l'Homme errant* *(id.)*
Jacqueline Marc-Chadourne, Paris: Pauvert, 1965.
(*Melmoth* had also been adapted for the stage in 1824: a mimo-drama in three acts by MM. Ferdinand and Saint-Hilaire, music by Sergent, ballets by M. Jacquinet. (First perf.: 16.3.1824, Cirque Olympique), Paris: Bezou, 1824. M. A. Ruff (op. cit.) also takes into account two unpublished adaptations, an opera by Paul Foucher, music by Zimmermann, and a 'pièce-féerie' by Gaspard de Pons.)

— LA FAMILLE DE MONTARIO, *ou la* *(Fatal Revenge)*
fatale Vengeance.
J. Cohen, Paris: G. C. Hubert, 1822, 5 v.

— LES ALBIGEOIS, *roman historique du XIIe* *(The Albigenses)*
siècle ... précédé d'une notice biographique
sur le Rév. Ch. R. Maturin.
Paris: Gosselin, Mame et Delaunay-Vallée, 1825, 4 v.

— LE JEUNE IRLANDAIS. *(The Wild Irish Boy)*
Comtesse de Molé, Paris: Mame et
Delaunay-Vallée, 1828, 4 v.

— CONNAL, *ou les Milésiens.* *(The Milesian Chief)*
Comtesse de Molé, Paris: Mame et
Delaunay-Vallée, 1828, 4 v.

— «LE CHATEAU DE LEIXLIP, *légende d'une*   (*Leixlip Castle*)
famille irlandaise».
Georgette Camille, in Roger Caillois: *Anthologie du Fantastique*.
Paris: Le Club français du Livre, 1958, pp. 87–94.

MAXWELL (Rev. William Hamilton)

LA DAME NOIRE DE DOONA.   (*The Dark Lady of Doona*)
Paquis, Paris: Allardin, 1834, 2 v.

MOORE (Thomas)

Information concerning Moore's French bibliography will be
found – scattered – in the two theses by G. Vallat and A. P.
Thomas (q.v. Moore: English bibliography) as well as in the work
by E. Partridge: *The French Romantics' Knowledge of French
Literature* (q.v. in the general bibliography) ...
All these data are collected here, with numerous additions,
sometimes with the help of the late E. Mac White.

(a) Poems: individual works:

— (*Lalla Rookh*)

LALLA ROUKH, *ou la Princesse mongole, histoire orientale*.
Amédée Pichot, Paris: Ponthieu, 1820, 2 v.
(With a notice on the author.)

LE PROPHÈTE VOILÉ, LE PARADIS ET LA PÉRI.
A. P. Rigaud, Paris: Bertrand, 1820.

LE PARADIS ET LA PÉRI.
Victor S., 1840.

LE PARADIS ET LA PÉRI, *conte oriental*.
A. Clavareau, Liège, 1857.

LE PARADIS ET LA PÉRI.
paroles par V. Wilder, musique de R. Schumann.
Paris: Durand, n.d.

LALLA ROOKH.
J. Thomassy, Paris: Leroux, 1887.

— *(The Loves of the Angels)*

LES AMOURS DES ANGES, *et les Mélodies irlandaises.*
Mme Louise Sw. Belloc, Paris: Chasseriau, 1823.

LES AMOURS DES ANGES, *poème en 3 chants.*
D. de Fontès, Paris: Pillet aîné, 1823.

LES AMOURS DES ANGES.
E. Aroux, Paris: A. Mesmer, 1829.

LES AMOURS DES ANGES.
L. Moutardier (a verse trans.), Angoulême: Laroche, 1830.

LES AMOURS DES ANGES, *poème traduit en vers français*
par Ostrowski, Paris: Gosselin, 1837.

LES AMOURS DES ANGES, *poème oriental.*
A. Clavareau, Liège, 1838.

La Légende de Jeanne d'Arc, suivie des Faits et Gestes du
Renard et des AMOURS DES ANGES.
T. Cabuchet, Paris: Bray, 1857.

— *(Irish Melodies)*

Les Amours des Anges, et LES MÉLODIES IRLANDAISES.
Mme L. Sw. Belloc, Paris: Chasseriau, 1823.

MÉLODIES IRLANDAISES; librement arrangées
et mises en accord avec le génie de la langue française
par T. G. de Mandelsloh (in verse), Marseille: Senès, 1841.

MÉLODIES IRLANDAISES traduites en vers français par
M. Henri Jousselin. Préface de Jules Janin.
Paris: E. Maillet, 1869 (An appendix in 1870).

QUELQUES MÉLODIES IRLANDAISES DE TH. MOORE.
Lyon: Pitrat, 1879.

— STANCES SUR LA MORT DE LORD BYRON par son ami Sir
Thomas Moore (sic).
Paris: Chez les Marchands de nouveautés, 1824, (in single
sheet 8°.)

(b) Poetry: Selected pieces:

CHOIX DE POÉSIES DE BYRON, DE W. SCOTT ET MOORE,
traduction libre pas l'un des rédacteurs de la Bibliothèque
Universelle, Paris et Genève: Paschoud, 1820, 2 v.
By Moore: *Le Prophète voilé du Khorasan*, cantos 1, 2, 3 (V.
II, pp. 137–233).

LA COURONNE LITTÉRAIRE,
composée de morceaux principalement extraits des poètes et
des prosateurs contemporains les plus distingués: ouvrage
essentiellement moral et religieux propre aux leçons de l'art de
lire à haute voix ... à l'usage des maisons d'éducation par
MM. A. Boniface, instituteur, D. Lévi, professeur, Paris:
Ferra jeune, 1824.
(contains 4 poems that already figure in Mme Belloc's 1823
translation: «Il n'est rien de vrai que le ciel» (31), «Sur la
Musique» (39), «Chant sacré» (45), «La Vallée d'Ovoca»
(sic) (51).)

MÉLANGES POÉTIQUES.
Ulric Guttinguer, Paris: A. Boulland, 1824.
(contains imitations of 3 melodies:
    'The Last Rose of Summer':

> Toutes les fleurs de la vallée
> Tombent sur le sol attristé ...
> La dernière rose d'été
> Fleurit encor, mais isolée!

'Though the Last Glimpse of Erin':

> Lorsque je ne vis plus la rive ...

'Fly not yet, 'tis just the hour':

> Ami ne t'en va pas encore.)

BALLADES, LÉGENDES ET CHANTS POPULAIRES DE
L'ANGLETERRE ET DE L'ECOSSE par Walter Scott, Th.
Moore, Campbell et les anciens Poètes ...
publiés et précédés d'une introduction par Loève Veimars,
Paris: A. A. Renouard, 1825.

POÉSIES EUROPÉENNES par Léon Halévy.
Paris: Delaforest, 1827–8.
(contains 4 melodies:
«A la Patrie» (61) ('Remember Thee').
«Le Passé» (85) ('Oft in the stilly night'):

> Souvent, pendant la nuit, dans l'ombre et le silence …

«Mélodie» (151) ('I'd mourn the hopes').

«Rêverie» (177) ('I saw from the beach').

BALLADES, MÉLODIES ET POÉSIES DIVERSES.
par A. Fontaney, Paris: Hayet, 1829.
(Contrary to Allen B. Thomas's affirmation, op. cit., p. 80, the book is in the Bibliothèque Nationale, number: Ye 9969. It contains more translations of the 'Irish Melodies' and 'National Airs' than the preceding anthologies. Among others:

«La dernière Rose» ('The Last Rose of Summer'):

> Voici la dernière rose
> De l'été qui fuit …

«Souvenir» ('Dost thou remember'):

> Te le rappelles-tu ce jardin solitaire,
> Où tu reçus l'aveu de mon timide amour? …

«Reviens» ('Come, rest, in this bosom'):

> Sois encore une fois contre mon sein pressée.)

LORD BYRON ET THOMAS MOORE.
Poésies traduites par M. A. Pichot, Mme Belloc, M. E. Henrion
avec notice par Ch. Nodier.
Paris; 20 rue Férou, 1829.

LES PRÉLUDES.
par Mme Caroline Pavlof, Paris: 1839.
(contains: «L'origine de la harpe» and «L'adieu à la harpe».)

CHEFS-D'ŒUVRE POÉTIQUES DE THOMAS MOORE.
Traduits par Mme L. Sw. Belloc, avec une traduction des poésies satiriques et burlesques de Moore, une notice sur la vie et les œuvres du même auteur, précédée d'un aperçu sur les antiquités et la littérature irlandaises par D. O'Sullivan, Paris: Gosselin, 1841.

ECRIN POÉTIQUE DE LITTÉRATURE ANGLAISE.
Traduction en vers français, avec notes historiques, de poèmes, épisodes et fragments choisis de Lord Byron, Thomas Moore, Gray, Graham, etc.
par D. Bonnefin, Paris: Hachette, 1841.
(contains by Moore: «La Péri» and a few «Mélodies»).

MORCEAUX CHOISIS EN PROSE ET EN VERS DES CLASSIQUES ANGLAIS, par F. G. Eichoff, traduits en français par M. Hauvette-Desnault, 1re série, Paris: Hachette, 1859.

(Attention is drawn to this anthology in which Moore figures:
cf. pp. 106–7: «Le Bon Sens et le Génie»
p. 152: «La Tombe du Proscrit» ('Oh, breathe not his
Name')
but, also, and perhaps for the first time, some other Irish
poets.)

BEAUTÉS DE LA POÉSIE ANGLAISE.
Le Chevalier de Châtelain, Londres: Rolandi.
Vol. I, 1860 (1857?). Vol. II, 1860 (1857?). III, 1863
(under the title *Rayons et Reflets*). IV, 1864 (under the title
Le Fond du Sac). V, 1872 (returns to the title *Beautés* ...).
Moore figures in:
Vol. I, pp. 187–89: «Le Miroir magique» ('The Magic
Mirror').
Vol. III, p. 277: «La Légende de Puck le lutin» ('The
Legend of Puck, the Fairy').
Vol. IV, p. 294: «Chante douce Harpe» ('Sing Sweet
Harp'); p. 295: «La Mouche Phosphorique» ('To the Fire-
Fly'); p. 296: «Stances» ('O thou! who dryest the mourner's
tear').
Vol. V, p. 220: «Matin et Soir»:

> Au matin d'un beau jour j'apperçus (sic) de la grève
> Une barque filant fièrement sur les flots.

(c) Prose:

— *(Sheridan)*

MÉMOIRES SUR LA VIE PRIVÉE, POLITIQUE ET LITTÉRAIRE
DE R. B. SHERIDAN.
J. J. Parisot, Paris: Bertrand, 1826, 2 v.

— *(The Epicurean)*

L'EPICURIEN.
A. Renouard, Paris: J. Renouard, 1827.

L'EPICURIEN, *ou la vierge de Memphis.*
Mme A. Aragon, Paris: Béchet, 1827.

L'EPICURIEN.
Ives Tennaec, Rennes: Marteville, 1847.

L'EPICURIEN, précédé d'une notice sur l'auteur,
traduction nouvelle. Avignon: A. Chaillot, 1861.

L'EPICURIEN.
H. Butat, mis en vers par Th. Gautier, préface d'E. Thierry,
dessins de Gustave Doré.
Paris: E. Dentu, 1865.

— *(Captain Rock)*

INSURRECTIONS IRLANDAISES DEPUIS HENRI II JUSQU'A
L'UNION, *ou Mémoires du Capitaine Rock.*
L. Nachet, Paris: E. Dentu, 1829.

— *(Byron)*

MÉMOIRES DE LORD BYRON.
Mme L. Sw, Belloc, Paris: Mesnier, 1830, 5 v.

'MÉMOIRES SUR LA VIE DE LORD BYRON' dans:
Œuvres complètes de Byron. Paris, 1830.

ŒUVRES COMPLÈTES DE LORD BYRON avec les notes et
commentaires de W. Scott, Th. Moore, etc.
Paris, 1836.

— *(Travels ... in Search of a Religion)*

VOYAGES D'UN GENTILHOMME IRLANDAIS A LA RECHER-
CHE D'UNE RELIGION avec notes et éclaircissements par Th.
Moore.
Abbé Didon, Paris: Gaume, 1833.
Republished in 1834 (Lyon), 1835, 1836; also in 1841 (Tours
Mame).

Also in MIGNE (Abbé): *Démonstrations Evangéliques,*
Paris: Migne, 1842–53, 20 v., Tome XIV.

— *(History of Ireland)*

HISTOIRE D'IRLANDE.
H. Bion-Marlavagne, Paris: Périsse, 1835.

HISTOIRE D'IRLANDE.
A. J. B. Defauconpret, Paris: Gosselin, 1835.

HISTOIRE DE L'IRLANDE.
Baron de Roujoux, Lyon: Pelagaud, 1836.

also: HISTOIRE D'IRLANDE d'après Th. Moore ...
by M. de Marles, Paris: Parent-Desbarres, 1840.

MORGAN (Sydney Owenson, Lady ——)

The author's French translations are given again even though I.
A. Moraud (*Une Irlandaise libérale*, q.v. in the English bibliography for Lady Morgan) has already listed them: the present
author adds several corrections or further information.

LA FEMME, *ou Ida l'Athénienne.*   *(Woman: or, Ida of Athens)*
P. L. Dubuc, Paris: H. Nicolle, 1812, 4 v., re-issued in 1816.

LE MISSIONNAIRE, *Histoire indienne.*   *(The Missionary)*
P. L. Dubuc, Paris: H. Nicolle, 1812, 3 v., re-issued in 1816.

GLORVINA, *ou la jeune Irlandaise.*   *(The Wild Irish Girl)*
P. L. Dubuc, Paris: Gide fils, 1813, 4 v.

SAINT-CLAIR, *ou l'héritière de Desmond.*   *(Saint Clare)*
H. Vilmain, Paris: J. G. Dentu, 1813, 2 v.

O'DONNEL, *ou l'Irlande, histoire nationale.*   *(O'Donnel)*
P. A. Lebrun de Charmettes, Paris: Le Normant, 1815, 3 v.

LA NOVICE DE SAINT   *(The Novice of St Dominick)*
DOMINIQUE.
Vtesse de Ruolz, Paris: H. Nicolle, 1816, 4 v. (according to
Monglond, there was a translation in 1805. It has not been found
by the present author).

FRAGMENTS PATRIOTIQUES SUR   *(Patriotic Sketches)*
L'IRLANDE.
Mme A. d'Esmenard, Paris: L'Huillier, 1817.

LA FRANCE.   *(France)*
Strasbourg and London: Trenthel & Würtz, 1817, 2 v.
Note also the same year, by the same publisher, Paris and London
this time, and translator named: A. J. B. Defauconpret, a 2nd
edition with critical notes by the translator and, in 1848, a 5th
edition 'dans laquelle on a réintégré toutes les suppressions faites
dans les éditions précédentes' ('in which have been reinstated all the
excisions made in the previous editions'). This time the publisher is
Tillois and there are three volumes.

FLORENCE MACARTHY.   *(Florence Macarthy)*
A. J. B. Defauconpret, Paris: H. Nicolle, 1819, 4 v.

FLORENCE MACARTHY.   *(id.)*
J. T. Parisot, Paris: Treuttel et Würtz, 1819, 4 v.

L'ITALIE.   *(Italy)*
Mlle A. Sobry, Paris: P. Dufart, 1821, 4 v.

ENCORE UNE VICTIME, *ou Caroline de Brunswick, reine d'Angleterre.*
Paris: Les Marchands de nouveautés, 1821.

MÉMOIRES SUR LA VIE ET LE   *(The Life and Times of*
SIÈCLE DE SALVATOR ROSA.   *Salvator Rosa)*
Mlle A. Sobry et M. Pierhuc.
Paris: A. Emery, 1824, 2 v.

LES O'BRIEN ET LES O'FLAHERTY, *ou*   *(The O'Briens and the*
l'Irlande en 1793, histoire nationale.   *O'Flahertys)*
J. Cohen, Paris: Gosselin, 1828, 6 v.

LE LIVRE DU BOUDOIR.   *(The Book of the Boudoir)*
A. J. B. Defauconpret,
Paris: Gosselin, 1828, 2 v.

LA FRANCE EN 1829–30.   *(France in 1829–30)*
Mlle A. Sobry,
Paris: H. Fournier jeune, 1830, 2 v.

SCÈNES DRAMATIQUES EMPRUNTÉES   *(Dramatic Scenes of*
A LA VIE RÉELLE.   *Real Life)*
Mlle A. Sobry,
Paris: H. Fournier jeune, 1833, 2 v.

LA PRINCESSE.   *(The Princess)*
Mlle A. Sobry et M.A.S.T. (3ᵉ vol.),
Paris: A. Bertrand, 1835, 3 v.

O'BRIEN (Fitz James)

QU'ÉTAIT-CE?, etc.   *(What Was It?)*
Jacques Papy, Paris: R. Marin, 1950.
(«L'envers du miroir»).

O'CONNELL (Daniel)

L'IRLANDE ET LES IRLANDAIS.   *(A Memoir of Ireland)*
G. de Coutance, Lyon: Blanc et Hervier, 1843.

MÉMOIRE SUR L'IRLANDE INDIGÈNE ET   *(id.)*

SAXONNE.
Ortaire Fournier, Paris: Warée, 1843.

POWER (W. G. Tyrone)

LE SECRET DU ROI.   *(The King's Secret)*
A. J. B. Defauconpret,
Paris: E. Renduel, 1832, 2 v.

ROCHE (Regina Maria Dalton, Mrs ——)

LE CURÉ DE LANSDOWNE, *ou les*   *(The Vicar of Lansdowne)*
Garnisons.
Paris: rue des Poitevins,
Hôtel Bouthillier, 1789, 2 v.

LES ENFANTS DE L'ABBAYE.   *(The Children of the Abbey)*
A. Morellet, Paris: Denné, 1797, 6 v.
reprinted by Maradan in 1798 and 1812.

A. Labaume, Paris: Le Prieur, 1801, 6 v.
a new translation in 1841.

CLERMONT.   *(Clermont)*
A. Morellet, Paris: Denné jeune, 1798, 3 v.

LA FILLE DU HAMEAU.   *(The Maid of the Hamlet)*
Dubergier, Paris: J. G. Dentu, 1801.

LA VISITE NOCTURNE.   *(The Nocturnal Visit)*
P. L. Lebas, Paris: Michel et Le Normant,
1801, 5 v.

LE FILS BANNI, *ou, la Retraite des*   *(The Discarded Son)*
brigands.
M. et Mme de Sennevas,
Paris: Chaumerot, 1808, 4 v.

LE MONASTÈRE DE ST COLUMBA,   *(The Monastery of*
ou le Chevalier des armes rouges.   *St Columb)*
Paris: J. G. Dentu, 1810, 3 v.

L'ENFANT DE LA CHAUMIÈRE DE *(The Munster Cottage*
MUNSTER. *Boy)*
Mlle L. Girard de Caudenberg,
Paris: Locard et Davy, 1820, 5 v.

L'ORPHELIN DE LA CHAUMIÈRE IRLANDAISE. *(id.)*
J. Cohen, Paris: J. G. Dentu, 1821, 5 v.

LE MARIAGE DE DUNAMORE. *(The Bridal of Dunamore)*
Dubergier, Paris: Haut-Cœur et Gayet jeune, 1824, 4 v.

LA TRADITION DU CHATEAU, *ou Scènes* *(The Tradition of the*
de l'île d'émeraude. *Castle)*
Dubergier, Paris: Tardieu, Boulland et Cie, 1824, 3 v.

LA CHAPELLE DU VIEUX CHATEAU DE *(The Castle Chapel)*
ST DOULAGH, *ou les Bandits de Newgate.*
Paris: Corbet aîné, 1852, 4 v.

id.
Fournier, Paris: Michel Lévy Frères, 1868.

Titles such as *L'Abbaye de Léolin* (1824), which is by Miss Alicia
Lefanu, *Le Père Coupable* and *Suzanne* have been mistakenly
attributed to the author.

SHEIL (R.L.)

SCÈNES POPULAIRES EN IRLANDE.
L. Sw. Belloc et A. de M.
Paris: Sédillot et Dondey Dupré fils, 1830.
(the author is given as R. L. Shiel).

SHERIDAN (Richard Brinsley)

It is beyond the present author's intentions to reproduce the
substantial French bibliography of Sheridan, details of which will
be found in J. Dulck (q.v. in the English bibliography of the
author).

Note only:

PIZZARE.   *(Pizzaro)*
A. J. Dumanian, Paris: Cailleau, 1793.

THÉATRE COMPLET.
Paris: Fournier, 1836, 2 v.

4

PRINCIPAL
IRISH PERIODICALS
from 1789 to 1850

ANCIENT IRELAND.
A weekly magazine (in fact appeared only very irregularly) established for ... reviving the cultivation of the Irish language and originating an earnest investigation into the antient history of Ireland by Philip F. Barron, Esq., Waterford.
   1 v. 5 numbers, 176 p. (1. 1st Jan. 1835; 2. 10 Jan.; 3. 31 Jan.; 4. April 1835; 5. May).

ANTHOLOGIA HIBERNICA.
or monthly collection of science, belles-lettres and history.
Dublin: printed for R. E. Mercier.
   4 v. I. Jan.–June 1793, 484 p. + index; II. July–Dec. 1793, 472 p. + index; III. Jan.–June 1794; IV. July–Dec. 1794, 479 p. + index.
Science and antiquities are given ample space. The poetical section, which is fairly restricted, includes pieces by Dermody and Th. Moore's first publications.

THE ANTI-UNION.
Dublin: 27 Dec. 1798–9 Mar. 1799.

THE ANTI-UNIONIST MAGAZINE.
Dublin: Nolan, 31 Jan.–30 May 1818.

THE BELFAST LITERARY JOURNAL.
Belfast: 1816.

THE BELFAST MAGAZINE AND LITERARY JOURNAL.
Belfast: Feb.–June 1825.

THE BELFAST MONTHLY MAGAZINE.
Belfast: 1808–14, 13 v.
(Ed. W. Drennan).

THE BELFASTMAN'S JOURNAL.
Belfast: 1850.
(Ed. F. Davis)

BOLG AN TSOLAIR, *or Gaelic Magazine.*
Belfast: Northern Star Office, 1795 (a single issue).

BOLSTER'S QUARTERLY MAGAZINE.
Cork: J. Bolster; Dublin: R. Milliken; London: Longman & Co, 3 v.
  I: 1828–Feb. (n° 1), May (2), Aug. (3), Nov. (4) 1826.
  II: 1828–Jan. (5), April (6), July (7), Oct. (8) 1827.
  III: 1831–May 1828 (9), Aug. 1828 (10), Dec. 1829 (11), Mar.
1830 (12).
In Vols. 1 and 3, the running title was 'The Irish Magazine' and in
Vol. 2, 'The Magazine of Ireland'.
  An important literary magazine in spite of its lifelessness. It is
balanced and a-political.

THE CASKET; *or, Hesperian Magazine.*
Cork 1797–8 (established by R. Milliken).
  Vol. I: printed by J. Daly, 3 numbers, April, May, June 1797,
216 p.
  Vol. II: printed by Edwards: n° 4, Aug. 1797; n° 5, Sept.; n° 6,
Oct., 216 p.
  Vol. III: id. n° 7, Nov. 1797; n° 8, Dec. 1797; n° 9, Jan. 1798,
216 p.
stories, poetry (neo-classical), biography, anecdotes.

THE CATHOLIC PENNY MAGAZINE.
Dublin: Coldwell, 1834–5 (weekly).

THE CHRISTIAN EXAMINER AND CHURCH OF IRELAND
MAGAZINE.
Dublin 1825–1869.
A partisan magazine launched by the Rev. C. Otway and which
had Carleton as one of its contributors.

THE CITIZEN.

Dublin: 1839–1840, 2 v.

A monthly publication continued successively under the following titles:

> The Citizen; or, Dublin Monthly Magazine: 1840–1.
> The Dublin Monthly Magazine: Jan.–June 1842.
> The Dublin Magazine (and Citizen): Jan.–April 1843.

An important place is given to music.

THE CLUBBIST.

Consisting chiefly of a selection of poems from the ... suppressed journals.

Dublin: 1849, 3 numbers.

THE COMET.

Dublin: printed for Browne and Sheehan, 3 v. folio.

   I. 1st May 1831–22 April 1832, n°s 1–52, 416 p.
   II. 29 April 1832, n°s 53–104, 416 p.
   III.   –1st Dec. 1833, n°s 105–135, pp. 417 to 640
(but the last 3 issues are unpaginated.)

A satirical weekly particularly opposed to tithes. Its editors published, with illustrations by S. Lover: The Parson's Horn Book, ibid., 1831, 136 p., a pamphlet of a similar tone.

THE COMIC OFFERING.

Dublin, 1832–5 (annual).

THE CONNOISSEUR; or, Dublin Weekly Gazette.

Dublin, 1827.

THE CONSTITUTION AND CHURCH SENTINEL.

A Protestant and Literary Journal.

Dublin, 1848–9.

THE CORK MAGAZINE.

Cork: 1847–1848, 14 issues (there had also been another newspaper with this title in 1819). Editor: Joseph Brenan.

THE CYCLOPAEDIAN MAGAZINE AND DUBLIN MONTHLY REGISTER.

Dublin: 1807–1809.

THE DRAMA.

A daily register of plays performed on the Dublin stage.

Dublin, 1821–2.

THE DRAMATIC ARGUS.
Dublin: 1824–1825, 2 v.

DUBLIN AND LONDON MAGAZINE.
London: James Robins & Co; Dublin: Joseph Robins, Jun. & Co, 4 v.
    I. 1825 (1st number: Mar.), 473 p. + index.
    II. 1826, 572 p. + index.
    III. (entitled *Robins's London and Dublin Magazine*. Sole publisher: Joseph Robins, London and Dublin). 1827 (Jan. to June), 680 p. + index.
    IV. 1828 (Feb. to June), 236 p. + index.
A very important Catholic magazine directed by Michael James Whitty. Th. Furlong contributed to it. *The Catholic Miscellany* (1828–9) seems to have taken it over.

THE DUBLIN EXAMINER; *or, Monthly Journal of Science, Literature and Art.*
Dublin: May 1816–Jan. 1817, 2 v., 9 numbers.

THE DUBLIN FAMILY MAGAZINE; *or, Literary and Religious Miscellany.*
Dublin: April–Sept. 1829, 6 numbers.

THE DUBLIN JOURNAL OF TEMPERANCE, SCIENCE AND LITERATURE.
Dublin: T. Tegg (for vol. I), G. R. Tracy (for vol. II), 2 v.
    I. 30 April–22 Oct. 1842, 26 numbers, 416 p.
    II. (The dates are no longer indicated), 27 issues, 430 p. 1843.

THE DUBLIN LITERARY GAZETTE; *or, Weekly Chronicle of Criticism, Belles-Lettres and Fine Arts.*
Dublin: W. F. Wakeman, 2 Jan.–26 June 1830 (26 numbers).
from July, a change of title: *The National Magazine*, etc.
    Vol. I. title: 'The National Magazine'; 2nd page: 'The Dublin Literary Gazette and National Magazine'. July.–Dec. 1830, 756 p.
    Vol. II. title: 'The National Magazine and Dublin Literary Gazette. Edited by P. D. Hardy'. Months not indicated, 1831, 488 p.

THE DUBLIN LITERARY JOURNAL AND SELECT FAMILY VISITOR, a Monthly Periodical.
Dublin: J. Abell, 3 v. in-4°.
    I. 1st April 1843–1st Mar. 1844, n°s 1 to 12, 192 p.

II. 1st April 1844–1st Mar. 1845, n°s 13 to 24, pp. 193–368.
III. 1st April 1845–1st Feb. 1846, n°s 25 to 35, pp. 369–560.
The aim of this magazine is 'to record and disseminate the reports of the various Irish literary and scientific societies'. It is of minimal interest however.

THE DUBLIN MAGAZINE, 1843. See *The Citizen.*

THE DUBLIN MAGAZINE AND IRISH MONTHLY REGISTER.
Being a repository of useful and entertaining knowledge including a review of new publications and an accurate register of the transactions literary, political and military of the times.
Dublin: printed for J. Moore, 5 v.
I. July–Dec. 1798.
II. Jan.–June 1799.
III. July–Dec. 1799.
IV. Jan.–June 1800.
V. July–Dec. 1800.
More interesting for history and politics than for literature, this magazine archaically printed in two columns, nevertheless published some poems by O'Keeffe and W. Oulton, translations from the German and 'Mackliniana'.

THE DUBLIN MAGAZINE; *or, general repertory of philosophy, belles-lettres,* etc.
Dublin: Jan.–Dec. 1820, 2 v.

THE DUBLIN MAGAZINE; *or monthly memorialist.*
Dublin: Nov. 1812–Sept. 1813, 1 v.

THE DUBLIN MONTHLY MAGAZINE.
Dublin: Jan.–June 1830, 6 numbers.

THE DUBLIN MONTHLY MAGAZINE. 1842. See *The Citizen.*

THE DUBLIN PENNY JOURNAL.
Dublin: J. S. Fold, 4 v., 4°, ill.
I. 1832 (from 30 June)–1833 (22 June), n°s 1–52, 416 p.+ preface + index.
II. 1833 (6 July)–1834 (28 June), n°s 53–104, 416 p.. + preface + table + supplement (A Guide to the Giants' Causeway).
   The publisher is, here: Penny Journal Office conducted by P. D. Hardy (a change, from n° 56: 26 July).

III. 1834 (5 July)–1835 (27 June), n°s 105–156, 416 p. + preface + supplement (Views in Dublin).

IV. 1835 (4 July)–1836 (25 June), n°s 157–208, 416 p. + preface + table + supplement (Views in the neighbourhood of Belfast).

The first 55 issues are of capital importance on account of the outstanding contributors to the paper: Mangan, Croker, Banim, Carleton, Ferguson, Hall, Lover, Petrie, etc.

P. D. Hardy compiled a selection of articles which appeared after he unfortunately took over.

Pic Nics From 'The Dublin Penny Journal' ... ill. with ten characteristic engravings by Mr B. Clayton, Jun.

Dublin: P. D. Hardy, 1836, VII + 328 p.

THE DUBLIN PHILOSOPHICAL JOURNAL AND SCIENTIFIC REVIEW.

Dublin: 1825–6, 2 v.

THE DUBLIN REVIEW.

London, Vol. I–III: W. Spooner, IV–V: Booker and Dolman, VI seq.: C. Dolman; Dublin: J. Cumming; Edinburgh: W. Tait.

I. May–July 1836, 667 p.

II. Dec. 1836–April 1837, 620 p. + index.

III. July 1837–October 1837, 570 p.

from 1838 (the 1st series continued until 1863; then 1863–78; then 1897, etc.) 2 volumes (4 issues) per year.

An essentially religious (Catholic) publication but also including some long and interesting articles on literature and on society.

THE DUBLIN SATIRIST.

edited by the Buckthorn Club, Dublin: printed and published for the proprietors.

Vol. I, n°s 1 to 52, 22 June 1833–14 June 1834, 416 p.

Vol. II *(The Dublin Satirist; or, Weekly Magazine of Fashion and Literature)*, n°s 53 to 104, 21 June 1834–13 June 1835, 416 p.

Vol. III (id.), n°s 105 to 136, 20 June 1835–23 January 1836, 256 p.

(A newspaper had also appeared under this title in 1809–10.)

THE DUBLIN UNIVERSITY MAGAZINE.

a Literary and Political Journal.

Dublin: W. Curry, Jun. & Co; London: Simpkin and Marshall; then Dublin: M'Glashan.

35 volumes up until 1850 (but the magazine lasted until 1877), a monthly publication, 2 v. per year. First issue: January 1833. Successive editors: C. S. Stanford, I. Butt, J. Wills, Ch. Lever, J. F. Waller, J. Sheridan Le Fanu, all of them Tories and Protestants. Despite its caricatural sectarianism, the *D.U.M.* is by far the most remarkable Irish magazine of the period.
See:

SADLEIR (Michael): *Dublin University Magazine, Its History, Contents and Bibliography*. Dublin, 1938 (*The Bibliographical Society of Ireland:* Vol. V, n° 4, pp. 59–82, 1 plate).

THE (DUBLIN) UNIVERSITY REVIEW AND QUARTERLY MAGAZINE.
Dublin: W. F. Wakeman, 1 v., 900 p.
4 numbers: I: 1 Jan. 1833.
    II: April.
    III and IV with no dates given in the copy in the British Museum.

DUFFY'S IRISH CATHOLIC MAGAZINE,
a monthly review, devoted to National Literature, the fine arts, ecclesiastical history, antiquities, biography of illustrious Irishmen, military memoirs, etc.
Dublin: J. Duffy, 2 v., 23 numbers.
    I. Feb. 1847–Jan. 1848, 336 p., n°ˢ 1–12.
    II. Feb.–Dec. 1848, 306 p., n°ˢ 13–23.
J. C. Mangan figured among the editors of this interesting magazine that, in England, can be found only in the Bodleian.

FREEMAN'S JOURNAL, Dublin, 1763–1924.

THE FRIEND OF IRELAND; *or, Monthly Visitor*.
Dublin: 1842 (P. D. Hardy, ed.)

THE HARP.
London: 2 Dec. 1810–3 Feb. 1811.
The first Irish periodical published in England.

THE HIBERNIA MAGAZINE AND MONTHLY PANORAMA.
Dublin: 1810–11.

THE HIBERNIAN MAGAZINE; *or, Compendium of Entertaining Knowledge,*

containing the greatest variety of the most curious and useful subjects on every branch of Polite Literature.
Illustrated with a great number of copper-plates.
Dublin: printed by J. Potts, 1 v. a year from 1771 to 1785.
Continued, from 1786 to 1811, under the title: *Walker's Hibernian Magazine.*
The oldest of the Irish magazines in the period under discussion.

IRELAND'S MIRROR; *or, a Chronicle of the Times.*
Dublin: Holmes & Charles, May 1804 to Dec. 1805, 2 v.
   I: 406 p.   II: 696 p.
It is of little interest except that it existed at a particularly meagre period: immediately after the Union.

THE IRISH DRAMATIC CENSOR.
Dublin: 1811–1812.

THE IRISH FELON.
Dublin: J. Martin, 24 June–22 July 1848 (5 numbers).

THE IRISH MAGAZINE AND MONTHLY ASYLUM FOR NEGLECTED BIOGRAPHY.
Dublin, 1807–1815, 8 v.
   I. Nov. 1807–Nov. 1808, 96 + 558 p.
   II. Jan. 1809–Dec. 1809, 573 + 3 p.
   III. 1810, IV. 1811, V. 1812, VI. 1813, VII. 1814, VIII. 1815 (all vols.: 576 p.)
   See:

O'CASAIDE (S.): *Watty Cox and his Publications.* Dublin: 3 Candles, 1935, 38 p., ill. (*The Bibliographical Society of Ireland.* Vol. V, n° 2.)

THE IRISHMAN.
Dublin: John Flanedy, 3 v.
   I. 6 Jan. 1849–29 Dec. 1849, n°s 1–52, 832 p.
   II. 5 Jan. 1850–25 May 1850, n°s 1–21, 396 p.
   (III.) Vol. I new series (smaller format), 2 numbers only: 10 Aug., 17 Aug. 1850, 32 p.
Numerous other Irish newspapers had previously adopted this title. They are not recorded here. Thus:
   London: 27 Feb.–27 Mar. 1831.
   Galway: 6 May–12 Dec. 1835.
   Dublin: 18 Jan. 1840–8 Oct. 1842.
   Dublin: 10 June–10 July, 1848 …

THE IRISH MONTHLY MAGAZINE, 1845–6. See *The Union Magazine*.

THE IRISH MONTHLY MAGAZINE OF POLITICS AND LITERATURE.
Dublin: May 1832–Sept. 1834, 3 v.

THE IRISH NATIONAL MAGAZINE AND WEEKLY JOURNAL OF LITERATURE, SCIENCE AND ART.
Dublin: 16 May–15 Aug. 1846.

THE IRISH PENNY JOURNAL,
containing original contributions by several of the most eminent Irish writers.
Dublin: Gunn & Cameron, 1 v., 4 July 1840–26 June 1841, 52 issues.
A weekly established by Petrie in the spirit of the *Dublin Penny Journal* of the early days, with similar presentation and format (in-4°). Carleton, Mangan, etc., contributed to it.

THE IRISH PENNY MAGAZINE.
Dublin: Coldwell, 2 v.
   I. 1833 (reprinted in 1841), 416 p.
   II. 1834 (continued in 1842), 104 p.
Interesting, among other things, on account of S. Lover's articles and illustrations. Same presentation and same format as the preceding.

THE IRISH TRIBUNE.
Dublin: printed for the proprietors by Denis Hoban.
10 June to 8 July 1848, 80 p., 5 issues, folio.
One of the organs of Young Ireland.
Editors: R. D. Williams, Kevin O'Doherty.
Contributions by Carleton, Mangan, Savage.

THE IRISH UNION MAGAZINE, 1845. See *The Union Magazine*.

KENNEDY'S BRITISH AND IRISH CATHOLIC MAGAZINE AND JOURNAL OF MISCELLANEOUS KNOWLEDGE.
Glasgow, 1836–7, monthly.

THE LITERARY AND POLITICAL EXAMINER.
Cork, Feb. 1818.

THE MILESIAN MAGAZINE.
Dublin: W. M. M'Donald. Extremely irregular publication:
   (I). April, May, June, July, 1812, pp. 1-158; Oct. 1813, pp. 159-190; Dec. 1813, pp. 191-230; May 1814, pp. 231-270; July 1814, pp. 271-312; Dec. 1814, pp. 313-352.
   (II). May 1815, pp. 1-40.
   (III). Feb. 1816, pp. 1-40; July 1816, pp. 41-80.
   (IV). Feb. 1817, pp. 1-40.
   (V). no date, pp. 1-40.
   (VI). no date but marked n° XV pp. 1-40.
   (VII). *The Milesian Magazine for 1825* unpaginated).
Medical matters are given much space (the editor is a certain Dr Brenan); Watty Cox (cf.: *Irish Magazine*) is constantly and violently taken to task.

THE MONTHLY MUSEUM; *or, Dublin Literary Repertory of Arts, Science, Literature and Miscellaneous Information.*
Dublin: Oct. 1813-Dec. 1814, 2 v.

THE MONTHLY PANTHEON.
Dublin: 1808-9, 3 v.

THE NATION.
Dublin: published every Saturday by the proprietor at the office 12, Trinity Street, afterwards: Duffy, 7 v., folio.
   I.   15 Oct. 1842-14 Oct. 1843, 848 p., n°ˢ 1-53.
   II. 21 Oct. 1843-5 Oct. 1844, 832 p., n°ˢ 54-104.
   III. 12 Oct. 1844-11 Oct. 1845, 864 p., n°ˢ 105-157.
   IV. 18 Oct. 1845-3 Oct. 1846, 816 p., n°ˢ 158-208.
   V.   10 Oct. 1846-24 Dec. 1847, 1024 p., n°ˢ 209-273.
   VI. 1 Jan.-22 July 1848, 480 p., n°ˢ 274-303.
Banned by the government and with its contributors imprisoned, the great weekly newspaper of Irish nationalism reappeared the following year:
   VII. (new series) 1 Sept.-29 Dec. 1849, 288 p., 19 numbers.
The prose, admirable for its passion, deserved better than the slender anthology:

— *A Voice from the Prison, or, The Voice of the Nation.*
Dublin: J. Duffy, 1844, 146 p.

The paper's patriotic poetry was immensely successful in the following anthologies:

— *The Spirit of the Nation* by the writers of The Nation Newspaper.
Dublin: J. Duffy, 1843, VIII + 76 p.

— *The Spirit of the Nation, Part II.* Being a second series of Political Songs and National Ballads by the writers of The Nation Newspaper.
Dublin: J. Duffy, 1843, VIII + 76 p.
The 1845 quarto brings together these 2 parts and provides the music. 1870 saw the 50th edition.

— *The New Spirit of The Nation; or, ballads and songs* by the writers of 'The Nation' ... published since 1845.
Edited with an introduction by Martin MacDermott.
London: Fisher Unwin; Dublin: Sealy; New York: Kenedy, 1894, XXI + 198 p. (Poems published between 1845 and 1849.)
The poets represented include:
Davis, Barry, Drennan, D. E. M'Carthy, Walsh, Mangan, Mitchel, as well as (in *The New Spirit*) Thomas D'Arcy Mc Gee, Lady Wilde, etc.

THE NATIONAL MAGAZINE. See *The Dublin Literary Gazette*.

THE NEW MAGAZINE.
Dublin: 1799–1800.
From July to October 1800, continued under the title: *The Strabane Magazine*.

THE NEWRY MAGAZINE, a literary and political Register.
Newry: 1815–1819.

NOLAN'S THEATRICAL OBSERVER. See *The Theatrical Observer*.

THE NORTHERN STAR.
Belfast: 4 Jan. 1792–29 Dec. 1794.
The daily newspaper of the United Irishmen.

THE ORIGINAL THEATRICAL OBSERVER. See *The Theatrical Observer*.

PADDY KELLY'S BUDGET; *or, a penny-worth of fun!!!*
Dublin: printed by Michael Bourke (Vol. 1), by James Bannon (Vol. 2 and 3).
  I. 14 Nov. 1832–22 Jan. 1834, 416 p.
  II. 29 Jan. 1834–21 Jan. 1835, 416 p.

III. 28 Jan. 1835–7 Oct. 1835, 296 p.
A famous humorous weekly of a frighteningly low level.

THE PRESS.

Dublin: 28 Sept. 1797–13 Mar. 1798, folio, 69 issues, the penulti-
mate destroyed by order of the government, the last censored. A
tri-weekly directed by Arthur O'Connor. Of very great interest for
the history of the 1798 rebellion. Was reprinted in book form twice.
F. J. Bigger, in an article in *The Irish Book Lover*, I, 5 (Dec. 1909),
p. 56, mentions the first of these books: *The Beauties of The Press*,
1800, 602 p.
The present author, for his part, has only been able to study the
second: '*Extracts from The Press* ... including numbers sixty-eight
and sixty-nine, which were suppressed by order of the Irish
Government before the usual time of publication'.
Philadelphia: printed by William Duane, Aurora Office, 1802,
VIII + 400 p.

THE PROTESTANT PENNY MAGAZINE.

Dublin: 1834–1836.

THE SENTIMENTAL AND MASONIC MAGAZINE.

Dublin: printed for ... John Jones, 6 v.
  I. July–Dec. 1792.
  II. Jan.–June 1793.
  III. July–Dec. 1793.
  IV. Jan.–June 1794.
  V. July–Dec. 1794.
  VI. Jan.–June 1795.

THE SOUTHERN REPORTER
Conservative.
Cork, 1813–71.
(M. J. Barry was editor from 1848 onwards and, in 1849, published
an anthology of the paper's poems:
Echoes from Parnassus
Cork: Southern Reporter, 1849, VIII + 92 p.
The publication seems to have continued under the title:
Irish Daily Telegraph, then *Waterford Mail.*)

THE STAGE.
Dublin: 1821, 2 v.
Daily.

THE STRABANE MAGAZINE. See *The New Magazine.*

THE TATLER AND THEATRICAL MIRROR.
Dublin: 1834.

THE THEATRE, then:
The Theatre; or, Daily Miscellany of Fashion.
Dublin: 1822–3.

THE THEATRICAL OBSERVER.
successively:
The Original Theatrical Observer.
Nolan's Theatrical Observer.
Dublin: 1821–1823.

THE ULSTER REGISTER, a political and literary magazine.
Belfast: 1816–1818.

THE UNION MAGAZINE.
A Dublin magazine that changed title several times:
    I. (1 n°): *The Union Magazine*, Mar. 1845.
    II. (n°s 1–6): *The Irish Union Magazine*, April–Aug. 1845, 466 p.; (n°s 7–12): *The Irish Monthly Magazine*, Sept. 1845–Feb. 1846, 494 p.

THE UNITED IRISHMAN.
Dublin: printed and published by John Mitchel.
12 Feb.–27 May 1848, 16 numbers, 248 p., folio.
One of Young Ireland's numerous newspapers, like *The Irish Felon, The Nation, The Young Irishman*, etc.

THE UNIVERSAL MAGAZINE AND ENTERTAINING MISCELLANY.
Dublin: Mar.–May 1802.

THE UNIVERSAL MAGAZINE AND REVIEW, *or repository of literature*, containing the literature, history, manners, arts and amusements of the age.
Dublin: printed by P. Byrne ... and W. Porter, 8 v. (twice yearly) 1789–1792.

THE VINDICATOR.
Belfast, 1 May 1839–5 February 1848.
909 numbers in 9 volumes:

I. (4) + 416 p.	III. (4) + 420 p.	
II. (4) + 420 p.	IV. (4) + 416 p.	

V. (4) + 420 p.   VIII. (4) + 428 p.
VI. (4) + 408 p.   IX. (4) + 300 p.
VII. (4) + 408 p.

WALKER'S HIBERNIAN MAGAZINE. See *The Hibernian Magazine*.

THE WEEKLY DUBLIN SATIRIST. Current title of *The Dublin Satirist*, q.v.

THE YOUNG IRISHMAN.
Dublin: 1848, 4 numbers from 25 March.